ALASDAIR MACINTYRE

on Practical Philosophy

ALASDAIR MACINTYRE

on Practical Philosophy

Essential Works

Edited by Kelvin Knight and Peter Wicks

University of Notre Dame Press
Notre Dame, Indiana

Copyright © 2026 by the University of Notre Dame
Published by the University of Notre Dame Press
Notre Dame, Indiana 46556
undpress.nd.edu

All Rights Reserved

Published in the United States of America

Library of Congress Control Number: 2025946668

ISBN: 978-0-268-21050-2 (Hardback)
ISBN: 978-0-268-21055-7 (Paperback)
ISBN: 978-0-268-21057-1 (WebPDF)
ISBN: 978-0-268-21056-4 (Epub3)

GPSR Compliance Inquiries:
Lightning Source France, 1 Av. Johannes Gutenberg, 78310 Maurepas, France
compliance@lightningsource.fr | Phone: +33 1 30 49 23 42

CONTENTS

Acknowledgements vii

Introduction xi

PART I
Rethinking a Tradition of Practical Rationality

1 Plain Persons and Moral Philosophy: Rules, Virtues and Goods   3

2 Does Applied Ethics Rest on a Mistake?   25

3 Are Philosophical Problems Insoluble? The Relevance of System and History   43

4 The Idea of an Educated Public   64

5 Interview with Dmitri Nikulin   86

6 The Recovery of Moral Agency?   104

7 Conflicts of Desire   125

8 Interview with Alex Voorhoeve   144

9 Danish Ethical Demands and French Common Goods: Two Moral Philosophies   157

10 On Having Survived the Academic Moral Philosophy of the Twentieth Century   177

PART II
Challenging Contemporary Politics

11	Breaking the Chains of Reason	**197**
12	The *Theses on Feuerbach*: A Road Not Taken	**229**
13	Politics, Philosophy and the Common Good	**244**
14	How Aristotelianism Can Become Revolutionary	**267**
15	The Irrelevance of Ethics	**276**
16	Four—or More?—Political Aristotles	**294**
17	Two Kinds of Political Reasoning	**312**
18	Happiness	**331**
19	Political Rhetoric in a Fractured Society	**350**
20	Common Goods, Modern States, Rights, and—Maritain	**366**
21	Practical Rationality and Irrationality and Their Social Settings	**388**

Notes **411**

Index **421**

ACKNOWLEDGEMENTS

The editors and University of Notre Dame Press would like to gratefully acknowledge their permission to reprint the following:

"Plain Persons and Moral Philosophy: Rules, Virtues and Goods." Originally published in *American Catholic Philosophical Quarterly* 66, no. 1 (1992), 3–19.

"Does Applied Ethics Rest on a Mistake?" Originally published in *The Monist* 67, no. 4 (1984), 498–513. Reproduced by permission of Oxford University Press.

"Are Philosophical Problems Insoluble? The Relevance of System and History." Originally published in Patricia Cook, ed., *Philosophical Imagination and Cultural Memory: Appropriating Historical Traditions* (Duke University Press, 1993). Reproduced by permission of Duke University Press.

"The Idea of an Educated Public." Originally published in Graham Haydon, ed., *Education and Values: The Richard Peters Lectures* (Institute of Education, University of London, 1987).

MacIntyre's interview with Dmitri Nikulin appeared in German translation as "Wahre Selbsterkenntnis durch Verstehen unserer selbst aus der Perspektive anderer," *Deutsche Zeitschrift für Philosophie* 44, no. 4 (1996), 671–84. The original English text is published here for the first time.

"The Recovery of Moral Agency." Originally published in *Harvard Divinity Bulletin* 28, no. 4 (1999), 6–10.

"Conflicts of Desire." Originally published in Tobias Hoffman, ed., *Weakness of the Will from Plato to the Present* (Catholic University of America Press, 2008). Reproduced by permission of Catholic University of America Press.

MacIntyre's interview with Alex Voorhoeve was originally published under the title "The Illusion of Self-Sufficiency" in Alex Voorhoeve, *Conversations on Ethics* (Oxford University Press, 2009). Reproduced by permission of Oxford University Press.

"Danish Ethical Demands and French Common Goods: Two Moral Philosophies." Originally published in *European Journal of Philosophy* 18 (2010), 1–16.

"On Having Survived the Moral Philosophy of the Twentieth Century." Originally published in Fran O'Rourke, ed., *What Happened in and to Moral Philosophy in the Twentieth Century?* (University of Notre Dame Press, 2013). Reproduced by permission of the University of Notre Dame Press.

"Breaking the Chains of Reason." Originally published in E. P. Thompson, ed., *Out of Apathy* (Stevens & Sons, 1960).

"The *Theses on Feuerbach*: A Road Not Taken." Originally published in Carol C. Gould and Robert S. Cohen, eds., *Artifacts, Representations and Social Practice: Essays for Marx Wartofsky* (Springer, 1994). Reproduced by permission of Springer Nature Customer Service Centre.

"Politics, Philosophy, and the Common Good." First published in Italian translation as "Politica, filosofia e bene comune" in *Studi Perugini*, no. 3 (1997), 9–30. The original English text, republished here, was first published in Kelvin Knight, ed., *The MacIntyre Reader* (Polity Press & University of Notre Dame Press, 1998).

"How Aristotelianism Can Become Revolutionary: Ethics, Resistance, and Utopia." Previously published in *Philosophy of Management* 7 (2008), 3–7, and in Paul Blackledge and Kelvin Knight, eds., *Virtue and Politics: Alasdair MacIntyre's Revolutionary Aristotelianism* (University of Notre Dame Press, 2011).

"The Irrelevance of Ethics." Originally published in Andrius Bielskis and Kelvin Knight, eds., *Virtue and Economy: Essays on Morality and Markets* (Routledge, 2016).

"Four—or More?—Political Aristotles." Originally published in Andrius Bielskis, Eleni Leontsini and Kelvin Knight, eds., *Virtue Ethics and Contemporary Aristotelianism: Modernity, Conflict and Politics* (Bloomsbury, 2020).

We are grateful to Alasdair MacIntyre for permission to publish the previously unpublished papers included here as well as those materials listed above for which he is the copyright holder.

INTRODUCTION

Alasdair MacIntyre has been one of the world's leading philosophers for over half a century. His two most lastingly important books will be *After Virtue: A Study in Moral Theory*, first published in 1981, and *Ethics in the Conflicts of Modernity: An Essay on Desire, Practical Reasoning, and Narrative*, published in 2016. The papers collected below were, with one exception, written between those two dates, a period in which he revitalized the Aristotelian tradition of practical reasoning about ethics and politics. In presenting them together, our intention is to provide a more comprehensive sense of MacIntyre's project in practical philosophy, illuminating its distinctive features and radical implications.

By the time *After Virtue* was published, MacIntyre had already established himself as an original and iconoclastic philosophical voice as well as a trenchant critic of contemporary politics. It has proven to be an enduringly influential work, although some accounts of that influence have the effect of obscuring the radicalism of the project it announced. One example of this is the tendency to describe *After Virtue* as a seminal text in the emergence of virtue ethics as a major rival to the various forms of consequentialist and deontological moral theory that dominated academic moral philosophy when the book appeared. That *After Virtue* played a major role in the renewal of interest in virtue among moral philosophers in the decades that followed its publication is not in dispute, but MacIntyre's goal had not been to develop a virtue-based theory to rival the prevailing moral theories of the day. Instead, he found in Aristotelianism a way to challenge dominant assumptions about how moral theorizing should be done and to show the need for ethics to be informed by an understanding of real social relations of power and practice. In turning to the Aristotelian tradition, he identified a conceptual scheme capable of recombining theory with practice.

The papers in Part I illustrate how MacIntyre continued to develop this Aristotelian tradition of practical philosophy. "Plain Persons and Moral Philosophy" shows how Aristotelian concepts represent patterns of ethical thought and judgment developed in the normal course of living one's life as an embodied, social being. It also makes clear that from an Aristotelian perspective any suggestion that we must choose between a morality of virtue and a morality of rules must be rejected as a false dichotomy; the pursuit of our individual and common goods requires both the cultivation of good character traits and the adherence to moral rules. In "Conflicts of Desire," MacIntyre elaborates on this account, showing how we typically learn to make judgments about our desires, distinguishing those which aim at that which we have good reason to desire from those that do not. Aristotelian practical reasoning takes as its starting point the fact that we continually make judgments that depend upon this distinction and are thus, long before any encounter with ethical theory, already committed to rejecting the view that our good is to be found in the satisfaction of desire as such. The idea that we can have or lack good reasons to desire is a familiar part of our everyday reasoning. Yet, as MacIntyre shows, it has implications that challenge conceptions of our agency and welfare that exert immense influence in modern thought and social structures.

A crucial theme throughout MacIntyre's writings is the importance of understanding the proper relationship between theory and practice. As he puts it in "The Recovery of Moral Agency?" we need "to begin with practice, for theory is the articulation of practice and good theory of good practice." We are all already committed in various ways to concepts and distinctions that provide us with valid grounds for judging how we should act. Having recognized such grounds, we can proceed in ethics the way that Aristotle proceeded. Within the range of materially and performatively productive activities that *After Virtue*'s fourteenth chapter calls *practices*, we learn which goods are most worthy of our pursuit and to judge how best to achieve them.

Another respect in which MacIntyre challenges the conventions of moral philosophy is in his insistence that contemporary moral disputes cannot be adequately understood except in a historical perspective. Moral philosophers should appreciate how and why their subject has changed and changes, which requires understanding of its historical and social context. As he wrote in *After Virtue*, "we all too often still treat the moral philosophers of the past as contributors to a single debate with a relatively unvarying subject-matter, treating Plato and Hume and Mill as contemporaries both of ourselves and of each other. This leads to an abstraction of these writers from the cultural and social milieus in which they lived and thought and so the history of their thought acquires a false independence from the rest of the culture."[1] In "Are Philosophical Problems Insoluble?" he elaborates on this point, seeking to show how history can play an essential role in understanding and eventually resolving otherwise intractable philosophical disagreements. "Danish Ethical Demands and French Common Goods" provides an example of this, showing how such Aristotelians as Jacques Maritain and MacIntyre may emulate Thomas Aquinas's theoretical practice by both criticizing and incorporating insights from rival traditions in ways that require a historical understanding of how and why such traditions came to disagree. On this understanding of the specifically *Thomistic* Aristotelian tradition in which MacIntyre now participates, enquiry is an ongoing and collaborative project of theoretical and practical reasoning that aims at the common good of human beings as such.

The papers collected in Part II address specifically political reasoning and practice. The first, "Breaking the Chains of Reason," is the only one in the book that predates *After Virtue*. First published in 1960, this once-famous Trotskyist intervention in what history knows as Britain's "first New Left" demonstrates both MacIntyre's political provenance and that even at this early stage his social and political criticism was already informed by philosophy, history, economics, and literary analysis. As a graduate in Classics, he already knew Aristotle's practical and theoretical philosophy. As a Marxist, he already knew the importance of correctly understanding theory's relation to action. What he did not yet appreciate was how Aristotelian resources enable such understanding. The second paper, "The *Theses on Feuerbach*: A Road Not Taken," uses those resources to expose the inadequacies of Marx's own understanding of how to relate theory to practice.

The difficulties confronting any project of social and political transformation were always apparent to MacIntyre. Practically, they are difficulties that he set aside upon moving to America to focus on getting ethics right. The theoretical view of politics he developed in and following *After*

Virtue is summarized in "Politics, Philosophy and the Common Good." A decade later, in 2007, he switched his focus back to politics. The remaining eight papers in Part II were presented over the following five years, back in England. Apart from "The Irrelevance of Ethics," which was delivered in Cambridge, all were presented at London Metropolitan University. "Two Kinds of Political Reasoning"—his inaugural lecture as a senior research fellow at London Met, which is published here for the first time—indicates the continuity of his practical philosophy. It should be read in the light of what he wrote in *After Virtue* about goods both "internal" and "external" to socially cooperative practices, the particular common goods of which need to be defended against their participants' managerial manipulation and institutionalized corruption.

The last four papers, previously unpublished, are parts of a research project on "Common Goods and Political Reasoning." Each was presented to a dedicated but critical symposium of political philosophers, ethicists, and social scientists. They analyze the ethical idea of common goods, the political idea of *the* common good, and some of the institutional and ideological obstacles to actualizing such shared goods. Even when such ends are clear, questions of identifiable means and agency will always remain. Theoretically, MacIntyre points such enquiry in the right direction; practically, he tells us why we must always be ready to engage in social and political conflict. Taken together, the papers in Part II facilitate the continuation of MacIntyre's project of political reasoning by those who share his understanding of shared goods and of our true, ethical end.

The original aim of MacIntyre's "Common Goods and Political Reasoning" project was to produce a book entitled *The Politics of the Common Good In and Against the Politics of the Modern State*; it instead became *Ethics in the Conflicts of Modernity*. Both this and *After Virtue* are products of many years of critical reflection and discussion, of arguments' construction and refinement, and of the drafting and careful redrafting of what he intends as contributions to a shared tradition of enquiry and action. The papers collected below may all be read as contributions to that same project of understanding and advancing the good life for human beings.

Alasdair MacIntyre speaking at London Metropolitan University on June 29, 2007, at the first of the International Society for MacIntyrean Enquiry's ongoing annual conferences. In it, Alasdair is responding to questions after delivering "How Aristotelianism Can Become Revolutionary: Ethics, Resistance, and Utopia," which is republished in this volume.

The manuscript for this book was already with the University of Notre Dame Press when MacIntyre passed away in May 2025. The many reflections on his career and influence published in the wake of his death testified to the enduring interest in his ideas among a wide and varied readership. They also demonstrated that there remains much disagreement over the philosophical significance and practical implications of those ideas, as well as a persistent tendency to classify his thought using the very categories he had sought to put into question. Much of the commentary following his death showed little engagement with the texts in which he continued to elaborate and develop his ideas after their revolutionary expression in *After Virtue*. By presenting a substantial selection of those texts in a single volume, this collection will help those seeking a more comprehensive understanding of MacIntyre's thought.

We, the editors of this collection, regret that so much time has passed since its original conception, given that MacIntyre has not lived to see its publication. We are grateful to him for his support and encouragement throughout the process of assembling it. We hope that gathering these papers together will help them to achieve the purpose for which they were written: advancing our understanding of moral agency, the cultural and institutional obstacles to its exercise and enhancement, and how those obstacles might be overcome.

PART I

Rethinking a Tradition of Practical Rationality

ONE

Plain Persons and Moral Philosophy

Rules, Virtues and Goods

What is the relationship between the moral philosopher's judgments about the life of practice and the everyday plain person's moral questions and judgments? Moral philosophers are of course themselves in most of their lives everyday plain persons, but on some views what they do and judge *qua* moral philosopher is very different from what they do and judge *qua* plain person. Some analytic philosophers, for example, have envisaged the relationship between moral philosophy and everyday moral judgments and activity as analogous to that between the philosophy of science and the judgments and activity of the natural scientist or that between the philosophy of law and legal practice. In each such case the philosophy is to

"Plain Persons and Moral Philosophy: Rules, Virtues and Goods," *American Catholic Philosophical Quarterly* 66, no. 1 (1992): 3–19.

be understood as detached second-order commentary upon first-order judgments and activity. But for moral philosophers at work in the Aristotelian Thomistic tradition this is not at all how that relationship is to be conceived.

For, on an Aristotelian view, the questions posed by the moral philosopher and the questions posed by the plain person are to an important degree inseparable. And it is with questions that each begins, for each is engaged in enquiry, the plain person often unsystematically asking: "What is my good?" and "What actions will achieve it?" and the moral philosopher systematically enquiring "What is *the* good for human beings?" and "What kinds of actions will achieve the good?" Any persistent attempt to answer either of these sets of questions soon leads to asking the other. The moral philosopher has to recognize that any true account of the human good is incomplete and inadequate, unless and until it enables us to understand how particular plain persons, including her or himself, are able to move towards their particular goods. And if I, as a plain person, ask persistently what good it is that is at stake for me here and now in particular situations, I will soon have to ask the further, already philosophical question "What in general is the good for my kind of person with my kind of history in this kind of situation?" and that in turn will lead to a fundamental philosophical question "What is the good as such for human beings as such?"

A plain person who begins to understand her or his life as an uneven progress towards the achievement of her or his good is thus to some significant extent transformed into a moral philosopher, asking and answering the same questions posed by Aristotle in the *Nicomachean Ethics* and by Aquinas in his commentary on the *Ethics* and elsewhere. Often enough, such a plain person will not recognize how far she or he has been transformed in this direction, but insofar as a plain person fails to recognize her or himself as a moral philosopher, to that extent that plain person is the more likely to be less competent as a moral philosopher than she or he needs to be and is able to be. So the question to which this lecture is addressed is: just how much of a moral philosopher does the plain person need to become?

At once it may be objected that I already seem to be assuming by my references to Aristotle and Aquinas that, insofar as the plain person becomes a moral philosopher, she or he will at least tend towards becoming an Aristotelian. And this may seem to be question-begging. For I am, it may be said, highhandedly usurping the role of the plain person and putting my philosophical words, or rather Aristotle's and Aquinas's philosophical words, into her or his prephilosophical mouth. But surely the plain person must be allowed to speak for her or himself and to become whatever kind of philosopher she or he chooses to be. Yet this at first sight plausible objection is in fact misleading.

Consider the image of the plain person which this objection presents: that of someone who initially is a stranger to all moral philosophies and therefore wholly unequipped with the resources provided by any particular philosophical standpoint. Such a plain person therefore begins from a position of philosophical neutrality, taking her or his first steps in the direction of this or that philosophical standpoint without the guidance of any reasons which presuppose some philosophical commitment. But this is to leave the plain person bereft of philosophically relevant reasoning. The counterpart of the neutrality of the plain person thus conceived is therefore a rationally unguided arbitrariness in that person's initial choice of which philosophical direction to take. And at this point we experience a shock of recognition. For we have met this particular plain person before, not in the street or on the farm, but in the pages of a number of philosophers since Kierkegaard, especially those of the Sartre of the late nineteen forties. This is a human being constructed by existentialist philosophical theory, disguised as a plain person; this image of the plain person is itself a philosophical artefact.

When I say this, I do not mean to deny that there are and have been real human beings in the condition represented by this image, human beings, that is, lacking the resources to make fundamental choices in any but a criterionless way. But the question is whether this type of human being is not her or himself a social artefact, someone who has undergone a process of social and moral deprivation, not a plain person as such, but someone who somehow or other has been stripped of the ability to understand her or himself aright. So this attempt to replace my apparently question-begging image of the plain person as someone who is from the very beginning on the verge of becoming a Thomistic Aristotelian by a philosophically untainted image of the plain person has failed. And it could not but have failed. For every conception of the plain person is at home in some particular philosophical standpoint and there is no way of thinking realistically about the plain person except as someone who is from the outset potentially a moral philosopher of one distinctive kind rather than another.

The history of philosophy confirms this. Immanuel Kant's plain person, who possesses what Kant calls an "ordinary rational knowledge of morality," is already a proto-Kantian. Thomas Reid's plain person does not possess mere common sense, but common sense as articulated philosophically by Reid. And when Henry Sidgwick appeals to "common moral opinion," its deliverances turn out to furnish a very Sidgwickian point of entry into Sidgwickian theory. So we have good reason to believe that attempts to portray the plain person as initially completely innocent of philosophy in her or his attitudes, presuppositions, beliefs and questionings are bound to fail. Let us then recognize instead that the plain person must always be conceived as already somehow or other engaged with philosophy in some determinate way, and that we need to ask what particular philosophical standpoint it is which is already implicit in her or his initial attitudes, presuppositions, beliefs and questionings. Is she or he perhaps a proto-Kantian or a potential follower of Reid? Or do plain persons vary a good deal in their initial philosophical allegiance? I want to answer these questions by defending the following theses: that plain persons are in fact generally and to a significant degree proto-Aristotelians, and that, insofar as they are not, it is from the standpoint of a Thomistic Aristotelianism that we can most adequately explain why they are not, and why they have become whatever it is instead that they are.

Characteristically and generally, individuals come to ask the question, 'What is my good?' in social contexts in which different aspects of human activity combine to make it difficult not at some point to raise that question explicitly, and impossible, whether one raises it explicitly or not, not to presuppose some answer to it by the way in which one comes to live out one's life. The first of these aspects is the goal-directedness which from a relatively early age one discovers in different types of norm-informed activity in which one has become involved. Some goals are biologically given, some are social. But in activities as elementary as those which sustain and preserve one's own life, as universal among human beings as those which arise from kin, familial and household relationships, and as open-ended as those which provide one's first education into productive, practical and theoretical arts, one inescapably discovers oneself as a being in norm-governed direction towards goals which are thereby recognized as goods. These norm-governed directednesses are what Aquinas calls *inclinationes* in a passage in which he says that it is in virtue of our relationship to these *inclinationes*, partially defining as they do our nature as human agents, that the precepts of the natural law are so-called (*Summa Theologiae* Ia-IIae q. 94 a. 2).

The connection between *inclinationes* and such precepts I take to be as follows. When I discover that my life is, as a matter of biological and social fact, partially ordered by regularities which give expression to these primary tendencies towards particular ends, I have it in my power to make these ends mine in a new and secondary way by self-consciously directing my activities to these ends and, insofar as I have rightly understood my own nature, it will be rational for me to do so. The rules to which I will have to conform, if I am so to direct my activities, are those expressed by the precepts of the natural law. What was mere regularity becomes rule-governedness.

If this is how Aquinas understood matters, then it is not difficult to respond to a charge levelled by T. H. Irwin that Aquinas entangles himself in contradiction in his account of the relationship between the virtues, inclination towards right ends and deliberation.[1] Irwin correctly ascribes to Aquinas the theses that what is in our power depends on our deliberative capacities and that ends are fixed nondeliberatively, and Irwin concludes that Aquinas is therefore committed to holding that what our ends are to be is not in our power. But Aquinas also asserts that an inclination towards right ends distinguishes virtue and vice and that to be virtuous rather than vicious is in our power, so that Aquinas is also committed to holding that what our ends are to be must be in our power. Hence, Irwin further concludes that Aquinas is guilty of inconsistency.

What Irwin has failed to distinguish are two distinct ways in which, on Aquinas's view, someone may have an end. We human beings are indeed by our specific nature directed towards certain hierarchically ordered ends, and it is not in our power to have a nature other than that which we have, and so not in our power to have ends other than these. But it is in our power whether or not in our rational decision-making to direct our activities towards the achievements of those ends. It is open to us to move in quite other directions. So, according to Aquinas, in one way our ends are in our power and in another way they are not, and there is no inconsistency in the conclusions to which he is committed. Irwin, however, has done us a service by compelling us to raise the questions: how does the plain person make of the ends which are her or his by nature ends actually and rationally directive of her or his activities? And in what social contexts do plain persons learn how to order ends rightly and to recognize their mistakes when they have failed to do so?

Such learning is generally achieved only through involvement in a type of activity which raises for individuals the question, "What is my good?" in a manner that is complementary to that in which that question is posed by *inclinationes*, a type of activity characteristic of practices, those cooperative forms of activity whose participants jointly pursue the goods internal to those forms of activity and jointly value excellence in achieving those goods. Such practices are of very different kinds. The activities of members of string-quartets, of the crews of fishing-fleets, of architects and construction workers jointly engaged in developing good housing, of members of families making and sustaining the familial community, of farmers and of physicists — to name only a few — are all practice-based and practice-structured. It is through initiation into the ordered relationships of some particular practice or practices, through education into the skills and virtues which it or they require, and through an understanding of the relationship of those skills and virtues to the achievement of the goods internal to that practice or those practices that we first find application in everyday life for just such a teleological scheme of understanding as that which Aristotle presents at a very different level of philosophical sophistication in the *Nicomachean Ethics*. It is by our finding application for this scheme in our practical activities, a scheme which provides the directedness of our *inclinationes* with a further rationale, that we first become evidently, even if unwittingly, Aristotelians. It is in doing so that we also acquire a capacity for becoming reflective about norms and goals.

This capacity is expressed in our learning how to apply two closely related distinctions. The first is that between what I would do, if I did what would please me most here and now, and what I would do if, in the light of the best instruction available to me, I were to do what would make me excellent in the pursuit of the goods internal to the particular practice or practices in which I am engaged. Failure in making this first distinction is characteristically a sign of failure in ordering the appetites and passions. A second distinction is that between what it would be to achieve what is good and best unqualifiedly and what is good and best here and now for me, at my stage in the education of my capacities, to do. Failure in making this second distinction is characteristically a sign of failure in evaluating how far I have progressed in ordering my appetites and passions. How to make these distinctions is something that each person has to learn, and what has to be learned always can be mislearned. So that through a process of learning, making mistakes, correcting those mistakes and so moving towards the achievement of excellence, the individual comes to understand her or himself as *in via*, in the middle of a journey. And as she or he also comes to understand how each practice in which she or he is engaged itself has a history in the course of which goals, skills and virtues have been variously identified, misunderstood and reconceived, so she or he comes to understand her or his own history of progress within that particular practice as embedded in the history of the practice. But no individual lives her or his life wholly within the confines of any one practice. She or he always pursues the goods of more than one practice, as well as goods external to all practices, and so cannot escape posing and answering the question, even if only by the way in which she or he lives, of how these goods are to be ordered, of which part each is to play within the structures of a whole life. The recurrent and rival claims of pleasure, of the pursuit of wealth, of power, of honor and prestige to be the ordering principle of human lives will each have to be responded to in turn; and in so responding, an individual will be defining her or his attitudes to those considerations which Aristotle rehearses in Book I of the *Nicomachean Ethics* and which Aquinas reconsiders in the opening questions of the Ia-IIae of the *Summa Theologiae*, in the course of their extended dialectical arguments on the nature of the supreme good.

Characteristically, the plain person responds to these claims not so much through explicit arguments, although these may always play a part, as by shaping his or her life in one way rather than another. When from time to time, the plain person retrospectively examines what her or his life amounts to as a whole, often enough with a view to choice between alternative futures, characteristically what she or he is in effect asking is, "To what conception of my overall good have I so far committed myself?

And, do I now have reason to put it in question?" The unity of her or his life about which each human being thus enquires is the unity of a dramatic narrative, of a story whose outcome can be success or failure for each protagonist. Were it otherwise, the notion of an overall good for that life, one which provides that life with its standards of success and failure, would lack application. When someone writes the narrative either of her or his own or of someone else's life, its adequacy can be judged by the extent to which it provides answers to such questions as: What did the person whose life has been thus narrated take to be her or his good? Did she or he misconceive that good? What obstacles and frustrations confronted that person and did she or he possess the qualities of mind and character necessary to overcome them? The conception of a *telos* of human life is generally first comprehended in terms of the outcomes of particular narratives about particular lives.

So when we as readers or spectators put such questions to a narrative, we look for the universal in the particular. Both plot and character have significance for us in so far as we can understand them in terms of universal conceptions of the good and of the virtues and vices which transcend, but inform, the particularities of *this* narrative. When however in the examination of our own past lives we proceed from the narrative structure of those lives, as they have been lived so far, to enquiry about what from now on we are now to make of ourselves, we are compelled instead to ask of the universal how it may be particularized, how certain conceptions of *the* good and of the virtues may take on embodied form through our realization of this possibility rather than that, posing these questions in terms of the specificities of the narratives of our lives. In so doing, we characteristically draw upon resources provided by some stock of stories from which we had earlier learned to understand both our own lives and the lives of others in narrative terms, the oral and written literature of whatever particular culture it is that we happen to inhabit.

An ability to put ourselves to the question philosophically thus in key part depends upon the prior possession of some measure of narrative understanding, but this ability transcends the limitations of such understanding. For in stories, as contrasted with theories, we encounter the universal *only* in and through the particular. What we need are stories which provoke us to move beyond stories—although everything then turns upon what direction it is that our movement takes. Narratives which point beyond themselves towards the theories that we in fact need are to be found in many places: in some folk-tales, in Sophoclean and Shakespearean drama, and above all in Dante's *Commedia*, which directs us beyond itself towards the kind of theoretical understanding provided by Aquinas's commentaries on the *Ethics* and *Politics*.

One of the things that we most need to learn, first from narrative and then from theory is that it is one of the marks of someone who develops bad character that, as it develops, she or he becomes progressively less and less able to understand what it is that she or he has mislearned and how it was that she or he fell into error. Part of the badness of bad character is intellectual blindness on moral questions. It is important therefore at an early stage to possess resources for right judgment and action, which include resources for explaining how we may come to fail and have come to fail and what we have to do to avoid failure. We need, that is, an extended, practically usable answer to the question "What is my good?" and "How is it to be achieved?", which will both direct us in present and future action and also evaluate and explain past action.

Such an answer will have to supply not only an account of goods and virtues, but also of rules, and of how goods, virtues and rules relate to one another. It will be an account which will answer not only the plain person's practical questions about how to achieve her or his good, but also the central question of this lecture, that of how much of a moral philosopher the plain person needs to become. For the plain person, so it has turned out, must become at least enough of a moral philosopher to understand her or himself, in all her or his particularities, as exemplifying the universal concepts of a theory which is not only both explanatorily and prescriptively powerful, but which also is able to justify a claim to be superior to such rival theories as may present themselves in one guise or another as claimants for the plain person's allegiance. What kind of theory then does the plain person need?

Let us begin with the place, in such a theory, of fundamental rules, of those precepts of the natural law whose evidentness to the plain person who aspires to direct her or himself towards her or his good in the company of other rational persons it is hard to disguise, even although it has often enough been denied. For, to violate these rules in one's relationships with other persons is bound to deprive one of their cooperation in the achievement of a good about which one still has much to learn from them. In the search for our good, everyone is a potential teacher and has therefore to be treated as one from whom I still may have to learn. So the rules governing my fundamental relationships with others are not affirmed as conclusions from some yet more fundamental set of premises. Allegiance to those rules cannot depend upon the outcome of theorizing. For suppose someone were to deny this and to embark upon the project of cooperating with others in constructing a theory designed to provide them with a rational justification. In order to do so successfully, she or he would first have to enter into cooperative relationships already informed by allegiance to just those rules for which she or he aspired to provide a justification. Hence, allegiance to these particular rules has to precede any set of arguments, any theorizing.

The same rules have another part to play in the plain person's initial education into the moral life. For a first primitive conception of each of the virtues that we need to acquire, if we are to achieve our good, can be articulated only through a set of rules which, turn out to be another application of the primary precepts of the natural law. We can only learn what it is to be courageous or temperate or truthful by first learning that certain types of action are always and exceptionlessly such as we must refrain from if we are to exemplify those virtues. The disposition which we need to acquire by habituation in the case of each virtue is of course a disposition not merely to act in certain rule-governed ways, but also to do more than the rules require. What more is required varies with time, place and circumstance. And knowing how to go beyond the rules in order to judge appropriately in particular circumstances is itself impossible without the virtue of *phronēsis*. So the order of learning is such that we first have to learn in certain initial situations what is *always* enjoined or always prohibited, in order that later we may become able to extrapolate in a non-rule-governed way to other types of situations in which what courage or justice or truthfulness, together with prudence, demand is more than conformity to the universal rule. Learning what the virtues require of us in a wide range of different situations is inseparable from learning which, out of the multiplicity of goods, more is at stake in any given situation. So we go on to learn more than we initially could learn from the rules, but part of what we then learn is that we can never dispense with the rules. And that this is so is integral to our understanding of goods and of virtues as well as of the rules themselves. Consider how those rules relate to our supreme good.

It has to be of the nature of whatever is genuinely the supreme good that it makes no sense to think of weighing it against other goods. The supreme good is not a good that just happens on some particular occasions, or even on every particular occasion, to outweigh other goods. It must be that it *cannot* be outweighed. Otherwise its status as supreme good would be contingent and therefore very possibly temporary. It would be vulnerable to displacement. Moreover, the rules, observance of which is required if *our* final good is to be achieved—that is, if we are to achieve whatever relationship to the supreme good it is in which our own final good consists—must define what is necessarily true of that relationship. Those rules, then, cannot be such as to bind us only so long as certain contingent circumstances obtain, that is, conditionally. So that if someone entertained the thought, as many of course have done, that we perhaps ought on some particular occasion, for the sake of achieving what is taken to be some other good only thus obtainable, temporarily to suspend the requirement of obedience to one or more of those rules, if, that is, we treated them as open to exceptions, we would have misconceived both the nature and function of those rules and the nature of the good and of our good. And in so misconceiving them we would have exhibited a defect both in our possession of and in our understanding of one or more of the intellectual and moral virtues. Virtues, rules and goods, so it turns out, have to be understood in their interrelationship or not at all.

Consider as an analogy the relationship of the rules governing activities of enquiry in mathematics or the natural sciences to the goal of those activities, that of attaining truth: for example, the rule that one should be scrupulous in laying out one's theses and putative proofs so that they are maximally vulnerable to objection and refutation. Suppose that someone were to propose that in the interests of obtaining some nonmathematical and nonscientific good, this rule should, from time to time, be suspended. Such a proposal, ignoring as it does the internal relation between truth and ability to withstand refutation, would make no sense, insofar as it was proposed as a rule for mathematicians *qua* mathematicians or scientists *qua* scientists. And a proposal temporarily to suspend the application of the precepts of the natural law, ignoring, as it would, the internal relation between the conception of the supreme good and those precepts, would similarly make no sense insofar as it was proposed as a rule for rational beings *qua* rational beings. Yet on many occasions, such proposals are made with great seriousness. The benefits of violating some requirement of the natural law are compared with the benefits of conformity. And that is to say that some good or set of goods is being weighed against the supreme good, as if in relation to it any question of weighing could arise. How does such a mistake come to be made?

Characteristically, it is the outcome of fragmenting into independent parts the conceptual scheme in terms of which the plain person had at first organized her or his moral understanding. Goods, rules and virtues are as a result of such fragmentation reconceived as isolable from one another, so that the problem is not that of how to articulate a preexisting relationship, but to construct a relationship apparently not yet established between the disparate parts of one's moral scheme. And the difficulty for the plain person in this situation is that once the different elements in her or his moral conceptual scheme have been thus torn apart, each of them thereby assumes a somewhat different character. Rules, conceived apart from virtues and goods, are not the same as rules conceived in dependence upon virtues and goods; and so it is also with virtues apart from rules and goods and goods apart from rules and virtues.

Observe now that in making these theoretical remarks I have already resorted to the narrative mode. I have begun to tell a story, the story of the decline and fall of the plain person. It is a story in four episodes, a story of a failed quest for what proves in the end to be an illusory grail. In the first of these, the protagonist sets out to discover what the final good for beings such as her or himself is and finds that, in asking 'What is my good?' and 'What is the good?' in any way that is well-designed to secure helpful answers, she or he has to define that quest in a way which already presupposes to a significant degree a particular kind of answer to those questions. For those rules and virtues which alone guide one reliably in the earliest stages of fruitful moral enquiry are structured, so that they already presuppose a great deal about the existence and nature of that same good about which one has only begun to enquire.

The circularity in which the protagonist is thereby involved is one which requires of her or him an asceticism or at least a temperateness about certain classes of less than supreme goods, which she or he will only be able to justify fully at some future time in the light later to be afforded by a more adequate conception of the good. Yet should she or he, solicited by a variety of such goods, physical, aesthetic and intellectual, fail in this temperateness, not only will she or he debar her or himself from ever reaching the point at which such rational justification would become possible, but she or he will, in according independent recognition to a multiplicity of more or less immediate goods, have adopted a set of standards of justification very different from that towards an understanding of which she or he had originally been moving. As a result in this second type of episode a radical discrepancy begins to appear between the rules in obedience to which the quest was originally to have been conducted and the multiplicity of goods now envisaged, possibly as rival candidates for the status of supreme good, possibly as by their very multiplicity excluding the notion of a single supreme good. And already any conception of a good that not only is not but could not be outweighed by other goods has disappeared from view.

In a third type of episode this discrepancy is resolved in either of two incompatible ways. *Either*, the authority of rules is made independent of all relationship to goods, so that obedience to rules is valued for its own sake, *or* the rules are reconceived so that they are authoritative only if and insofar as obedience to them is causally effective in attaining what are taken to be goods.

Whichever of these two resolutions is adopted, new problems are engendered. If conformity to moral rules is now to be valued only for its own sake, as Kant, for example, held, then the question inescapably arises of why and how a rational person should be moved to value such conformity. If rules are only a means to the achievement of goods, and a multiplicity of competing goods are acknowledged, as they are by utilitarians, then it will be necessary to decide how to respond on those occasions when the actions necessary for the attainment of some one particular good violate the rule or rules necessary for the attainment of some other good.

During this third type of episode therefore the protagonist of our story discovers not only that she or he must take sides on these issues, but that other similar persons take opposing sides. The protagonist consequently confronts one or more antagonists and becomes involved in intellectual and moral conflict. And this conflict may extend beyond the initial opposition, in which the upholder of rules independent of goods confronted the upholder of rules as nothing more than a means to the achievement of goods, to further questions about what place the virtues are to have in each of these rival schemes and how the problems internal to each scheme are to be resolved. Our protagonist therefore now confronts a variety of antagonists and perhaps her or himself with a divided mind on these divisive issues.

A fourth and final type of episode opens with the protagonist's discovery that the major issues over which conflict has been joined are not rationally resolvable. It is not that each of the contending parties does not have arguments to deploy, but rather that each gives a different weight to different types of consideration, and that there are no rational criteria, shared between the contending parties, to which appeal can be made in deciding what weight should be so given. Fundamental disagreement turns out to be ineliminable. There is more than one way in which our protagonist might respond to this discovery, perhaps by acting out the part of a wholly prephilosophical and now cynical plain person, standing outside and pouring scorn upon all philosophical points of view, or perhaps by becoming a plain person's version of a proto-Nietzschean, one devoted to unmasking a will to power disguised by the proponents of each contending moral standpoint.

I have told this story of the transformations of the plain person only in bare and skeletal outline. But I hope that I have said enough at least to suggest that this story could be told with sufficient detail to explain both how those changing portraits of the plain person which decorate the history of moral philosophy do in fact correspond to social realities—hence the immense plausibility in one time and place of Kant's portrait of the plain person, in another of Reid's, in a third of Sidgwick's, and in a fourth of Sartre's—and how, nonetheless, the plain person is fundamentally a proto-Aristotelian. What is the force of 'fundamentally' here? What it conveys can be expressed in three claims, first that every human being *either* lives out her or his life in a narrative form which is structured in terms of a *telos*, of virtues and of rules in an Aristotelian mode or has disrupted that narrative by committing her or himself to some other way of life, which is best understood as an alternative designed to avoid or escape from an Aristotelian mode of life, so that the lives of those who understand themselves, explicitly or much more probably implicitly, in terms set by Kant or Reid or Sidgwick or Sartre, are still informed by this rejected alternative. Secondly, I have told the story of the decline and fall of the plain person as the narrative of a single life. But the story could have been told, and I have told it elsewhere (in *After Virtue*), as a claim about the narrative history of a set of successive periods in Western culture from the sixteenth to the twentieth century. This partial mirroring of the fate of individuals in the history of the larger social order and of the fate of that larger order in the narratives of individual lives testifies to the inseparability of the two stories.

Thirdly, as these first two claims imply, I am also committed to holding that every human being is potentially a fully-fledged and not merely a proto-Aristotelian and that the frustration of that potentiality is among his or her morally important characteristics. We should therefore expect to find, within those who have not been allowed to develop, or have not themselves allowed their lives to develop, an Aristotelian form, a crucial and ineliminable tension between that in them which is and that which is not, Aristotelian. The standard modern anti-Aristotelian self will be a particular kind of divided self, exhibiting that complexity so characteristic of and so prized by modernity.

We can now say something more not only about how much of a moral philosopher the plain person has to be, but also about what kind of a moral philosopher the plain person has to be and how this may differ from situation to situation. The plain person needs as much of a theory as will enable her or him to identify what the significant alternatives are which now confront her or him, and to understand why and how it was in the past that she or he did or did not make mistakes in acting in one way rather than another. That need may not be met, not only if the plain person is insufficiently a theorist, but also if the theory which is made available to her or him, even if true and adequate *qua* theory, is stated in too much abstraction from the specificities and particularities of her or his historical and autobiographical situation.

This is why we would not meet the practical needs of contemporary plain persons by simply providing them with copies of the *Nicomachean*

Ethics and of Aquinas's commentary, nor even of the Ia-IIae of the *Summa*. What such persons would still lack is a capacity for reading or hearing what is written in such texts as providing answers to their own specific and particular questions. Such texts may be theoretically powerful, but still remain practically idle, for they do no work for us, until and unless we learn how to read them in such a way as to generate specific and particular answers to the practical questions of all of us, moral philosophers and plain persons alike, since in her or his practical life a moral philosopher is just one more type of plain person. But those texts do, if we read them aright, meet us, so to speak, half way. They are responsive to this kind of practical reading, because their authors' expectations of this kind of reader already inform those texts. The reader still, however, has the work to do of constructing her or his own specific and particular reading of the text at the points at which her or his practical questions and the text intersect. What form do such specific and particular readings take?

A practical reader can only approach a text with the resources for questioning it which are afforded by her or his social context and relationships. Such resources always limit as well as focus our initial questioning and an effective practical text begins by subordinating our questions to its own. It responds to our interrogation by interrogating us. So it is at the outset in the *Nicomachean Ethics*. So it is at the beginning of the Ia-IIae, a work designed for teachers, confessors and other intermediaries between its text and the readings of the practical reader or hearer. Such a reader is forced back upon questions to which her or his own questioning has to be subordinated and by which it is likely to be transformed.

Consider the sequence of questioning as expounded in the Ia-IIae and its shadow counterpart in the sequence of questioning of some particular practical reader. Where Aquinas asks what the ultimate end is towards which the activities of any human being qua rational person are directed and explains why wealth, honor, pleasure, power, the goods of the body and the goods of the soul cannot be that end, the practical reader will be concerned with these particular pleasures, with that particular opportunity for enriching her or himself, with the attractions of this or that specific type of power, as these present themselves as the ends of possible courses of action. Where Aquinas presents the most powerful arguments against his own conclusions through a wide range of earlier voices, including those of

Plato, Aristotle, Cicero, Boethius, and Augustine, the contemporary practical reader cannot but also hear the practical advice of the major voices of her or his own time, those of, say, Diderot, Rousseau and Kant in the eighteenth century or of Hegel and Mill in the nineteenth, often perhaps in vulgarized and diminished form, presented in the conversation of one's neighbors, rather than in philosophical texts, but not necessarily the less powerful for that. Such a reader needs to learn what Aquinas has to teach us in each of his dialectical responses about how to respond to these contending voices. She or he needs to learn through this process of argumentative debate to identify in concrete terms what here and now she or he must do, if she or he is not to confuse the supreme good with some lesser good.

It was precisely at this point and over this question that the protagonist in my earlier story of the decline and fall of the plain person made a large initial mistake, and the practical reader of the Ia-IIae will be able to avoid this same error only by learning how to arrive, in practice, at those conclusions which Aquinas reaches theoretically, in moving from his answer to Question 5 about where happiness is to be found, through the conclusions of Questions 18–21 about what makes an act good and evil, to Questions 24–48 about the function of the passions in making her or him act well and badly, and on to Questions 49–66 about the habits which have to be developed as virtues, so that her or his passions are ordered and transformed, so that she or he, in consequence, acts well rather than badly, so that she or he, in further consequence, is directed towards her or his true final end. But if such a person moves successfully through this process of practical enquiry, embodying in the dramatic sequences of her or his life a highly particularized counterpart of the ordered sequences of moral learning presented in the questions and answers of those parts of the Ia-IIae, she or he is bound to discover the very same circularity that was evident also in the story of the decline and fall of the plain person.

Such a person, that is, will have to recognize that the point in her or his practical enquiry at which recognition of the nature of and the need for the virtues has been achieved could not have been reached, if she or he had not already at a much earlier stage possessed and valued those same virtues to some significant, even if less than perfect degree. Unless the activities in which her or his initial questioning was embodied had been in appropriate measure courageous—both patient, when necessary, and daring, when necessary, just in giving what was due to other participants in those activities, temperate in restraining desires, so that a multiplicity of solicitations liable to distract the course of enquiry were put aside for the sake of a good thereby already implicitly judged to be supreme, and always prudent in the ordering of these activities, she or he could not have achieved any adequate understanding of why without courage, justice, temperateness and prudence her or his enquiry was bound to fail. So a reader making her or his way through the Ia-IIae will learn only later what it was in her or his earlier relationship to the text which enabled her or him to make of the narrative of her or his own life a particularized version of the progress of Aquinas's argument. How the text is read depends, that is to say, in key part on the incipient virtues of the practical reader and on what incipient virtues the reader is able to bring to her or his reading depends in turn on the resources on which that reader can draw in and from the particular social context. What kind of resources are these?

In order to answer this question it is worth considering two important objections that may be advanced against my argument so far. The first of these might begin by pointing out that many plain persona have fared very well morally without ever encountering philosophy. With the moral resources afforded by sound, plain, practical teaching, by the cultivation of the virtues and by an instructed conscience, what need is there for philosophy? It may be thought that it is part of the arrogance of an intellectual to project onto plain persons a need for theory. It is however no part of my case that the plain person needs to become anything like a professional theorist. It is central to my argument that the practice of the moral life by plain persons always presupposes the truth of some particular theoretical standpoint and that, when confronted by rival claims to her or his moral allegiance, the plain person's reflective practical choices will implicitly at least be a choice between theoretical standpoints. In our own society common plain persons who have never heard of John Stuart Mill offer as the deliverances of what they take to be their common sense maxims of hedonistic utilitarianism. Other such plain persons, equally ignorant of Kant, will insist on the irrelevance of consequences to the rightness of their actions. A good deal of ordinary conversation and debate bears out the epigram that common sense is a graveyard of past philosophies.

Plain persons then exhibit their allegiances in their actions and in their reasons for action, not in their theorizing. But this does not deprive those allegiances of a philosophical dimension. It might however be objected that those allegiances could never rightly be described as Aristotelian or even proto-Aristotelian. For Aristotle himself took plain persons to be incapable of philosophical reflection. Aristotle's exclusions of not only barbarians, but also women (*Politics* 1259b21–1260a33) and productive workers (*Politics* 1328b33–1329a2) from the life of citizenship and of the virtues is surely enough to show that he could not have taken plain persons to be proto-Aristotelians. But Aristotle has of course no worthwhile arguments to support these exclusions, and the Thomistic Aristotelianism of a Maritain or a Simon rightly ignored them. And so do I.

What the first of these objections does draw to our attention is the danger to someone holding my position of too easy an assimilation of the theoretical to the practical life and therefore of the preoccupations of the philosopher to those of the plain person. I have, for example, emphasized how the plain person's moral understanding is of goods, rules and virtues in his or her interrelationships. And the practical need to understand these together, although real, is very different from the philosopher's need to develop a theoretical understanding of each of these in its own terms. So that often enough, if we are to make what philosophers say relevant to the practical concerns of plain persons, including philosophers in their own practical lives, we need first to reorganize and rethink the philosophers' arguments. Some topics which were, for good analytical and didactic reasons, treated separately in Aristotle and Aquinas need in contexts of practice to be treated together. Aristotle considers the acquisition of the virtues in one set of passages and the nature of practical reasoning in another; and Aquinas, in the *Summa*, not only considers these separately, but discusses the character of the natural law in yet a third set of passages. Both provide in their discussions much that suggests the importance of the relationships between them. But subsequent teaching about practical reasoning, virtues and natural law has often enforced a separation of topics which has obscured the fact that at the level of practice, especially initial practice, the ability to judge and to act in accordance with the precepts of the natural law, the ability to acquire an increasing set of dispositions to act virtuously, and the ability to judge rightly about goods are all exercised as aspects of one and the same complex ability, the ability to engage in sound practical reasoning. How is this so?

To reason practically, I must always set in front of myself some good which will be specified in the major premise of my practical reasoning and, if my practical reasoning is in any particular instance not to obstruct my attempt to answer the question 'What is my ultimate good?' alternative immediate goods must from the outset be ordered so that no lesser, but more immediate good can be thought to outweigh my ultimate good. My ultimate good, that is to say, will have to be conceived from the outset as a good than which no greater can be pursued by me, in order to ensure the integrity of my practical reasoning.

At the same time, the various relationships into which I will have to enter, in order to achieve the kind of understanding of myself and others without which I will be unable to learn what the human good is, will themselves have to be informed by those virtues and governed by those rules without which the activities of enquiry will be barren. Any ordering of goods which involves my conceiving of my ultimate good as a good than which no greater can be pursued will have to be matched by an ordering of my life in terms of virtues and rules which is consistent with the affirmation of the true nature of the good and the best as the first premise of my practical reasoning. The movement from that first premise to a conclusion which is right action requires from me a correspondingly ordered character and a correspondingly ordered set of social relationships. This connection between what kind of person I have to become in order to achieve a given end and what the character of that given end is is of course not peculiar to this kind of enquiry. It is a connection embodied in the structure and reasoning of all practice-based activity; what the need for it in enquiry by particular human beings designed to answer the questions "What is my good?" and "What is *the* good?" confirms is that such enquiry is itself a practice.

So it is not just that, as I said earlier, practices have an Aristotelian structure. It is also that in engaging in the practice of asking seriously and systematically the question "What is my good?" plain persons engage in a reflective practice with an Aristotelian content as well as an Aristotelian structure, a practice in which both Aristotle and Aquinas preceded them.

So it is less surprising than we may have thought that those who first come to a reading of the *Nicomachean Ethics* or Aquinas's commentary or the Ia-IIae of the *Summa* may already exhibit the cardinal virtues without as yet knowing the reasons for needing them, and it is not after all paradoxical to assert that we must already have those virtues at least to some degree if we are to understand why we need to have them. The *Nicomachean Ethics* and Aquinas's commentary upon it and the Ia-IIae are texts in which readers are able to discover themselves as characters, or rather to discover types of character which to some significant degree they already exemplify. And they may also discover that what they are now able to learn about themselves in universal terms from such texts, in beginning to comprehend a philosophical theory of the moral life, is what they had already learned in part through practice-informed activities concerning the particularities of their own lives. If their subsequent practice becomes informed and enriched by philosophical theory, they may feel that they have transcended certain limitations of that past learning, limitations rooted in the relative inarticulacy of the merely practical. But they need never disown, indeed they could not without incoherence disown, the first stages of the enacted narrative of their lives. We are thus able to set beside the fable of the decline and fall of the plain person the story of the plain person who does not go astray, or rather who finds the resources for correcting her or his errors as she or he proceeds towards both an understanding of, and the achievement of, her or his good.

Those stories, it needs finally to be remarked, have genuine application to human lives only if and because certain metaphysical as well as moral claims can be sustained within philosophy. For those stories not only draw explicitly and obviously upon concepts and theses having to do with rules, regularities, passions, dispositions and ends, but also, if less obviously, upon rules and concepts having to do with substances, essential and accidental properties, potentiality and act, and form and matter. They involve explanations of what it is for someone to succeed in progressing towards or to fail in progressing towards their ultimate end, and such explanations are of interest only if and insofar as we have good reason to believe that they are *true*. But such explanations will be true if and only if the universe itself is teleologically ordered, and the only type of teleologically ordered universe in which we have good reason to believe is a theistic universe.

Hence, the moral progress of the plain person towards her or his ultimate good is always a matter of more than morality. And the enacted narrative of that progress will only become fully intelligible when it is understood not only in terms of metaphysics but in an adequate theological light, when, that is, the particularities of that narrative are understood to embody what is said about sin and about grace in the Ia-IIae of the *Summa* as well as what is said about law and the virtues. The moral progress of the plain person is always the beginnings of a pilgrim's progress.

TWO

Does Applied Ethics Rest on a Mistake?

'Applied ethics', as that expression is now used, is a single rubric for a large range of different theoretical and practical activities. Such rubrics function partly as a protective device both within the academic community and outside it; a name of this kind suggests not just a discipline, but a particular type of discipline. In the case of 'applied ethics' the suggestive power of the name derives from a particular conception of the relationship of ethics to what goes on under the rubric of 'applied ethics'. Not everyone who conducts activities under that rubric owes allegiance to this conception and there are doubtless some who would repudiate it as strongly as I do. But it is that dominant conception from which most work in this area derives or aspires to derive its philosophical legitimacy. What is that conception?

"Does Applied Ethics Rest on a Mistake?" *The Monist* 67, no. 4 (1984): 498–513.

Ethics as such, on this dominant view, has as its subject-matter *morality as such*. Morality as such imposes requirements upon human individuals *qua* human individuals. It has the function of regulating the relationships of anyone whatsoever with anyone else. It thus moves at a level of abstraction and generality which detaches its concerns and its formulations from all social particularity. Being concerned with persons *qua* persons its formulations make no reference to particular social roles or institutional forms. It is not however without explicit social content. Society is understood as an arena of rival and competing interests and what morality supplies are rules which from a neutral and impartial point of view set constraints upon how these interests may be pursued. The rules are neutral and impartial in that they are such that any rational person who had detached him or herself from the distorting causal influence of his or her interests would assent to them. It follows that in the formulation of such rules only concepts available to rational persons as such may be employed: either concepts whose application is involved in any evaluation whatsoever of discourse as rational—concepts such as those of consistency, truth, universality, necessity and the like—or concepts which specify either universal or near universal features of desired states of affairs ("being found pleasant" is one frequent candidate for this status) or universal or near universal objects of desire ("liberty to get what one wants" might be claimed to be such a concept).

Morality as such thus concerns what is true of everyone and anyone in their capacity as rational persons. The requirement of agreement by rational persons removes from the realm of morality one area that has been sometimes thought to be central to it. Our social order is not only an arena for competing interests; it is also one for competing views, religious and nonreligious, as to the best way for human beings to live. On the dominant view it is held that either because rational agreement on the nature of the good life for human beings cannot be reached or just because as a matter of fact it has not been reached or because it is a key part of the freedom of each individual to choose whatever he or she takes to be the best life for him or herself, the rules that constitute morality must be neutral between alternative and conflicting views of the good for human beings. Pluralism about the good is to coexist with rational agreement on the rules of morality.

There are of course many versions of this dominant view of morality: Kantian, utilitarian, contractarian, Kantian-cum-utilitarian, Kantian-cum-contractarian and so on. But the adherents of all such views agree in attempting to specify universally binding principles or rules whose universality has the scope of humanity itself. Detachment from and disinterestedness towards all social particularity and positivity is thus a defining mark of morality. It follows that morality can be formulated and understood independently of any considerations which arise from highly specific forms of social structure. Ignorance of sociology and history will not be a defect in the student of morality as such. But what then of those areas of human life in which the regulation of conduct requires the framing of rules which specify how institutionalised relationships are to be conducted? Examples are the contemporary and shifting relationships of physician, nurse and patient, of lawyer, client and judge, of elected public officials to civil servants and to the public. The answer, according to the dominant standpoint, is that the rules of morality as such have to be *applied* to this kind of socially and institutionally specific subject-matter to yield socially and institutionally specific rules. The academic discipline of *ethics as such*, which enquires into the nature of morality as such, has to be supplemented by the discipline of *applied ethics*. Applied ethics derives its conclusions from sets of premises in which conclusions drawn from ethics are conjoined to factual findings about some specific social and intellectual area. Its rational claims upon our attention depend first then upon the justifiability of the account of morality which it presupposes; secondly, upon the warranted character of its account of the structures of medical or legal or political or military or business institutional and social relationships; and thirdly, upon its ability to derive its conclusions rationally from its premises. It is upon the first and third of these that I shall focus attention.

I

The central requirement of the dominant conception of ethics is then that the rules of morality are such as any rational agent would agree to. But it is an equally notable fact about the moral philosophers who share this conception of ethics that they are in fact unable to agree either upon the precise content of the rules of morality or upon the appropriate way in which such rules are to be rationally justified. Kantians or post-Kantians, utilitarians of different schools, contractarians and the various mixtures of these remain intractably at odds with one another. And in the extent of both ranges of disagreement they mirror the dominant trends of that liberal culture of which they are the articulate spokesmen.

Of course in the culture at large the range of disagreements on both counts is even wider, for all the dissenters from the dominant point of view, theological and nontheological, also have to be counted in. If then, in spite of the dominant requirement of rational agreement, disagreement on what the rules of morality actually are is rampant and in the foreseeable future unresolvable *and* if applied ethics is in fact an application to cases falling within particular social spheres of what are taken to be the rules of morality, then we should expect to find that the disagreements over moral rules reproduce themselves within applied ethics. Doubtless to some extent and on some issues they do: for example, in many debates over abortion. But in an interestingly high proportion of examples either large disagreement on what the rules of morality are turns out to be compatible with large agreement on issues within the domain of applied ethics or, where there is disagreement within that domain between contending parties, it does not reproduce the disagreements between them on the fundamental rules of morality.

Since the former type of example is the more striking, let me discuss one particular report of such a combination of disagreements and agreements. Commenting on the work of the National Commission for the Protection of Human Subjects of Biomedical and Behavioral Research, Stephen Toulmin, who was a staff member for that commission, has described how the commissioners found it relatively easy to reach agreement, or in a minority of intractable cases at least local and isolable disagreement, on particular concrete issues raised by specific difficult types of case, but continued to have fundamental and radical disagreements on matters of moral principle, on what the rules of morality actually are, even although each of them individually aspired to justify his or her views on the concrete issues by appeal to his or her principles.[1]

This type of situation is recurrent within applied ethics and there are three possible explanations for it. The first is that rival and conflicting moral principles do, when applied within applied ethics, surprisingly and unexpectedly yield the same answers. But were this to be true more than very occasionally, grave doubt would be cast on whether the principles or rules being invoked really were in conflict with each other. And since we do seem to have independently adequate grounds for holding that the principles and rules in question are rival and conflicting, we do have grounds for rejecting this explanation. The discrepancy between the agreements on the issues that fall to applied ethics and the disagreements over the principles and rules which constitute morality is just as radical and disturbing as it appears to be.

The second and third types of explanation agree on one central contention: that in such cases the various parties involved in the disagreements at one level and the agreements at another are not in fact applying the moral principles or rules about which they disagree. One possible explanation, which is, I take it, Toulmin's own in the case of the National Commission, is that a very different type of moral reasoning is at work—one in which the fundamental appeal is not to rules, but to cases. On this view, on occasions on which this explanation holds, the participants are behaving rationally in reaching their agreements within applied ethics, but may misrepresent to themselves the nature of their own moral reasoning. A third possible explanation is of a different order. It is that in some such cases at least—although not necessarily of course in that of the National Commission—there is indeed a misrepresentation by the participants to themselves and to others of how agreement is being reached, but that a central feature of the misrepresentation is that what is in fact a nonrational social transaction is being presented as though it were a process of rational argument. I shall want to suggest that in some at least, although certainly not in all of the cases falling under the rubric of 'applied ethics', this third type of explanation needs to be seriously considered.

II

One reason for this last suggestion is that it seems clear that in applied ethics the rules or principles which on the dominant conception constitute morality cannot be being applied in the way that is commonly supposed.

For the relationship between a rule and its applications *cannot* be what on the dominant view it is taken to be; that is, it cannot be the case that we can first and independently comprehend the rules of morality as such and then only secondly enquire as to their application in particular specialized social spheres. For, were this to be the case, the rules of morality as such would be effectively contentless. On the dominant view, for example, we are first and independently to frame a rule or rules about truth-telling and honesty in general and then only secondly need to enquire how it is, or they are to be applied in such relationships as those of physician to patient or lawyer in respect of his or her client's affairs and so on. But no rule exists apart from its applications and if as we approach the question of whether a physician on a particular type of occasion ought to answer a question by a patient truthfully or not it must be in the light of previous applications of the rule. But these applications will have been to situations and relationships quite as socially specific as is the physician-patient relationship. It is characteristically and generally in such relations as those between parent and children, teacher and pupils, clergy and congregation that rules of truthfulness are first learnt. And in extending the rule so that it applies to new situations there are only three possibilities. The first is that, although the rule was first learned and formulated in a certain socially specific type of situation, it was learned and formulated as applying to persons as such independent of what type of situation and relationship each may be involved in at any given time. But if so, there is no new, secondary task of applying the rule to the physician-patient relationship: what the rule says is already clear. Physician-patient relationships in this case are simply part of the subject-matter of morality as such. There is nothing left over for applied ethics to study. A second possibility is that the rule *is* formulated with specific reference to what has been the range of its applications so far, that in its function as a rule of morality as such it does make reference to certain particular socially specific rules and relationships and that in extending it to the physician-patient relationship we are moving beyond the type of case hitherto covered by that rule. But, if so, the task of now reformulating it so that it covers this new class of relationships will be no different in kind from the task already performed of formulating it with reference to those relationships to govern and regulate which it was originally brought into being. In this latter type of case the conception of the rules which constitute morality as such differs from that appealed to in the framing of the former type of case, but, just as in the former type of case, the rule that covers the physician-patient relationship turns out to be a rule of morality as such, no different from any other such rule. And once again after we have understood how the rules of morality as such are formulated and function, no task remains over for something called 'applied ethics' to perform.

Both these possibilities are exemplified of course in actual moral practice: the first by strict, practising Kantians and also for example by the kind of pietist Christian believers from whom Kant's parents learned the rule about truthfulness which they taught to Kant; the second in the extension of rules specifically prohibiting, and providing penalties for, the slaying of an identified member of another kinship group, and rules specifically prohibiting the slaying of strangers, to rules prohibiting homicide in early English society. Is there or could there be a third possibility, a third type of case, which would provide tasks specific to applied ethics? Or do the two types of case which I have sketched in outline exhaust the possibilities, so that in essence the case against applied ethics is already complete? These questions could only be adequately answered by a fuller account of what is involved both in rule-following and in the extension of a preexisting rule to some new class of cases.

III

No rule exists apart from some range of applications. But the relationship of a rule to the specification of its applications varies of course with the type of rule. At one end of the scale there are those rules which the conditions of discourse as such enforce upon us, so that we cannot escape the logical consequences of violating them: such is the rule forbidding the assertion of a statement conjoined to the denial of that same statement. The penalties of inconsistency in the statement and bafflement in the understanding of those who hear or read it are inescapable. In these cases there is no such thing as understanding the rule and not knowing how it is to be applied. This is also true at the other end of the scale where the type of rule is such that to understand it involves the identification of particulars and the specification of context. "Do not enter the greenhouses except by the side doors" as an item in the list of rules governing use of a particular botanical garden is a rule not to be grasped except in terms of particular identifications in a particular context. The rule and its applications are necessarily grasped together.

There are of course crucial differences between these two extreme types of rule: an understanding of some particular rule of the former type can be exhibited quite independently of a knowledge of any formulation of it, whereas understanding and following a rule of the latter type depends upon grasping that there *is* such a rule, something that does require knowledge of its formulation. Moreover, rules of the latter kind are examples of pure positivity. They have their status as rules purely in virtue of the fiat of some authority. Whereas rules of the former kind have no taint of positivity at all; each rational agent must utter them, as it were, to him or herself.

Moral rules—in any useful sense of 'moral'—are and must be of some intermediate type. It is characteristic of moral reflection, as of some other centrally important kinds of thinking, that we move to and fro from the rule to some range of examples of its application and from these particular applications back to the rule; and this movement is an important clue to the nature of moral reflection. For this kind of rule cannot be adequately understood by any individual agent apart from some set of particular exemplary applications. But to grasp some particular rule is nonetheless also to go beyond *any* set of particular applications, for no one has grasped a given rule adequately until he or she has learned how to extrapolate justifiably from the cases in which he or she has understood that rule so far to an indeterminate range of possible future applications of that same rule. The justification for extrapolating in one way rather than another may be a complex matter. It must be partly retrospective, a matter of some tolerably high degree of consistency with past applications of the rule; but it will also be partly prospective, a matter of bringing out crucial or at least relevant resemblances and differences between cases that apart from this kind of application of the rule would have to go unremarked or obscured. And since all rules occur in sets, it is also partly a matter of the implications for other members of the same set—new applications for an expression used in the formulation or reformulation of one rule have to have some kind of consonance with uses of the same expression in other rules.

What is crucial is to be able to distinguish between cases in which a rule is extended in its applications but remains one and the same rule from cases in which a rule by the nature of the extension of its applications has had to be to lesser or greater degree reformulated, so that what we have is a new rule, which however is in some strong sense the successor to its predecessor, and both of these in turn from cases in which a rule has simply been abandoned, perhaps being replaced by no rule at all, perhaps by a rule which embodies a quite different standpoint. What are the criteria in virtue of which we are able to make these distinctions?

It may seem trivial to begin by asserting that the same rule is being applied only if it is applied to the same kind of instance of whatever it is, in virtue of those instances possessing the same characteristic or characteristics in virtue of which it was applied to earlier instances. But this is not the same as saying that it is the same rule which is being applied only if the characteristic or characteristics of instances in virtue of which it is being applied to them are being *understood* as identified in the same way that they were understood in those earlier instances. Continuity in the use of some particular rule does not require continuity in the understanding of that use. And sometimes when prospectively the extension of a rule to some apparently new class of instances seems to create grave problems as to whether after application to this new class of instances the rule could possibly be the same, retrospectively it may become clear that what had to be changed was not the use of the rule, but the understanding of its use.

Consider two very different examples. One is that of the proposal, whenever it was first made (perhaps by some Indian anticipator of Bhāskara in the twelfth century), to extend the rule of subtraction so that some operation of subtraction, that of -1 perhaps, could be performed upon the number 0. The other is the proposal (made perhaps by some Alexandrian Jew to the local Aristotelians in the second century) to extend to cases of infanticide and abortion a prohibition upon the taking of human life which had hitherto been understood not to exclude these. In each case the appeal made by whomsoever was proposing the extension of the rule would have been *to* that in virtue of which in fact the rule had previously been applied to the instances to which it had been applied and *against* that in virtue of which it had been understood to have been so applied. So in the first example the argument would have been that it was the properties of integers *qua* integers and not their properties as *positive* integers in virtue of which the rule had been applied; in the second example it would have been that it was the property of being an innocent individual member of the human species which brought someone under the prohibition of killing and not, for example, the property of being a potentially useful human individual (by being, say, male rather than female; it was female infants who were most often abandoned to their deaths in the ancient classical world). Thus the justification of the extension of the rule derives from a particular kind of reexamination by the members of the community whose rule it is of their understanding of their own rule, one which characteristically involves *both* an enquiry into how the rule had been applied in the past and the nature of the reasons adduced for applying it *and* an enquiry into what members of the community would have said, had the rule been applied to certain types of case to which it had not in fact been applied. Such an enquiry can of course have a variety of outcomes. Because it involves counter factual considerations, its outcome may be indecisive; and even if decisive, what it discloses may be that agreement on the understanding of the rule has not in fact been present, or at least has not been present to the degree requisite for an appeal to it. Nonetheless it is clear that the requirements for a justified extension of a particular rule to cover some particular new type of case can be applied with sufficient clarity for us to be able to discriminate cases which clearly are those of justified extension from cases which equally clearly fail to satisfy the requirements and both from cases in which no verdict can be justified.

What then of the second type of case, that in which we are concerned not with a new application of some particular established rule, so that it is still one and the same rule that is being obeyed, but rather with what is a reformulation of the old rule? Here again there are clear and applicable requirements. For some new rule applied to some new class of instances to be accepted as a reformulation of some other rule to which hitherto allegiance had been given, the justification of the new reformulated rule and of its applications must be auxiliary to and parasitic upon the justification of its predecessor. So the movement from the several prohibitions of several distinct types of killing to a single comprehensive prohibition of homicide, a movement actually made in a number of earlier societies, could satisfy the requirements for a justified reformulation if not only could the set of more limited prohibitions embodied in the earlier rules be deduced from the new reformulation, but the reasons which provide the grounds for obedience to the rule in its new reformulation either give a more fundamental insight into the grounds adduced earlier for the several independent prohibitions or provide more adequate grounds for those prohibitions. To speak of a reformulation in this respect is of course to understand the new rule as more and other than a mere conjunction of the earlier prohibitions. Moreover the reformulation need not forfeit its status as a reformulation if in addition to its greater comprehensiveness, it in some small measure has to correct the older prohibitions or injunctions in order to make them deducible from the new formulation. What matters is that those corrections should not be of what was at the core of the older formulation, but should concern only their more marginal aspects; and thus correction is only in place where it is possible to distinguish the central intention of a prohibition or injunction from the details of its embodiment in a particular rule.

As with the cases where one and the same rule is being applied to some new class of instances, so also in the cases where a rule has been replaced by a rule that is clearly a reformulation of *that* rule, the criteria are adequate to enable us to distinguish those cases of rule innovation which clearly do fall under that description from those which equally clearly do not, and both from those cases where difficulties in applying the criteria hinder or prevent any decisive verdict. What is crucial in the cases where the new rule is a justified reformulation of some older rule or rules is that it was possible to appeal in the course of the reformulation to some shared background of evaluative beliefs. What kind of background must this be?

When the issue of extending a rule to cover some new class of instances arises, whether the outcome is that one and the same rule continues to be used, but with a new understanding of its point and purport, or it is that the rule is reformulated or it is that no change whatsoever is made, it must always be because members of that particular community could agree in seeing some substantial good at stake in responding in one way rather than another. The following of rules and the understanding of rules, implicit and explicit, is always correlative to the apprehension of goods and evils and what the rules are is in any given community a partial, although only a partial specification of goods and evils as understood in that community: a specification of, not a derivation from. So it is true that all rules are to be understood as instantiations of *Bonum est faciendum, et prosequendum et malum vitandum*.[2] Notice that we are speaking here of goods generally: what is at stake in moral rules is good generally, not some special kind of good to be called 'moral good'. Notice also that if the making and remaking and extending and amending of rules is to be a rational activity the goods by appeal to which these activities are carried on must themselves be rationally ordered in some hierarchy. A shared theory of goods of some fairly extensive kind is presupposed, and the notion that genuine rules could be neutral between rival theories of the hierarchy of the goods is ruled out.

Rules and goods both generally find their place within some more comprehensive moral scheme, within which goods ordered hierarchically, virtues, duties, obligations and liberties all find a place. It is with reference to their place in such a scheme that changes in the understanding of rules, reformulations of rules, formulations of new rules and the like are or are not rationally justifiable. It follows that at the core of all issues of rational moral justification is the question of whether the scheme as a whole is or is not rationally justified. When I speak of an overall moral scheme of this kind, I do not merely mean a theory, but rather a theory that is actually embodied in the practices and relationships of a specific society, a theory which if and when it is articulated at the level of explicit theorising will have to be able to give an account of its own embodiment, if it is to sustain its claims.

Such moral schemes themselves have histories and part of that history is the dialectical movement between the consideration and apprehension of higher order goods and principles. It is within this movement that the consideration of individual cases finds its place, either as exemplifying the application of some existing rule, or as providing an occasion for the reformulation of a rule or a set of rules, or sometimes as proving unamenable to treatment in terms of rules and calling for the exercise of judgment of a different order. For no rule or set of rules can cover every relevant contingency; and the discovery of a case not so covered need not provide and on occasion cannot provide adequate reason for extending or reformulating these particular rules. Nonetheless even such cases are defined in terms of and acquire their significance and their status from the rules in question.

Thus the notion that there could be systematic disagreement about moral rules or principles, but agreement about particular cases without some irrationality on someone's part is at the very least highly implausible. But if this is so, the notion of a "case method in ethics," as championed by Toulmin, makes no sense.[3] There is no method of handling cases except in the context of some large degree of agreement upon rules and, for the reasons already given, on a good deal more than rules.

What makes a rule a specifically *moral* rule? This is a question to which an answer has been presupposed throughout my argument, but never spelled out. The answer is that a rule is a moral rule if and insofar as obedience to it is required in exercising the virtues of character, among which the virtue of justice is preeminent in its rule requirements. It may seem however that the account which I have given of how rules may be extended, reformulated to greater or lesser degree (and even abandoned or replaced) is incompatible with the kind of regard for rules which justice requires. Does not justice require us to regard some rules at least as holding for all human beings throughout time, so that my discussion of changes in the understanding and formulation of rules, let alone any more radical kind of moral change, will be ruled out in advance for *those* rules? This is after all not only the doctrine of some modern liberal thinkers, but also of Aquinas and Scotus, and Aristotle himself was surely committed to some such thesis by his belief in natural, as against conventional, justice.

The relevance of this objection to my central thesis is clear. I first suggested that when ethics and morality are rightly understood, the concept of applied ethics loses all application. This suggestion depended for its force upon what the relationship of a moral rule to its applications is. The investigation of this relationship has so far at least confirmed the original suggestion. Moral rules exist only in and through their range of applications and the history of moral rules in key part is the history of the changes in their applications. The conception of morality articulated in this account of moral rules is one according to which moralities are social phenomena, each of which has its own peculiar history of growth and change, of learning and failing to learn, of victories and defeats. But the conception of morality which both generates and underpins the dominant contemporary conception of applied ethics is one according to which morality, not moralities, provides the subject-matter for ethics and according to which morality has at its core a set of timeless principles or rules. It is indeed just because these principles or rules are ahistorical and independent of social change, that the changing realm of the social and the historical raises problems about their application, problems specific to particular sets of social institutions in particular times and places. And such problems are precisely those that provide modern applied ethics with its domain. Hence it may seem to follow that the case for applied ethics and the case for timeless, ahistorical moral principles or rules stand or fall together.

To this argument I concede at once the following: the argument which I have deployed against the very concept of applied ethics does indeed entail the rejection of any conception of moral principles or rules as timeless and ahistorical. What it does not rule out is the possibility of there being enduring moral principles or rules. An enduring moral principle or rule is one which remains rationally undefeated through time, surviving a wide range of challenges and objections, perhaps undergoing limited reformulations or changes in how it is understood, but retaining its basic identity through the history of its applications. In so surviving and enduring it meets the highest rational standard that can be imposed, and there clearly comes a time in the history of a morality when the possibility of some particular principle or rule being either overthrown or radically emended, although still open in principle—quite new forms of challenge can never be finally ruled out—provides no ground at all for any limitation upon our practical allegiance to that principle or rule. And it is no more and no other than this kind of allegiance to this kind of rule that the exercise of the virtue of justice requires.

The theory of knowledge presupposed by this account of the central principles or rules of justice is that set forth in germ by Plato in the *Gorgias* (509a) where Socrates is represented as saying that he does not *know* what is in fact the case with regard to the matters about which he is speaking, but that no one has so far been able to maintain an incompatible view without manifestly falling into error, and that in consequence he holds that matters are as he takes them to be. The Socrates thus represented by Plato was also represented by him as a moral rigorist. And if moral rigorism required principles that could in the Socratic sense be "known," Socrates would have been deeply inconsistent; but, as he himself notices in the same passage, what he requires are principles supported by arguments as enduring as "iron or adamant," enduring, that is, in the face of counter-arguments, counter-examples, rival theories of knowledge and the like. This is the same requirement that the conception of morality which I am defending imposes upon its fundamental principles and rules.

IV

My central claim in this paper is that applied ethics cannot be the kind of activity that it is so often claimed to be, for there is not and could not be any such kind of activity. But what then does go on under that highly misleading rubric? I shall want to suggest that at least two quite different types of activity are being conducted; but a necessary prologue to making this suggestion is a scrutiny of what the morality of our contemporary liberal individualist, morally pluralist society is. For what applied ethics actually comprises turns out to stand in an illuminating relationship to the condition of contemporary morality. What then is the morality actually embodied in those transactions and relationships which are of central importance to the social order of our modernity?

It cannot be the morality spoken of by contemporary liberal moral philosophers; for that morality is constituted by a set of principles or rules to which any rational agent would assent and, as I pointed out earlier, no such set of rules has as yet been identified. It does not of course follow that this conception of morality is without social influence; and what it tends to provide are a set of standards by means of which each contending party in fundamental moral disputes is able to discredit the rational pretensions of its opponents. And this is one more source of the systematically inconclusive character of debate over fundamental issues in our contemporary moral culture. But the ongoing necessities of social life require that these fundamental rifts and conflicts be kept out of view so far as possible; hence the everyday practical life of our social institutions has to be insulated so far as possible from fundamental debate. The phenomenon, which Toulmin noted in the members of the National Commission, of an ability to combine disagreement on moral issues at theoretically fundamental levels with agreement at the level of immediate practicality is in fact and has to be pervasive in our social lives. One central way in which this is achieved is by conferring a high degree of indeterminacy upon our actual shared moral principles.

By our actual shared moral principles I do not mean a set of principles formulated as persons of anyone highly determinate point of view—let alone moral philosophers—would formulate what they regard as their own moral principles. I mean a set of principles which have been rendered indeterminate in order to be adequately shared, adequately shared for the purposes of practical life, that is, with persons of quite different and incompatible standpoints. What those principles then amount to has to be expressed in sentences without any clear ending; "One ought to tell the truth, but there are a range of occasions on which truth-telling is problematic and then. . . ." or "One ought to obey the law, but there are a range of situations in which law-abidingness is problematic and then. . . ." It is of the essence of such principles that although they may list a number of the types of situation in which the application of the principle is not straightforward, such a list will always end with an "etc." for the class of possible exceptions to the rule can never be made fully determinate.

If these were genuine moral rules, they would indeed furnish a decisive counter-example to my thesis about such rules, namely that this kind of rule can never be specified apart from the range of its applications. For these principles can indeed be fully specified in all their indeterminacy prior to their applications; and no finite number of applications will remove that indeterminacy. A decision to apply the principle in one way rather than another in one particular situation does not characteristically and generally make it any less problematic how the principle is to be applied the next time a similar situation recurs. Why is this? It is first of all because characteristically and generally what renders the relevant type of situation problematic is the adducing of a number of rival and incompatible considerations and hence in arriving at a decision how to act the idiom of "a balancing of considerations" is often and appositely used; only—there are no scales—and so the metaphor of balancing, if thought of as a rational process, is a misleading and disguising fiction. And secondly it is because there is no social process of accumulating precedents, of understanding rules as emerging from a history of successful and unsuccessful attempts at reformulation. Socially made decisions are treated in the vast majority of cases as occurring historically *in vacuo*. We do not bind our successors and we are not bound by our predecessors. Nor indeed could we if this account of our shared principles and rules is true, for the indeterminacy of our principles or rules is such that they do not in any substantial sense at all bind us. This is why these are *not* genuinely moral principles or rules.

It is crucial to reiterate that I am not here speaking of the principles or rules of those clear-headed adherents of highly determinate moral standpoints who provide our society with its deviant moral subcultures: Catholics or Southern Baptists, pacifist members of the Society of Friends or radical feminists. What I am speaking of are those simulacra of moral principles that are what moral principles are transformed into in the great pluralist mishmash of the shared public life of liberal societies. And if I am to any large degree right about this, it is not difficult to understand why what is named 'applied ethics' should have been called into being. For there are of course centrally important areas in our social life where there has to be shared public agreement and agreement of a kind incompatible with the indeterminacy and imprecision of what function as, or perhaps rather instead of, shared moral principles in our general public social life.

What areas are these? Unsurprisingly they are just those areas in which applied ethics has flourished: medicine, law, the world of such professions as accountancy and engineering, the military. These are areas in which highly determinate types of action of great moral import have continually to be taken. It is impossible most of the time at least to fudge the question of what one is actually doing. These are also areas in which public confidence in professional activity is required and a necessary condition for such confidence is a high degree of warranted expectation. Such warranted expectation can only be provided by relatively uniform behavior on the part of those engaged in such professional activities within any one particular profession. And such uniform behavior requires a high degree of uniformity of moral education and of ways of handling the problematic. Hence the ubiquity in those areas of codes, explicit and implicit; and hence also the unimportance of these codes being in agreement with one another.[4] The scope required of warranted expectation is by and large no greater than the single profession.

Yet for each profession of this kind the task of showing that it is morally credible and morally accountable has to be an important one. Thus the need to affiliate its particular code or procedures to morality in general arises and with it the need for applied ethics. And at once the ideological function of the dominant conception of applied ethics becomes clear. If and insofar as the codes and procedures of particular professions, of physicians or lawyers or corporate executives, actually were the application in their specific sphere of the rules of morality as such, then those codes and procedures would have all the justification that morality can provide. It is small wonder that in a time of relative economic hardship applied ethics should have flourished financially as well as in other ways. But if the conclusion that I have reached in this paper is correct, applied ethics cannot in fact be achieving what, on the dominant view, it purports to achieve. What actually is going on?

The answer is: at least two quite different kinds of activity. In some areas the ideological function of the dominant conception of applied ethics masks transactions in which professional power and authority are being asserted in a way that will protect professional autonomy from general moral scrutiny. But in other areas what the dominant conception of applied ethics partially conceals from view is a rediscovery of morality as such, and this is notably so in the case of a great deal of work in medical ethics and among the military in the last decade. Such work has been hampered, although often only marginally, by the need to think of it in terms of applied ethics. When physicians or nurses for instance discuss truth-telling, honesty, trust, and allied subjects it is almost always the case—I speak from experience of such discussions in a number of hospitals—that they are doing nothing other than reopening that general discussion of truth-telling in which Aristotle, Maimonides, Aquinas, Kant and Mill are among their predecessors. Their questions concern what the rules are and whether they need to be extended or reformulated, questions perhaps occasioned for them by peculiarly medical issues and questions peculiarly urgent for physicians and nurses, but not at all peculiarly medical questions.

The rubric of 'applied ethics' is thus in both areas a barrier to understanding what is actually going on. In some instances it protects power from scrutiny, in others it disguises the general moral importance of what is occurring. Applied ethics is not only based upon a mistake, but upon one that has proved to be harmfully influential.

THREE

Are Philosophical Problems Insoluble?

The Relevance of System and History

Nobody ever became rich by being a professional academic philosopher. But we academic philosophers are all supported, directly and indirectly, by the labor and earnings of others—this much was true long ago even of the unprofessional Socrates, who scorned to take fees for teaching—and from time to time the question naturally enough arises: why should quite so much in the way of private and public resources be devoted to supporting the inquiries of philosophers and the teaching of philosophy? When we are thus invited to justify ourselves and our activities, there is something of a tendency to stammer and stutter. Philosophy after all is not

"Are Philosophical Problems Insoluble? The Relevance of System and History," in *Philosophical Imagination and Cultural Memory: Appropriating Historical Traditions*, ed. Patricia Cook, 65–82 (Duke University Press, 1993).

technologically useful; it does not supply us with ever more adequate agreed empirical results, as chemistry does; much of it is arid and dry, lacking the charms of literature and the arts. "What good then can philosophy be?" it will be asked.

How we respond to this question will depend in key part upon how we understand the relationship between ourselves and those who pose it. If we think of ourselves as philosophers by profession and those who question us as lay nonphilosophical and unphilosophical persons, ourselves as insiders and them as outsiders, then the problem will be that of how to construct a justification of philosophy in nonphilosophical terms, terms available to those external to what is conceived as a specialized and professionalized activity. To justify philosophy to nonphilosophers will be like justifying engineering to nonengineers or golf to nongolfers. And there are those among our colleagues who have supposed that this is what needs to be done. What they sometimes say is that an education in philosophy is useful. It provides excellent training in lucid writing, in analytical skills, and in problem-solving. This is true; but this was how the teaching of Latin in secondary schools used to be justified, and Latin then disappeared from the secondary school curriculum.

Yet what is wrong with this appeal to the external utility of philosophy is not only that it is likely to be ineffective. In asking, "What good can philosophy be?" those who are asking for a justification have themselves posed a specifically philosophical question in a way which suggests that the distinction between insiders and outsiders is deeply misleading. Philosophical assumptions, theses, arguments, and questions are already present, in one way or another, in the idioms, actions, beliefs, forms of cooperation, and conversation that constitute everyday life. What the academic philosopher does is to make explicit and to pursue with some persistence questions that are posed to and answered by everyone. So a first stage in the justification of academic philosophy has to proceed by bringing those who have not yet recognized this to understand that their choice and ours is not between doing philosophy or not doing philosophy, but between doing it badly and doing it well. And a second stage will be that of showing how the inquiries of professional academic philosophers not only achieve the relevant kind of excellence, but, in addition, provide the resources to enable those who are not professional academic philosophers, in their own nonprofessional way and at whatever level they need or desire to do so, also to achieve the relevant kind of excellence. But can this be shown?

This is the hard question, and part of what makes it hard is a salient and continuing feature of academic philosophy, of which those outside academia are often very well aware, the large inability of professional academic philosophers to arrive at agreed solutions to their own central problems and the corresponding apparent lack of substantive progress within philosophy. Let me begin from an example.

A central fact of our culture is the extent and fundamental character of moral disagreement. Such disagreement arises, in part, from the multiplicity of considerations that are generally recognized as relevant in deciding what it is right to do in particular situations and, in part, from the seemingly incommensurable standards that are invoked in assigning weight to particular claims. So appeals to the rights of one particular group will compete not only with appeals to the rights of other groups, but also with claims based on utility. What some people *deserve* will be weighed against what other people *need*, and rival sets of needs will compete with one another for generally scarce resources. Some among us appeal to exceptionless moral rules, taken to have authority independently of circumstance and consequence; others are sometimes or often prepared to rewrite their rules in the light of circumstances and consequences. Hence, it is unsurprising that to some people at least, the moral life appears as pervasively problematic, a source of recurring dilemmas, while others avoid dilemmas by invoking some particular highly determinate moral scheme, but only at the cost of equally recurrent contention both with those who uphold some rival and incompatible scheme, and with those who oscillate between one position and another. So it is with disputes about abortion. So it is over issues of distributive justice and the morality of war. So it is on occasions when the claims of truthfulness compete with those of responsibility for the well-being of others or of oneself or of the state.

It is therefore unsurprising that distinctively philosophical questions about morality are often enough nowadays explicitly posed by ordinary plain persons who have discovered that they need to learn, if they aspire to be rational, how to argue their way through these apparently problematic situations. And one such central question is: are these situations genuinely or only apparently problematic? Are irreducible, perhaps irreducibly tragic, moral dilemmas an ineliminable feature of the moral life, or is belief in such dilemmas itself an illusion to be dispelled by adequate analysis? Is there perhaps for every human being in every moral situation something to be done that it is unambiguously best and right to do, even if it is sometimes difficult to discern what it is? It is at this point that a recognition that she or he is asking questions with a philosophical dimension may lead an ordinary plain person to turn to professional academic philosophy for assistance. And at first sight a great deal of assistance is available.

Since 1962, more than a hundred articles in philosophical journals, chapters of books, or whole books have been published either directly on the subject of moral dilemmas or on some closely related topic. The problem therefore is not that the lay person will have difficulty in finding philosophical advice. It is that the range and variety and fundamental character of the disagreements in recent and current philosophical literature about moral dilemmas, about whether or not they are real or only apparent, and if real what their character is, and if only apparent, why they are taken to be real, and how they are to be resolved, not merely match the range of disagreements already present in everyday moral debate, but extend and sharpen those disagreements. Nor are there in this large and growing literature any signs of converging agreement on the substantive issues, signs of what a lay person would take to be progress. Thus, to the external observer irresolvable disagreement may appear, in this case as in others, to be the permanent and irremediable condition of academic philosophy. But if so, then the kind of justification of academic philosophy on which I have embarked must seem doomed to failure. For what, it will be asked by the plain person, is the point of rendering explicit what is philosophically implicit in everyday discourse, if the outcome is only to replace one set of seemingly insoluble problems by another set of even more intractable problems?

At this point, a defender of academic philosophy may well reply that *some* progress has in fact been made on these questions in the philosophical literature, even if no agreement on the substantive issues has been arrived at. Some arguments have been discredited, some concepts have been clarified. Ruth Barcan Marcus, for example, has successfully answered the accusation that the very statement of a moral dilemma involves fatal inconsistency, inasmuch as it seems to provide grounds for holding of one and the same person at one and the same time that it is and is not the case that he or she ought to do such and such and therefore cannot describe a possible state of affairs. And Marcus did so by providing a conception of consistency that avoids this charge. Again, Bas C. van Fraassen has provided a novel interpretation of and new rules for deontic logic, which in another way rescue the statement of moral dilemmas from charges of inconsistency.

Yet although these are both clearly examples of philosophical progress, the plain person will be apt to observe that their effect has been not to eliminate or reduce the range of philosophical disagreements, but to sustain and even increase them by rendering certain positions in contention less vulnerable to refutation by their rivals than they previously were. So that what is accounted progress from the standpoint of professional academic philosophy turns out to be quite consistent with what will be accounted lack of progress by the everyday person looking to philosophy for help.

There is, however, another conclusion that emerges from this particular set of philosophical discussions which may not at first appear hopeful to that plain person, but which in the longer run is highly significant for his or her quest. It has been suggested both by Bernard Williams and by van Fraassen that one can appeal against certain theses that deny the possibility of genuine moral dilemmas to what Williams calls "the facts" about moral dilemmas and van Fraassen "the kind of fact of moral life on which ethical theories founder." But what emerges from recent discussions is that there are no such facts about dilemmas independent of and antecedent to all theories. Whether we take it to be a fact that genuine moral dilemmas do occur turns out to depend on how and from what theoretical standpoint we characterize the relevant types of situation.

Consider three very different kinds of moral theory and the different ways in which they will classify and describe one and the same type of moral situation, first taking it to be an instance of a genuine dilemma—that is, of a situation in which two mandatory moral rules prescribe incompatible conduct and there is no rational way of adjudicating between their claims, so that some important rule has to be disobeyed, a second, by contrast, taking that same situation to be an example of a hard case, that is, one in which the relevant mandatory rule unconditionally prescribes an action the performance of which involves a very high cost to the agent or to others or to both in suffering, a cost that however provides no good reason for either disobeying or revising that particular rule, and a third taking this very same situation to exemplify that type of occasion which provides sufficient grounds for revising one or more of our moral rules, as they have hitherto been understood, so that all appearance of a dilemma is removed, and the revision of the rule has taken into account the suffering otherwise involved.

So, for example, from the standpoint of the first type of theory, someone faced with the choice between telling a lie on a matter of some import and being unable otherwise to prevent an innocent person from suffering significant harm will be understood to be in a genuine dilemma in which the good of truth-telling is judged incommensurable with that of preventing harm to innocent people. Yet in that same situation adherents of the second type of theory will judge this a hard case, but one that provides no ground whatsoever for disobeying that exceptionless categorical precept which prohibits all lying. And those who espouse the third type of theory will see neither a dilemma nor a hard case here; they will instead argue that such circumstances justify a revision of the rule which prohibits lying in general, in order to add one more type of exception to a rule formulated in more and more complex ways to accommodate more and more types of situations.

Characteristically and generally, utilitarians will provide examples of this third type of standpoint; Thomists and Kantians in somewhat different ways, are examples of the second; and a variety of recent moral philosophers, such as Stuart Hampshire and Bernard Williams, who take there to be a number of independent sources of incommensurable values, the first. These rival standpoints are, it is clear, not merely those of the adherents of rival sets of moral standards. Their fundamental disagreements extend to the question of how the facts on which their standards are to be brought to bear are to be characterized and classified. Hence, each of these theoretical standpoints has internal to itself its own systematic way of understanding the relevant facts, and no neutral appeal to the facts as they are in themselves, independent of all theorizing, is available. We are thus confronted by three incompatible types of large-scale theory whose adherents have been unable so far to settle their disagreements.

Clearly, something further has emerged from the literature about moral dilemmas, but once again it is something that may appear to make the issues which divide the contending parties less rather than more resolvable. Is this perhaps confirmation that permanent, wide-ranging disagreement is an ineliminable condition of philosophy? A first step in answering this question is to ask what those things are about which in general philosophers do find it possible to secure agreement and correspondingly what it is about their enquiries that engenders and perpetuates conflict and disagreement. Philosophers often *are* able to agree about the structures of the concepts and theories that they study and even more often about the relationships of entailment, implication, and presupposition that hold among statements playing key parts in the elucidation of such concepts and the statement of such theories. Generally, that is, they agree about what follows from what, about what else one is committed to asserting if one asserts some particular statement. And they often, although not always, agree in their diagnoses of incoherence.

The sources of their disagreements are threefold. First, they do not agree on where to begin, either in the initial definition of the philosophical project or on what concepts should be taken to be primary and central in those constructions of philosophical theory that are their intended end product. And, of course, where one begins determines in key part where one ends. Even those philosophers who agree that we ought to begin by criticizing our best predecessors are not of one mind as to who those predecessors are.

Secondly, they do not agree on what weight to assign to different types of consideration, something that divides not only philosophers of vastly different perspectives, such as Heideggerians and Wittgensteinians, but even philosophers whose methods and insights are largely the same. For example, among the theorists of the semantics of possible worlds, David Lewis, Alvin Plantinga, and Robert Adams arrive at some strikingly different conclusions. This is, I take it, because, although philosophers may agree on what further commitments are involved in adopting this or that thesis, or relying on this or that argument, they do not share any overall set of standards by which to evaluate the intellectual costs attached to or the intellectual benefits to be derived from such commitments.

A third type of disagreement among philosophers concerns what they are *against*. A good deal of philosophy is by intention polemical, and some feminist philosophers have suggested that this adversarial character is the result of male domination of the discipline. But I note that they themselves have all too often advanced this thesis in a characteristically adversarial way. (I am happy to concede to such feminists that the too often unnecessarily disagreeable character of philosophical polemics may well arise from typically male vanity and petulance.) What is true is that much central philosophical theorizing has been informed by hostility to some chosen adversarial figure. Think of the very different ways in which Descartes has been used as a whipping boy by Maritain, by Ryle, and by Rorty, or of the way in which Hegel functioned for Russell, Husserl for Derrida, or the earlier for the later Wittgenstein. Whom and what one chooses to be *against* thus has one key part in determining both the direction of one's philosophy and some of the ways in which one will consequently differ from other philosophers.

Given this range of sources of disagreement, the interminability of philosophical conflicts and disagreements is not surprising. But philosophers may at this point be inclined to comment that persistent and apparently ineliminable disagreement is not peculiar to philosophy; it is also a feature of other disciplines. Psychologists have been unable to resolve the conflicts between behaviorists, psychoanalysts, and cognitive theorists, and internal to each of these parties there are also continuing disputes. Economists are able from their professional ranks to provide corporations and governments with equally expert advisers of widely disparate and incompatible points of view. And similar ranges of disagreement are to be found in literary studies, in sociology, and elsewhere. But this appeal to the conflict-ridden character of other disciplines may make the prima facie case against philosophy stronger rather than weaker.

For what are the sources of these conflicts in other disciplines? They arise, I suggest, at just those points within those other disciplines at which specifically philosophical issues become inescapable. The issues that divide psychoanalysts and behaviorists are inseparable from, even if not restricted to, issues in the philosophy of mind; the issues that divide Keynesians and monetarists are inseparable from, even if not restricted to, issues in the philosophy of social science. And so it is also in literary theory and sociology. The appeal to the condition of other disciplines may therefore turn out only to reinforce belief in the distinctively unsettlable character of specifically philosophical quarrels. So how then is the philosopher to respond?

I have identified three main sources of philosophical disagreement in assumptions about what philosophy's starting point should be, about what kind of weight should be attached to different kinds of consideration, and about what types of error we especially need to avoid and to refute. Notice now that characteristically and generally there is a systematic connection not only among what positions are taken up in each of these three latter areas, but also among those positions and what is accounted a conclusive solution to a particular problem or an adequate treatment of a particular issue. And notice also that to insist on the explicit statement and articulation of these systematic connections would be to transform the appearance of the philosophical landscape. Where, previously, stances on particular issues and theses about particular problems had seemed to have been adopted and formulated in a piecemeal, issue-by-issue, and problem-by-problem way, so that each disagreement was apparently framed, in large part at least, in terms specific to each problem situation, it would now become clear that very many of these, at least, are the expression in particularized, small-scale terms of a much smaller number of large-scale, systematic disagreements. To understand this does not make the small-scale, more detailed disagreements any the less important; but it significantly alters our conception both of how they are to be characterized and of how questions concerning their resolution ought to be formulated.

Initially, of course, it may well seem that little or nothing is to be gained by adopting this type of systematic perspective. After all, the history of philosophy is in large part a history of philosophical systems engaged in conflict with one another, Aristotelians criticizing Platonists, Scotists attempting the refutation of Thomists, Cartesians deploring all of the above, empiricists savaging Cartesians, and so on. Thus, it may appear that we have merely added to the catalog of types of philosophical disagreement, rather than having made a first move toward an understanding of how such disagreement can be rationally resolved. But this would be a mistake, as I shall try to show by defending three theses.

The first of these is that adequately determinate solutions to philosophical problems and resolutions of philosophical issues are to be had only from philosophical inquiry within and from the standpoint of some system. Only the constraints afforded by systems supply the requisite kind and degree of determinateness. Secondly, conflicts among philosophical systems, contrary to appearances, are in fact rationally resolvable, but the character of these resolutions has still to be widely understood. And thirdly, the identification of the systematic character of philosophical disagreement enables us to formulate a sufficient rational justification for the activities of the academic philosopher to the layperson outside academic philosophy, even before such a resolution has been achieved and even in spite of the fact that such a resolution may well not be achieved within the lifetimes of the relevant set of laypersons and the relevant set of academic philosophers.

I turn first then to ask what difference it makes to pose philosophical questions from within the context and perspective afforded by the construction of a system rather than by posing such questions as though askable and answerable one by one, in minimal, separable units, the type of unit provided by that distinctive genre of piecemeal philosophy, the contemporary journal article, so that we make explicit not only to the characterization of what whole the characterization of each subordinate part or aspect of each topic or issue is to contribute, and in the light of what overall canons of method an answer to a philosophical question is to be deemed adequate and adequately well-grounded, but also to the standards set by what philosophical predecessors we are to be held accountable. In so doing, we make available a strong set of criteria, conformity to which characteristically provides conclusiveness, or at least relative conclusiveness in evaluating alternative formulations of philosophical issues and alternative solutions to philosophical questions. Consider in this light the questions posed about moral dilemmas.

I noticed earlier that what characterization a particular philosopher gives of that type of situation about which, characteristically, disagreement arises in answering the question of whether it does or does not confront us with a moral dilemma will depend on what large-scale theoretical standpoint such a philosopher either invokes explicitly or tacitly presupposes. And in a similar way, the answers to other questions about aspects and details of the problems treated under the rubric 'moral dilemmas'—problems, for example, about the logical status and structure of the rules that do or do not generate such dilemmas, or about the reactions appropriate to certain types of action that infringe on what is normally taken to be required of us, whether regret, remorse, or guilt—also turn out to differ with the type of theoretical standpoint invoked or presupposed.

It is then in fact the case, whether recognized or not, that in these controversies what systematically confront one another are rival, large-scale theoretical standpoints, such as those of utilitarianism, Kantianism, and Thomism, including as one more such standpoint the antitheoretical moral theory of such as Bernard Williams. Abstract the issues of detail from the contexts provided by such theoretical standpoints, and detach the various points of view expressed on those issues of detail from the premises and presuppositions afforded by such standpoints, and the outcome will be a set of necessarily interminable disagreements among positions whose truth or falsity is underdetermined by the only kinds of reasoning then apparently admissible, as indeed the literature shows that it is. It is not of course, as I also noted earlier, that a good deal of worthwhile clarification has not been achieved through the discussion of those disagreements; but the point and purpose of such clarification only emerges in those larger systematic contexts. So the move to or toward doing philosophy systematically issues in the replacement of a multiplicity of interminable disagreements by the emergence of a number of solutions, each taken to be conclusive, or at least relatively so, from within its own theoretical perspective. But what then of the charge that it is just the level of disagreement which has changed, but not the fact of its intractability? Now everything turns on whether or not the claims of one large-scale theoretical standpoint can or cannot be vindicated against its rivals.

In order to answer this question, let us for the moment put it on one side, and consider further some characteristics of philosophical systems. Such systems often enough arise out of an attempt to exhibit to some particular prephilosophical audience why they are finding some particular type of difficulty or problem of their own peculiarly intractable or some particular type of fundamental disagreement obstinately unresolvable, by providing a systematic philosophical setting within which those problems and disagreements can be reformulated in a way that makes them amenable, or at least more amenable, to rational solution. Philosophical systems, that is to say, are initially responses to prephilosophical questions.

An example is provided by Aristotle's ethics and politics—ethics and politics understood as having a systematic metaphysical dimension. What was it outside philosophy to which Aristotle in formulating his ethical and political views was responding? A variety of competing types of political constitution, oligarchic and democratic, rival adherents of which sometimes engaged in civil war; a variety of competing diagnoses of past Greek political failures invoked to support rival policies; a variety of well-established opinions held by poets, dramatists, and statesmen about what the human good is, what the virtues are, and how particular virtues are to be understood. To whom was Aristotle speaking? Primarily and immediately to young men who would by the time they were thirty share in the rule of some *polis* and who were confronted not only with this range of rival and competing opinions, but with disagreements about what kind of education would best enable them to act well, disagreements most notably between a range of sophistic views, Plato's philosophical antipolitics, Isocrates's defense of a rhetorical training informed by revived Periclean ideals, a defense which disdained philosophy as unpractical, and Aristotle's own theory and practice.

Aristotle also had, of course, a secondary audience: the ruling elites of the *polis* from whom these students were drawn and to whose ranks they would return. And we, belated members of a tertiary audience, need to understand how it was in virtue of his addressing these particular primary and secondary audiences, confronting this particular range of problems and issues, of *aporiai*, that Aristotle had to understand his relationship to these audiences. First, it was crucial to the kind of conversation in which he was engaging that his accounts of constitutions, of established rival opinions and of the *aporiai*, the problem and issues, arising from them should be recognizably accurate. And secondly, he had to enable his audience to recognize its own initial incompetence, including an incompetence to understand the nature of that incompetence, in confronting those *aporiai*. That is, the young and immature, the inexperienced and undisciplined, had to be induced to subject themselves to an education into a set of moral and intellectual virtues, the point and purpose of which they would be able to appreciate only once they had acquired them. So, according to Aristotle, in coming to understand the human good, the truths about that good which are finally to be attained through arduous inquiry must themselves already be presupposed in the earliest phases of that inquiry, by the way in which inquiry has to be organized at its outset. This type of circularity involved in initiating and carrying through philosophical inquiry, which Aristotle makes so plain to us, I take to be an ineliminable feature of systematic philosophy. Our *telos*, our end, theoretical or practical, is already in our beginnings.

That this is so has two important consequences. First, systematic philosophy cannot commend itself to members of its prephilosophical audience by arguing that what they are going to learn from it will serve their preexisting preferences and purposes, at least as they initially understood them. For almost the first thing they will have to learn is that until they have put those preexisting preferences and purposes in question, they will be debarred from genuine participation in the philosophical enterprise. So it turns out once again that the case against justifying philosophy by appealing to its external utility, as utility is prephilosophically understood, is from the standpoint of systematic philosophy illegitimate. What philosophy does and can speak to in our prephilosophical condition are those incoherences and unintelligibilities of which we become aware in the course of making explicit those philosophical assumptions that already informed our prephilosophical discourse and beliefs. Yet in learning from philosophy how to address these difficulties, we have to act in ways that presuppose what we have yet to learn. It is common enough not to recognize this point, sometimes because all circularity in philosophical inquiry is thought to be vacuous or vicious. And circularity in rigorous demonstrative argument is, of course, vacuous and vicious; but in dialectical inquiries of the kind from which systematic philosophy begins, one sometimes already has to presuppose, without recognizing it, what one is going to put in question, in order to be able to put it in question rationally. This is notoriously how Aristotle proceeded in *Metaphysics K* in defending the principle of noncontradiction, but he also proceeds in this way elsewhere, although sometimes less obviously. And we find the same type of fully defensible circularity in as different a philosopher as Descartes. That circularity has often enough been remarked, but characteristically in order to impugn Descartes. Descartes, it is rightly said, derives his fundamental criterion of clarity and distinctness from the *Cogito*. And, it is then equally rightly remarked, that he relies upon these criteria in determining the truth of the *Cogito*. And this clear and distinct circularity with respect to clarity and distinctness is then adduced by some critics as a ground for rejecting the structure of Descartes's argument. But what such critics once again fail to distinguish are the standards appropriate to demonstrative arguments and the standards appropriate to those dialectical arguments by means of which demonstratively structured systems of thought are brought into being. What the historical narratives of the *Discourse* and the *Meditations* recount is a story of how progress in dialectical inquiry had brought Descartes to a point at which he could from within what had now become Cartesianism—the "I" who had once been the historical René Descartes had been rendered into the timeless "I" internal to the *Cogito*—reject both history and dialectic. Like the Wittgenstein of the *Tractatus*, he threw away the ladder by which he had mounted. And in this, of course, he was quite unlike Aristotle. But so far as the circularity by which he had reached his goal is concerned, Cartesian circularity is no more objectionable than Aristotelian.

This, then, is how systematic philosophy begins. It deserves to be called systematic only when as large a range as possible of the problems, incoherences, and partial unintelligibilities of prephilosophical discourse, action, and inquiry are made the subject matter of an inquiry in which the questions to be answered are of the form: How are all of these to be understood in the light of the best unified and integrated conception of rationally adequate inquiry possessed so far? Every well-developed conception of rational adequacy is a conception internal to some particular philosophical system; indeed, from one point of view a particular philosophical system just is a well-developed, unified, and integrated conception of rational adequacy. But at the same time, rational adequacy is what we all aspire to in our prephilosophical arguments, assertions, debates, and inquiries. Yet it is at this point that another serious objection has been advanced. For it has been thought that if philosophical systems are informed by circularities of the type that I have identified, then they will be inherently defective in providing ideal conceptions of rational adequacy.

Each philosophical system will from the outset in developing its ostensibly rational accounts of this or that area of discourse, action, or inquiry tacitly presuppose or explicitly invoke just that conception of the *telos* of inquiry which in turn it will support by appeal to the findings derived from those accounts. So Aristotle's account of the ultimate human good supports his account of the virtues and is in turn supported by them. So his account of practical deliberation in choice supports his account of the good and is in turn supported by it. And so it is also with thinkers other than Aristotle. But then it seems that each such system will have internal to it its own conception of rational justification, and that therefore there will be no point at which the conception can itself be put in question. This has the consequence that two or more rival philosophical systems, with substantively different conceptions of what rational justification is, Aristotelianism, say, on the one hand, and Cartesianism on the other, will each provide for appeal only to its own standards of rational evaluation, and so the adherents of each will be confirmed in their belief in the superiority of their own system, but in a way that makes the encounter between such rival systems rationally barren. We shall end up with too many rationalities, too many conceptions of rational adequacy, each self-confirming and none able to provide genuinely good reasons for preferring it to its rival.

That this is indeed the case has been a powerfully influential view. In one form it underpinned a good deal of the logical positivist objection to metaphysics. But it has also been in a different way an influence on Heideggerian and post-Heideggerian evaluations of past philosophy. In the logical positivist version, the rejection of past philosophical systems depended on the alleged undecidability of the claims of rival metaphysical theses. In the Heideggerian and post-Heideggerian versions, the rejection depends on the ascription to past metaphysical systems of a claim to a kind of grounding that they cannot in fact have. The positivists impugned the credentials of past philosophical systems because their adherents were not able to appeal to some criterion that could be established independent of and prior to the particular claims of any systematic philosophical theory; the Heideggerians have impugned the credentials of past philosophical systems by ascribing to them just such an appeal, albeit an entirely illegitimate one, to something external to and independent of their systematic theories, which could provide those theories, and discourse and action issuing from them, with grounding.

Both positivists and Heideggerians are mistaken. Philosophical systems do not need, in order to provide themselves with rational justification, to appeal to some external, theory-independent standard of justification; and they did not in fact do so. But in what, then, does their own rational justification consist? In the way in which and to the extent to which within each system provision has been made, explicitly or implicitly, for the possibility that by putting itself to the question in its own terms it will break down and exhibit a variety of forms of internal incoherence and resourcelessness, so that that system will fail by its own internal standards of rational justification. It is one of the marks of the rise of a major philosophical system, that its initial large-scale statement always engenders a new set of problems internal to that particular system. The internal problematic of each system provides its adherents with a set of tasks; their progress in or failure to make progress in dealing with those tasks provides initially a more important measure of intellectual success or failure than do the tasks of responding to external critics. And the merits of a system depend on and are relative to its problem-engendering character. What makes it possible for the adherents of a philosophical system to claim that it has been rationally vindicated is just that about it in respect of which it is also open to the possibility of rational defeat. Hence, it is one of the essential virtues for a major philosophical system that it will be stated in a way that renders it maximally vulnerable to refutation from its own point of view. This is a standard judged by which Plato, Aristotle, Descartes, Hume, Spinoza, and Kant excel; if we were to apply it to such postmodernist thinkers as Lyotard, Rorty, and Fish, they would fare very badly.

The radical criticism and rejection of a major philosophical system is then something that is able to and proceeds from its own point of view. But to say this is not to say that such criticism and rejection can be achieved only through the work of adherents of that particular philosophical system. Philosophical imagination enables us to inhabit temporarily a diversity of systems other than our own, and thus to participate both in the criticism of rival systems and of our own as though we were external critics; and the development of a philosophical imagination is a central part of a philosophical education.

Philosophical systems, then, can be rationally defeated—self-defeated. But, it may be retorted, this does not fully respond to the objection. For it might still seem that, although within each such system the activity of rational criticism of that system can go on, each system cannot but be isolated from criticism from the standpoint of its rivals. But this too is a mistake. For the claims of any developed, would-be comprehensive system depend in key part upon its ability to provide within itself, in its own terms and in a way that accords with its own standards, a representation of the relevant theses and arguments of its rivals. So there is a Kantian account of

Plato and a Hegelian account of Aristotle and equally an Aristotelian account of Kant and Hegel, provided by modern Thomists. We have therefore moved to the point at which it is possible to understand how two theses often thought to be incompatible can both be true.

The first is that there are indeed no standards or criteria of rational evaluation in any area, no matter how fundamental, that are theory-independent and inquiry-independent, neutral between rival theoretical standpoints, whether philosophical, natural scientific, moral, or whatever, and available therefore to intelligent persons of any point of view. The second is that it is nonetheless possible on occasion to decide rationally between the claims of two rival competing schemes of thought and/or practice in a way that is equally rationally compelling to the adherents of both the rival standpoints. And this is possible because some particular scheme of thought and/or practice can be rationally defeated both by its own standards *and* by the standards of one of those competing rivals. When, in addition, that particular rationally victorious rival possesses the resources to provide an illuminating identification and explanation of just those limitations and inadequacies, the recognition of which as irremediable in the light of that system's own standards had led to the acknowledgment of its having failed by its own standards, something which that self-defeated system did not itself possess the resources to provide, then that particular rival will have satisfied the conditions jointly necessary for its rational superiority to have been established in the strongest terms possible.

In this respect there is no difference between philosophical systems and large-scale bodies of scientific theory—and sometimes, of course, although not always, such bodies of scientific theory themselves are, or are constituent parts of, philosophical systems. Galilean and later Newtonian physics rationally defeated Aristotelian physics not by appealing to some philosophically and scientifically neutral, theory-independent criterion, for there is none such, but because not only did Aristotelian physics, as it had developed into late medieval impetus theory, fail by its own standards in a way in which Galilean and Newtonian physics did not fail by their own standards, but also Galilean and more especially Newtonian physics were able to explain, and to explain precisely, just why and how Aristotelian physics, if developed to a certain point, had to fail in the way that it did.

It follows from all this that the history of philosophy can be written as a history of rational progress, provided that three conditions are satisfied. The first is that that history should be conceived primarily not as a history of problems or as a history of texts, but as a history of systems, of their rising, flourishing, and declining, within which problems and texts find their place. A second condition, implicit in the first, is that systems themselves should be understood as historical: there is no such thing as Aristotelianism or Cartesianism, but only Aristotelianism at each successive stage of its development, only Cartesianism in its first formulations, in its mature formulations, and in its uses by Descartes's successors. To inhabit a philosophical system is to be a participant in a history, a history in and through which some particular conception of rational adequacy in theory and in practice is formulated, developed, tested, revised, and perhaps finally defeated, but perhaps instead one that survives its encounters with both internal and external critiques, so that it remains a contender in philosophical debate.

A third condition, implicit in the first two, is that such a history should be written from the standpoint of some one particular system. For if it is to be justified as history, it must itself meet standards of rational adequacy, both theoretical and practical, and the particular set of such standards to which the historian will have to appeal will be standards developed within some particular system. No system, of course, will be able to provide a standpoint from which an adequate history can be written that is not itself conceptually rich enough to provide from within itself representations of those other systems that have been or still are the major contenders in philosophical debate. And indeed it will have to be rich enough also to provide adequate representations of their representations of it. So no Aristotelianism will be qualified to provide a standpoint for writing the history of philosophy that lacks the resources to furnish adequate and accurate representations not only of Cartesianism and Kantianism and Hegelianism, but also of Cartesian and Kantian and Hegelian representations of Aristotelianism.

One further characteristic, not only of such a history, but of the history of the various philosophical systems that provide it with its subject matter must now be noted. I have suggested that philosophical systems are elaborations of ideals of rational adequacy, both theoretical and practical, but of the rational adequacy of *what*? The answer is: those multifarious beliefs, arguments, assertions, and practices, persistent features of which forced on everyday plain persons a recognition of their need to raise philosophical questions about those beliefs, arguments, assertions, and practices. But this relationship between the initial self-questioning of the prephilosophical plain person and the answers delivered by those speaking from the standpoint of some philosophical system is not something that occurs at the inception of systematic theorizing, but thereafter disappears. It is only because and insofar as there are a more or less continuous set of dialectical interchanges between those philosophers who are engaged in articulating some particular system and those plain prephilosophical persons who are engaged in posing questions about the rational adequacy of their beliefs and practices, questions that arise out of their everyday discourse and interaction as well as from scientific and theological inquiries, aesthetic and legal and political activities, and so on, that philosophical systems continue to have an identifiable subject matter.

It is at this point that yet one more version of a difficulty which in different forms has arisen again and again in this chapter can be relevantly advanced. Even if plain persons do come to understand, it may be said, that philosophical systems articulate ideals of rational adequacy which provide answers to some of their own central questions, they cannot but notice that rival philosophical systems persist, and that the disagreements and conflicts among major systems have not yet been resolved. So the justification of philosophy still has to confront continuing large-scale disagreement among philosophers. But these disagreements must now surely appear in a new light.

For if there are recognizable within our culture philosophical systems that articulate rival and conflicting conceptions and ideals of rational adequacy, it is now clear that this must be because disagreement on these fundamental matters is deep-rooted and pervasive in our culture. It is these disagreements, so often concealed behind the platitudes of official rhetoric, that philosophy enables the plain person to identify and to understand, so enabling her or him to engage with these disagreements more rationally and less confusedly than would otherwise be the case. When understood thus, the continuing disagreements of philosophy no longer stand in the way of a rational justification of philosophy.

So it is that in satisfying the conditions for the successful development of a philosophical system or systems of any depth and sophistication, the conditions are simultaneously satisfied for answering the question of how and in what terms the philosophical enterprise is to be justified to those not professionally engaged in it. It is because and insofar as a particular system articulates ideals of rational adequacy, which in successive formulations provide more and more satisfactory answers to the continuing questions of some particular prephilosophical public, that it both flourishes as a philosophy and can be seen to discharge its responsibilities in the world at large, even if it is in continuing conflict with other such systems. Hence, there is a social dimension to the history of philosophy, one generally omitted or very largely so from the history of philosophy when studied as an academic discipline. And this is an omission that deforms the history of philosophy. For philosophy does not generate its own most fundamental questions, even when it is a philosopher who, as Socrates did, initially guides others into posing questions that they might well not otherwise have asked, so revealing the extent to which those others had already been concerned with and perhaps entangled by distinctively philosophical issues.

Insofar as there are those among them who continue to reformulate and reiterate those questions, so constituting a continuing public for some particular developing philosophical system, a public of everyday plain people for whom the standards by which they judge the rational adequacy or inadequacy of their own reflective discourse and inquiry are standards furnished at different stages by that system, the relationship of academic, professionalized philosophy needs no further justification. For insofar as some plain people in a social group discharge their part as a public in bringing their own questions about the rationality of what they judge and do to philosophy, to that same degree philosophers are able to discharge their part in eliciting, revising, and sustaining the standards of rationality required by a variety of types of human activity, and indeed by human activity as such. And in this lies the only justification of philosophy.

Yet if this is so, the rational justification of philosophy is not something that can be carried through for anyone whatsoever at any time or place. Only when philosophy is in a particular condition, and that social group to the members of which philosophy is to be justified is in a corresponding condition, is the enterprise of justifying philosophy a possible one. There have, of course, been a variety of times and places when the necessary kind of symbiosis between the life of systematic philosophy and the life of the corresponding social group or groups has been achieved. So it was at certain times in ancient Greek city-states and in Islamic medieval caliphates and in medieval Christian universities both in their agreements and in their conflicts; so it was in a number of periods in Chinese and Japanese history. In each such case, a justification of philosophy was possible in terms of the highly specific character of some particular philosophical system or systems and the nature of the sustained interchanges between those engaged in explicitly philosophical inquiry and other key members of the relevant social groups.

It follows, of course, that, in times and places where either or both of these two conditions go unsatisfied, it will not be possible to provide any rationally compelling public justification of philosophy. If and when philosophy is no longer a largely systematic activity, but is instead, at least for the most part, conducted piecemeal, and if and when social and cultural life is such that there is a widespread inability or reluctance—for whatever reason—to press questions to the point at which their inescapably philosophical character becomes evident, then the claims of philosophy on scarce academic and educational resources, in competition with other claimants, will become difficult to vindicate. Those of us who are committed to philosophy should pray not to live in such a time.

FOUR

The Idea of an Educated Public

There are very few invitations which I could have been more pleased to accept than one to participate in a series of lectures honouring Richard Peters. The period which he and I have lived through from the Second World War to the present, or in philosophical terms from Ryle and Sartre to Derrida and Davidson, has been one in which it has been common enough for lip-service to be paid to the notion that philosophy is a form of activity of crucial relevance to success or failure in our other activities, but not very common for this thesis to be exemplified in a cogent and creative way. Richard Peters' professional life has been just such an exemplification; and by it he has put us all in his debt. I have myself in addition some more particular reasons to be grateful. I have learnt continually from what he has

"The Idea of an Educated Public," in *Education and Values: The Richard Peters Lectures*, ed. Graham Haydon (University of London Institute of Education, 1987).

written and said ever since his paper on 'Motives and causes' in 1952;[1] and he has been kind enough on occasion to be a trenchant but careful critic of my own work. My gratitude for his criticism is perhaps all the greater because generally, although not of course always, reflection upon his criticisms has both convinced me of the inadequacy of the formulations in which I had expressed what I was trying to say and yet confirmed me in a good deal of the substance of the views which he has so vigorously rejected. But if I have been thus obdurate, it has certainly not been because I am ungrateful and I hope it has not been because I have not appreciated the force of his arguments. J. L. Austin once said, 'I am not sure importance is important; truth is.'[2] Richard Peters is one of those who has shown us that a care for truth is all the more important when one is dealing with important questions. It is to a question on the importance of which I am sure that he and I have always agreed, and on the truth about which I am equally sure that he and I would always have been likely to disagree, that I now turn.

I

Teachers are the forlorn hope of the culture of Western modernity. I use that expression in the original sixteenth-century Dutch sense (*verloren hoop*) of an assault party sent out on some dangerous offensive mission in advance of the main forces, as well as in its later English sense of an enterprise on whose success we have to depend, but which is in fact bound to fail. For the mission with which contemporary teachers are entrusted is both essential and impossible. It is impossible because the two major purposes which teachers are required to serve are, under the conditions of Western modernity, mutually incompatible. What are those purposes?

The first is one that is among the purposes of almost all education almost everywhere: it is to shape the young person so that he or she may fit into some social role and function that requires recruits. Athenian sophists, masters in medieval Dominican houses of study, Prussian ex-sergeants turned village schoolmasters and T. H. Green's colleagues in the teaching of *Literae Humaniores* at Oxford all served this purpose quite as faithfully as any teacher of automechanics in a trade school. The second purpose is derived in its more specific form from the culture of the eighteenth-century

Enlightenment, although it has of course its earlier antecedents. It is the purpose of teaching young persons how to think for themselves, how to acquire independence of mind, how to be enlightened, as Kant understood 'enlightenment'. These two purposes can be combined only if the kind of social roles and occupation for which a given educational system is training the young are such that their exercise requires, or is at least compatible with, the possession of a general culture, mastery of which will enable each young person to think for him or herself.

Thinking, on Kant's view—and here he spoke for the whole Enlightenment—is an activity the end-product of which requires rational justification; it is an activity in which we exhibit our power of rational objectivity. Where there are no standards of rational objectivity, there is no place for thinking and *a fortiori* for independent, enlightened thinking. And where there is no widespread social agreement either upon what such standards are, or upon what subject-matters it is important that thinking should be exercised, there will be no general culture of the requisite kind. For thinking, as Kant and indeed as the majority of his Enlightenment peers understood it, is not a specialized activity, exercised upon specialized subject-matters. It was, on Kant's view, not in the professional faculties of law or theology, but in the faculty of philosophy that thinking was to be learnt. And philosophy was not then a specialized discipline.

When I say that the two overall purposes of modern educational systems are to fit the young person for some particular role and occupation in the social system and to enable him or her to think for him or herself, I mean at least two things. First, the claim that these are the purposes to be served by an educational system takes its place among the undeniable platitudes of the age—uttered in speeches by ministers of education, chairpersons of local authorities or head teachers, it will be so familiar as not even to be heard. Secondly, these aims are in fact presupposed, whether consciously or not, as providing the final answers to a chain of questions of the form: 'For the sake of what is that being done?', when and if such questions are posed about the immediate, everyday tasks which each teacher faces in the classroom.

That these two overall purposes are mutually incompatible, that success at one is bound to ensure failure at the other, is not a timeless conceptual thesis. I am not claiming that the concept of being taught to think for oneself necessarily can only have application when the concept of being fitted for one's part in social life lacks it or vice versa. For I am going to argue that under certain types of social and cultural condition both concepts can indeed find application within one and the same educational system. But I shall also argue that as a matter of contingent fact specifically modern post-Enlightenment societies and cultures now exclude the conditions which make this coexistence possible.

What modernity excludes is the possibility of the existence of an educated public; and I shall be arguing that it is only where an educated public exists, and where introduction into the membership of that educated public is the goal of education, that both the overall purposes presupposed in modern education systems can be realized. What am I going to mean by an educated public? Let me begin by giving a paradigmatic example.

II

It is in the eighteenth century that the modern concept of an educated public first finds application; and the example of such a public which has most and immediate relevance to our own concerns is that of the public created by the remaking of the Scottish universities in the first half of that century. Scotland, after the loss of political sovereignty in 1707, had simultaneously to redefine its national identity and provide a milieu for nationwide debate on its future development. Its culture was a culture in which the specific institutions of Scots law, of the Scottish educational system and of the Presbyterian Church of Scotland as established in 1689 required justification in the face of continuous pressure from forces of Anglicization. But it was not only that these Scottish institutions had to be vindicated as superior to their English counterparts. They had to be vindicated in a way that dissociated this distinctive Scottish identity from, on the one hand, the claims of Gaelic Scotland, largely Jacobite, and Roman Catholic or Episcopalian, and on the other, the claims of those Evangelicals within and without the Church of Scotland who saw in the settlement of 1689 a betrayal of the theocratic ideals for which their predecessors had fought.

At the same time Scotland confronted alternative economic and social futures. Its way of life was that of a nation of small local communities for whom possibilities of large-scale economic growth had now begun to open up. Could the values of small communities be preserved in a period of commercial and industrial expansion? Was it desirable that they should be? Were the conflicts of the past detrimental to society? Or would their eradication itself be detrimental? These were the questions to which a variety of mutually incompatible answers were to be given by Andrew Fletcher, David Hume, Adam Smith and Adam Ferguson, to pick out only the greatest names. But a debate between a few outstanding protagonists is something very different from a discussion carried on by and within an educated public. What conditions are required for the existence of such a public?

They are of at least three kinds. There must first of all be a tolerably large body of individuals, educated into both the habit and the opportunity of active rational debate, to whose verdict appeal is being made by the intellectual protagonists. These individuals must understand the questions being debated as having practical import for generally important aspects of their shared social existence. And in their communication with one another they must recognize themselves as constituting a public. Thus an educated public is to be contrasted both with a group of specialists, participation in whose controversies is restricted to their peers, and with a passive mass public of readers or listeners who merely provide an audience for the debates of others.

A second type of requirement is shared assent, both to the standards by appeal to which the success or failure of any particular thesis or argument is to be judged, and to the form of rational justification from which those standards derive their authority. So the debates of an educated public are to be contrasted with those very different controversies in which disagreement extends so far into the question of how disagreement is to be rationally resolved that no effective terminus to debate is possible. And they are also to be contrasted with those debates in which there are indeed shared standards of success and failure in argument, but where the authority of those standards is afforded no rational justification, but derives merely from local precedent and custom. The undue prevalence either of a certain kind of scepticism or of a certain kind of dogmatism destroys the possibility of an educated public.

Both these types of requirement presuppose a third. An educated community can exist only where there is some large degree of shared background beliefs and attitudes, informed by the widespread reading of a common body of texts, texts which are accorded a canonical status within that particular community. When I speak of a canonical status, I do not mean that such texts provide a final court of appeal. I mean only that appeal to them has to be treated with a special seriousness, that to controvert them requires a special weight of argument. This common possession by a community of such a shared body of texts is only possible when there is also an established tradition of interpretative understanding of how such texts are to be read and construed. So not every literate and reading public is an educated public; mass literacy in a society which lacks both canonical texts and a tradition of interpretative understanding is more likely to produce a condition of public mindlessness than an educated public.

In the creation of an educated public in eighteenth-century Scotland, it was the movement of reform in the universities largely initiated by William Carstares, who was Principal of Edinburgh University from 1703 to 1716, which in some large measure provided for the satisfaction of all three types of requirement. A shared model of rational justification was provided partly through the way in which logic was taught, but more importantly by the requirement that all undergraduate students read the first six books of Euclid early in their academic careers. The application of the model of justification learned from Euclid to substantive non-mathematical issues was primarily pursued in the philosophy, and more especially the moral philosophy, classes, and in those classes the place of student debate and discussion was crucial. In addition to the two hours devoted to lecturing, an hour a week was given over to the questioning of members of the class by the professor, and on occasion to arguing with them over the subject of the lectures. Sometimes the students were made to debate among themselves.

This discussion within the classroom was reinforced by the practice of both formal and informal debate within student societies, societies which at their best were remarkable centres of intellectual life. When it is remembered how many of these students would either become lawyers, within a legal system in which debate over appeal to first principles was at home in a way completely foreign to English law, or ministers in a church whose courts from the local kirk session up to the General Assembly were similar forums of debate, the continuities between undergraduate education and the creation of a larger educated public become clear. And it is important to notice that the legal and ecclesiastical communities were united not only by the fact that members of the legal profession were by and large also members and often office-holders in the kirk, and not only by their shared modes of dispute and justification, but also by the fact that one and the same set of first principles were appealed to by both, those first principles which provided the subject-matter of moral philosophy.

Moral philosophy was thus to some degree the keystone of the curriculum and it was moral philosophy of one particular kind. A shared allegiance to its principles was the constitutive belief crucial to the existence of the educated public of eighteenth-century Scotland. These principles received their classical statement in the lectures and books of Thomas Reid and Dugald Stewart. But Reid did not invent the role of the professor of moral philosophy as rational apologist for a morality that would be at once secular and yet both consonant with and supportive of the Christian religion. In so far as any one individual had invented that role it had been Francis Hutcheson. What Reid had discovered was that if you began in moral philosophy where Hutcheson began, you were bound to end where Hume had ended. Indeed it was part of Reid's greatness to have understood that the whole movement of modern philosophy from Descartes onwards was inexorably towards the Hume of the *Treatise*. And on Reid's interpretation, or perhaps misinterpretation, of the *Treatise* the outcome was a scepticism, both metaphysical and moral, which fatally undermined the type of moral belief of which both Hutcheson and Reid aspired to be defenders.

Reid identified what he took to be the error committed not only by Hutcheson, but by all the adherents of 'the way of ideas' as deriving from a mistake about the nature, content and status of first principles. The mind of every rational being is stocked with a set of principles which provides premises from which all other justified beliefs can be derived. These principles have the role in the structure of our beliefs in general that axioms have in geometry. They cannot therefore be derived from any more ultimate principles. But their status is not a matter of their not being deniable without contradiction. Only two classes of person are, however, liable to deny them: the insane and philosophers—in the insane of course because they are incapable of reflection on the import of such principles; philosophers because either they mistakenly look for further justifications where none is needed or they equally mistakenly suppose that, because such justifications are lacking, sceptical conclusions are in order.

What are these principles which furnish mankind with its reasonable common sense? They include: that every physical event has a cause; that the willing of rational agents is not determined by any external cause; and that duty is a notion independent of that of interest. Conjoined with other more specialized conceptions, they and others such yielded the principles appropriate to international law, and those required for political economy, both still conceived as part of the moral philosophy curriculum. And in so doing they define the boundaries of the shared outlook which constitutes the educated public of the Scottish Enlightenment. What doctrines are excluded by those boundaries? On the one hand, Hume represents a type of morality which is understood as not merely secular, but anti-Christian in its implications; on the other, the sermons of the Evangelical theologians of the Secession of 1740, Ebenezer and Ralph Erskine, represent a dogmatic appeal to a neo-Calvinist understanding of scripture which is incompatible with the whole project of rational justification. And at one level Hume and Ebenezer Erskine coincide: both are determinists of the same kind and where Hume claims that 'reason is, and ought only to be, the slave of the passions'[3] Erskine asserts that it is an effect of the Fall that 'corrupt inclinations of the soul rule and govern, instead of the understanding, in all its actions'.[4] Thus, against what was taken to be the scepticism of Hume and the dogmatism of Erskine, Reid and Stewart articulate in explicit philosophical terms the stance of the Presbyterian clergy of the Moderate party and of their social allies.

It is important to emphasize that this articulation had as its content continuous debate. I have already noticed how Reid's views emerged from the criticism of both Hutcheson and Hume, but it is crucial to recognize what a wide variety of points of view from both within and without the Moderate Presbyterian consensus took part in the debate. Adam Smith, Adam Ferguson, John Millar and Thomas Brown were all in varying degrees at odds, sometimes radically at odds, with what Reid and Stewart taught. None the less I do want to claim that the rise and fall of Reid's and Stewart's philosophy of common sense provided the philosophical debates with their central focus, and that the rise and fall of the educated public of the Scottish Enlightenment was coincident with the rise and fall of that philosophy.

This coincidence suggests strongly that the existence of an educated public requires a widespread shared philosophical education. Who shared in that education?

First, there were of course those young men who became the Moderate clergy. The word 'moderate' was originally used to define a political stance; King William III used it in his first message to the General Assembly of the Church of Scotland and it became the badge of the party who espoused the Williamite settlement. But their claims to hegemony soon became cultural. In a speech at a General Assembly, Alexander Carlyle, minister of Inveresk, was able to proclaim that

> We are rich in the best goods a Church can have—the learning, the manners and character of its members . . . Who have wrote the best history ancient and modern?—It has been clergymen of this Church. Who has wrote the clearest delineation of the human understanding and all its power?—A clergyman of this Church. Who has written the best system of rhetoric and exemplified it by his own orations?—A clergyman of this Church. Who wrote a tragedy that has been deemed perfect?—A clergyman of this Church. Who was the most profound mathematician of the age he lived in?—A clergyman of this Church . . .[5]

Notice the praise of mathematics. Newton's protege, Colin Maclaurin, had introduced the teaching of Newtonian physics at Edinburgh in 1725, and soon divided his mathematics classes into four stages, at the highest of which the students read the whole of the *Principia*. Alexander Carlyle had himself taken three successive years of instruction from Maclaurin. And when Maclaurin undertook the refutation of Berkeley's scepticism about the calculus, he confronted his task in the same way that Reid confronted his when he undertook to refute Hume. So that Newton provided yet another part of the shared outlook of the educated public.

How widely did that public extend? I have already spoken of the Moderate clergy and of the lawyers. But who else was included? And who was excluded?

The larger farmers and smaller gentry, the merchants, especially the more prosperous, and the schoolmasters, especially in the better schools, must all be included. Where were the better schools? School provision varied a great deal. A city such as Edinburgh provided a number of excellent schools, but only catered for a very small segment of the population. The grammar schools in the burghs, and the academies founded in the later part of the eighteenth century, provided in a number of towns and cities an education that was still for a minority, but which enabled a small but increasing number of the children of artisans and small farmers to attend universities. Intelligent literacy was provided by the parochial schools to a very large number indeed. So that in local communities ministers, lawyers, merchants, the smaller gentry and the schoolmasters provided a microcosm of the larger educated public. And the schoolmasters provided a vital link. University entry to a four-year course was at age sixteen, or even fifteen, in the earlier part of the eighteenth century and in the seventeenth century younger still. The teaching of geometry, Latin and sometimes elementary Greek, afforded the preparation for university; and the educated schoolmaster understood the *telos* of his activity with his pupils as their introduction, if possible, to the condition of a member of the educated public. So it was the whole educational curriculum and not merely that in the universities which was given a sense of direction by the dominant philosophical *Weltanschauung*.

Who by contrast was excluded both from the educated community and from its *Weltanschauung*? A large number of the uneducated took their view of the world from the ministers of the Evangelical party, both inside and outside the established church. The educated leaders of that party, which finally became dominant, did in time come to annex parts of the philosophy of common sense to their theology, but only in a form which no longer allowed it to furnish a background to continuous intellectual debate.

Four other groups were either excluded or excluded themselves. Of the latter kind were those Anglicizers of the upper classes who exercised power on behalf of London and had little interest in maintaining a substantial, rather than a merely sentimental, Scottish identity. This group included many of the larger landowners who increasingly were to have their children educated at English public schools or Scottish imitations thereof, a reversal of the eighteenth-century trend which had sent English Dissenters, barred from Oxford and Cambridge, to Edinburgh.

A second excluded group consisted of the growing numbers of the labouring classes who were outside both the church and the educational system, those who were to become the nineteenth-century industrial proletariat. And thirdly there are the always diminishing numbers of the Gaelic-speaking, often Roman Catholic, impoverished fishermen and small farmers of the Highlands and the Hebrides. Finally, also excluded are a set of people who can scarcely be called a group, since they are members of every social group: women. This particular educated public was a public composed of the male middle classes, a spectrum that could range from the sons of the minor nobility to the sons of shopkeepers.

It is now possible to understand how the requirements for the existence of an educated public were to some substantial degree satisfied in eighteenth-century Scotland; and it is also possible to understand how they enabled one and the same education to fit individuals for their social roles and to make them, in Kant's sense, enlightened. To be enlightened is to be able to think for oneself; but it is a familiar truth that one can only think for oneself if one does not think by oneself. It is only through the discipline of having one's claims tested in ongoing debate, in the light of standards on the rational justification of which, and on the rational justification afforded by which, the participants in debate are able to agree, that the reasoning of any particular individual is rescued from the vagaries of passion and interest. This is a truth that no one is likely to deny in the context of specialized academic disciplines; it is a truth embodied in such institutions as the seminar or the scholarly journal. But that a large segment of a whole society should institutionalize its informal debates over the best way for its members to live, so that the conversation of that society is to some notable degree both an extension of and an interchange with the discussions within its universities, so that that same truth is to that degree exemplified in the society at large, is a relatively rare phenomenon. And it required for its exemplification not only the kind of university curriculum that eighteenth-century Scotland supplied, and not only the agreement upon issues of philosophical debate that obtained, but also an understanding of their social roles by ministers, lawyers, merchants, schoolmasters and others which enabled them in such local forums as town councils, presbyteries, boards of bank directors and law courts to look beyond immediate questions to issues of first principles.

There is in third-rate English fiction of the late nineteenth and early twentieth centuries a stock, comic character, the needlessly disputatious Scotsman, whose activities, usually as an engineer or an administrator in the outposts of empire, have in fact nothing to do with the kind of cosmic issues which he insists on raising. This absurd character is the shadow cast by eighteenth and early nineteenth-century Scottish philosophical education. It is what results when you detach the product of that education from the social roles in which it can genuinely be exercised and transplant him into an environment impervious to general ideas.

This relationship of Enlightenment to social roles is often overlooked. When Kant enjoined us to think for ourselves, it could never have occurred to him that thinking, in the sense in which he was talking about it, might be deformed into a professionalized activity, largely unavailable except in specialized contexts. Yet just this is what has happened in modern society. Thinking has become the occupational responsibility of those who discharge certain social roles: the professional scientist, for example. But those topics thinking about which is of general social concern, thought about goods and the good, about the relationship of justice to effectiveness or the place of aesthetic goods in human life, about the tragic, the comic and the farcical not only in literature, but also in politics and economics, *either* are handed over to certain disciplined, but limited because professionalized, specialists, *or* are dealt with in forums in which the constraints of disciplined exchange are almost entirely lacking. The link which Scottish eighteenth-century culture forged between the particular responsibilities of particular social roles and the ability to appeal to principles about the general good and to participate in debate about these principles has been broken. The educated public has been replaced by a heterogeneous set of specialized publics. But could it have been otherwise?

III

To answer that question we have to identify the agencies that subverted the Scottish Enlightenment. They are at least five in number. The order in which I take them implies no judgement as to either their relative importance or their relationship. But we may notice at the outset the extent to which the forces that were finally to be effective in their destruction of this particular educated public had already been identified in the controversies which provided it with so much of its intellectual life. And this should not be surprising. The existence of an educated public requires a degree of self-awareness about its own condition which is likely to produce this kind of result.

A first agency that undermined the Scottish Enlightenment was the further progress of the philosophical debate that had constituted the core of its intellectual discussion. Partly this was a matter of the raising of questions, the pursuit of which could not be contained within the philosophy of common sense. Brown cast doubt on whether Hume had really been answered by Reid; Hamilton tried to blend Reid and Kant. And as the philosophy of common sense became more complex in its response to a variety of questionings, it ceased to be able to articulate a common educated mind. One response was simply to refuse the movement towards complexity and to retreat from debate into assertion. At Edinburgh Stewart discontinued the hour allotted to class discussion and lectured for three instead of two hours a week. His heirs in the United States, such as Francis Wayland and James McCosh dictated their lectures to a passive audience.

It can be argued that this outcome could have been predicted, that philosophical enquiry exhibits a continuous history of the displacement of one point of view by another and that to allow one philosophical standpoint to play the constitutive social part played by the debates around the philosophy of common sense is to ensure sooner or later either the dissolution of the philosophical presupposition shared by members of the educated public or a collapse into dogmatic assertion which excludes debate and so equally conclusively puts an end to the existence of an educated public. But one assumption of this argument can be challenged: it is that philosophy must necessarily, if it is true to its aims of enquiry, exhibit this kind of instability. This assumption was of course challenged by Reid and Stewart themselves: they believed that, just because their philosophy expressed those beliefs to which any rational person unimpaired by either mental defect or false philosophy would assent, it was a philosophy capable of withstanding any reasonable challenge. But a more radical challenge to the same assumption and one that, if it had been successful, would have prevented the rise of the philosophy of common sense, had been made at the beginning of the eighteenth century by Andrew Fletcher of Saltoun. Fletcher believed that the ideal models for both society and philosophy were to be found in the ancient world and that modern philosophy could not by its very nature provide shared beliefs of a socially cohesive kind. Yet what he recommended in its stead could never have articulated the underlying beliefs of the eighteenth-century professional and mercantile classes. Aristotle's *Ethics* and *Politics*, Fletcher's prescribed texts, presuppose a kind of state and a kind of economy far too alien to eighteenth-century Scotland. None the less in his defence of the Greek *polis* Fletcher fastened upon two more of the factors which in time were to contribute to the downfall of the educated public.

The first of these was size. Fletcher believed that Scotland could only flourish as an independent small-scale community which was itself an association of small-scale local communities. Whether the virtues necessary to a flourishing common life, intellectual as well as moral, could be widely enough engendered outside small local communities became matter for a debate to which both Adam Smith and Adam Ferguson were to make major contributions. It was unsurprising that there was debate: in 1700 Edinburgh University had about 400 students in a city of about 30,000; around 1830 the University had nearly five times as many students, in a city more than five times as large. The university population had to exercise such influence as it had on much larger numbers of the excluded, whose social life was carried on in much larger units.

The second factor was economic growth. Fletcher was the champion of economic self-sufficiency; but he was thereby compelled to propose that poverty should be dealt with by the imposition upon the poor of forced labour at public works. For Hume by contrast it was only by commercial transactions with the larger world that Scotland could be rescued from isolation, and Adam Smith included among the benefits of the free trade of the market that it rescued the labourer from arbitrary local subjection as well as from poverty. Smith understood some of the dangers of economic growth. But it was Adam Ferguson who saw that the specialization of different trades and professions in commercial society eroded the civic virtues by means of which individuals understood their primary loyalties as being to the society as a whole.

We have then identified so far three types of change which were incompatible with the continued flourishing of the educated public of the Scottish Enlightenment: the change inherent in philosophical debate was destructive of the necessary degree of agreement in fundamental belief; the change in the scale of political institutions meant that educated individuals less and less tended to encounter each other in small local communities in which the type of network of relationships first established in university discussions was in some sort reproduced; and the changes brought about by economic growth created more and more specialized and narrowly defined social roles with narrowly focused interests. The effect of the conjunction of all three types of change was to make the attempt to appeal to and to debate the character and content of first principles socially and culturally irrelevant. And this irrelevance was confirmed by two further types of change.

One of the major effects of economic growth was to increase the size and importance of those social classes effectively excluded from the eighteenth-century educated public: both the owning and employing class and the labouring class in mining and manufacturing industry. And although Smith and Millar charted the emerging class structure in striking and insightful ways, it was in fact a class structure which made the educated class impotent and functionless in the face of the new class conflicts.

At the same time the effects of growth, of specialization and of the division of labour became increasingly apparent not only in manufacturing industry, but also in the realm of knowledge and of the curriculum. Sometimes exaggerated importance is attached to sheer quantity in the growth of knowledge and it is suggested that the reason why no overview of the disciplines is any longer possible is that there is just too much to be known, especially in the natural sciences. But quantity is not in itself very important. What is "more important is the kind of professionalization which makes the specialized content of each discipline a subject-matter for enquiry; but excludes from any discipline the subject-matter of the relevance of the disciplines to each other. And what is perhaps most important is the lack of resources possessed by our culture for securing rational agreement on what it would be relevant and important for members of a contemporary educational public to share in the way of belief, in the way of perspective, in the way of debate. We possess in our culture too many different and incompatible modes of justification. We do not even have enough agreement to be able to arrive at a common mind about what it is that we should be quarrelling about.

IV

To this it may be retorted: even if you have succeeded in showing that the causes which brought to an end the educated public of the Scottish Enlightenment have operated in post-Enlightenment modernity to prevent the re-emergence of such a public, you have not shown that the making and remaking of an educated public is in fact the presupposed *telos* of our modern educational systems. Certainly our educational systems presuppose some aim beyond those of training in basic skills, on the one hand, and those of inculcating the specialized disciplines of the professions, academic and non-academic, on the other; but this aim is simply to provide, to varying levels, an education in the liberal arts and sciences. And these, so it will be urged, are characteristically worth pursuing in and for their own sake. But my thesis is that the liberal arts and sciences can only be effectively appropriated and developed in the arena provided by an educated public. Take away such a public with shared standards of justification, with a shared view of what the past of the society of which it is a nucleus is, with a shared ability to participate in common public debate, and you reduce the function of the liberal arts and sciences, so far as those who are not specialists are concerned, to the provision of a series of passively received consumer products. The consequent impoverishment extends beyond the general public to the content of the specialized disciplines. And unless we notice this we may draw the wrong moral from the story so far.

In 1961 George Elder Davie published *The Democratic Intellect*, an account of the Scottish universities in the nineteenth century and of the battles that raged between the protagonists of the curriculum which had been inherited from the Scottish Enlightenment and those who aspired to anglicize the Scottish curriculum by introducing specialized honours programmes that would place the Scottish universities in the same relationship to the curriculum of Oxford and Cambridge in which the new English universities of the nineteenth century were placed. Davie's exposition of the merits of the older curriculum was remarkably powerful and deservedly influential. But unfortunately its influence was almost entirely due to what I take to be a misreading. The Robbins Committee was at the time of publication already engaged in its enquiries; and *The Democratic Intellect*, or at least reviews of *The Democratic Intellect*, became required reading for the ruling class of the British academic world. What they took away from their reading of Davie was a belief that the strength of the eighteenth-century curriculum had derived from its generalist character, and some of them concluded that the moral to be drawn was one of curricular reform, a reform which would consist in replacing the specialized honours school in the undergraduate degree with multidisciplinary studies. There is certainly a good deal to be said in favour of some patterns of multidisciplinary study. But curricular reform of this kind cannot in any way reproduce the eighteenth-century Scottish curriculum and so cannot take us even one step towards the restoration of an educated public. And the reason for this is crucial to my whole argument. For it is not just the case that an educated public can only be sustained by a particular kind of curriculum and by a particular mode of teaching both in the universities and in the schools. It is also the case that when the academic disciplines are no longer organized so that their teaching will serve the needs of an educated public, they too are transformed and transformed in ways that are in part detrimental. The crucial case is of course that of philosophy, and more particularly of moral philosophy. And I want to argue that when moral philosophy no longer had the function of both providing the presuppositions for, and defining the controversial issues within the debates of, an educated public, it was not just that that educated public was deprived of one of the necessary conditions of its flourishing, but also that moral philosophy suffered a certain kind of loss.

What kind of loss? That question can best be answered by giving examples. One important set of examples would be that of the fates suffered by the philosophy of common sense itself when it was successively deprived at different stages of its history of its relationship to an educated public, first in Scotland and later on both in the France of the Restoration and in the United States. But to use those examples might suggest that the kind of transformation which I am trying to characterize was peculiar to the philosophy of common sense. Let me therefore instead, in order to avoid lending plausibility to that misleading suggestion, show how the same kind of transformation is exemplified in the history of a very different kind of moral philosophy in a very different type of social context, a philosophy sharply opposed to the philosophy of common sense on many issues. I refer to the utilitarianism of John Stuart Mill.

Mill's doctrines are all too often presented in a way that abstracts them both from their social milieu and from Mill's own fundamental projects. The context of those projects was defined for Mill in large part by Coleridge in his writings about a problem to which a whole range of contemporary English thinkers, including Thomas Arnold and F. D. Maurice, had addressed themselves, that of how the Church of England could become again in some substantial sense a church of the whole English people. Coleridge, typically enough, had provided both the most radical and the most impractical of solutions. What the nation required was a clerisy or body of clergy who would provide each local community with

> a resident guide, guardian and instructor; the objects and final intention of the whole order being these—to preserve the stores and guard the treasures of past civilization, and thus to bind the present with the past; to perfect and add to the same, and thus to connect the present with the future; but especially to diffuse through the community . . . that quantity and quality of knowledge which was indispensable both for the understanding of . . . rights, and for the performance of the duties correspondent . . .[6]

The clergy of the established church, that is to say, are to constitute the core of an educated public. Had Coleridge known what had happened in Scotland in the previous century, he could indeed have seen in the examples of the Moderate clergy a foreshadowing of his clerisy. But Coleridge, so untypical in other respects, was typically English in his ignorance of Scottish history.

Mill understood very well what Coleridge intended; the endowment of a National Church as understood by Coleridge would be, Mill asked, 'for what purpose? For the worship of God? For the performance of religious ceremonies? No; for the advancement of knowledge, and the civilization and cultivation of the community.'[7] But Mill also understood that the Church of England as an actual institution with its own past history and present structure could never constitute such an educated public as Coleridge envisaged: 'by setting in a clear light what a national church establishment ought to be, and what, by the very fact of its existence, it must be held to pretend to be, he has pronounced the severest satire on what in fact it is.'[8]

What Mill hoped to put in place of Coleridge's clerisy was a different kind of educated public that could none the less stand to the rest of English society in the way in which Coleridge had hoped that a reconstructed Church of England would. That educated public would not be constituted by agreement in fundamental belief of the kind shared by the educated public of eighteenth-century Scotland; for such agreement was not to be had in nineteenth-century England. It would instead be founded on a particular kind of agreement to disagree. It would be constituted by its agreement to participate in a particular ongoing debate, and allegiance to the purposes of the debate would have to be as important to the participants as their allegiance to their own point of view. Coleridge and those who thought with him and after him represented one point of view, the presence of which was essential for the flourishing of the debate; Benthamism in the form in which it had descended through Austin and Grote was another. And these were not the only standpoints to be presented. It is crucial to understanding Mill's own attitudes that this project of debate required him to speak with two distinct voices, and requires his listeners and readers to recognize with which voice he is speaking on any given occasion and to hear how what he says in the one voice relates to what he says in the other. To do this is possible only if in our reading we do not isolate his works from one another or from the context of his project. Consider in this respect the relationship of the *Autobiography* to *Utilitarianism*.

Although the *Autobiography* was only published posthumously, it is most of all of Mill's writings that in which he presents his credentials to be a leading participant in the debate and expresses his allegiance to the debate rather than merely to his own point of view. For the *Autobiography* is the narrative of how Mill's own opinions had themselves changed and developed stage by stage through a process of debate. What *Utilitarianism* represents by contrast is one of Mill's contributions to the debate, a contribution which responds to earlier points made by others. It is thus intended to state what Mill judges to be the best argument available in the debate so far. If we ignore this, we shall misread Mill in two ways. We shall misunderstand the tenor and import of his argumentative stance and we shall also misunderstand the force of some of his particular arguments.

Consider, for example, the force of the paragraph in which Mill declares that we have now 'an answer to the question of what sort of proof the principle of utility is susceptible'[9] and of the relevant passages which precede and follow it. Mill has often been supposed in this passage to have offered us one inference in which he passes from the premise that everyone desires only happiness to the conclusion that only happiness is worthy of being desired and another in which he passes from the premise that each of us desires happiness to the conclusion that each of us ought to promote the greatest happiness of the greatest number. And those who have understood that it was a mistake to attribute either of these invalid inferences to Mill have tended to suppose that the greatest happiness principle must then be for Mill what Sidgwick found himself compelled to take it to be, an unargued first principle, an intuition. But in fact Mill presents the principle of utility, understood as he was able to understand it by 1861, as what had emerged from a debate in which it had been modified, but not refuted by continuous criticism. He presents it as a principle which has been vindicated because it has withstood dialectical assault so far. In particular he defends it as a principle which must be conceded by anyone who has understood what the empirical conditions of pursuing his or her own happiness in rational co-operation with others must be in the light of the diversity of rational goals disclosed by the debate so far. Thus the principle of utility is defended neither as an inference from more ultimate premises nor as an underived first principle. How did it come to be misread as being either one or the other?

By being read as though it was the conclusion of an argument being offered for the inspection and assent of any rational person whatsoever, independently of any particular social context, and in particular independently of that context of debate constitutive of an educated public to which Mill understood himself to have been contributing. For the treatment of moral concepts and arguments as timeless and contextless was what moral philosophy was transformed into when it became in the last decades of the nineteenth century a professionalized and specialized academic discipline. And perhaps when moral philosophy lost its social function of articulating the presuppositions of, the debates within and the challenges to, specific social groups, there was nothing else left for it to become. But academic moral philosophy thus conceived in terms of would-be conceptual abstraction from all specific time and place, has of course all too little to contribute to the remaking of an educated public. To include it within a multidisciplinary curriculum will do little to restore the functions served by the eighteenth-century Scottish curriculum.

It would therefore be a misunderstanding of my central thesis if it were interpreted as even in part a call for curricular reform. Such reform may on other grounds be a good or a bad thing. But both the persistence into our own time of the causes already at work in the larger society which destroyed the educated public of the Scottish Enlightenment, and the effects upon the academic disciplines of the disappearance of that public and of its counterparts, real or projected, at various times in England, France, the United States and elsewhere, ensure that the concept of an educated public has no way of taking on life in contemporary society. It is at most a ghost haunting our educational systems.

V

None the less it is a ghost that cannot be exorcized. Our inheritance from the culture of the Enlightenment is so pervasive that we cannot rid ourselves of attitudes to the arts and sciences which presuppose that introduction into membership of an educated public of at least some of our pupils is one of the central aims of our educational systems. But, so I have claimed, there is no such public for them to be a member of. And I have also claimed that it is only where there is an educated public that two other central aims of all modern educational systems can be compatibly pursued: to fit young persons for their social role and occupation or to teach them to think for themselves. If the truth of this thesis came to be acknowledged, then where we have so far believed that our teachers could pursue both these aims with a success limited only by the resources available to them and by their own abilities and training, we should have instead to conclude first that a certain kind of failure is inherent in modern educational systems, a kind of failure that no type of educational reform can be expected to remedy, and secondly that in respect of these two aims teachers confront not a both/and, but an either/or. Either they can continue to pursue the aim of fitting their pupils for the type and level of social role and occupation prescribed in their society for the products of that part of the educational system in which they are at work, or they can continue to pursue the aim of enabling their pupils to think for themselves, but they cannot coherently pursue both aims. Yet even this mis-describes the choice that would confront teachers, if ever they came to accept the substance of my argument. For I have suggested that the possibility of thinking for oneself, other than as a professional specialist, only opens up in the context of a certain kind of community and that that kind of community is no longer available, indeed has not been generally available to post-Enlightenment culture for quite some time. Such teachers would therefore have to ask themselves how that kind of community is to be reinvented. Where could they look for answers?

It would be both historically mistaken and anachronistic to ascribe to Andrew Fletcher of Saltoun a prophetic prevision of this outcome in any detail. However, he emerges in the end as the hero of this narrative. For Fletcher does seem to have understood in some degree that the culture of the Enlightenment would be in a remarkable way self-dissolving; and that the protagonists of growth, development and largeness of scale in state and economy were engendering a type of society in which they themselves would no longer be possible. And so it proved: the success of Hume and Adam Smith in convincing their countrymen produced a society in which the type of culture of which Hume and Adam Smith were so distinguished a part became impossible. I also happen to think that Fletcher was in the right against his opponents in contending that a revival of the reading of Greek philosophical and political texts would necessarily be central to any form of education that could enable a community to resist this outcome successfully or to recover from it. But happily even to begin to move towards a statement of this thesis lies beyond the scope of this lecture.

FIVE

Interview with Dmitri Nikulin

DMITRI NIKULIN   Professor MacIntyre, I am really glad to introduce you to the readers of *Voprosy filosofii*, many of whom already know your writings. Could you first say some words on your own spiritual and intellectual development? Who are those thinkers which influenced you most? And what is the cultural and historical background of your philosophy? What was *A Short History of Ethics* for you?

ALASDAIR MACINTYRE   My family background was in small communities in the North of Ireland and the West of Scotland—my father belonged to the first generation in his family who did not have to learn English as a second language. And, that is to say, I come from the fringes of modern

Published in German translation as "Wahre Selbsterkenntnis durch Verstehen unserer selbst aus der Perspektive anderer," *Deutsche Zeitschrift für Philosophie* 44, no. 4 (1996): 671–84. The original English text is published for the first time here.

Western culture and I have tried to provide an articulate voice for some of those who do not belong to and cannot identify with the metropolitan mainstream. But, paradoxically, I have only been able to do this, and I only became aware of the need to do this, because I myself spent most of my adult life in universities that belong to that mainstream. Much of my university training in philosophy predisposed me to accept some of the standard analytic positions of what has been the dominant trend in English language philosophy. But I was also exposed to other philosophical influences more eccentric to twentieth century modernity: that of Aquinas and more generally of Catholic thought, that of Marxism and that of the philosopher of history, R. G. Collingwood. A central problem for me in my earlier career was that I did not as yet know how to integrate what I had learned from such different sources into an overall view, and so there were tensions within my work that I was not always able to acknowledge.

Much of what is unsatisfactory in my *A Short History of Ethics* (1966) derived from those tensions. I have recently written a new preface for the Polish translation of the *Short History* and in it I point out how in the *Short History* I asserted two positions that I was unable to reconcile, although I was not then aware of this. For on the one hand I held—rightly—that each fundamental standpoint in moral philosophy not only has its own mode of conceptualizing and understanding the moral life, one that gives expression to the claims of some actual or possible social order, but also has its own set of first principles, to which its adherents appeal to justify the claims of their own standpoint to universality and to rational superiority over its rivals. Yet on the other hand, especially in the last chapter, I mistakenly treated the choice between fundamental standpoints as though it could be characterized independently of one's own particular moral and philosophical standpoint and I failed to understand that how choice between standpoints is conceived also varies from standpoint to standpoint.

What this for a long time prevented me from recognizing was the possibility of a kind of debate between the adherents of rival standpoints in which theoretical and practical argument could exhibit the rational superiority of one standpoint over another, not merely by its own standards of justification, but also by the standards of its rival. One consequence of this failure was that until the nineteen seventies my most effective philosophical work was negative and critical, rather than constructive. This is the work collected in *Against the Self-Images of the Age* (1971).

DMITRI NIKULIN   You were once much interested in the Marxist tradition. What development did your understanding of it undergo from *Marxism and Christianity* (1953, 1968) to your most recent paper, published this year, where you present a new interpretation of the *Theses on Feuerbach*, especially of the famous 11th one? This could be especially interesting for Russian readers since there are now many debates on the post-Marxist future of the former Soviet Union and Eastern European countries, and knowledge of Marx's theses was formerly required for every schoolgirl and schoolboy.

ALASDAIR MACINTYRE   *Marxism and Christianity* will be published in a new edition this year (1995). For it too I have written a new preface in which I argue that the present is a period in which what is most important is no longer the critical rejection of that in Marxism which ought to be rejected—by now that work has been done—but rather that we begin once again to learn from Marxism what we badly need to learn from it, and this especially in two areas. First Marx's errors about socialism must not be allowed to blind us to the penetrating character of many of the insights embodied in his critique of capitalism. Marx himself was not concerned with the criticism of capitalism as a system of gross social injustice, but there are central Marxist concepts—of labor, of exploitation and of the function of money—that need to be put to work in the construction of such a criticism. And secondly Marx posed for us, but did not himself pursue adequately, questions about the relationship of philosophy to social practice which urgently need to be reopened. This is what I have attempted to do in my recent paper on the *Theses on Feuerbach*.

Moreover, while great quantities of Marxist writing since 1917 can safely be consigned to the garbage collectors, it is important not to forget how much interesting philosophical work was nevertheless done by Marxists in Italy, France and Russia. Among Russian philosophers, I think particularly of E. V. Ilyenkov, from whose writings over the years I have learned a great deal, most of all perhaps when I have most disagreed with him.

DMITRI NIKULIN   In your famous and widely discussed book *After Virtue: A Study in Moral Theory* (1981) you argue that the Enlightenment project of identifying a rational foundation of morality has failed (moreover, it had to fail). Do you see any possibility of a foundation and rational justification of morality which would fit modernity?

ALASDAIR MacINTYRE   Let me begin with a characterization of Western modernity. It is first of all individualist. Those who inhabit it learn to conceive of society as an arena in which each individual pursues whatever it is that she or he takes to be her or his good. In order to be effective in that pursuit, each needs to form cooperative alliances with others. And in order that each individual should not be treated merely as a means to the ends of others, each individual needs to be protected from such victimization by others. This individualist understanding of social life is articulated through a set of concepts that are embodied in the social practices of modernity—of the market, of liberal democratic mass politics and of personal relationships—and that also receive expression in those philosophical theories that provide modernity with its ideological justifications. What are those concepts?

They are those of individual autonomy in the making of choices, of individual utility and its maximization, of the general utility of the sum of individuals, of contract, of rights specifying basic liberties and protections, of duties as required by regard for individual autonomy and for rights, and of the nation state as enforcer of contracts, protector of rights and custodian of the public interest.

These concepts are a heterogeneous set and any attempt to apply them systematically generates such problems as these: If there is a conflict between some individuals' rights and some other individuals' utility, how is this conflict to be resolved? If the maximizing or even the satisficing of my utility is incompatible with my fulfilling the terms of some contract into which I have entered, are there any conditions under which I am entitled to violate that contract? If there is a conflict between some individuals' rights and the general utility, how is such a conflict to be resolved? How, if, in some type of situation. respect for the rights of one set of persons is incompatible with respect for the rights of some other set of persons, are such conflicts to be adjudicated? Can considerations concerning utility ever outweigh the requirement of respect for autonomy? And so on.

The thinkers of the eighteenth century Enlightenment aspired to provide an account of morality, compelling to all rational beings, which would enable us to supply rationally justifiable answers to such questions. What in fact emerged from the Enlightenment was a set of competing accounts, each appealing to its own standards of theoretical and practical rationality and each unable to defeat its rivals, except in its own terms. And the controversies generated by the philosophers who were the authors of these accounts—Locke, Rousseau, Hume, Smith, Bentham, Kant, Mill and a number of others—continue unresolved to the present day. There is therefore no single set of rationally justifiable standards available, by appeal to which on each particular occasion that disputes over the answers to these questions arise, such disputes can be rationally settled. Instead we have a set of contending principles and, generally speaking, which principle is invoked depends upon whose interests are involved, upon how power is distributed, and upon how effective various kinds of nonrational persuasion are.

Western modernity is thus a condition in which, while rational debate about moral issues continues interminably, rationality—except for its function in calculating the consequences for each individual of implementing this preference rather than that—is in general morally powerless. The notion therefore of supplying what you call in your question "a foundation and rational justification of morality which would fit modernity" is inherently paradoxical. And I am not in favor of embracing paradoxes.

DMITRI NIKULIN In *After Virtue* you argue in support of an ethics of the virtues. Do you mean that we can and have to come back to Aristotelian or Thomistic ethics or should we adapt it for the modern world? Is it possible to combine such ethics with the achievements of liberal and Enlightenment traditions?

ALASDAIR MacINTYRE What in *After Virtue* I called the tradition of the virtues was not and is not grounded in nor is it primarily a matter of any particular theory of the virtues. Theories of the virtues, including those advanced by Aristotle and by St. Thomas Aquinas, are important only because and insofar as they provide expression at the level of philosophical enquiry and debate for modes of social activity that are structured in and through practices. By a practice I mean a type of cooperative activity, extended through time, that has its own goods internal to itself, into which beginners have to be initiated by those who already possess not only the skills, but also the qualities of character required for the achievement of those goods. Examples of practices, thus understood, include the productive activities of farmers, fishing crews, painters, sculptors, and musicians, practitioners of crafts such as house-building and furniture-making, the enquiries of natural scientists and historians and games as different as football and chess.

The skills required vary enormously from practice to practice. The qualities of character required, the virtues, especially the cardinal virtues of practical intelligence or prudence, justice, temperateness and courage, turn out to be very much the same in all practices, although of course the courage to confront physical danger, for example, while never irrelevant is more immediately relevant in some practices than in others. One consequence of this is that, so long as practices flourish, the virtues will continue to be recognized in practice, if not in theory. The ethics of the modern world is of course one inimical to the flourishing of practices. The dominance of capitalist markets and of bureaucratic structures of corporate organization has the effect that activities are understood and valued as means to the achievement of economic and social aggrandizement, rather than for the sake of the goods internal to practices. But even within distinctively modern societies human nature is such that practices, even when marginalized, are continually regenerated, and with their regeneration there cannot but come renewals of the virtues.

The claim to be made on behalf of Aristotle and of the Aristotelianism of St. Thomas Aquinas is that their theories afford us the best starting-point for the understanding of practices and virtues by articulating at the level of theory the concepts embodied in practices, thus understood. But, as Aristotle himself remarks, philosophical conclusions have to be tested against practice, and there are notable respects in which the outcome of that test has to be the revision and correction of theories. So it is with Aristotle's own theories, since he had radically erroneous views about women, about slavery and about the place of productive work in human life. But the grounds on which these need to be rejected are Aristotelian grounds and later Aristotelian and Thomistic tradition has rightly rejected them. I think, for example, of the instructive sixteenth century debate between Sepúlveda, editor of Aristotle's *Politics* and defender of Aristotle's errors, and that great Dominican Aristotelian, Las Casas, in which Las Casas on Aristotelian grounds championed the cause of the indigenous peoples of the Americas against those Spaniards who attempted to justify—on grounds also drawn from Aristotle—their enslavement.

So there is no question of our now going *back* to the ethics of Aristotle or Aquinas. There is only the question of what resources they can afford us for our own contemporary understanding of ourselves, of our relationship to practices and of our need for the virtues. One thing that we can learn from them is that practice-based communities, that is, communities in which the goods of various practices are ordered within a way of life aimed at the good and the best, cannot but have a very different political structure from that of modern nation-states. The politics of practice-based communities is a politics of relatively small-scale and local forms of community, within which agreement about goods and about their ordering is presupposed. It is a type of community whose shared conceptions of goods and virtues makes possible a conception of the communal life as a shared enterprise, within which an understanding of justice in terms of desert—"from each according to her or his ability, to each according to her or his contribution", as that partial Aristotelian, Karl Marx, almost put it—can find application. The construction and expansion of such local forms of community, where they do not yet exist, and their sustaining and defense, where they do already exist—in a myriad of different situations: fishing villages, farming cooperatives, schools, clinics, parishes, laboratories—is the central task of my contemporary protagonist of practice-based communities in which the virtues can flourish and be taught effectively. It is a task that puts such a protagonist at odds politically with the dominant structures of the market and the nation-state, structures in which the qualities of acquisitiveness and aggrandizement are valued in such a way as to undermine any teaching of the virtues.

Liberalism by contrast is at home in modernity. The liberal aspiration is to provide maximal freedom for each individual within societies in which there is little or no agreement about goods or about their ordering.

Indeed most liberals regard the prospect of such agreement as itself a threat to liberty and believe that the type of community that I have just described must be oppressive and stifling. So that between liberalism and my own standpoint there can be little common ground. But on one matter I am in complete agreement with liberals. No large-scale modern nation-state could have or should try to have the characteristics of a community in which there is agreement on goods. For such agreement—or rather the appearance of such agreement—could be achieved on the scale of a nation-state only by being coercively and unjustly imposed. When a modern nation state claims to be the locus and source of community, it is always a dangerous threat to its own citizens and often a dangerous threat to others. Contemporary nationalisms are of a number of different kinds and some of them are deeply inimical to genuine community, substituting for the bonds of the common good the bonds of ethnic prejudice.

DMITRI NIKULIN Supporting a teleological ethics of virtue, do you see any possibility of combining it (or of a synthesis) with deontological ethics of duty? In other words, do you see a possibility to overcome Kant's rigid distinction of *Soll* and *Sein*? And what is in this perspective your attitude towards utilitarianism?

ALASDAIR MACINTYRE An ethics of virtue requires certain kinds of social relationship for its embodiment. Those social relationships have to be rule-governed, and the rules conformity to which constitutes them are the precepts of what Aquinas called the natural law. The negative precepts of the natural law, those, for example, that forbid the taking of innocent life or the violation of another's property in situations in which this is not required in order to save a life, are exceptionless and unconditional in their application to human beings. They are those rules which direct us to our common good and the exercise of the virtues itself requires conformity to them. Central to them are the rules of justice, rules that define what we owe to others and so lay down our duties to them.

One reason why Kant rejects any teleological grounding of moral rules is that he supposes that, if the justification of such rules is that they direct us towards the attainment of happiness, they will lose their unconditional character. And he supposes this because he identifies happiness with the maximal satisfaction of our inclinations. If this were indeed how happiness is to be conceived, then Kant would be right. And insofar as utilitarians do understand happiness in just this way, I agree with Kant in rejecting utilitarianism. But Aristotle and Aquinas understood happiness (*eudaimonia, beatitudo*) quite differently and therefore understood the relationship of rule-observance to happiness correspondingly differently. The precepts of the natural law are constitutive of that mode of activity in which happiness is achieved and unconditional respect for them is therefore a necessary condition of the achievement of happiness. If a rational being is to *be* happy, then that rational being *ought* to do what the precepts of the natural law require and to do so just because the precepts of the natural law direct her or him to that good which she or he shares with others. The antithesis of *Soll* and *Sein* disappears.

There is indeed a remarkable correspondence between what Kant's deontological ethics of duty requires and what Aquinas's ethics of natural law requires. And historically this is no accident. Kant was the heir of a succession of later natural law theorists and one way to interpret his ethics is as an attempt to restate natural law theory without the older teleology. Yet of course in the section of the *Critique of Practical Reason* on the presuppositions of pure practical reason that teleology reappears in Kant's account of the *summum bonum*, even if in a very different form.

Finally, let me note that among utilitarians John Stuart Mill had a conception of happiness much closer to Aristotle's than to those of most modern consequentialists. Mill recognized the kinship of his own views to those of Aristotle.

DMITRI NIKULIN Do you see a possibility or necessity for ethics to be religious? Can an ethics of the virtues be justified and practised without the notion of God?

ALASDAIR MACINTYRE The questions that you ask here are large and general. Let me replace them with two more specific questions. The first is: Is a catalogue of the virtues importantly incomplete, if it omits all reference to the theological virtues of faith, hope and charity? The answer to this is: in one way, yes, in another, no. I follow Aquinas in holding that human beings are capable of acquiring the natural virtues of prudence, justice, courage and temperateness and of understanding why those virtues are the excellences peculiar to rational animals without having any particular theological commitments. But I also follow Aquinas in holding that supernatural charity is the form of all the virtues, that is, that no virtue can be genuinely exercised, unless its exercise is also an exercise of charity. And charity is impossible without God-given grace. But that does not mean that those whose exercise of the virtues is also an exercise of charity do in fact recognize that grace is at work in their lives. The virtues can only be *fully* understood theologically, but the exercise of the natural virtues and an understanding of what it is that makes them excellences is compatible with atheism.

A second question is: can the final good that provides the life of the virtues with its end be specified without reference to God? And once again, for parallel reasons, the answer is: in one way, yes, in another, no. The Aristotelian conception of human activity as directed towards a final end, so that human beings can achieve the kind of flourishing specific to their nature, if and only if they are not frustrated or diverted from the achievement of that end, is one that presupposes a strong realist understanding of truth and falsity. It is, as Nietzsche well understood, deeply incompatible with any kind of perspectivism. And it was also Nietzsche who recognized that an inability to abandon a strong realist conception of truth is a sign of an inability finally to separate oneself from belief in God. For the belief that there is not just reality-as-perceived-and-interpreted-from-this-or-that-partial-point-of-view, but that there is reality-as-such, that over and above how things seem to be from this or that partial standpoint there is how things in fact are, is a belief inherited from a metaphysics that is open to the possibility of divine existence. And I take it therefore that someone consistently committed to an Aristotelian ethics of the virtues has to be open to the possibility of divine existence.

Being open to the possibility that God exists is not of course the same as believing in God. But because God acts so as to make those who are genuinely open to His existence aware of Him, being open to the possibility of God's existence is characteristically a prologue to acknowledging His existence. It is important however to remember that, just as grace may be at work in someone's life without that person being aware of it, so also someone's life may give expression to her or his belief in God without that person recognizing that she or he is a believer.

DMITRI NIKULIN One of the central notions of your philosophy is that of a tradition [e.g., as presented in *Whose Justice? Which Rationality?* (1988)]: rational debate and inquiry are possible and meaningful only inside certain traditional discursive patterns. Thus, in *Three Rival Versions of Moral Enquiry* (1990) you consider three different paradigms of moral philosophy— that of Aristotle and St. Thomas, of St. Augustine and of Hume and Scottish philosophy. Are such different traditions incommensurable, as Spengler and Danilevsky suppose them to be—or can there be a possibility for meaningful dialogue and understanding?

ALASDAIR MACINTYRE Any flourishing tradition of inquiry will develop within its own conceptual framework its own modes of theoretical and practical argument and its own standards of rational justification. When it encounters some other tradition that has developed independently, the question must always arise as to whether the adherents of the two traditions share enough by way of concepts, beliefs, modes of argument and standards of justification to resolve rationally disagreements between them and more especially fundamental disagreements. Sometimes of course they do. But in a number of very important instances not enough was or is shared for there to be any resolution of crucial disagreements. Hence the outcome of encounters between the representatives of such rival traditions has sometimes been a set of disappointingly sterile debates, at least initially.

Two kinds of philosophical error have been generated by the history of such encounters. There are on the one hand philosophers who have wanted to insist that, since so very much must be shared by any two groups of language-users—just because of what is required for the use and the interpretation of language—there must also be, at some fundamental level at least, shared standards which already embody agreement of some basic kind. The appearance of any radical form of incommensurability in respect of standards is always therefore an illusion. There are on the other hand philosophers who, because they are impressed by examples of encounters between adherents of rival traditions in which no common ground in respect of concepts, beliefs and students, sufficient to allow for a resolution of fundamental disagreements, could be discovered, have no difficulty in acknowledging the reality of incommensurability. But they sometimes fall into error by concluding that in such encounters incommensurability is a surd and ultimate fact, an ineliminable obstacle to any further rational dialogue between the protagonists of the rival traditions. Why is this a mistake? It is so, because it blinds us to the possibility of a kind of transformation of either or both of the traditions engaged in such a confrontation.

This is a possibility that can emerge only if at least some of those who are involved in such an encounter are able to learn to understand it, not only from the point of view of their own tradition, but also from that of the rival and hitherto alien tradition. Such learning will often require the acquisition of a new language, and it always requires immersion to some significant degree in the modes of practice and thought of the other tradition, and an ability to identify imaginatively with the beliefs and judgments of a standpoint not their own. So, by coming to understand the other in the others' own terms, from the others' point of view, they will become able to identify what it is that is untranslatable from the one language into the other and more generally what the barriers and obstacles to wider understanding are. But this is only a first stage.

What they may also learn—and whether and how far this is so will of course vary from case to case—is that from their newly acquired point of view they are able to identify and to understand better what they themselves and those who share their tradition had already recognized—by the standards of their own native tradition—as problems, difficulties and limitations in and of their own modes of thought and practice, problems, difficulties and limitations which had proved irresolvable and intractable, if responded to only with the resources of their own tradition. In making this discovery they will have found good reason—by the standards of their own tradition—for treating with respect the insights afforded by the concepts, beliefs, modes of argument and standards of justification of what had hitherto been a tradition at once alien and rival. Commensurability will have begun to emerge and with it new possibilities of rational dialogue.

Incommensurability between two particular traditions may then characterize no more than a stage in the development of either or both of those traditions and the response to that initial incommensurability may have important consequences for the further development of either or both traditions. There is a not uncommon pattern, when an encounter is between traditions rooted in very different cultures, whereby at first each insists on understanding the other in its own terms and so on systematically misunderstanding it. At a second stage these misunderstandings are exposed and are replaced by an awareness of the very different standards governing thought and practice in the two different cultures and of some large degree of incommensurability. Happily this second stage is sometimes a prologue to a third in which, as some of those who belong to each culture come to understand the other in depth, each party finds good reasons by the standards of their own culture to value modes of understanding and practice that had hitherto been alien, to master with greater fluency and depth the language of the other culture, and to recognize what is indeed, at least for the present, unresolvable in the differences between the two cultures and traditions.

A danger in the modern world is that instead negotiation between the representatives of rival traditions and cultures takes place in the neutral modern idiom of internationalized discourse, a type of use of language that seems to be neutral between all particular cultures and traditions, because rooted in none. This is, for example, the idiom of much simultaneous translation at international conferences. And it has become in fact the idiom of a new culture of those engaged in internationalized commerce, politics and intellectual exchange, from within which every point of view appears commensurable, because no point of view is taken seriously until its concepts, beliefs and judgments have been translated or rather mistranslated into this new culture's idiom. One, although only one, major source of the misunderstandings by Western communities of developments in Russia is to be found in just this type of mistranslation. Internationalism, sometimes in the guise of a cosmopolitan liberalism, has its harmful varieties, just as nationalism does.

DMITRI NIKULIN Your works, unlike most other contemporary philosophical studies, are remarkable for constant references to both ancient and modern history, literature and philosophy. What role does ancient culture play for you? Do you see any possibility of overcoming the contemporary tendency towards extreme specialization in philosophy?

ALASDAIR MACINTYRE One of the striking features of Western twentieth century philosophy has been the way in which philosophers of very different and strongly opposed philosophical tendencies have agreed in rejecting the history of philosophy, except insofar as they can abstract from it this or that thesis or argument to serve their own contemporary purposes. So the adherents of twentieth century positivism and some of its analytical heirs have dismissed the whole metaphysical tradition that stems from Parmenides and Plato as a tissue of errors, but so too have Heidegger and his disciples with their very different project of overcoming metaphysics and returning to an archaic sense of being. These at least in their profoundest versions are the errors of geniuses—and the errors of geniuses are always instructive—but they are nonetheless errors.

At every stage in its history Western philosophy has presented those who engage in it with a set of questions formulated in terms that are in key part specific to that particular stage: in the fourth century BCE the questions are largely Socratic and Platonic, in the twelfth century they are largely Augustinian, in the thirteenth they are both Augustinian and Aristotelian, in the later seventeenth and the early eighteenth century they are Cartesian, in the early nineteenth century they are Kantian. But it is characteristic of philosophy that the difficulties that we encounter in trying to answer its questions at every stage compel us, or should compel us, to question the questions. And putting the questions to the question compels us, or should compel us, to recognize that every particular formulation of a philosophical question is adequately intelligible only because of its place within a history of philosophical enquiry, a history that reveals the questions of each stage as generally both reformulations of earlier, sometimes philosophical, sometimes prephilosophical questions and precursors of later questions, later questions whose formulations often reveal what was hidden or partly hidden in earlier formulations. So to cut oneself off from the history of philosophy, as positivists and analytical philosophers have so often done, or to suppose that we can go behind the history of philosophy to a condition of naive, premetaphysical closeness to being, as Heideggerians have generally done, is to debar oneself from an adequate understanding of philosophical questions. Enquiry into the history of philosophy, and perhaps now especially into the history of ancient and medieval philosophy, is integral to philosophical enquiry. But a failure to understand this is not the only major defect of twentieth century philosophy.

Philosophy has become—with some gain, but also with a good deal of loss and usually unrecognized loss—a specialized, professionalized discipline. In so doing it has become marginal to the dominant culture of modernity, an academic sideshow, lacking the prestige of technology and the natural sciences, of economics and political science, and even of literary studies. There are a number of reasons for this, most of them to do with the nature of the dominant culture. But philosophy has been an accomplice in its own marginalization.

I remarked earlier, when speaking about Marx, that part of Marx's importance lies in his insistence on the connection between philosophical thinking and social practice. And I said about Aristotle and Aquinas that the significance of their theories of the virtues arises from the extent to which they articulate at the level of philosophy concepts embodied in various types of practice. Philosophical questioning—and not only on ethics and politics—arises from difficulties and perplexities that arise within contexts of cultural and social practice. Philosophy does not have a special subject-matter of its own, and philosophical questions are not and cannot be the exclusive concern of some particular group of academically trained and licensed persons. Philosophical questions are the questions of plain persons who have become, perhaps have had to become, unusually reflective about the difficulties and perplexities of the everyday life of the practices in which they engage and of the culture in which they are at home.

Philosophers therefore need continually to return to those contexts of social and cultural practice to reexamine how particular philosophical questions are generated and to make sure that crucial aspects of those questions have not been ignored in the course of abstracting and isolating them for philosophical attention. This is why it is necessary for philosophers to be educated in more than philosophy. They need, if possible, to be immersed not only in the history, literature, science and language of their own culture, but also in the history, literature, science and language of some alien culture, one that will provide them with a view of themselves and their own culture from an external standpoint. A recognition of the need for a conversation between traditions should be part of the education of every philosopher. Genuine self-knowledge of any depth always requires an understanding of ourselves from the perspective of others.

DMITRI NIKULIN   Russian culture tends to understand itself through its intelligentsia as marginally European but as having some peculiar and important insights which could be useful (and, as Dostoyevsky argued, even indispensable) for the whole of European culture. Has Russian culture had any influence on you?

ALASDAIR MacINTYRE   All relatively homogeneous cultures are initially and often for a very long time ethnocentric and apt to understand what is foreign as inferior and even barbarian. European cultures in this respect are no different from a variety of others. But the victories of Western European imperialisms, cultural as well as political and economic, led to a situation in which too many members of non-European elites treated Western European modernity as though it had some kind of unique universality, as though its condition was the *telos* towards which all rational progress in every society tended. And this in turn has reinforced the tendency of some members of European and post-European societies, such as that of the United States, to treat certain beliefs and modes of thought and practice inherited from the Enlightenment and the Industrial Revolution as though these deserved the allegiance of rational humanity everywhere.

This was indeed the attitude of some members of the nineteenth-century Russian intelligentsia. And the Slavophile critique of those attitudes, from Dostoyevsky to Solzhenitsyn, is, just as Dostoyevsky asserted, an indispensable corrective not only for Russians tempted to adopt this attitude, but for other Europeans too. This is why reading, not only Turgenev, Dostoyevsky, Tolstoy, Chekhov, Pasternak, and Solzhenitsyn, but also such thinkers as Soloviev and Berdyaev, has to be part of any adequate European education. What has to be learned from that reading is that it contributes to a still ongoing debate in which both sides need to be heard, so that we may have some possibility of transcending the limitations of the earlier participants in it. But how to do this we have not yet learned. So my answer to your question: 'Has Russian culture had any influence on you?' is 'Not enough as yet.'

DMITRI NIKULIN   In what direction do you expect your future work to develop?

ALASDAIR MacINTYRE In what I have written about the possibility of rational dialogue between different traditions of enquiry, and in the conclusions that I have defended about the nature of practical reasoning, and also in what I have said—far too briefly—about the relationship of theory to practice, I have presupposed the possibility of an adequate statement and defense of a strongly realistic conception of truth. Such a conception of truth is very much at variance both with the dominant views of truth in analytic philosophy—disquotational views, for example, or the very different antirealist views of Michael Dummett or Crispin Wright—and with the various treatments of truth by Foucault and Deleuze and Derrida.

What we need to understand a good deal better than we do is the place of truth in human life, that is, both of truth as the goal of various types of enquiry, of truthfulness, a systematic regard for truth, as a necessary condition for various types of relationship, and of the relationship between these. To do so we will need to be able to characterize more adequately the difference between someone whose beliefs not only correspond to how things are, but are as they are *because* that is how things are, and someone whose beliefs cannot be so explained, and what it is in virtue of which judgments are characterized as true or false. We also need a better understanding of why any adequate concept of God requires that we represent Him as one whose word cannot fail in respect of truth. In each of these areas there is of course already a vast body of literature. But it is remarkable how seldom those who have conducted their own investigations in one of these areas have asked what bearing upon their own conclusions investigations in other of these areas might have. And this is a task in the achievement of which I hope to make a beginning, although at best it can be little more than a beginning.

I have made a few remarks relevant to this issue in my Aquinas lecture in 1990 on *First Principles, Final Ends and Contemporary Philosophical Issues* (Marquette University Press) and said a very little more in an essay on "Moral Relativism, Truth and Justification" (in Luke Gormally, ed., *Moral Truth and Moral Tradition: Essays in Honour of Peter Geach and Elizabeth Anscombe,* Four Courts Press, 1994), but these do no more than gesture at the direction in which I hope to proceed. I am now engaged in writing a book on truthfulness and truth that will, I hope, take the enquiry one stage further. But this is certainly not a project that I have any hope of completing—and, if I were thirty years younger, I would still have no hope of completing it. All the philosophical projects on which I have worked have been ones inherited from our philosophical predecessors and they are all projects in which a great deal will remain to be done by our successors. Generally, even if not quite always, that is how it is with philosophy.

SIX

The Recovery of Moral Agency?

The overall argument of this lecture will move through three stages. In the first I identify two contrasting styles of moral utterance that dominate our present public discourse and spell out their shared presuppositions, remarking that both modes are characterized by an absence of self-questioning, a certain type of thoughtlessness. This, I'll suggest, renders those whose modes of utterance they are responsive to vulnerable to a range of nonrational influences that operate upon desire, influences that make us, unless we have acquired certain powers of practical discrimination, victims of our own desires and of those influences rather than genuine moral agents.

Those same powers of practical discrimination, powers exhibited in self-knowledge and self-directedness, are, I shall argue, generally to be ac-

"The Recovery of Moral Agency? The Dudleian Lecture," *Harvard Divinity Bulletin* 28, no. 4 (1999): 6–10.

quired only through training in and engagement with certain kinds of disciplined practice through which moral character is formed. And in the second part of this lecture I'll discuss what kinds of practice those are and offer two examples. Finally and briefly, I shall contrast the styles of moral utterance characteristic of those whose moral character has been formed through this kind of practice with the culturally dominant styles of moral utterance.

It is because we still do engage in types of practice that do provide resources for recovering from the afflictions of contemporary morality that I speak in my title of the recovery of moral agency. And it's because it is far from clear that we are able to give those types of practice anything like their due place in our common life that I speak of the recovery of moral agency only with a question mark.

I

Consider two very different modes of and attitudes to moral judgment, both characteristic of present-day North American public debate. One is self-confidently assertive and apparently innocent of any sense of moral complexity. The other is characteristically tentative in its expression and, even when not so, often presents its judgments on particular acts or choices without giving determinate form to whatever universal and general principles might be presupposed by those judgments.

For these latter, complexity often seems to be a refuge from finality of judgment, a warrant for hesitation and qualification. By contrast, the speech-acts characteristic of those whose mode is confidently assertive are generally those of either unproblematic condemnation or unproblematic confession. Moral indignation or moral self-laceration are its emotions of choice, while the practitioners of the tentative mode, bent as they are on finding some way of judging without being what they're apt to call judgmental, often seem to exhibit in their feelings the same cloudy indefiniteness that their judgments betray. For the one, a sense of outrage is instantly available; for the other, when some act—a lie, for example—is allowed to be wrong, the word "wrong" is uttered almost as if it were a word from some imperfectly known foreign language.

Neither of these psychological modes is to be identified with any particular point on the political spectrum. And indeed, sometimes within one and the same individual both attitudes are found, so that dogmatism and assertiveness about issues of, say, distributive justice or individual rights may coexist with tentative and indeterminate attitudes to issues of truth-telling and lying. Yet, on any particular subject of moral controversy, those who judge in the one mode generally identify those who judge in the other as among their antagonists. And each, in rejecting the other, tends to see its rival as the only alternative to itself. Neither seems open to the thought that a moral culture in which choice is so often defined by these two alternative types of attitude might itself be defective. And this is perhaps unsurprising. For both modes generally provide a terminus for thought. Neither seems open to self-questioning, to entertaining doubt about, in the one case, their certainties or, in the other, their uncertainties and qualifications. So, generally neither appears willing to undertake the work of identifying, let alone putting in question, their shared presuppositions.

Part of the work of disclosing those presuppositions, so that they can be put to the question, is historical. For both sets of attitudes seem to have been generated, at least in part, as responses to predicaments characteristic of post-Enlightenment moral cultures. Those predicaments are the effect of combining a continuing allegiance to Enlightenment standards for the justification of moral judgments with an awareness of the outcome of the moral debates of the Enlightenment.

Enlightenment standards require of those who give them their allegiance that they should be able to justify their particular moral judgments by appeal to some unique set of universal and general principles, principles such that they couldn't reasonably be rejected by *any* rational agent. Enlightenment inquiries, however, have provided us with just too many different and rival conclusions as to what those principles should be: principles enjoining the maximization of utility, principles enjoining the exceptionless prescriptions and prohibitions of the categorical imperative, principles ascribing universal and inalienable natural rights, principles appealing to contractarian considerations. And Enlightenment debates, both debates between different and rival protagonists of Enlightenment—Diderot, Bentham, Rousseau, Kant, and not only these—and debates between the protagonists of the Enlightenment and its critics resulted in an uneasy awareness that, although none of these positions was, or is liable to be, anything like conclusive refutation by its rivals, none had been able to provide resources for the refutation of those rivals, except in its own terms and by its own standards.

Consequently, the self-aware inhabitants of a post-Enlightenment moral culture have had to combine a claim to the rational superiority of their own positions over against those advanced by rival claimants with a recognition that those same rival claimants are, by and large, as intelligent and well-informed and morally self-aware—that is, as rational—as they are. And this isn't just a predicament of philosophers. For the thought of plain persons, to some large degree, is in the same condition. For them, too, when they're confronted by large issues of principle, implicit or explicit claims to the rational superiority of their own positions coexist with a similar awareness of disagreements with others who are advancing claims to the superiority of rival and incompatible positions. And this in a situation in which each party, while judging itself to be argumentatively victorious in its own terms and by its own standards, is nonetheless recurrently reminded that its rivals also, and in just the same way, take themselves to be the victors.

It is not surprising that those who find themselves in this type of situation should tend to respond either with self-confident and adversarial reiterations of the superiority of their own standpoint or else with a certain distancing of themselves from all contending points of view, so their judgments become tentative expressions of unsure and indefinite commitments. But there's another feature of their situation that needs to be remarked. It's not only that both contending parties exclude from view the historical roots of their situation. Neither seems able to engage with questions about the social and psychological factors that are at work in making them what they are.

The setting of limits to self-questioning is reinforced by another feature of our social order. Our institutions provide a number of different kinds of forum for moral debate. But it is very rarely indeed—outside academic, and that's to say, in this respect irrelevant, contexts—that there are opportunities for ordinary citizens, for plain persons, to engage together in systematic and extended inquiry into the issues posed for them by debate. So, for example, there are recurrent occasions on which public debate takes place over a lie told by some official person, over whether that lie was or was not justified—or if not justified, was at least excusable, or if not excusable, was perhaps too trivial to censure. And there are a range of opportunities, both for political and religious spokespersons, and for plain persons, to express judgments on such occasions. But these are judgments that must, in very many cases, be mindless, just because those who express them have, like the vast majority of their fellow citizens, never been afforded any opportunity to consider, together with others, in any systematic and extended way, what different and alternative views have been taken and might be taken of what rules ought to govern truth-telling and lying and why, and of how the virtue of truthfulness is to be conceived.

Absent such opportunity, what we're bound to have is, to a significant extent, a morality of public thoughtlessness—a thoughtlessness too often evident in both the mode of moral dogmatism and the mode of moral indeterminacy.

When I speak of thoughtlessness here I refer to a lack of will to carry reflection beyond a certain point. It is exemplified in a type of debate that is inescapable in many areas in which adjudication between rival claims of certain types is central to our decision-making. Those claims concern, on the one hand, rights; on the other, utility. And there are therefore three different kinds of conflict that require adjudication: conflict in which the rights of one contending party can only be upheld if someone else's rights are violated; conflicts in which the utility of this or that set of individual or corporate persons can only be maximized at the expense of the utility of some other set of individual or corporate persons, and conflicts in which the decision must be either to give priority to someone's rights over someone else's utility or vice versa.

Let's attend for the moment only to conflicts of this third kind, supposing, even if only for the sake of the argument, that we're in fact in possession of some rational method for assigning priorities to rights, so that we can decide whose rights should prevail over whose, and some rational method for maximizing utilities, so that we can decide which out of alternative courses of action will genuinely maximize the general utility. How then are conflicts between rights-based claims and utility-based claims adjudicated?

When those who adjudicate such conflicts report upon how in fact they make their decisions, they almost invariably speak in terms of the weight to be given to each of the relevant-considerations and of balancing one set of considerations against another. That is, they resort to metaphor. But how is this metaphor to be understood? What plays the part of the scales that provide some measure of weight and balance? And how are those scales calibrated? The short answer is: there are no such scales. There is no rationally justifiable method for making such decisions. And the mind that allows thought to terminate with this metaphor disguises this fact from itself. What is also disguised is the nature of the nonrational influences that are at work in the making of such decisions—the influences concealed by the metaphor. And an unwillingness or an inability to recognize and to understand those influences is an unwillingness or inability to confront the sources and the inequalities of power.

For at those points at which agents for no further reason give weight to this set of reasons rather than to that—something that characterizes *all* the types of moral attitude that I've so far identified—we always need to ask: To what particular influences are they being responsive? Whose power is at work in making them responsive to those influences and not to these? And what are the distributions of power that determine whose power is effective and whose ineffective in this particular area of decision-making?

It is only through asking and answering these questions that we become able to identify the otherwise often unrecognized pressures exerted on individual agents to become what the social order needs them to become if they are to enact the roles presented for them in this or that area of social life in a way that doesn't call into question those distributions of power, and to engage in those debates that define what had been socially determined to be the range of acceptable attitudes and choices. If we leave these questions unasked, we deprive ourselves of a crucial dimension of self-knowledge. And what I've called thoughtlessness is a quality of minds so deprived.

What's the effect of this kind of thoughtlessness? It is that individuals without being adequately aware of it are molded by forces at work in their social environment, so that their judgments express uncritically attitudes that they've never had an opportunity to make genuinely their own. They don't exhibit bad character so much as lack of character. They are no longer fully responsible agents, having become too responsive to this or that set of pressures. Thoughtlessness is then a mark of loss of moral agency. And the types of moral judgment that I've described are symptoms of that loss.

What then is it instead to be thoughtful? It is to be unwilling to allow thought to rest content with unscrutinized metaphors or unidentified presuppositions, especially when these function as obstacles to further moral inquiry. But at this point there's a mistake that would be easy to make. For we might suppose that in order to deal with those nonrational influences that have, for the most part without our recognizing it, molded our character and set limits to the alternatives between which we choose in our decision-making, we need to embark on sociological and psychological inquiries—inquiries whose end product would be a set of generalizations about how power is distributed and about how nonrational influences are exerted in contemporary social and cultural orders.

But while such inquiries are certainly of value, it is possible for someone to be very well-informed about their findings without having moved in any way toward the kind of self-knowledge without which we'll be able to understand our own habits and choices adequately and to distinguish that in them which is genuinely directed toward our good as rational agents and that in them which derives from a variety of unacknowledged nonrational influences.

The knowledge that we need for moral agency is not theoretical, but practical. And practical knowledge is not applied theoretical knowledge. The relevant practical knowledge is the knowledge of how to discriminate among the various objects of attention presented to us by our desires. And it's in the first instance our own desires of which we have to learn to beware. For the nonrational influences that may make us, for example, responsive to advertising rather than to reliable sources of information, or that render us vulnerable to the selectivity of television news programs because we are not aware of the principles governing that selectivity, or that lead us to form our ambitions in response to the aura of prestige and glamour surrounding the rich and the powerful, those influences, all of them, operate on our desires. Arousing them, magnetizing them, focusing them, strengthening them, and determining what is taken to be frustration or deprivation in respect of desire, so that in an important way those passions are no longer wholly ours but have become in part a medium by which we are possessed, so that desire desires through us, so that what have become the objects of our strongest desires dictate to us. The Japanese have a saying about alcohol: "First the man takes a drink, then the drink takes a drink, then the drink takes the man." This, I take it, captures very well the way in which we may more generally become victims of a variety of forms of desire that operate upon us as though they were impersonal forces.

The condition of victims of dictatorial desire is one that we're all able to recognize easily enough when it takes the extreme form of an addiction, but of which we're much less often aware in other cases. There's a whole range of influences upon character and decision that, even when we acknowledge their power at the level of theory and generalization, we largely and often entirely ignore in the particularities of practice. The questions then are: What kind of a human being would I have to become in order not to be so influenced? And what would I have to do or what would have to happen to me for me to become such a human being?

The aim isn't, of course, to arrive at a point at which one's desires are no longer subject to external influences. That would be an impossible, even a silly, aim. It is instead to aim to make one's desires truly one's own, by making them, so far as possible, responsive only to those influences to which it is for the agent's good to be responsive. It is to aim at educating one's desires, so that they are discriminatingly responsive, giving expression to those powers of rational discrimination that are one mark of moral agency. So how then should we proceed?

II

Here I might, as a certain kind of Aristotelian, a Thomist Aristotelian, be tempted to make another mistake: that of turning to the texts and developing answers to these questions based on what is said by Aristotle, and by Aquinas in his commentaries on Aristotle. But to proceed in this way would tend to preserve the illusion that such questions can be addressed adequately at the level of theory. And by introducing Aristotle's moral theory as one more contribution to contemporary moral debate, I would be transforming Aristotle into one more post-Enlightenment moral philosopher, so enlarging the controversies of post-Enlightenment moral philosophy by adding yet another contending standpoint, but not changing their character. So, Aristotelian ethics would become understood, as too often it has been understood, as just one more set of theoretical positions whose adherents are engaged in one more set of inconclusive debates with utilitarians, Kantians, and contractarians. But theory of and by itself, reasoning of and by itself, good theory just as much as bad theory, never made anyone a better human being. Indeed, Aristotle suggested that theorizing is sometimes a device of those anxious to avoid habituation into the virtues: "They take refuge in discourse and think that they are philosophizing and in this way will become good."

We need instead to begin with practice, for theory is the articulation of practice and good theory of good practice. Moral debate is therefore not primarily between theories as such, but rather between theories that afford expression to rival forms of practice. And we do not understand any theory adequately until we've understood in concrete detail the form of practice of which it's an articulation. Note that I'm not at all suggesting that theory has no practical relevance. There are types of practice that are atheoretical, forms of practice from which theory is absent or even excluded, and that thereby set narrow limits to the possibilities of reflection upon practice, limits that inevitably themselves produce what I have called thoughtlessness. Theory, when it is recognized to be the articulation of practice, enables practice to be reflectively thoughtful and so to remedy what have been its defects and limitations.

One function of such theory is to enable those who engage in relevant forms of practice to address questions to themselves about their practice—questions posed by theory, but to be answered in practice, by acting in one way rather than in another. So that what theory may provide—what good theory should provide—is an agenda for practical reflection. Hence what we need to take from Aristotle's texts are not primarily theses, but rather questions, questions whose answers would enable us first to reformulate and then to address in practice those issues that concern the transformation of our desires and of our attitudes to our desires, so that we may no longer be victimized by them. Consider four such Aristotelian sets of questions.

A first set concerns how I am to make the distinction between those objects of desire that I seek to attain just because they are objects of my desire, and I want my desire to be satisfied, and those objects of desire that I seek to obtain because I judge it to be good in general for human beings to obtain this kind of object, and good in particular for me here now to do so. In the former case I value the object just because and insofar as it's an object of my desire. In the latter, I take the desire to provide a good reason for action just because and insofar as it's a desire for what is good and in these circumstances best. So a form of practice that's to educate the desires will be one that enables those engaged in it to make this distinction in their practice. (And here, of course, at the level of theory Aristotle has to be able to provide resources for a reply to Hume, who allows no place for this distinction.)

A second set of Aristotelian questions concerns how we are to acquire the ability to act for the best here and now, in situations in which there isn't enough time for deliberation, so that the agent has to draw upon past deliberations that have prepared her or him to act spontaneously and immediately in this type of situation. The agent needs to have learned how to act with good reasons and from good reasons without making those reasons explicit. And the agent's appetites and passions have to be such that the agent is moved only by the desire to act immediately for the best and is not distracted by irrelevant fearful or hopeful wishes. So that when the agent is presented with someone else's gross and urgent need—a child needs to be rescued from imminent danger, a persecuted individual or group is threatened with death—she or he does not have to calculate, but finds it unproblematic to respond, even when the risk may be to her or his own life. What matters is whether such an agent has embodied in her or his dispositions to feel, to judge, and to act a rank ordering of goods, a conception of human flourishing that issues in this kind of response to gross and urgent need. It matters not at all whether she or he is able to articulate that rank ordering, that conception, in theoretical terms. It does matter, of course, that it should be articulatable, that it should be expressible in the form of theses and arguments, so that it can be put to critical question. But an inability of any particular agent to do this on some particular occasion is never of itself a moral defect. (And here, of course, at the level of theory Aristotle has to be able to reply to Kant, who denies that the concept of human flourishing can have this kind of place in our rational practice.)

To these two marks of adequate practice conceived in Aristotelian terms—an ability to discriminate those objects of my desire that it is here and now good for me to pursue from those that solicit my desires simply as objects of desire, and an ability on occasion to act when there is good reason to act without having to remind myself of what that good reason is—a third must be added. For we also need to ask questions about how an agent's practice is to embody features that belong to the overall unity of that agent's life. The episodes through which these and other abilities are developed must be understood as part of a narrative that the agent is enacting, in which the agent's success or failure in understanding at the level of practice what it would be to complete that narrative well or badly is itself one important aspect of completing that narrative well or badly. The agent's life, thus, should exhibit and exhibit increasingly some degree of overall directedness, a certain narrative unity, so that retrospectively earlier stages in that life can be understood as just that, stages on the way to something not yet adequately but increasingly characterizable.

The agent progresses toward making her or his activities intelligible, both to her or himself and to others, through her or his emerging conception of a final telos toward which those activities are directed and from which they get not their only point and purpose, but further point and purpose. Desire, that is to say, will have been directed toward a further and ultimate object, one in which, were it to be achieved, it could rest satisfied, and one in which, were it not to be achieved, it would be permanently unsatisfied. (And here, of course, at the level of theory Aristotle has to be able to reply to Hobbes, who holds that there is no such object.)

A fourth mark of good practice in an Aristotelian view is supplied by answering questions about the types of social relationship in and through which the goods of such practice are achieved. We can only initially engage in good practice through putting ourselves into the hands of others who will be able to teach us what we need to learn. And we can generally achieve the goods of practice only in systematic and structured cooperation with others who also recognize that only insofar as we and they achieve our common good can we achieve our individual goods. My actions are to contribute to activities and projects that are not only mine, but ours, so that we have to deliberate with others. And on this view, insofar as I think of the actions to be engaged in and the goods to be achieved as primarily mine, I will tend to act in such a way as to frustrate my achievement of important types of good.

Any kind of competitiveness that encourages egoistic thinking is therefore an enemy of good practice. So we have to learn that while it is important to care about excelling, it's corrupting to care about who is ranked higher than whom in respective excellence. Desire has to be detached from the badges of such rank ordering—prizes, fame, money—while directed toward those achievements of excellence for which, ostensibly at least, such badges are awarded.

We need then to be educated into the relevant kind of relationship with those others who participate with us in particular practices. And to be so educated we have to entrust ourselves to others who will act both as instructors and exemplars. Note that they won't so instruct us by professing to teach us something whose name is "ethics." Practical moral instruction is incidental to instruction in the tasks of many types of practice—farming and fishing, building houses and staging plays, playing football and conducting scientific inquiries. It is in such contexts that desires that we initially bring to these tasks—often desires to please parents or teachers and to obtain goods that are the external rewards for success in this or that particular activity, prizes, fame, money—are displaced by and transformed into desires for the goods internal to each particular activity, and more especially, for the good of excellence in performing those tasks.

This displacement and transformation of desire is then also something achieved incidentally and not by being directly aimed at. And it is generally achieved only by those whose teachers have themselves, at some earlier period, experienced just such a displacement and transformation. If those teachers are successful, they make of their students or apprentices future teachers. Having entrusted themselves to the authority of their teachers, those students or apprentices become able to exercise authority as teachers of others. Having had exemplars, role models, they in turn become exemplars. Good practices are transmitted through traditions of good teaching.

So far then, I've tried to supply, from within a generally Aristotelian framework, proposals for an outline account—a very bare outline account—of some of the conditions that would have to be satisfied by our practice, if we were to become able to direct desires toward our goods and our good, so that we would no longer be rendered vulnerable to the nonrational solicitations and influences that are determined by distributions of power. Earlier I suggested that the dominant forms of contemporary morality do not rescue those who give them their allegiance from this vulnerability, and I tried to identify some sources of that vulnerability. Now I add the suggestion that the dominant forms of our culture may provide too few opportunities for education into the kind of practice through which the desires become directed in such a way that they are less liable to be responsive to and perhaps corrupted by the stimuli of nonrational influences. But my discussion, as I noticed earlier, has remained, could not but have remained, at the level of theory. What I can do, however, is to identify examples of the type of practice articulated by this kind of Aristotelian theorizing and in so doing allow theory to direct our attention beyond theory to practice. What then are one or two relevant contemporary examples of practice?

III

Every stable form of human life within which goods are achieved depends for its continuing existence, let alone its flourishing, upon there being those who provide it with security from external and internal aggression and who therefore must be prepared to sacrifice their lives, if necessary, in that cause. And one measure of the moral substance of a way of life is what answer it gives in practice to the question: What do the rest of us owe in justice to those who are so prepared? Our attitudes to police officers, firefighters, prison guards and the military are therefore significant, and not only because we have entrusted our lives and our security to them. For in trusting them we have to recognize that, if they are to perform their duties adequately, they have to be authorized to use coercive violence of a kind forbidden to the rest of us. But this power can very easily be misused. So those who are so authorized have to be trained, so that they use their power for the sake of achieving the relevant goods rather than misusing it. And we have to trust not only in them but also in the effectiveness of their training.

It is obvious that the training of such individuals will have to involve just that kind of redirection of the desires about which I've been speaking. They will have to become disposed to act, so that they unhesitatingly prefer on occasion the safety of the community to their own safety, and also so that if the opportunities afforded to them by their power they avail themselves of those that involve no misuse of it. What kind of training inculcates such dispositions? The answer to this question given by the United States Marine Corps in the 11 weeks of basic training is among the most interesting answers ever given.

The recruits who receive this training are, by the standard of our society, generally very unpromising material: often those with whom their high school teachers have failed, nearly half of whom have used drugs, had brushes with the law or experienced other problems. (For the data here, particularly the statistical data, I am relying heavily on Thomas E. Ricks's splendid 1998 book *Making the Corps*, published by Touchstone.) At the end, those who have survived their basic training are not only excellent at what they do, but some at least have made significant initial progress toward becoming the future noncommissioned leadership of the Corps, including those who, as drill instructors, will train future recruits. How did they make this transition? It could not have happened without strenuously enforced discipline throughout their working hours, without their being screamed at, harassed, and subjected to the pains of punishment, until they had become self-directed toward and narrowly focused upon succeeding at each successive task.

But during this period they will also have learned both that they will be given every assistance possible to succeed and also that they are capable of high levels of practical achievement that they had for the most part never realized. They will also have learned that these achievements were made possible only by the contributions of others and that their value lies in enabling them to achieve shared tasks with the rest of their platoon—that it is, in the end, the shared success or failure that counts and not just their own. So they'll have learned that they're accountable to others for their actions and especially for their failures. Why does it matter so much that they shouldn't fail? Because others have put their lives in their hands and this in two ways.

First the people of the United States have put their lives and their security into the hands of, among others, the Marines. There have been perhaps 15 serious attempts to abolish the Corps. All have failed, and all failed because of public opinion. "You know why America has a Marine Corps?" the recruit training regiment commander is quoted as saying to recruits. "Because she wants one." And their training is designed to make marines aware of how they serve the needs of the wider society. But secondly, all marines will have learned that if their own lives are at risk, then any other marine at hand is bound to come to their aid, even at the possible cost of life, and that in turn each of them is under the same obligation.

These two bonds of responsibility—to their fellow marines, and to the wider society—are both formed by their training, but they are, of course, very different types of bond. And it is difficult to resist the conclusion, even from the most favorable accounts of marine attitudes and actions, that the strength of the first bond is to some extent achieved by means that weaken the second. Solidarity with one's fellow marines is at the expense of solidarity with the wider society. For becoming a marine, at the same time as it inculcates some sense of a responsibility to the wider society, seems to alienate marines, not only from those aspects of the wider society about which they may be quite right to be dismissive, but also from any external standpoint that might put their own values seriously in question. A narrow limit to the possibility of moral reflection has been imposed. And from a military standpoint this may be all to the good. Battlefields are generally not places for reflection, moral or otherwise. But the limitations of marine culture are as instructive as its achievements.

Earlier I identified four distinguishing characteristics of the kind of practice participation in which would provide individuals with the ability to discriminate among and to transform and redirect their desires, so that they would, as far as possible, no longer be open to being influenced by nonrational solicitations. The practice that is the outcome of Marine Corps training exhibits three of these four, although not all to the same degree. What it signally lacks, however, is one of these characteristics, the kind of directedness that has to inform not merely a term in or a career in the military, but a whole life, and this not only because time spent as a marine is only an episode, even if sometimes a prolonged episode, within a more extended narrative of a marine's life, but also because there are such important areas of human activity that fall outside the scope of marine training. Principal among them are those activities that are crucial to participation in the life of family and household and the life of a local community. What marine training doesn't provide is the discipline of reflection upon what part each of these types of activities should play in an overall human life—that is, reflection upon a wider range of goods, upon how those goods relate to one another, and upon how the importance each of them is accorded by a particular individual in her or his life answers at the level of practice the question of what that agent takes human flourishing to consist in.

An adequate moral education, then, will have some of the features of marine training, but it will unite these with education into a capacity for reflection upon goods that provides those engaged in the tasks of redirecting and transforming their desires with an additional resource. What kind of practice might provide this? Like a marine training, it will have to be demanding and to enable its practitioners both to extend their powers and to test themselves against high standards. It will have to teach individuals to excel without making them value winning over others rather than excelling. It will have to do this while inculcating a strong sense of dependence on others, of having had to put your life into the hands of others, thus warranting in others an exception that they'll be able to depend on you. And yet, unlike marine training, it will not merely leave one open to reflect on how goods should be ordered, and upon whether they are ordered rightly within this kind of training, but will provide a stimulus for such reflection and, if possible, make such reflection inescapable.

One salutary example of just such an education is that provided by the experience of members of some types of fishing crews who are at home in local communities where fishing has been a or the primary occupation through several generations. I could have taken examples from the northeast of Scotland or the northwest of Ireland or from Newfoundland. If I focus attention on fishing crews from New England towns to the south and north of Boston, and among them on some of those crews who fish for giant bluefin tuna, it's because Douglas Whynott's remarkable 1995 book, *Giant Bluefin* (Farrar, Straus and Giroux), asks and provides a starting point for answering more of the relevant questions than do most books on fishing. But first let me make a more general point about deep-sea fishing as an activity.

It is the most dangerous of American industries, with a death rate of 178 workers per 100,000 per year—significantly more dangerous than logging (155 deaths per 100,000 workers a year), and generally a good deal more dangerous than being a marine. Members of fishing crews, therefore, have to be able to rely on one another, on other fishing crews, and on the Coast Guard. They have to develop a range of skills, a capacity for hard manual labor, and a temperament that allows them to live at close quarters with others without friction that would be damaging to the enterprise.

What makes the recent history of tuna fishing really interesting is the way in which extreme and unpredicted changes made it more difficult than usual to resolve issues about the relationship between competitiveness and cooperativeness in the lives of crews. Both the extreme of prosperity, as Japanese markets opened up from the 1970s onward, and the extreme of restriction, due to the imposition of quotas in the early 1990s, fostered competitiveness. In the early times of prosperity, fortunes could be made or lost. In the later times of restriction, "reduced quotas, the shortened season, an increase in participants, migratory patterns that favored one region over another and the abuse of the rules all brought conflicts."

Both kinds of competitiveness put two kinds of strain on those engaged in fishing. On the one hand, cooperation was endangered. On the other, the question arose for many individuals of whether to stay with fishing or to engage in some other occupation. And these are questions with large import not only for those engaged in fishing, but also for their families and their communities. So for those engaged in fishing problems about how a variety of goods are to be rank-ordered arise inescapably from time to time. And it's difficult to remain a member of a fishing crew for any length of time without becoming to some extent reflective. What the outcome of such reflection is depends in key part upon varying qualities of character as well as of intelligence that individuals bring to the tasks of reflection and what those qualities of character are depends in turn upon how each particular individual has resolved the tensions between competition and cooperation.

Whynott reports on the view of those qualities taken by one Cape Cod fisherman, Robert Sampson. The danger for a tuna fisherman is an egotism that is generated by the need to have confidence in his or her own decisions, but that, by fostering a lack of confidence in others, "doomed cooperative ventures from the start because of lack of trust." What has to replace egotism is a confidence grounded in self-knowledge of one's individual strengths and weaknesses—a self-knowledge that not only makes one independent but enables one to contribute to cooperative enterprises and not to allow competitiveness to undermine cooperation. So envy and greed are viewed as threats. Bob Sampson's thought about what lack of such self-knowledge and lack of such independence entails is summarized by Whynott: "Otherwise you watched other people and you made your decisions according to what they were doing . . . . You became a blend of what others had thought and decided."

I am not of course suggesting—Sampson doesn't suggest, Whynott doesn't suggest—that the experiences and activities of fishing crews always have so admirable an outcome. What can go well can always go badly, and this is as true of fishing as it is of marine training. To engage in such a mode of life is never sufficient for the formation of the kind of character that enables individuals to stand back from and reflect on their desires, so that they are not, through lack of self-knowledge and self-directedness, the victims of those desires and of the influences that mold them. The question is: How difficult is it to acquire the virtues without some such mode of life?

Aristotle would have been astonished and appalled by this line of argument. Fishermen were, in his view, laborers whose banausic occupation made them unfit for citizenship and so for any part in public deliberation. And he would more generally have found it difficult to acknowledge any close connection between the nature of the occupation in which someone engages and that individual's likelihood of developing the virtues. Jefferson, by contrast, would not have been surprised: he took it that, by and large, a society of virtuous individuals, a society capable of sustaining the politics of a republic, would be a society of independent farmers. His farmers were also to act as a citizen militia, willing to put their lives on the line for the sake of their community. And in their ability to recognize the importance of both independence from and dependence upon others in their lives, the farmers envisaged by Jefferson resemble in important ways the marines described by Thomas Ricks and the fishermen described by Douglas Whynott.

If we ask what relevant features are and were shared in these three ways of life, we will soon recognize that they can be found, although with varying degrees of salience, in a considerably wider range of occupations. Those features include an ability and a willingness to take risks, possibly at great cost to oneself, for the sake of others; the kind of integrity that justifies others in trusting one; an ability to recognize common goods through which one's individual good is to be achieved and to contribute to shared enterprises designed to achieve those goods; justice in recognizing such contributions and fairness in assigning merit; a desire to excel, rather than to win; an ability to reflect upon one's own judgments and those of others, so that one becomes capable of the reflective correction of errors of judgment; and—what I've been principally concerned with here—an ability to focus one's desire on the relevant common and individual goods, so that one is neither distractible nor seducible by agencies seeking to attract and focus one's desires at the expense of one's self-knowledge and one's independence.

It therefore becomes possible for us to ask more systematically which types of work in our society, through their structures of training and apprenticeship and through the social relationships that engagement in them requires, provide systematic opportunity for education into the relevant virtues, which, by contrast, provide a setting that leaves it open to the individual and those immediately around her or him whether or not to make of the workplace a place of moral education, and which are, by their nature, inimical to growth in the virtues and favorable, therefore, to the acquisition of those vices that leave us open to the deformation of our desires. And of course; it is not only the activities and relationships of the workplace that conduce to or fail to conduce to character formation. The activities and relationships of households and families are also such as to favor or disfavor the development of character. So our inquiry will have to widen its scope. But, having noticed the importance of proceeding with such inquiry, I put it for the moment on one side, to ask further about the characteristics of those whose education into some practical discipline of the relevant kind has resulted in the self-knowledge and self-directedness that are prerequisites for independent moral agency. What kinds of moral judgments do such individuals make? What do they take to be the point and purpose of the actions of moral judgment? And what is their style of utterance?

When such individuals of character remark to themselves or to others that it is wrong to act in such and such a way, either in some particular occasion or generally, they remind themselves or those others that, by so acting, the possibility of achieving some recognized good has been obstructed or frustrated and that the individual responsible for such a wrong has defected from, has excluded her or himself from, any relationship that is informed by such a shared recognition of goods. A moral judgment gives expression to self-criticism or to action or potential change in relationships. The utterance of such judgments presupposes that those who utter them, and those to whom they're addressed, are both able to recognize that this is how moral judgments function, just because they share, to some large degree, the same abilities and the same dispositions to recognize goods, to distinguish between objects that are desired simply qua objects of desire and objects that are desired qua goods, to rank order goods and to direct themselves toward the achievement of the common good. There will always, of course, be room for some measure of disagreement, but such disagreement presupposes a background of more fundamental agreement, including agreement on those means by which disagreement is, if possible, to be resolved.

Such agreement is practical, and it is, so I have claimed, the expression of the kind of character that is generally and characteristically formed only by participation in those kinds of apprenticeship and training I've attempted to characterize. Where in some particular culture such participation is widespread, there will be correspondingly widespread agreement, not only on the content of moral judgment, but also on how its point and purpose is to be understood.

Where, however, this isn't so, or is no longer so, where such widespread agreement is now lacking, we should expect to find not only diversity and disagreement in the content of moral judgments, but also a transformation in the modes of their utterance. To utter a moral judgment can no longer have the purpose of reminding ourselves, or others who share our moral dispositions and recognitions; of what it is that we share, when we have come to share too little. Instead, the utterance of moral judgments will tend to acquire just those characteristics that I identified at the beginning of this lecture. In the mouths of those whose modes of utterance are, for whatever psychological reasons, assertive and adversarial, judgment will receive its characteristic expression in speech acts of condemnation. Their utterances will become in this way acts of self-expression, the striking of individual attitudes. Others, for whom disagreement is not a stimulus to self-assertion, but instead an occasion for puzzlement and reconsideration, will, in consequence, be increasingly apt to resort to tentative modes of speech and to hedging their judgments around with qualifications. To them, those who speak in the first mode will appear unwarrantedly and intolerably dogmatic, while those who are aggressive in their judgments will take this latter mode of utterance to exhibit a reprehensible failure to stand fast on moral issues. But in neither case will moral judgment function as the expression of well-formed moral character, but rather of lack of character, a sign of thoughtlessness. And those of us who find both modes of utterance inappropriate will do best perhaps to fall silent.

For I have tried to suggest that the unhappy condition of a culture dominated by these two modes of moral utterance is not to be remedied by further pursuit of those recurrent and inconclusive debates between rival and alternative points of view that have been so central to our moral thinking since the Enlightenment, either at the level of philosophy or that of everyday moral judgment. The recovery of moral agency depends rather upon what types of practice it is in which we and others find ourselves engaging, and not on what type of theoretical standpoint we adopt. Moral theorizing does, of course, have distinctive and valuable functions, but there are times at which it may have the effect of distracting us from our practical responsibilities. And perhaps this is one of those times. Perhaps what I should have learned from my own theorizing in this lecture, and elsewhere, is no longer to give such lectures. And what you should have learned is no longer to listen to them.

SEVEN

Conflicts of Desire

To be human is to suffer from unresolved, or at least from imperfectly resolved, conflicts of desire. Yet we are of course under considerable pressure to suppress the expression of such conflicts, so that we may be able to function in a socially acceptable way in a variety of contexts, making choices, pursuing projects, acting and responding to the actions of others, in coherent and what are taken to be normal ways. In order to be able to function acceptably and effectively we need almost all of the time to present ourselves to ourselves as well as to others as unified or very nearly so, and not as divided selves. So in every culture there is generated some image of what is taken to be the normal undivided self, a social artifact that enables us both to interpret others and to present ourselves to others as interpretable.

The normal self is understood as one who makes judgments and choices, pursues projects, and acts and responds to the actions of others in a principled and consistent way—except for what are taken to be

"Conflicts of Desire," in *Weakness of the Will from Plato to the Present*, ed. Tobias Hoffman, 276–92 (Catholic University of America Press, 2008).

very occasional lapses. There are of course individuals who fall outside the bounds of normality thus understood: the alcoholic, the psychotic, the gravely neurotic, the autistic. But, so far as individuals who suffer from none of these conditions are concerned, their lapses from normal coherent and principled functioning are treated as occasional, exceptional, out of character, in need of special explanation, rather than as what they generally in fact are: signs of deep fissures and fractures in the self.

The normal self with its occasional lapses is then a socially important fiction, one that commonly has great power over us. And it is this fiction that gives much of its interest to, even if it did not generate, the philosophical problem often characterized as that of weakness of will. To be sure, in its first and original version the problem was a theoretical response by Aristotle to Socrates' claim that no one willingly errs, that genuine knowledge of the good wholly precludes bad action. But it is not only philosophical considerations that have given continuing life to the problem, so that it has remained central to moral enquiry over an extraordinarily long period, but also a presumption prior to all theorizing that action in conformity with what are taken to be one's best founded judgments as to what one ought to do does not stand in need of explanation, but that actions at odds with those judgments stand in need of special explanation. Or, to put it another way, actions in character are taken to have an intelligibility that actions taken to be out of character lack. It is this presumption that I am going to argue against, rejecting with it the conception of character that informs it.

Social fictions are generally more powerful than philosophical arguments. So that, although most of this paper will be given up to argument, it is important also to say something about what gives this social fiction its power and why to unmask and displace it would cause psychological unease and discomfort. I shall proceed as follows. First, I will give a brief—too brief—account of the relationship of actions, reasons for action, and desires. Then I will say something about the nature of conflicts of desire and their place in our lives, as a prologue to considering and rejecting a currently influential view of what it is to be a rational agent and to order one's desires rationally. the view elaborated by rational decision theorists. I will propose a different account of practical rationality, one that is, I hope, able to accommodate the place that conflicts of desire have in our lives.

And finally I will suggest why attempts to think about ourselves in the light of that account will be apt to encounter psychological resistance.

I

It is important to say how the word *desire* is going to be used in this paper. Sometimes in everyday English usage we ascribe wants or desires solely on the basis of the performance of some action. Someone does something and we ask "What did he want to do that for?" This is not how I am going to use such words as *want* or *desire*. As I will use these verbs, it is true of someone that she or he acted from some desire, only if her or his failure to achieve the object of that desire does or would result in some feeling of frustration or disappointment. Desires are individualized by their objects and the frustration or disappointment must have as its intentional object the lack or absence of whatever it was that was desired. My use of *desire* also differs from Hume's, since Hume uses *desire* to name just one of the passions, whereas, as I use it, desire is a constituent of every passion. To be angry or resentful is to respond to some frustration or disappointment in respect of desire. To be joyful or elated is to respond to the achievement of some object of desire.

Are all actions motivated by desire thus understood? There are clearly actions not so motivated, of at least three kinds. Waiting to go into a meeting, I stroll in the corridor, whistling a half-remembered tune. Is either my strolling or my whistling motivated by some identifiable desire? It would be absurd to think so. A different kind of case is that in which we are afflicted by lack of desire—there is nothing that we particularly want to do or to achieve, no object that strikes us as desirable. Listlessly we go through the motions of our everyday activities, unmotivated by any identifiable desire. Thirdly and much more commonly we all of us, in performing the routine actions of our everyday lives, getting out of bed, brushing our teeth, putting on our clothes, and so on, do these things with minimal attention and without any identifiable desire motivating us. Notice, however, that in all three types of cases, that of the idle time-passing action, that of those afflicted by lassitude, and that of routine everyday activity, we act as we do only until or unless we are motivated by some desire to do otherwise.

Absence of desire is a key part of the explanation of our action in all three cases. We act as we do only because we have no desire to act otherwise. So desire is of crucial importance to our motivation even in these cases.

Some philosophers have argued in respect of all actions other than these that only desire motivates and that therefore the having of a sufficiently good reason for action cannot motivate by and of itself. Others have argued that the having of a sufficiently good reason can motivate by and of itself and that therefore it is not true that only desire motivates. I shall want to argue that, apart from the types of case that I have put on one side, only desire motivates, but that the nature of desire is such that we can become agents who, when we have a sufficiently good reason to act, are motivated by that reason.

We need first to think about how we come to distinguish between objects that we have reason to desire and objects that we do in fact desire. As children we desire many things that we are rightly told are not good for us: to eat junk food, to grab other children's toys, to watch TV. The first is damaging to our health, the second to our capacity for social relationships, the third to the development of our intellectual and aesthetic powers. If we learn what parents and other adults want us to learn, we learn not only that it is bad for us to have these things, but bad also to go on wanting them. To eat healthy food, keep one's hands off other people's possessions, and read Lewis Carroll or C. S. Lewis, while all the time wishing that one was doing otherwise, is also inimical to the development of bodily, social, intellectual, and aesthetic powers. We not only have good reason to want certain things, we also have good reason to want to want them, good reason to want to want what is for our good. But having reason to want, even having reason to want to want, is never by itself sufficient to generate desire. What else is needed?

For this we need to develop three kinds of habit: a habit of stopping and thinking before we act on a desire, a habit of feeling as much of a sense of achievement about letting some desires go unsatisfied as satisfying others, and a habit of being able to give ourselves wholeheartedly to the achievement of desires that are for our good, just because and insofar as they are for our good. Every normal human being has by nature the potentiality for acquiring these habits and by doing so transforming and redirecting her or his desires, although for some this acquisition is difficult, while for others it is relatively easy. And some have excellent teachers and role models, while others do not. What is true of everybody, however, is that the development of the relevant habits and the transformation and redirection of our desires is not something that happens once for all. It takes place over long periods of time and during that time part of what we discover are new obstacles and distractions.

Let us catalogue some of these difficulties by reminding ourselves of four familiar contrasts. The first is between objects of desire that are achievable in the short term and objects of desire to be achieved only in some longer term. It is notoriously dangerous to satisfy one's desires for what is immediate, so that one becomes unable to achieve future goals. But it is also dangerous to sacrifice the present to the future, so that the achievement of the object of desire is always deferred. And there are no rules to guide one here in making one's choices between present and future satisfactions, but only the exercise of fallible judgment.

A second contrast is between the care of oneself and the care of others. Without a suitable regard for others one will be unable to develop the types of social relationship and the type of character that are required if one is to be able to achieve one's own good. It is notoriously dangerous to sacrifice others to the satisfaction of one's desires for oneself, but it is also dangerous to sacrifice oneself for the sake of satisfying the desires of others. Yet the dangers here are different from those that derive from the first contrast. For here the tension is between, on the one hand, thinking in terms of *either* the-pursuit-of-my-good-at-the-expense-of-others *or* the-pursuit-of-the-good-of-others-at-the-expense-of-my-good and, on the other hand, thinking in terms of the pursuit of goods that are neither mine nor theirs, but ours, both mine and theirs, the common goods of human beings. For my care for family members or friends or strangers in need is in fact integral to my care for myself as someone in relationship to those others, someone who achieves her or his own good in achieving both what is good for me and what is good for those others. But this is something that we have to learn and we are so constituted that, even when we have understood it and to some significant measure embodied it in our lives, we are still apt to lapse into either the vices of selfishness or the vices of altruism, for the desires that find expression in those vices tend to survive, even when unrecognized.

A third contrast presents different possibilities of error and frustration. Even when we have successfully identified certain objects of desire as goods, and as goods that it is appropriate for us to pursue here and now, we are apt to care for these goods either too little or too much. Both excess and defect are signs of disorder in our desires. To care for something too little is to be too easily diverted from attempting to achieve it, to be too willing to give up on it. To care for something too much is to place it too high on the rank ordering of our goods, to project onto it a desirability that it does not in reality possess, and so to delude ourselves into believing that we have better reasons for putting on one side other projects and purposes than in fact we do.

Both these failures have extreme versions: that of treating something as the ultimate object of one's heart's desire, when it lacks the characteristics that such an object would have to possess, and that of treating nothing as the ultimate object of one's heart's desire because of a belief that such an ultimate object is an impossible object. The first of these attitudes involves illusion and disappointment, the second a desperate fear of illusion together with an insistence that nothing can be finally satisfying, an insistence designed to enable one to avoid disappointment. This of course is not the only strategy for avoiding disappointment. One way to ensure that one always gets what one wants is always to want only what one gets. Diminished desires and diminished expectations that issue in this often pathetically low level of satisfaction are sometimes the result of prolonged deprivation. Ferdinand Lassalle, the nineteenth-century German social democrat, spoke of "the damned wantlessness of the poor."

This condition of wantlessness is not so much a matter of treating this or that object of desire as less desirable than it is as of a lack of any but minimal desire for any object. And so we arrive at a fourth contrast, that between having too few and too weak desires and that of having too many and too strong desires, so in the latter case being too open to movement in too many directions, to a life of zigzags rather than one of deliberate progress. Here, as in the other three cases, we need to steer a course between two bad extremes and here again individuals differ in how difficult it is for them to steer such a course, either because of their biochemistry or because of their early childhood upbringing. Yet, no matter how favorable these are and no matter how good the habits that we develop, we are all of us liable to suffer from continuing contradictory influences that are the result of imperfect resolutions of tensions between incompatible desires. Where we differ from one another is both in the extent to which we are subject to such influences and in the degree to which we are aware of them, able to confront them, and to make choices that are not distorted by them. But how are we to do this? One answer to this question we owe to the exponents of rational decision theory.

II

To be practically rational, according to rational decision theorists, is to have rank-ordered one's preferences and assigned numbers to their relative strengths, to have assigned numerical probabilities to the outcome of each alternative course of action open to one, and to choose that course of action that scores highest when one combines the relevant numbers. It would, for example, be rational to choose a course of action such that there was a very high probability of satisfying some preference that ranked high in one's ordering rather than a course of action directed toward the satisfaction of some preference that one ranked a little higher, but where the probability of a favorable outcome of any course of action designed to achieve it was near zero. By so choosing one maximizes one's expected utility. To rank-order one's preferences is a matter of answering the question for each of what costs one would be prepared to pay to secure the satisfaction of that particular preference: the higher the cost, the higher the ranking of that preference. Such ordering has to conform to three conditions. First, a certain kind of asymmetry must hold, so that if I prefer x to y, then I must not prefer y to x or be indifferent as between x and y. Second, in the set of outcomes being considered, every outcome must be connected to every other by some state of the agent's preferences, so that of any outcome compared with any other we can say which of these two the agent prefers or if the agent is indifferent between them. Third, to these asymmetry and connectivity conditions we have to add a transitivity condition. If an agent prefers x to y and y to z, then the agent must prefer x to z, and if the agent prefers x to y, but is indifferent between y and z, then the agent must prefer x to z.[1]

Given an ordering of our preferences that satisfies these conditions and an adequate method for assigning probabilities to outcomes—and there are alternative ways of doing this—we can determine which course of action will maximize the satisfaction of these preferences. A background assumption is that our preferences will remain stable at least over the period during which we are engaged in trying to secure the maximum degree of satisfaction of this particular set of preferences. And it is of course the case that our estimation of probable outcomes will generally be more accurate the shorter the period between our choice and the expected outcome of our action. But these are not so much difficulties for the theory as limits on the powers of rational choice thus conceived. And there are of course many types of situation in which it is uncontroversial that to proceed as rational choice theory dictates is to proceed reasonably. But there are two large questions to be raised if that theory is taken to be an account of rationality as such.

The first concerns its inability to find any place for a concept of rational desire, a concept of objects of desire that we have reason to desire. The exponents of rational decision theory as a theory of practical rationality treat our preferences, and with them also our desires, as given, as surd realities from which rational decision making begins. In so doing they remind us of course of Hume, although their rhetoric is very different. Where Hume announces dramatically that "[r]eason is, and ought only to be the slave of the passions, and can never pretend to any other office than to serve and obey them" (*Treatise of Human Nature*, 2.3.3), they less dramatically presuppose an account of reason in our practical lives that is wholly instrumental, enabling us to satisfy as efficiently as possible the preferences by which we happen to be motivated. What we lack on both views is any practically effective conception of our individual and common goods that would allow us to distinguish between preferences and desires that it would be good that we should satisfy and preferences and desires of which this is not true.

What is it, then, at the level of practice to have such a conception of one's goods? It is to know how to engage in two kinds of rank ordering and not just one, a rank ordering, on the one hand, of preferences and desires and, on the other, of goods. Examples of these types of rank ordering and of the conflicts that they may and often do generate are familiar to everyone who has reflected on the difference between how they would live, if they acted as their present desires and preferences bid them, and how they would live if they were directed toward the good of their own bodily health. If I consulted only my own preferences, I would omit my annual physical examination with all the tests, some of them invasive, that generally lead to no particular result. I would consume large quantities of rich food and drink. And I would take only sporadic exercise. But I know that to live like this would be to be inadequately concerned with the good of my health. That good provides me with a standard and if I have developed the prudential habits and the desires that I need that will motivate me to act for the sake of that good.

To this the reply may be: insofar as you are motivated by your conception of your good, this is in each particular case just one more preference, to be rank-ordered together with your other preferences. This is therefore a type of case that rational decision theory can easily accommodate, although in characterizing your preference as one for your own good health, nothing more could be meant by "good" than perhaps "such as would be found desirable by many people." But this reply misses the point. For, when I say that bodily health is a good, I make an assertion about a matter of fact, something that is true or false independently of my preferences and desires. What kind of matter of fact is this?

Members of every animal species, except for the very simplest, pass through some natural line of development. And at each stage of their development they may flourish or fail to flourish. To flourish is for an animal to develop and to exercise its specific powers, so that it attains those goals that are its in virtue of its nature. And for rational animals, human beings, those powers are physical, moral, aesthetic, and rational. It is moreover the work of reason to govern, so far as it can, the exercise of our nonrational powers. And it is the work of reason to instruct us, among other things, as to what we do and do not have good reason to desire. To say that I have good reason to do whatever contributes to my flourishing is therefore to say that I have good reason to act only on good reasons, for to flourish is to act, so far as possible, only on good reasons.

Put this another way. Someone who is puzzled as to whether she or he has good reason to do what contributes to her or his flourishing has an inadequate grasp of the concept of human flourishing and such an inadequate grasp is itself a symptom of failure to flourish. It can therefore be the case that someone has good reason to desire, to choose, or to act in some particular way, without having any desire so to desire, to choose, or to act, and moreover without any awareness that this is so. But this is a possibility that those who take rational decision theory to be an account of practical rationality as such exclude from view. And, by excluding it, they exclude any possibility of a practically effective critique of desire that is not itself desire-based.

A second objection to rational decision theory as an account of practical rationality concerns the insistence by rational decision theorists on consistency as a requirement of rationality, a requirement embodied in the asymmetry, connectivity, and transitivity conditions that I noted earlier. And they are far from alone in thinking that in both theoretical and practical reasoning consistency is an obvious requirement. To this I reply that consistency must indeed be a goal of both rational enquiry and rational practice, but that there is always a danger of imposing a requirement of consistency prematurely. In theorizing we may well find ourselves with apparently good reason to affirm two or more inconsistent positions, but not yet know which to reject and which to affirm. In some contexts we find ourselves driven to the conclusion that p, while in other contexts we find ourselves driven to the conclusion that q, which we know very well entails $\sim p$. We never of course allow ourselves at any time and in any context to assert $p \cdot q$ without qualification. Nonetheless, an observer might seem to have reason to accuse us of inconsistency. Yet, if we were to try to rebut this accusation by a premature resolution of the issue, rejecting p in order to affirm q or vice versa, we might well find later on that we had closed some door to theoretical progress.

So it can be too an occasion with desires. Of two or more alternative and incompatible goals defining alternative and incompatible courses of action we may find ourselves in some contexts driven to the conclusion that we have sufficiently good reason to desire one and in other contexts equally driven to conclude that we have sufficiently good reason to desire the other. We never of course allow ourselves to conclude that we have sufficiently good reason to desire the conjunction of these incompatible sets of reasons. But once again an observer might seem to have reason to impute inconsistency. And once again if we were to try to rebut this accusation by abandoning one of these goals we might well find later that we had made a premature and unfortunate choice. Sometimes, then, rationality requires us to live on the edge of practical as well as of theoretical inconsistency, something of which rational decision theory seems to be able to offer no account.

Having recognized this we need to return to the question of what the relationship is between, on the one hand, having a good reason to act and, on the other, being motivated so to act, just because there is good reason to act. What we first need to understand, if we are to answer this question, is how we learn to desire what it is that we have reason to desire, a third notion that rational decision theory cannot accommodate. When we are infants our desires are for the immediate satisfaction of our own most strongly felt needs and they are clamorous. We begin, that is to say, at one extreme of each of the four contrasts that I identified earlier. Interaction with caring adults, especially and overwhelmingly our mothers, moves us away from those extremes, so that we learn to defer satisfaction, to become minimally patient, to respond to expressions of desire or need by others, and to have a wider range of types and strengths of desire. Mothers shape their children's desires, sometimes perhaps being too anxious to satisfy the child, sometimes perhaps teaching the child to be too compliant, but generally negotiating their way between these extremes and teaching the child how to negotiate her or his own way between them. So children begin to learn that they have reason to desire this and not that, to desire this strongly and that only moderately, to have neither too many nor too few desires. And learning to desire what we have reason to desire and as we have reason to desire is inseparable from learning how to rank-order goods, since to say of something that it is better than something else is to say that we have more or better reason to desire it.

Here again of course we are at odds with those whose conception of practical rationality is drawn from rational decision theory. Just because they can find no place for the concept of *having good reason to desire* and just because they understand the resolution of inconsistencies as a precondition for practical reasoning, rather than as something to be achieved by practical reasoning, so too they cannot find a place for such notions as those of learning how to desire and, in the course of that learning, learning how to resolve conflicts of desire.

This learning can be something that continues through the whole of one's life or it can be something that breaks off at some point, so that thereafter we leave our desires unexamined and our conflicts unresolved. And sometimes it may scarcely begin, so that we are liable to be passive in our responses to numerous stimuli that we encounter, victims of our own desires and of our conflicts of desire, a state that it is the intention of advertisers to induce in as many of us as possible. Advertising, like a good deal of contemporary political rhetoric, is not designed to engender calm reflection of the form "Do I really want this? And, whether I do or not, do I have good reason to want it?" yet it is only through such reflection, continued throughout our lives, that we over time through our rank ordering of desires and goods and through our resolution of conflicts acquire a more or less spelled-out conception of what a life would be that was directed toward the achievement of what is good and best for us as human beings, of *the* good and *our* good.

III

The progress toward such a conception is not, however, a straightforward one. For at different stages in our lives the issues presented by such questions as whether or not to focus on the short term at the expense of the longer term and whether or not to narrow down one's interests or to widen them may take very different forms. And having learned how to answer them more or less adequately at one stage in our lives is no guarantee that we will know how to answer them equally well at subsequent stages. Even when we have identified some misdirection of desire and know what must be done to redirect that desire, desire is not always immediately amenable to redirection even in the best of us. Occasional lapses from what we know to be best are therefore part of the normal human condition. They are not necessarily signs of a weak will, but may instead testify to the strength of some desire that we have not yet sufficiently transformed or redirected. So many of the cases that have been considered under the rubric "weakness of will" should instead have been considered under the rubric "strength of desire"—but not all. What, then, is the difference between them?

Weakness of will in someone is not so much a matter of the lapse itself, but of someone's attitude to her or his lapses. When we act other than as we know to be best, we may stop short, stand back, and express disappointment and, if appropriate, contrition, so making the lapse an occasion for resolving to do better. Or we may pass over it, excuse ourselves, and hurry on to something else. The differences between these two is a difference in direction. To will rightly is to be directed toward our good, since the will is appetite for the good. And to fail to be so directed is a failure of, a weakness in, will.

To be directed toward our good is then compatible with certain kinds of lapse, although certainly not with others. Actions that involve gratuitous violence toward others or treachery and betrayal of a friend, even when apparently out of character, are never mere lapses. They exhibit untamed and untrained desire. But we should not infer that someone who is never tempted to perform such actions or indeed any actions that violate the prohibitions of the moral law is therefore directed toward her or his good. Their condition may instead be simply one of absence of desire of any significant strength, including absence of desire for their own good, an unhappy condition that we need to distinguish from moral rectitude, even when its outward appearance is the same as that of moral rectitude.

To have a strong and sustained desire for one's good is compatible with large misconceptions of what one's good is and this in part because of the complexity of the concept of one's good. So each individual life embodies a narrative in which, if we do well, we move through a series of less than adequate understandings—sometimes gross misunderstandings—of our good and, that is to say, less than adequate understandings of what we will have to achieve if we are to perfect our lives according to the standard of specifically human flourishing. It is the mark of a desire for the good that insofar as we identify something hitherto desired as involving a misunderstanding or even a less than adequate understanding of our good, we become dissatisfied with that object of desire and our desire moves beyond it in search of another more adequate object, indeed in search of a fully adequate object. I move beyond thinking that this particular job, that particular set of material possessions, the enjoyment of this friendship or of the achievement of this child could in some way complete my life toward a thought of what I conceive of originally perhaps as something I know not what, something that would perfect and satisfy my life without qualification. To speak of this is on, for example, Lacan's view to speak of an illusion. But here I shall simply assume that Lacan is mistaken, for my immediate concern is not with what end would or would not complete the narrative of my or your life, but with the nature of our progress toward that end.

That progress will seldom, if ever, be straightforward for reasons that I have already suggested. Let me give just one example. Some of us, perhaps all of us, have within ourselves both a tendency toward risk taking and a tendency toward caution. In some the risk taking is so pronounced a trait that caution becomes something urged on the self by others and perhaps by an internalized voice, an other to whom either too little or too much heed may be paid. In others it is caution that has the upper hand, so that impulses toward risk taking are apt to be instantly suppressed. But for individuals of both types learning involves recognizing the need to strike a balance, to find a mean, and this need is something of which individuals characteristically become aware when they fall into disorder and frustration because of either too great risk taking or excessive caution. But they also learn, sometimes painfully, that one cannot hit on the mean between risk taking and caution once and for all so that thereafter one always or almost always gets it right. As one's circumstances change, as one finds oneself in new and unfamiliar contexts in which a balance has to be struck, one learns that what is now demanded of one by way of risk taking and caution may be so different from what was demanded in previous contexts that past experience hinders rather than helps. So that one also has to learn how to be neither too dismissive of nor too reliant on one's own past experience. And such complexities of learning are possible only for those whose desires have been ordered and directed in a particular way. To say what that particular way is is also to say something important about practical reasoning.

Someone who, as a rational agent, is moving toward her or his good through the conflicts engendered by her or his desire to take appropriate risks and desire to be properly cautious has to reckon with at least three motivations that may have to be integrated in choice and action. She or he may have an inclination to take the same bold and unexpected step toward her or his goal, one that, if it succeeds, will make further steps much easier, but that, if it fails—and there is a significant chance of failure—will make it necessary to begin all over again. She or he may also have an inclination to take a more arduous and much slower way of reaching her or his objective, but one that has less chance of failure. Yet in addition she or he will have a desire for her or his own good, a good the achievement of which requires that she or he becomes a particular kind of person, someone whose desires are rightly proportioned to their objects. So that a rational agent has to ask what kind of person she or he will be shown to be by her or his choice between risk taking and caution, and whether that is the kind of person that she or he needs to be, if she or he is to achieve her or his good. She or he has to ask, that is, whether in this respect she or he has reason to desire what and as she or he does desire. And this is possible only if and insofar as her or his desire for her or his good is her or his overriding motivation.

The desire for one's own good is a desire to desire only what one has good reason to desire. If we lacked any such desire, we would lack any motivation to transform and redirect our other desires, so that what we in fact desire might come to coincide with what we have good reason to desire. And it is in part because they can find no place for this desire for our own good in their account of the psychology of human agents that so-called internalists, who hold that the only practically effective reasons for action derive from within the set of our present desires (broadly construed), remain vulnerable to the criticisms of so-called externalists, who hold that we can be motivated to act in this or that particular way by having sufficiently good reasons so to act, independently of the state of our desires, and that such externalists remain similarly vulnerable to internalist criticism. The prudent reasoning and motivation of genuinely rational agents are fully intelligible only if we ascribe to such agents a desire for their own good.

What, then, is the structure of the practical reasoning of such agents? We can best answer this question by considering first an example that Aquinas employs in his discussion of incontinence, then Davidson's criticism of Aquinas's use of that example, and finally how the issue between Davidson and Aquinas should be addressed. Aquinas argues that someone under the influence of a passion may ignore the truth of the major premise of the relevant practical syllogism and supply instead an alternative major premise for a practical syllogism that will permit him to yield to the passion (Ia-IIae q. 77, a. 2). So someone envisaging a genuinely pleasing act of fornication supplies himself with a true minor premise, 'This will be pleasant,' supplies as a major premise 'Pleasure is to be pursued,' and concludes 'This act is to be pursued,' turning his mind away from other premises that he knows to be true, the minor premise, 'This is an act of fornication,' and the major premise 'No act of fornication is lawful,' judgments to which when not directed by passion he assents, and with them what follows from them, that 'This act is unlawful,' and therefore not to be performed.

Davidson has two closely related criticisms of Aquinas.[2] The first is that we need to represent the condition of the incontinent agent not just by two, but by three arguments. For if an agent were to rehearse the two rival arguments with their incompatible conclusions what he would arrive at is a blank contradiction, which cannot be a prescription for action. And of course, even if he attempts to proceed beyond the two arguments to a further third argument yielding a practical conclusion, he cannot do so via a blank contradiction. Hence we need to reword the two arguments as well as to go beyond them. And so Davidson reconstructs the two arguments, making of the principles that supply the major premises not unconditional, but merely prima facie assertions. With Davidson's reconstruction we do not need to be concerned. For Davidson's critique of Aquinas misses the point instructively. What Davidson has not recognized is the importance of time in Aquinas's representation of the arguments of the incontinent human being. And in omitting this element Davidson is following the example of almost all writers on practical reasoning.

Consider someone who, unlike the incontinent man, rehearses to himself each of the two practical arguments identified by Aquinas. He will do so successively, taking whatever time he needs, and in, as it were, different voices. He will be in dialogue with himself and at the point in time at which he has rehearsed only these two arguments his dialogue will be as yet incomplete. How then should he continue? He may of course not continue, but instead break off the dialogue, recognize that if he stops here he is faced with a blank contradiction and resolve matters by a choice, either, as passion bids, to do what is unlawful, or instead to obey reason and the natural law and put aside the bidding of pleasure. If he does the latter, it will surely be as a result of a habit, that of responding to moments of this kind by stopping and thinking, so that he is able to carry his dialogue with himself one stage further. With what thought might it continue? Perhaps with the thought of Aristotle and Aquinas that the pleasures of the good human being are not the same as those of the bad and that to find the unlawful pleasant is a sign of something in himself that still needs remedying.[3] If he does continue in this way, his lapse into temptation, even if not into action, becomes an occasion not only for an immediate practical conclusion, but also for further reflection.

Practical reasoning, then, commonly takes the form of temporally extended dialogue and the history of any practical reasoner is a history of ongoing dialogues, always with her- or himself and often, if she or he is prudent, with others. The dialogues with her- or himself are expressions both of conflicting desires and of rival sets of judgments as to what she or he has reason to desire. They will be dialogues to which others are invited to contribute, if the agent follows the dictates of reason, partly because it is often from others that we are able to learn how to correct the one-sidedness and partiality of our own particular point of view and to see things as they are, rather than as our desire-driven phantasies represent them, and partly because in so many of our enterprises we need to consult with others about their and our common good.

Accounts of practical reasoning generally ignore its dialogical character, just as they ignore the dimension of time. What they do provide is a statement of the final stages of practical reasoning, those that more or less immediately precede choice and action. And this is understandable, since generally all that honest and self-aware agents themselves provide when put to the question, whether as explanation or as justification for their choices and actions, is the reasoning of this final stage. But we also need to know how this final stage was arrived at.

This is not always a matter of those states of mind and desires that were immediately prior to this final stage. What determined the final stage of my reasoning on some particular occasion may or may not have occurred immediately beforehand. It is often the case that crucial dialogues that resolved tensions between conflicting desires, in the light of judgments about what we have good reason to desire, took place at some time well in advance of those situations whose practical reasoning they determine. And it is always the case that the patterns of our practical reasoning on particular occasions are the outcome of a lifelong history of conversations with ourselves and others, devoted to resolving conflicts of desire and to arriving at judgments about what we have reason to desire.

IV

What, then, is the case that I have advanced against what I take to be conventional conceptions of weakness of will? It is twofold. First, I have claimed that lapses and inconsistencies are in fact characteristic of the normally virtuous individual, of the normally genuinely virtuous individual, that is. They are signs not of weakness of will, but of that imperfect ordering of our desires that continues to mark the lives of the very best of us.

Second, I have suggested that what matters is not so much the occurrence of these lapses, important though that is, but our responses to them. Insofar as we are virtuous, we will take note of them, reflect on them, and try to make sure that they do not recur. But if we either pass over them, failing to take note, or actively assent to them, then we have taken a direction that is other than that toward our good and there is something amiss with the will, a weakness, a lack of strength to persevere in directedness toward our good, something that may properly be called "weakness of will."

I said at the beginning of this paper that the conventional view of weakness of will presupposed a socially influential conception of the normal self and that the alternative account that I was going to offer is one that there would be resistance to accepting. Now that I have sketched that alternative account it is possible to ask why this is so. Apart from my reference to Davidson's criticism of Aquinas, I have put forward my alternative account in an idiom that owes as little as possible to Aquinas, even though his thesis that every wrong act "proceeds from inordinate desire" (*Summa Theologiae* Ia-IIae q. 77 a. 4) is presupposed in my argument. I have, for example, spoken of strength of desire rather than, as Aquinas does, of weakness in not resisting such desire (Ia-IIae.77.3). And my hope has been by so doing to present philosophical arguments and a philosophical conclusion that are and are seen to be independent of any theological assertions or presuppositions. But at this point some reference to Thomist theology cannot be avoided. Consider what Aquinas says as to whether human beings without grace can avoid sin (Ia-IIae.109.8).

Without grace, says Aquinas, human beings can avoid each, but not every, act of sin. Any one particular act of sin could have been avoided. The agent did not have to perform it. Nonetheless, in the life of any human being there cannot but be acts of sin, acts that violate the precepts of the natural law. The human condition without grace is such that a normal human life is one in which lapses from principles to which agents are firmly committed occur recurrently. Aquinas, that is to say, describes what I have described as the normal human condition as the condition of original sin. But this is something that moral theorists are generally unwilling to allow, something indeed that normal human beings are deeply reluctant to acknowledge. For to agree that this is so would be to acknowledge that there is a humanly unbridgeable gap between what we know that we ought to do and what we do, a gap that can disappear only through the action of grace. The conception of the normal self presupposed by conventional views of weakness of will has the effect of disguising this aspect of the human condition. It functions as a defense against a theological understanding of human nature. Small wonder then that it is seldom put in question.

EIGHT

Interview with Alex Voorhoeve

ALEX VOORHOEVE How did you come to regard Aristotelian philosophy as basically right?[1]

ALASDAIR MacINTYRE I can give you a retrospective account of my thought, but it will be what [the philosopher of science] Imre Lakatos called a 'rational reconstruction'. That is, it may not be history as it actually happened, though it is an attempt to be that.

   As a graduate student, I was struck not just by the inability of moral theorists to resolve their fundamental differences—most notably the differences between Kantians and utilitarians—but also by the fact that these differences were about issues that were at stake in policy decisions in the latter days of World War II, decisions that resulted in the fire-bombings of

---

Excerpted from Alasdair MacIntyre, "The Illusion of Self-Sufficiency," in *Conversations on Ethics*, by Alex Voorhoeve, 115–22, 124–30 (Oxford University Press, 2009).

Dresden and Tokyo. I was and am convinced that those are prime examples of actions that should never be done. The official case was that the end of the war would be hastened by so acting and that those fire-bombings could therefore be justified by appealing to the utilitarian aim of the maximization of aggregate well-being. Clearly, some kind of consequentialism ruled in public policy. Yet the most compelling justification for going to war against the Nazis had derived from what seemed to be Kantian principles, according to which there are certain ways in which no one should ever be treated, whatever the consequences. So I asked myself 'How is it that we have these two incompatible moral views, each of which provides a rational justification for its moral judgements, but neither of which appears to be able to come to terms with the other?' This led me to examine more closely the characteristics that made each view objectionable.

ALEX VOORHOEVE What is most objectionable in utilitarianism?

ALASDAIR MACINTYRE Utilitarianism appears to provide no place for genuinely unconditional commitments—yet such commitments play a crucial role in human life. Take, for example, the commitment of a parent to a child of the form: 'However things turn out, I will be there for you.' Such a parent is committed to caring for his or her child, even if the child is gravely retarded or delinquent. *This* parent accepts that *this* child is *her* or *his* responsibility, whatever the consequences of assuming that responsibility. It is essential for a child's development that the parental attitude should take this form, for only in a relationship structured by this commitment does the child enjoy the security and recognition it needs to develop. And this type of commitment—there are quite a number of others—is not compatible with a utilitarian calculation of the overall expected balance of good over bad consequences of devoting oneself to caring for the child.

ALEX VOORHOEVE And what is wrong with Kantianism?

ALASDAIR MACINTYRE For a start, I do not think that Kant's derivation of the categorical imperative succeeds, either in his own version or in any of the versions elaborated by his followers. But, more importantly, Kant's conception of moral motivation is flawed. On Kant's view, the basis of moral motivation lies not in one's desires, but in a recognition that some type of action is morally required or prohibited. But I was and am unable to understand how we could be motivated to act as we should by anything but our desires. The hard work of morality consists in the *transformation* of our desires, so that we aim at the good and respect the precepts of the natural law.

I therefore knew very early in my enquiries what I rejected, but I had at that stage no idea what I wanted to say instead. And then, partly under the influence of Marxism, it occurred to me that although philosophers present moral theories as if they were free-standing, those theories generally are articulations of concepts and presuppositions embodied in forms of social life. By articulating those concepts and presuppositions, moral theorists open them up to criticism and so make it possible to question what has hitherto been taken for granted in a culture. So the emergence of moral philosophy in a culture—indeed the emergence of philosophy in general—is a mark of that culture having reached a point at which it can become self-critical. (As an aside: one way to think about cultures is in terms of the degree to which they are self-critical; and they may fail to be self-critical, not because philosophy does not flourish in them, but because philosophy has become such that it can have little effect on the dominant modes of practical thinking—which is the case here and now in our own culture.)

If moral theories articulate the presuppositions and concepts that are embodied in our everyday judgements, then one interesting way to begin our enquiries in moral philosophy is to ask ourselves what it is to which we are already committed by our everyday life and our everyday judgements. This is often not an easy question to answer, especially if you inhabit the morally fragmented culture of modernity. But when I began to ask myself this question, I discovered quite soon that I was and had been—without knowing it—an Aristotelian. For when I identified more precisely the reasons why I had rejected both utilitarianism and Kantianism, it became clear that those reasons stemmed from Aristotelian attitudes. Aristotle's account of the virtues entails that there are certain types of action that one will never perform, whatever the consequences, unless one has already gone badly wrong—unless one has become the kind of human being who is unwittingly or perversely frustrating himself in developing those relationships needed to achieve his good or goods. Aristotle also enables us to understand how and why it is that our desires, as they develop through and from early childhood, need to be transformed so that we acquire the virtues. My initial reasons for rejecting utilitarianism and Kantianism had been inchoately and unconsciously Aristotelian. Now they became explicitly Aristotelian. And so I found myself at work within a particular philosophical tradition and committed to undertaking two kinds of philosophical work. First of all, I needed to ask why in the past history of our culture a broadly Aristotelian standpoint had been displaced by those heirs of the Enlightenment, utilitarianism and Kantianism. It was by pursuing an answer to this question that I came to write *After Virtue*. Secondly, I had to spell out further what was involved in Aristotelianism, not only the Aristotelianism of Aristotle, but also that of his greatest interpreters, especially Aquinas.

ALEX VOORHOEVE   What was the source of your Aristotelian commitments?

ALASDAIR MACINTYRE   Perhaps autobiography may get in the way here, but obviously this happened in part as a result of how I had been brought up, of how some older family members and friends had influenced me by passing on thoughts and judgements from a still older way of life. Yet to tell this story would not be particularly interesting philosophically. I should instead focus on how my thinking developed.

One concern was with the place of rules in ethics. Rules must be a constituent of any morality, but rules can never be formulated so that they can be brought to bear unproblematically on all the cases to which they are relevant. And there are always situations in which no rule will give us the guidance that we need. So we cannot do without a capacity for judgement that is not itself rule-governed, that capacity to which Aristotle gave the name *phronēsis*, or 'practical intelligence'. This is the capacity that enables us to identify in each particular situation which rules, if any, are relevant and then to frame our choices accordingly. And it became clear to me that the exercise of *phronēsis* is always informed by some conception both of a good at which we are aiming in these particular circumstances and of a further good at which we are aiming as our ultimate good. So I needed to elucidate both the concept of *a* good and the concept of *the* good.

Consider the range of evaluations that we make in calling something good. We may evaluate something as instrumentally good—good as a means to further ends—and we may also call 'good' a range of things worth pursuing for their own sake, including goods internal to particular activities, such as those goods that are to be achieved in the playing or the enjoyment of music, in scientific enquiry, or in the activities and relationships of the family. With respect to this range of goods, we need to judge which of them to pursue and in which combination. In thinking about this question, I made a characteristic Aristotelian thought my own: that when I am assessing how such goods should be ordered, I am considering what part they play in human flourishing, what contribution they might make to my flourishing as a human being. I took and take this to be a quasi-biological question, like the questions 'What is it to flourish as a wolf?' or 'What is it to flourish as a dolphin?' In each case—humans, wolves, dolphins—what an individual needs to flourish is to develop the distinctive powers that it possesses as a member of its species.

ALEX VOORHOEVE What are these distinctive powers for humans?

ALASDAIR MACINTYRE The crucial difference between human beings as rational animals and other animal species is that human beings are able to reflect on the norms that govern their lives, on the nature of the activities they engage in, and the experiences they have, and can ask: 'Is there a better way to live than the way I am living now?' Indeed, in all sorts of ways, each of us recurrently asks this question, even though we do not usually make it explicit. So any human life is going to be impoverished without the exercise of this reflective, critical, and constructive capacity for practical reasoning. To have this capacity is to be able to stand back from one's desires and to evaluate them in the light of one's knowledge of goods and of the good. It is to be able to evaluate the reasons for action that others propose to me and that I propose to others.

ALEX VOORHOEVE What, if anything, follows from recognizing that part of my good is to engage in practical reasoning?

ALASDAIR MACINTYRE One thing that follows is the importance of friendship. For rational deliberation is essentially social. To think constructively about my own good in practical terms in everyday life, I need to deliberate along with and in the company of others. This is not only because I will have to make shared decisions with people around me, but also because my own thinking is likely to be defective unless it is exposed to criticism by others who are, to some significant degree, concerned about my good in the same way that I am, and who know that I am concerned about their good in the same way that they are. What is the consequence of not having critical friends? It is that one becomes the victim of one's hopes and fears, of wishful thinking and fantasy. I have learned from psychoanalysis that, to an extraordinary but generally unrecognized extent, unless we are very careful, we tend not to see things as they are, but as our fantasies predispose us to see them. And we can only be rescued from this by a certain kind of friendship. One important type of such friendship is marriage. It is crucial that husband and wife know enough and care enough about each other to be able to make perceptive, even if harsh, judgements. It is therefore also crucial that marriage be an unconditional commitment, because otherwise one may not have the security to give and take such criticism. But one always needs critical friends to rescue one from a distorted view of oneself.

I should add that reasoning together with others about my and their good requires some significant measure of agreement on our goals—where there is no common ground concerning ends, there can be no useful common deliberation. Fortunately, the range of goods about which we and others are able to agree without much difficulty is impressive. They include, as I indicated earlier, the goods of community life and of the workplace, the goods of enquiry, and various kinds of artistic and athletic goods. All of these enrich a life, and a life lacking all of them would be unhappy and impoverished. And since it is as practical reasoners that we achieve those goods, it is undeniably a good to engage in practical reasoning and to reason well.

Now, what we share with others depends crucially on the social relationships in which we find ourselves. When Aristotle discussed human flourishing, he was talking about flourishing in the context of the relationships of a *polis* [a Greek city-state] when it is in good order. When *we* are thinking about virtues, norms, and ends, we always have to begin where *we* are, with our having been brought up in a particular way and in a particular set of social relationships with its own conception of virtues, norms, and ends.

When we are engaged in this type of enquiry, the following questions arise: Why should we continue to give to this particular conception of moral requirements the authority that hitherto it has enjoyed? Is it for our good to continue to live in these ways? How these questions are answered in particular social circumstances will be, in part, a matter of the extent to which there is a shared conception of their good that is available to members of that particular group.

ALEX VOORHOEVE Your way of phrasing the question about the authority of moral norms as one about whether we think they serve our good differs from the typical way of asking the question, which is: Does regarding certain moral norms as authoritative serve my good? That's the way the question is put by Glaucon in Plato's *Republic*, for example. Why don't you phrase it that way?

ALASDAIR MACINTYRE We need to distinguish two kinds of goal and two kinds of deliberation. Some goals are peculiarly mine, so that I take others into account as people with independent goals, whose cooperation I might need or who might stand in the way of achieving my goals. In such cases, I deliberate with others in order to coordinate our actions so that we can each best pursue our independent goals. But many of our important goals are not like this. For most of us, in such contexts as the family, the workplace, and many other areas of social life, the goods that we try to achieve are common: in the family, educating and nurturing our children well; in the workplace, doing one's work according to some standard of professional excellence; and so on. Such goods are common because each participant recognizes their achievement by others as well as by her- or himself as part of her or his overall good. They are also common because what the relevant goods are is not up to each participant independently of others; instead, we identify these common goods and our shared goals only in the course of our transactions with others in the family, the workplace, or elsewhere.

Each individual therefore has a variety of common as well as individual goods, and we have to be able to order the various goods that we acknowledge, finding the place of each good in a life aimed at achieving the overall good. There is therefore one more type of good that each of us has in common with others: that of creating and sustaining the larger communities within which such shared deliberations about the overall good of human life can take place. In sum, our lives are structured by asking 'What do *we* want?', not 'What do *I* want?'

ALASDAIR MACINTYRE   In order to flourish, we must receive the kind of care that we need when we are very young, ill, injured, disabled, or very old. Acknowledging this means not sharing, in certain respects, the attitudes of Aristotle's *megalopsychos*. It involves, as Aquinas knew, being able to ask for and graciously receive others' help. It also means acknowledging what we owe to others as a consequence of what we have received.

ALEX VOORHOEVE   Your focus on dependence differs not just from Aristotle, but, as you say, from much of the tradition in Western moral philosophy. John Rawls is an example of a contemporary author who takes the central case for an account of justice to be the relationship between healthy adult citizens who can be fully cooperating members of society. The question of what we owe to adults who are barred from being fully cooperating members of society because of illness or disability is then meant to be dealt with by a supplementary account. Why can't we proceed in this way?

ALASDAIR MACINTYRE   The kind of vulnerability that is experienced by children, the very old, and adults who are sick or injured is indeed absent from Rawls's discussion. What is wrong with this way of proceeding is that when one *does* consider this vulnerability, it becomes clear that Rawls's 'central case' is *not*, in fact, the central case for developing an account of justice. What's more, it is a *misleading* case. For the individual who has been made the focus of the enquiry is someone who has been a child and who will, if she lives long enough, become old and infirm.

It is interesting that Rawls begins his account of justice with *society* and not with families or schools. For all of us first encounter questions of justice in the family and at school, and it seems plausible that the questions of what justice is in the family and what it is at school are good places to start an enquiry into justice. Consider two things that are not given their due place in Rawls's account. First, family members' needs, particularly the needs of children, but also the needs of parents. And second, the contributions that each person makes to the common enterprise of the family and what, in consequence, each deserves. Both provide grounds for allocating goods.

Now, once we bring needs into view, we discover that justice in the family—and elsewhere—requires generosity: it requires that we give to those with whom we share common goods in an unstinting, non-calculating way. The kind of care that we need, and that others need from us, does not have the character of a *quid pro quo*. In order to become independent practical reasoners, we needed from our parents, teachers, and others a kind of care that was not conditional on the expectation that we would render them some service in return. Moreover, the people to whom we owe assistance when we have become independent adults may be people who never have done and never will do anything for us. So a certain generosity beyond justice is required if justice is to be done. And one needs to have this virtue of 'just generosity', as I call it, in order to participate in a community that achieves the common good of caring justly for those in need.

ALEX VOORHOEVE   I don't fully understand this concept of just generosity. Can you give a further example?

ALASDAIR MACINTYRE   Consider the United States penal system. The United States locks up a larger proportion of its residents than any society in history. Moreover, the conditions in most prisons are bad in all sorts of ways, and for many who deserve punishment it is bad to be in prison because the experience contributes to their moral decline. Just generosity therefore requires us to help people newly released from prison, so that they may find their way back into society. I have an admirable colleague who devotes a substantial part of his spare time to meeting people on their release from prison, footing the bill for a meal, taking them to the place where they will be staying, making sure that they have enough money in their pockets, and so on. This is the sort of thing that it is necessary that some people do without thinking of any return. Moreover, people who do not contribute to this kind of enterprise are not acting unjustly. But they *are* failing to *sustain* justice.

ALEX VOORHOEVE   Isn't it the case that we need this kind of generosity only because the penal system is unjustly organized? So it would seem that this case doesn't show the need for a generosity beyond justice; it merely shows that when a society is unjust, it is a good thing that there are people who are willing to relieve some of the effects of that injustice.

ALASDAIR MacINTYRE   If the penal system of the United States were justly organized, then there would be less need of generosity towards ex-prisoners. But, no matter how well organized, it could not dispense with the exercise of the virtues of justice and generosity. I would go so far as to say that there is no real justice where there is no generosity.

ALEX VOORHOEVE   In *Dependent Rational Animals,* you claim that we must extend this type of generosity to those with severe mental disabilities. At the same time, you write that we do not need to show such generosity towards non-human animals with the same cognitive capacities. Moreover, on your view, we are permitted to do things to non-human animals that we are not permitted to do to humans with similar capacities. Peter Singer has famously challenged this type of thinking as a form of unjust discrimination against non-human animals, which he calls 'speciesism' in order to draw out the analogy with racism. He proposes that our tendency to view animals like chimpanzees as having lesser claims on us than those humans who have the same mental capacities stems from similar psychological tendencies as racism, such as that a person with a disability looks more like us, and that it is easier to sympathize with him. Now, by way of justification for the claim that we must care generously for and protect humans with severe mental disabilities in ways we need not care for and protect non-human animals with similar capacities, you write that our attitude towards these humans should be governed by the thought, 'That could have been me,' and that no such thought applies in the case of non-human animals. Isn't this just an expression of the type of unduly partial sympathy of which Singer complains?

ALASDAIR MacINTYRE   If I come across a severely injured chimpanzee, I should certainly do something about it. What I do not have to do is weigh its suffering on the same scale as human suffering. It is never a matter, for example, of judging that this chimpanzee is more severely injured than this human so that I should help the chimpanzee if I cannot help both. I do not share a form of life with chimpanzees in the same way that I share a form of life with other humans. I do not have the same relationship to them. Here I differ not only from Peter Singer, but also from some animal rights campaigners. For I take it to be an important question what kind of relationships we have with particular members of other species, rather than with non-human animals in general. As a farm worker, I may have particular relationships with this cow, that dog, this horse. And so I will acquire responsibilities to those particular animals in the course of working with them and living alongside them, of depending on them and having them depend on me. These relationships are part of our form of life, and someone involved in this form of life needs to know how to behave in relation to the animals that live alongside him. But I would not want to generalize from such cases to our duties to all animals.

So I do not think that the tendencies that Singer refers to ground our commitment to those who are severely disabled. The thought is, rather, that this is one more example of human vulnerability and that our form of life is such that coping with the vulnerabilities of others, and of ourselves, is one of the central tasks that confront us. In order to flourish, each of us needs to live in a community in which we are committed to meeting others' needs. And this commitment is, in certain respects, unconditional. I am *never* entitled to turn away from someone in great need if the need is urgent, I am at hand, and no one else is going to fulfil it. This is something that Aquinas makes clear in his discussion of the virtue that he calls *misericordia*, which we imperfectly translate as 'taking pity'. Such immediate and urgent need trumps other obligations and duties, always. A person who cannot see and feel this cannot fully enter into the relationships of giving and receiving that characterize a community in which these commitments are accepted, and so cannot achieve the common goods of that community.

ALEX VOORHOEVE So for someone in such a community, the thought 'That could have been me' expresses his recognition of two facts. First, in becoming who he is, he depended on others being prepared to care for him if he had ended up with a severe disability. And second, in his everyday life, he still relies on others to care for him should he end up in that position.

ALASDAIR MacINTYRE Yes. And if somebody said, 'I need an argument that will show that from this it follows that I have special duties towards the disabled,' the response should be: 'This is not something for which there could be an argument. If you genuinely need an argument, you must be lacking in a kind of responsive sensibility that is crucial to human life.' Many people who *do* ask for an argument will, of course, not be so lacking. They will just be academic philosophers, whose professional training has misled them into asking for arguments in situations where arguments are not to the point. They are better people than their theories suggest. As indeed is Peter Singer, whom I regard as an admirable human being even if he is, in my view, a wrong-headed theorist.

ALEX VOORHOEVE In closing, I would like to turn to your discussion of Aquinas's concept of 'natural law', which adds an account of moral rules to the Aristotelian account of the virtues. Can you explain how, like the virtues, the rules of natural law can be derived from your account of human goods?

ALASDAIR MacINTYRE On Aquinas's view, the precepts of the natural law are justified as rules that agents must observe in order to be able to participate in those social activities and relationships without which they cannot achieve their goods and their good. In these activities and relationships, each rational agent must treat others as rational agents, acting together in order to achieve their common goods. But to treat someone else as a rational agent is to engage in shared deliberation, in which my or the other's reasons for belief and action are to be advanced and evaluated solely as better or worse reasons. If instead we are moved in our deliberations by fear of the other, or if we try to inculcate such fear, or if we are merely charmed and seduced by the other, or if we attempt merely to charm and seduce, we have ceased to treat the other as a rational agent. We have also ceased to treat our common goods—the goods of families, of schools, of political societies, and so on—as the goods of rational agents. So the precepts of the natural law prohibit those attitudes and activities that violate the relationships of rational agents in pursuit of such common goods.

ALEX VOORHOEVE   I wonder whether this concept of natural law really provides a secure foundation for the kinds of prohibitions of deceit, manipulation, and harm that, intuitively, seem morally right. For it seems that basing these prohibitions on what is necessary for our pursuit of common goods will give us reason to follow the natural law only with regard to those people with whom we might productively deliberate or otherwise pursue common goals. It seems to give us no reason to accept these prohibitions as absolute vis-à-vis those from whom we have nothing to learn or to gain.

ALASDAIR MACINTYRE   Yes, but we always potentially have something to learn and to gain from any other person.

ALEX VOORHOEVE   Even if that's true, I might be able to deliberate and pursue various cooperatively generated goods more successfully, on balance, if I exclude certain people from consideration and adopt the relevant moral attitudes only towards those with whom I can engage especially productively.

ALASDAIR MACINTYRE   Something that we badly need to learn is that that is false. We may start by writing off lots of people as those from whom we have nothing to learn, but then, if we are fortunate, we will discover that we were wrong. We are apt to find out that what we have to learn from and about others is unpredictable and surprising. And to act towards others in certain ways prevents us from learning this. So, for example, purely coercive relationships frustrate us and prevent us from learning what it is that we have to learn from those we coerce. And a great many people initially write off the disabled, not recognizing how much there is to be learnt only from them and with them. Only by learning from such others can we rid ourselves of illusions of self-sufficiency, illusions that stand in the way of our recognizing our need for some of the virtues that we need to flourish.

Danish Ethical Demands and French Common Goods

Two Moral Philosophies

When two incompatible moral philosophies confront us, how should we evaluate their rival claims? We might be tempted to suppose that we could match each of their alternative accounts of morality against *morality itself*, but that temptation will last only until we remind ourselves that what is accounted *morality itself* in one particular culture is treated as distorted or impoverished morality in others, and that one of the tasks of moral philosophy is to enable us to distinguish moral claims which we, whatever the culture we inhabit, should acknowledge from those which we should reject. So how to proceed?

"Danish Ethical Demands and French Common Goods: Two Moral Philosophies," *European Journal of Philosophy* 18, no. 1 (2010): 1–16.

We will not do well if we remain at so abstract and general a level of enquiry. Let me therefore consider the rival claims of two particular moral philosophies of different kinds, at home in two different European national cultures, but responsive to some of the same historical experiences. Knud Eiler Løgstrup published *Den Etiske Fordring* in 1956, while a professor at Aarhus University, but the lines of thought from which that book developed had engaged him for more than twenty years, and its impact on students, colleagues, and more widely in Denmark made it evident that he was giving a voice to an importantly shared moral standpoint. In the same period in which Løgstrup was developing and expanding his positions renewed versions of Thomist moral philosophy, drawing upon the earlier work of Garrigou Lagrange and others, and beyond them on the sources of the Thomist revival, were being taught in French-speaking educational institutions, among them Dominican Houses of Study, at Louvain, at the Institut Catholique in Paris, and elsewhere in France, no longer from textbooks *ad mentem Divi Thomae*, but through commentary on Aquinas's texts, especially on questions 90–97 of the first part of the second part of the *Summa Theologiae*, so that Aquinas became a contemporary moral philosopher.[1]

The concepts central to that Thomistic moral philosophy are those of the common good and the natural law. The concept central to Løgstrup's thought is that of the singularity of the ethical demand. And on a first scrutiny—indeed even on a second or a third—if what Løgstrup says about the ethical demand is true, then the Thomistic concepts are nothing but sources of illusion, while, if what the Thomists assert is true, then what Løgstrup offers is a distorted and perverse account of the claims of morality. We need therefore to set out each set of claims in detail, noting in both the moral landscape which they take for granted and the type of philosophical background that they presuppose, in Løgstrup's case phenomenological, in the case of the Thomists Aristotelian. I begin with Løgstrup.

1.

Løgstrup's phenomenology he learned from Hans Lipps, Husserl's student and critic and Edith Stein's friend. When Løgstrup first encountered Lipps in 1931, he was twenty-six years old, a graduate in theology from Copenhagen and at work or about to be at work on a prize essay criticizing Scheler and a dissertation criticizing Husserl, a dissertation that was to be strongly influenced by Lipps. So let me tell a brief and therefore oversimplified story about Husserl and Lipps. Husserl had contended that what is presented to consciousness is always at once particular and universal. To see *this* house is necessarily to see *a* house. And we understand *this* house as *a* house by grasping what it is for anything to be a house, by grasping the essential properties of a house, something only to be achieved by adopting the distinctive phenomenological stance. That stance requires of us that we separate ourselves from our natural everyday attitudes and prejudices, attending only to what is given in immediate experience, so that our judgments are not influenced by our prephilosophical beliefs.

Those of Husserl's students who had resisted his move into transcendental phenomenology, such as Ingarden and Stein, continued to agree with Husserl both in his contentions about the apprehension of essences and in his methodological stance. With Lipps it was otherwise. He had left the university for a soldier's life in 1914, a convinced follower of Husserl, indeed he had taken Husserl's *Ideen* with him into the trenches, where his reading and rereading convinced him that Husserl was deeply mistaken. What was Husserl's fundamental error? It was to project on to the objects presented to consciousness characteristics that in fact belong to our descriptions of those presentations. What is presented is concrete and particular; it is language that is irremediably general and universal. And the form of the problem that this posed for Lipps was: How, given that language is so, can we speak so as to identify and to communicate concerning the particularities and singularities that we encounter?

So Lipps embarked on the enquiries of his linguistic phenomenology, arguing that, instead of substituting the phenomenological stance for our everyday engagement with people and things, it is in and through those everyday engagements that we become aware of the multiplicity of ways in which language can be used to direct our attention to this or that particular. The meanings of linguistic expressions cannot be understood apart from their uses in speech-acts. It is by abstracting meaning from use and then considering meaning in isolation from use that we are deceived, as Husserl was deceived. It is not of course that we can dispense with universal generalizations and other generalities. And there are indeed expressions for the correct application of which necessary and sufficient conditions can be supplied, the expressions used in the natural sciences, uses whose justification is pragmatic. But outside the natural sciences we exercise our linguistic skills in knowing not only how to capture what is particular in and to this or that situation, but how to communicate it to others. Unsurprisingly, having learnt these lessons from Lipps, Løgstrup became attentive to the uses of language characteristic of novelists, who are exemplary in their exercise of just those skills.

It is not just because what I have said about Lipps is brief and oversimplified that difficult questions about the contrasts that Lipps emphasized remain unanswered. But, since I am concerned here only with the use that Løgstrup was to make of Lipps' work, I put those questions on one side[2] and turn to the moral landscape of post-war Denmark.

In 1940 Denmark had been occupied by the German army. Its subsequent condition differed from that of other countries under German occupation until 1943, in that it continued to be ruled by its own elected government. The lives of the great majority of Danes were surprisingly unaffected by the occupation. And Danish farmers, receiving the same prices for their products as German farmers, prospered. Yet there was from the very first days of occupation in 1940 some small resistance and from 1943 a well-organized resistance movement. Traditional Lutheran teaching has it that subjects are prohibited from rebelling against their legitimate rulers and it had therefore been argued within the established church that participation in resistance to the German occupiers, sanctioned as that occupation was by an elected government, was theologically and morally forbidden. Løgstrup, by then vicar of a country parish on the Island of Funen—he became a professor at Aarhus in 1943—was one of the leading protagonists of the view that the evils of National Socialism were such that armed resistance to the occupiers was morally required and he himself worked as a courier for the resistance and made his house available for wireless transmissions to England. To belong to a secret and illegal organization, activities for which render one liable to torture and death, requires a remarkable willingness to trust those others who know of one's activities—among them some who are otherwise strangers—not to betray one, even though on occasion they may have to choose between themselves enduring death and torture and such betrayal. And Løgstrup, perhaps through this experience and certainly from his wife's and his own earlier experiences of life in Nazi Germany, became unusually aware of the all-important place of trust in human life, an awareness that provided a starting-point for his moral philosophy.

We find ourselves as small children relying on others for almost everything. And trust in others remains an indispensable part of the fabric of our lives. To trust others is to lay oneself open to them. To respond to others who invite our trust is to respond to an unvoiced demand. And in the various exchanges of everyday life how we respond to those unvoiced demands and to those others defines our relationship to them. So I may respond to someone by purposefully trivial conversation, designed to keep the other at arm's length. Or I may tentatively open up questions, so that I can test their response. Or by the use of harsh words I may deliberately invite conflict with the other. Or I may try to impose on the other my own expectations and purposes. And in all these cases I move either towards or away from a relationship of trust.

The place of trust and therefore also of mistrust in our lives can be obscured by too great an emphasis on rules, on social norms. Løgstrup had been impressed by historical and sociological studies of such norms, including Westermarck's, which made it clear how they have changed over time and how they differ from society to society. So we should not treat the rules of our own society as sacrosanct, although to a relativist who points out that, had we lived in ancient Rome or the contemporary Andaman Islands, we would have had different rules, the reply should be that we live now and here. But, although the social norms of our own society provide a necessary starting-point for dealings with others, they are at best insufficient to direct our lives and we need to decide what attitude to take to them. Crucial to those attitudes is whether or not we are open to and acknowledge what Løgstrup called the ethical demand. When the ethical demand is heard, it is a demand that concerns some particular other in gross need, it is a demand that I allow her or him to trust me without reservation, and that I take her or his life into my hands. So it may be, for example, when I come across a stranger seriously injured in an automobile accident and there is no one else to take responsibility for seeing that she or he receives whatever medical and other help that they need.

Six characteristics of the ethical demand, as Løgstrup understands it, are important. First, it is unvoiced, it is silent. It is not a demand made by those others whose need I confront and they have no right to make such a demand. I have to hear and to respond to *the* demand, not *their* demand. Secondly, the demand is radical. It may require me to put on one side for an unpredictable amount of time my own legitimate preoccupations, in order to meet the need of these particular others: 'it intrudes disturbingly into my own existence'.[3] Thirdly, the demand is that I do what is best for the other, that I supply what that other needs, not what that other wants. I have to take charge. But I have to do this, so far as possible, in a way that allows the other to remain sovereign in her or his own world. 'The demand is always also a demand that we use the surrender out of which the demand has come in such a way as to free the other person from his or her confinement and to give her or his vision the widest possible horizon'.[4]

Fourthly, in judging what it is best for me to do for and with the other, I must act in the light of established social norms, but what I may have to do in responding to the ethical demand is such that sometimes I will find myself at odds with those norms. Fifthly, the demand is not limitless. Although, when I acknowledge and respond to the demand, I may not be in a position to predict how far my responsibilities will extend, but my resources and my other responsibilities have to be taken into account. I need to exercise judgment as to where I draw the line.

Sixthly and finally, in acknowledging and responding to the ethical demand I am not following a rule, let alone a rule that prescribes that like cases be treated alike. Were I to view the actions elicited by the demand as required by some rule, I would, on Løgstrup's view, be acting for the sake of conformity to that rule and because the other person or persons, to whose need I am responding, fall under some general description of the type of person to whom I should furnish aid, while by contrast what the demand requires of us is that we act for the sake of and in response to that particular other person and to act *only* for her or his sake. It is to them in their particularity and in the particularity of their situation that we must respond, if we are to acknowledge the authority of the demand. Accounts of morality as a kind of rule-following, whether utilitarian or Kantian, are therefore not merely philosophically mistaken, they are morally distorting, in that they distract us from attention to and action in terms of the singularity of this or that particular situation. We are summoned by the demand not to act so as to maximize preferences, nor to act so as to conform to the norms of rationality, but to act so as to discharge a particular responsibility to this or that particular other, who happens on this particular occasion to have been given into our hands.

There are of course a variety of ways in which we can refuse to acknowledge the ethical demand. I may make myself deaf to it, I may close myself off from the other, insisting that my life is my own, my property, with which I am free to do as I will, *qua* rational being, *qua* happiness-seeking being, *qua* whatever. In so doing I fail to understand my own life as a life that I have received as a gift, an understanding that finds its expression in giving freely to others in response to the demand, in giving without expecting anything in return. And for so giving I can have and can give no reason, except that I have heard this unvoiced demand. Indeed even the unvoiced demand does not provide a reason, since, when I hear it, part of what I learn is that I have not yet begun to do what I should already have been doing.

One way therefore to evade recognition of the demand is to insist on having and giving reasons for morally required actions, invoking perhaps some notion of reciprocity or of self-fulfillment.[5] To do so is, on Løgstrup's view, to try to manage one's life by appeal to a theory, so concealing what is at stake for each of us in responding or failing to respond to the demand. And at this point, if I followed Løgstrup's own order of exposition, I would move on to consider other facets of his account, especially those concerning the sense in which and the way in which the demand is unfulfillable, and the question of whether or not Løgstrup's view has theological presuppositions. But to do so might distract us from attending to something of the first importance, that, in giving us his account of the ethical demand, Løgstrup is not advancing an argument or expounding a theory. He is, as phenomenologists often do, inviting us to an act of recognition. Failure by someone to recognize the phenomenon that Løgstrup describes may tell us something illuminating about that someone, not something about Løgstrup's account. And one way to proceed further would be to ask if there are cases where response to or failure to respond to the ethical demand can itself be recognized. I think that there are.

Those few Europeans who put themselves at risk of torture and death during the years 1941 to 1945, in order to rescue Jews from their Nazi murderers, had a wide range of moral and religious viewpoints: Catholic, Protestant, Jewish, Moslem, atheist, positivist, Marxist, Kantian, utilitarian, even the odd principled Polish antisemite, who thought it right to exclude Jews from universities, but not to murder them. (We should of course note that very much the same range of views can be found among that much more numerous group who condoned or assisted the Nazis.) Some of those who rescued Jews were notably virtuous in other areas of their lives, others were not. A significant number of those who survived their own heroism were later interviewed and what is initially surprising is the extent to which, when asked why they had acted as they did, they gave the same type of response. They did not invoke their wider moral or religious beliefs, they did not appeal to rules or theories, they answered, characteristically briefly, saying such things as that it was the only thing to do or that anyone in their situation would have acted likewise, or that there was no alternative to doing what they did.[6]

These answers I take to be a sign of the inadequacy of words to express what they were in fact doing in responding to the gross and urgent need of particular Jews, sometimes friends or neighbours, often strangers, Jews whose lives had suddenly been put into their hands, who had no one else to trust, who confronted them with the singularity of the ethical demand. And we can perhaps recognize in their responses acknowledgement of the peculiar authority of that demand. I therefore find myself strongly inclined—although not only in the light of that acknowledgement—to assent to Løgstrup's central claims. But I cannot give you an argument to provide grounds for that assent. And were I to do so, I would, just by so doing, have abandoned Løgstrup's position. It does not follow that argument is irrelevant to the defence of Løgstrup's view. For there are arguments that seem to provide solid grounds for quarrelling with Løgstrup's claims, among them arguments drawn from the Thomistic moral philosophy that had been widely taught in much of Catholic French-speaking Europe, for nearly half a century both before 1940 and during the period in which Løgstrup was writing *The Ethical Demand*.

2.

That moral philosophy shares Løgstrup's rejection of Kantianism and utilitarianism. But it is at odds with Løgstrup's claims in the central place that it gives to a set of rules, the precepts of the natural law, precepts which forbid us to take innocent life, to make our own what is the legitimate property of others, to lie, to break promises, and so on. Løgstrup rejected, and his position required him to reject, any conception of the natural law,[7] seeing it not only as part of a mistaken account of the authority of rules, but also as an inheritance from the metaphysical tradition which, following Heidegger and Lipps, he took to have been discredited. What then is the Thomistic case for upholding the precepts of the natural law?

It is that only insofar as we obey these precepts are we able to achieve such common goods as those of family and household, of school, of workplace, of local community, of a wide variety of shared activities and projects, and perhaps above all of political society. Common goods are goods that we can only achieve and enjoy *qua* family member or *qua* participant in this or that practice or project or *qua* citizen or subject of some political community. Why so? To direct ourselves rightly towards common goods, let alone to achieve them, we need to deliberate in the company of those others with whom we share those goods in common. And rational deliberation is possible only among those whose social relationships are structured by a regard for the natural law. They and we can only be partners in rational deliberation, if we do not threaten or coerce each other, if we speak truthfully to each other, if we honour our commitments, if force and fraud are excluded from our relationships.

Why then should each of us, as rational agents, accept the constraints of the natural law? It is because only insofar as we are directed towards the achievement of the relevant set of common goods—not themselves reducible to individual goods—are we also directed towards the achievement of our own individual good, the good of each of us *qua* human being. So runs the Thomistic account. Thomists therefore were and are in disagreement with Løgstrup not only over the nature and place of rules in the moral life, but also because, where they take it that right action is action undertaken for the sake of achieving this or that end, Løgstrup held that we are to act only for the sake of this or that particular human being and not for the sake of anything further. Add to this a third and fourth area of contention.

The third concerns spontaneity and reflection. To act as the ethical demand bids us act, is, on Løgstrup's view, to act spontaneously. Spontaneous acts, Løgstrup was to say 'are elicited solely by the condition or situation in which the other finds himself'.[8] But spontaneity, as Løgstrup understands it, although it does not exclude thinking about the particularities of the matter in hand, does exclude the kind of reflection on principles that sometimes precedes and always should inform those shared practical deliberations which are central to the Thomistic account of action. And it also excludes both habit and *habitus*, those dispositions which, on a Thomistic view, include the virtue of *misericordia*, the virtue expressed in our responses to those in urgent need.

Add to this a fourth and fundamental disagreement. Thomistic moral philosophy, in this at least like Kantianism and utilitarianism, presents right action, when it is properly understood, as conforming to judgments which have argumentative justifications. Yet, on Løgstrup's view, as I noted earlier, where the ethical demand is concerned, argument is not to the point. A response to the ethical demand is never a conclusion inferred from a set of premises. A failure to respond could never be remedied by a compelling argument. It therefore appears that the disagreements between Løgstrup and those who have followed him and the Thomists are of the deepest kind. And this is unsurprising when we consider how different and incompatible the philosophical backgrounds to those two moral philosophies are. The Aristotelian perspective of the Thomists and Lipps's linguistic phenomenology provided very different starting-points for the enquiries of these two sets of moral philosophers. So we might conclude that they are bound to be antagonistic. But now let me begin to think about these two moral philosophies in a somewhat different way.

I have emphasized how far Løgstrup is in disagreement with Thomism of any kind, but I have had especially in mind some of Løgstrup's contemporaries, the French Thomists of the 1940s and 50s. Neither party was in the least aware of the other. For Thomists, as for French philosophers in general, Kierkegaard was the only Danish philosopher of whom they had any awareness. Danish philosophers were more likely to be aware of French than French of Danish, but the only French language philosopher named by Løgstrup in *Den Etiske Fordring* is the Swiss Denis de Rougemont. And it is clear that, if Løgstrup thought of Thomism at all, it was as something that belonged to a remote and now irrelevant past. His own Lutheran roots make this dismissive attitude unsurprising. Nonetheless I hope to show that it is philosophically and morally profitable to bring these two standpoints into belated conversation.

3.

A starting-point for that conversation is Aristotle's thesis, endorsed by Aquinas, that, unless you have already developed the requisite habits, habits that incline you to virtue, you will not in fact be open to argument on moral matters.[9] But just what habits are these? Among them, I want to suggest, is a disposition, unrecognized by Aristotle, to be open to and to be responsive on occasion to the particularities of urgent human needs of others for whom there is no one else to take responsibility. What kind of disposition is this?

It is a readiness to be interrupted in one's projects, a willingness to turn aside from whatever good one is at that moment aiming to achieve or is in the course of achieving, so as to provide aid to those in urgent need. Why is this disposition so important? One reason is that every one of us all the time may suddenly and unexpectedly find ourselves in need of such aid. I am standing in line to buy a ticket or walking casually along a street and I suffer a heart attack or a slate falls on my head from a roof or an angry drunkard lashes out at me. I become a helpless victim whose life choices will be determined by the response or lack of response of strangers. So it is for each of us a deeply ingrained hope that, if our lives are so disrupted, there will be at hand someone, perhaps a stranger, perhaps not, who will interrupt her or his life to come to our aid, someone whom we can trust to act for our good. In the background of all our attempts to achieve our goods is this usually unvoiced reliance on others.

It is because of our shared reliance on this habit that we have the best of reasons to make sure that we ourselves are so disposed and that our children are brought up so that they too are thus disposed. For without this virtue we will be unable to enter into some of those social relationships without which we will be unable to achieve our common and individual goods. We will be excluded from, we will have excluded ourselves from the society of moral reasoners. So it is not in the least paradoxical to assert that we have good reason to become the kind of person who responds spontaneously, who responds without having or requiring justifying argument, in certain situations. Nor is it paradoxical to recognize that our reasoning will have no hold upon anyone who does not already possess this virtue to some significant degree.

The contrast between the moral agent as portrayed by Løgstrup and the moral agent as portrayed by the Thomists is therefore less sharp than it first appeared to be. To act for the sake of the other in urgent need may also be to act for the sake of my own good. About this the Thomists are right. But, if on some particular occasion I act for the sake of some other in urgent need, I need no further reason or motive and I should allow no further reason or motive to distract me. About this Løgstrup is right. The two positions, far from being in conflict, complement one another. French Thomists of the post-war period, had they encountered Løgstrup's moral philosophy, would have enriched their Thomism by integrating into it Løgstrup's phenomenological account of the ethical demand and Løgstrup would have rendered his own position both more intelligible and more defensible, if he had allowed that in responding to the ethical demand we may also be acting for the sake of our own good. (Løgstrup did believe that acting in response to the ethical demand was for our good, even if it was not acting for the sake of our good.) And this is not the only respect in which Løgstrup and the Thomists needed each other. Consider the apparent conflict over rules.

Løgstrup recognizes the importance of rules in ordering our social life and coordinating our activities. But he takes the attitudes of trust in which our moral lives are rooted and the particular forms of trust that are involved in our responsiveness to the ethical demand and in our caring for those who are in urgent need to be prior to and independent of all rule-following. And, as I also noted earlier, he supposes that to act in accordance with the ethical demand is to act in a way that excludes rule-following. But consider now what expectations are involved in trusting someone and what it is to be trustworthy.

If I trust someone, I trust them to answer questions that I put to them without guile or subterfuge. I trust them to tell me how things are. I trust them not to equivocate or mislead. And, if they do not conform to these expectations, I treat them as untrustworthy. But, if this is so, then only those persons are trustworthy who are bound by the rule not to lie. (Note that to be bound by a rule in acting does not involve having that rule in mind when acting.) Obviously to be bound by that rule is not sufficient for someone to be trustworthy. They must also be promise-keepers, observant of yet another rule, honouring their commitments. And they must possess such traits as reliability in their ongoing concerns and prudence in making commitments. Their rule-following will only be one aspect of their virtues, but a crucial aspect. Yet note that, in making this point against Løgstrup—that he cannot consistently combine his account of rules with his account of trust—I am not merely making a negative point. For Løgstrup is not mistaken in the importance that he attaches to trust and what emerges from this critique is that much, although not all of the point of the rules that enjoin truth-telling and promise-keeping is that without conformity to them trust between individuals and groups cannot be secured.

Thomist moral philosophers have argued that conformity to those rules that are the precepts of the natural law is required, if we are to be able to achieve a variety of common goods, most notably those of political society. What Løgstrup brings out is that there is a lacuna in the Thomist accounts, a failure to spell out the relationship between on the one hand conformity to rules and on the other the achievement of common goods. Løgstrup makes a beginning in supplying what is lacking with his account of the role of trust in human life. Aristotle and Aquinas had both noted that trust is among the requirements for friendship and Aquinas had added that it is involved in our everyday transactions with strangers.[10] What neither however remark upon is the crucial role that trust plays in the life of political societies. Consider a type of situation in which shared rational deliberation about the common good of some particular political society is in danger of being frustrated by the extent of radical disagreement about what the common good of that society here and now is. What may decide whether or not that danger can be overcome is the extent of the trust that each of the contending parties is able to place in the good will of the other. Absent some large degree of trust, suspicion will almost certainly make it impossible to continue to engage in shared good faith deliberation. And absent shared good faith deliberation appeals to the common good will become empty and pointless, something recurrently confirmed in the history of post-war France.

4.

Radical disagreement about the nature of the common good, conjoined with a deep lack of trust, sometimes with suspicion as a mode of life, had afflicted French politics for a long time before the defeat of 1940. And after that defeat two rival contending causes claimed the allegiance of the Catholic community, including its Thomists: the adherents of Pétain's Vichy government with its program for the restoration of an hierarchically ordered rural France, invoked one particular view of the common good, not only of political society, but also of the family, while, bitterly opposed to that program, the followers of de Gaulle's tough minded revival of Péguy's vision of a France whose republican inheritance was not incompatible with Catholic loyalties, advanced a quite different conception. Each defined themselves not only in opposition to the other, but also and inescapably in opposition to yet other rival conceptions of the French common good, both Communist and secular republican. But their greatest hostility was reserved for each other. And Thomist thinkers were to be found politically engaged on both sides of the divide, on the one side Réginald Garrigou-Lagrange, whom Mauriac had called 'the sacred monster of Thomism', and on the other Jacques Maritain and the self-styled '*sans-culotte*', Yves Simon.

What became evident between the liberation of 1944 and de Gaulle's resignation from the presidency in 1946 was the distance between the realities of French post-war politics and either of these conceptions of the common good, indeed *any* conception of a political common good. What had emerged in postwar French politics was a set of power sharing arrangements, in which the mutually distrustful parties of the moderate left and right, representing a variety of conflicting interests, bargained and enacted compromises, compromises designed to exclude both communists and

Gaullists from power, compromises that had the aim of ensuring continued American support and of bringing about some degree of European integration, and all this in a society where widespread untruthfulness about what happened between 1940 and 1945 was protected by a pact of silence. The concept of the common good had become irrelevant, had become a concept that, so it seemed, could no longer find application, certainly in the sphere of politics, and to varying extents elsewhere.

It is not that the expression '*bien commun*' was used any less frequently in French rhetoric, but that what it was used of were what have been called public, rather than common goods. Public goods are reducible to and constructible out of individual and group interests. Their identification and characterization emerges from compromises and bargaining between individuals and groups. Common goods differ in both these respects. (Individualists of course deny that there are any such things as common goods.) And the achievement of public goods, far from requiring conformity to the precepts of the natural law, often requires violation of those precepts, notably with respect to truth-telling and lying. So any genuine notion of the political common good was effectively erased from French public discourse—as it was also often erased from public discourse elsewhere—until the crisis that brought de Gaulle back to power. And de Gaulle's second tenure of power wrote its final epitaph.

At the same time one aspect of the economic transformation of French life in the 1950s was a strengthening of individualist attitudes in everyday life, one articulated at the level of theory by those devoted to the renewal of the distinctively French liberal tradition, most notably by Raymond Aron. And those who resisted individualism and liberalism did so in the name of conceptions of *solidarité* to which the idiom of the common good was equally alien. (Maritain and Simon were by now in North America. Garrigou-Lagrange was in Rome.) But the social erasure of the notion of the common good seemed to make irrelevant the whole moral scheme in which it had played a central part.

What happens when a theoretical framework which has provided the conceptual presuppositions for some particular way of reasoning practically, of choosing, and of acting is thus taken away from those who had employed it? There are a number of possibilities. One is that those whose presuppositions they were find themselves continuing to view particular situations just as they have done in the past and responding to them just as they have done, but no longer having, let alone advancing, reasons for so responding. Plainly, if and when this comes to be, it will be over some extended period of time, during which, when those who are changing in this way have occasion to articulate their moral attitudes, they are likely to do so in less than wholly coherent ways. (Studies of the morality of the incoherent, studies that respect such incoherence and recognize that it is sometimes preferable to a premature reduction to consistency by, say, the Rawlsian method of equilibrium, are long overdue in moral philosophy.)

What will sometimes—not always—survive in those who have undergone this kind of transformation will be a set of dispositions to respond to situations such as those in which they encounter someone in urgent need, for whose plight there is no one else available to take responsibility. The way in which they view that someone, that plight, and that need and the way in which they respond to that someone, will not be significantly different from the ways in which they, or their parents or grandparents, had previously viewed and responded, in the days when they presupposed, say, the rational authority of the precepts of natural law, and justified their conformity to those precepts by referring to their common goods. Their dispositions to view, to judge, to feel, and to act remain what they had been. But now, if they were asked to reflect upon what was involved in their moral commitments, and if they were sufficiently articulate to respond, they would have to give a very different description of what they were doing than they themselves or their parents or grandparents would have done previously. What once would have been an expression of the virtue of *misericordia*, as prescribed by the natural law, would have remained a response, but a response to what? What kind of description of it would they now have to give?

It would be a phenomenological description of how certain types of situation present themselves to consciousness and elicit or fail to elicit appropriate responses. There is a danger however in our characterizing what such agents would say in terms of 'types of situations' and 'appropriate responses'. For this might suggest that the agent her or himself was or might be following a rule in so responding. Yet from the standpoint of the agent her or himself their response will not be rule-governed. It will be and will be experienced as a response to the singularity of *this* particular individual or group of individuals in *this* particular plight with *these* particular needs. And the phenomenologically sensitive describer will resist all attempts to assimilate what she or he is describing to any morality of rules or of virtues.

Løgstrup was of course just such a describer and was able to draw on the resources of Hans Lipps's phenomenology to make his point. But Løgstrup would of course have had to resist the suggestion implicit in the line of argument that I have developed that the experience of the ethical demand is a residue, a survival, and moreover a form of moral experience that can only be fully understood as such a residue, as such a survival. That it is such does not entail that the ethical demand is not authentic, that it is not, just as Løgstrup argued, at the core of moral experience. But on the view that I am suggesting the appeal to the ethical demand is not only not a rival to Thomistic appeals to the precepts of the natural law and the common good, but is what remains at the end of a process of transformation when something like that Thomistic appeal has lost its force and its rational hold on some population of moral agents. (It can of course be argued against this interpretation, as Hans Fink has argued, that what remains is indeed the core of genuine morality, now at last freed up from distorting connections to rules and goods. But this is a disagreement that I will not enter on here.)

I say 'something like' because obviously, if we were to ask for the historical antecedents of Løgstrup's moral philosophy, we should find not a trace of Thomism among them. And, if we were to look for the historical consequences of the loss of application for key Thomistic concepts in French public and everyday discourse and life after 1946, we should not find any invocation of Løgstrup. But my thesis would clearly be not just wrong, but absurd, if there were not in the antecedents of Løgstrup's moral philosophy something corresponding to the Thomistic conception of the natural law, and if there were not in the consequences of the fate that befell Thomism in France at least the possibility of something corresponding to Løgstrup's conception of the moral demand. And in each case there is.

5.

Løgstrup was not only a moral philosopher, but also a Lutheran pastor and a professor of theology. He himself had broken decisively with Luther's political ethics in the debates over Danish resistance to the German occupiers. And by the 1940s Danish society's relationship to the Lutheran Church was already that characterized by Jørgen I. Jensen: the church may by now be a building on the horizon, but it is still part of the landscape.[11] Danes by and large are not churchgoers, but by and large they voluntarily pay church taxes. Theirs is a residual, but a real Lutheranism, so that Knud J. V. Jespersen can speak of 'evangelical-Lutheran attitudes' as having 'permeated Danish mentality' and provided 'the ethical foundation of the modern Danish welfare state'.[12]

The Ethical Demand begins with a theological—one might almost say antitheological—discussion in which Løgstrup follows Friedrich Gogarten in claiming that 'the individual's relation to God is determined wholly at the point of his relation to the neighbor'[13] and then, for most of the next eleven chapters, answers the question of what my relation to my neighbour should be in the wholly secular terms of the ethical demand, before finally giving an account of the authority of Jesus and of his proclamation that leaves intact the secular character of the ethical demand itself. The ethical demand is then what is left when the framework of Lutheran ethics is no longer available. The last great exponent of that ethics had been Emil Brunner, who in 1932 had defended Luther's conception of the orders of creation, orders that supply norms governing the various areas of human life, for knowledge of which revelation is not necessary.[14] Those norms are the Lutheran equivalent to the Catholic and Thomist conception of the natural law, sharing much of its content, although differing in their purported justification and Løgstrup himself in an earlier period had appealed to such norms.

They are the norms that Danish Lutherans, including Løgstrup, had generally repudiated in the post-war period[15] and that the generality of Danes had no longer recognized as *their* norms for quite some time. So what is left of Lutheran ethics when the norms are subtracted? The answer is: the ethical demand, responsiveness to the voice that speaks to one out of the singularity of someone's need.

Is there a French history corresponding to this Danish history? If so, it is a history whose end-point would be a widespread openness to something like Levinas's claims. It was Zygmunt Bauman who first recognized the affinity between Levinas and Løgstrup. And the resemblances and differences between Løgstrup's claims and Levinas's claims are easy to catalogue. Bauman summarizes what they share by saying 'For both thinkers the *sine qua non* of moral stance is the assumption of responsibility', a responsibility that 'is under-defined and needs to be given content', by an act that always risks failure. To act instead from conformity to a rule or a command is to avoid such 'responsibility and risk'.[16]

The philosophical presuppositions of both Løgstrup and Levinas are phenomenological, but what Løgstrup and Levinas describe they describe in notably different terms. For Løgstrup the demand, although unvoiced, is heard or unheard. For Levinas that other which resists our self-aggrandizing appropriation is seen and what is seen is a face. Nonetheless what is demanded as response and as responsibility by voice and by face is remarkably the same. (It is worth noting that, although it is not possible here to do more than note that, in Hans Lipps's phenomenology 'the look' and 'the face' play significant parts.) So I follow Bauman in taking their accounts to be relevantly alike. Diane Perpich has aptly characterized Levinas's conception of the ethical as one of 'normativity without norms'[17] and this characterization could as aptly be used of Løgstrup. What I have been suggesting is that normativity without norms is intelligible only as the end result of a history during which the relevant set of norms had lost whatever it had been that had once made those norms compelling. What remains is an awareness and a mode of response that can only be described through phenomenological techniques. About that phenomenologically apprehended and described awareness I have been advancing two theses and this so as to formulate a question.

The first is that, rightly understood, Løgstrup's account of the ethical demand is complementary to rather than incompatible with a Thomistic account of the precepts of the natural law, a thesis that Løgstrup would have fiercely resisted. And I am of course committed by my argument to holding that what is true of Løgstrup's account is perhaps also true of Levinas's. My second thesis is that such phenomenological accounts of core experiences of the moral life, accounts which have found their way into the mainstream of moral philosophy only in the 20th century, are reports of historical residues, reports of what remains when some larger scheme for understanding the moral life has, for whatever reason, lost its credibility. To this it will rightly be replied that the history which I have employed to illustrate this thesis is, to put it kindly, far too brief and sketchy. The relevant historical work largely remains to be done and this kind of social history of morality is not easy to write. But it is important to write it.

Part of that importance is that we need to understand a good deal better than we do how under certain circumstances the moral life can be fragmented, so that different aspects of it—on the one hand, schemes of reasoning about goods and virtues which enable us to be practically reflective, on the other, capacities of feeling and judgment that enable us to be immediately responsive to urgent need—take on a life of their own and by so doing perhaps become distorted. If we were to understand that fragmentation a good deal better than as yet we do, we might also begin to understand how to reintegrate those two aspects. How we might become able to do that is the question that issues from the overall argument of this paper.[18]

TEN

On Having Survived the Academic Moral Philosophy of the Twentieth Century

HOW I DISCOVERED THAT, BY THE STANDARDS OF CONTEMPORARY ACADEMIC PHILOSOPHY, THOMIST CLAIMS *MUST BE* PROBLEMATIC

I was already fifty-five years old when I discovered that I had become a Thomistic Aristotelian. But I had first encountered Thomism thirty-eight years earlier, as an undergraduate, not in the form of moral philosophy, but in that of a critique of English culture developed by members of the Dominican order. Yet, although impressed by that critique, I hesitated, for

---

"On Having Survived the Moral Philosophy of the Twentieth Century," in *What Happened in and to Moral Philosophy in the Twentieth Century?: Philosophical Essays in Honor of Alasdair MacIntyre*, ed. Fran O'Rourke, 17–34 (University of Notre Dame Press, 2013).

those Dominicans made me aware of the philosophical presuppositions of their critique, of a set of Thomistic judgments about the relationships between body, mind, and soul, about passions, will, and intellect, about virtues and reason-informed human actions. And those theses I found problematic. Why so?

From 1945 to 1949 I was an undergraduate student in classics at what was then Queen Mary College in the University of London, reading Greek texts of Plato and Aristotle with my teachers, while also, from 1947 onwards, occasionally attending lectures given by A. J. Ayer or Karl Popper, or by visiting speakers to Ayer's seminar at University College, such as John Wisdom. Early on I had read *Language, Truth and Logic*, and Ayer's student James Thomson introduced me to the *Tractatus* and to Tarski's work on truth. Ayer and his students were exemplary in their clarity and rigor and in the philosophical excitement that their debates generated. And I became convinced that the test of any set of philosophical theses, including those defended by Thomists, was whether it could be vindicated in and through such debates. Yet I also had to learn—and this took a little longer—that in the debates of academic philosophy in the twentieth century no set of theses is ever decisively vindicated.

To excel as a contemporary academic philosopher is a matter of the quality of one's analytic and argumentative skills, especially in their negative use to expose failures in the distinction making of others or gaps in their arguments, together with an ability to summon up telling counterexamples. Conceptual inventiveness is also valued. Excellence in the exercise of these qualities is compatible with holding different and incompatible sets of beliefs about which of the various philosophical positions in contention in one's own specialized area is to be regarded as true and rationally justified, including those positions in contention over how truth and rational justification are to be understood. Disagreement on fundamental issues is in practice taken to be the permanent condition of philosophy. The range of continuing disagreements is impressive: realists versus anti realists in respect of mathematical, moral, perceptual, and historical judgments; dualists versus materialists in the philosophy of mind; utilitarians versus Kantians versus virtue theorists in ethics; Fregeans versus direct reference theorists in the philosophy of language; and a great many more. Add to these a range of disagreements in religion and politics that, themselves nonphilosophical, are closely related to philosophical disagreements: theists versus atheists, conservatives versus liberals versus libertarians versus Marxists.

It is not that there is no progress in philosophical inquiry so conceived. Arguments are further elaborated, concepts refined, and creative new ideas advanced by the genius of a Quine or a Kripke or a Lewis. But this makes it the more striking that there is *never* a decisive resolution of any central disputed issue. So how should we think about this and respond to it? David Lewis wrote that "whether or not it would be nice to knock disagreeing philosophers down by sheer force of argument, it cannot be done" and that "once the menu of well-worked-out theories is before us, philosophy is a matter of opinion."[1] Each philosopher, that is, considers the costs of accepting this body of philosophical theses and arguments or rejecting that, tries to bring her or his judgments, philosophical and nonphilosophical, into equilibrium, and in so doing take sides in one of these irresolvable disputes. My own immediate response to my recognition of the conditions of academy philosophy was more modest. It was that, however strong the case for Thomism, there was bound to be a strong case against it.

HOW I DISCOVERED FROM SARTRE AND AYER THAT THOMIST CLAIMS ARE PROBLEMATIC

Very soon I was impressed by the force of one such case. In 1947, while visiting Paris, I had been introduced to Sartre's 1945 lecture "L'existentialisme est un humanisme," in which Sartre argues that although we may have reasons for making our choices as we do, those reasons have only such weight as each of us chooses to give to them. What makes a particular reason a good or a sufficient reason for me to act depends on my decision to treat that reason as good or sufficient. The practical reasoning of any individual derives its conclusions from premises that that individual has chosen to make the premises of her or his practical reasoning. And on this Ayer concurred, even though he and Sartre disagreed about much else. "It is one of Sartre's merits," Ayer wrote, "that he sees that no system of values can be binding on someone unless he chooses to make it so."[2]

What Ayer and Sartre had combined to put in question was a set of theses central to Thomism according to which what makes a reason a good reason for action is independent of the agent's choices. It is, on the Thomist view, a good reason for acting in this way rather than in that, that by so acting one will achieve some good or avoid some bad and whether that at which one aims is good or bad is a matter of fact, a matter of whether the object aimed at contributes to or is constitutive of some aspect of one's flourishing as a human being. For Ayer and Sartre, by contrast, there are acts of choice, implicit or explicit, that are prior to and determinative of one's judgments of good and evil. For Thomists acts of choice are themselves to be evaluated by logically prior judgments concerning the good to be achieved or the evil to be avoided by those acts. How, I asked, was I to decide between these rival claims?

It was not that I could not find a number of reasons for favoring something closer to a Thomist view than to Ayer's or Sartre's. But I was well aware that none of these reasons were conclusive, were such that they could not be rationally resisted. So it seemed that the only reasonable conclusion about this particular disagreement was to agree with what David Lewis was to say: that this, like other disputed issues, "is a matter of opinion." But so to conclude was to conclude against Thomism. For it is crucial to the Thomistic view that such disagreements are not, in the sense that Lewis gives to that expression, matters of opinion, but rather matters on which reason renders a decisive verdict, even if highly intelligent people continue to disagree.

HOW MARXISM MADE IT POSSIBLE FOR ME TO RECOGNIZE THE NATURE OF THE DOMINANT CONTEMPORARY MORALITY

Thomism had also become problematic for me for another reason. The Communist Party at Queen Mary College had introduced me to the texts of the Marxist canon, and I had become and to this day remain convinced of the truth and political relevance of Marx's critique of capitalism and of his historical insights as presented in the narrative of the *Eighteenth Brumaire of Louis Bonaparte*. To how much else of Marxism I was thereby committed I was unclear, although I greatly admired both the work of

George Thomson, author of *Aeschylus and Athens* and translator of Plato into Irish, and the writings of Lucien Goldmann. Since one thing on which Marxists and Thomists seemed to agree was that Marxism and Thomism were incompatible, I found myself confronting yet another set of question marks. Nonetheless it was on the basis of Marxist insights into the nature both of morality and of moral philosophy that I began to formulate another, more constructive kind of question.

Marx and Engels had argued that every morality is the morality of some particular social and economic order and that every moral philosophy articulates and makes explicit the judgments, arguments, and presuppositions of some particular morality, either in such a way as to defend both that morality and the social and economic order of which it is the expression, or in such a way as to undermine them. And my acknowledgment of the truth of this thesis was reinforced by my encounters with social anthropology, especially first with the work of Franz Steiner and later with that of Rodney Needham. I therefore asked: What is the distinctive morality of this social and economic order that I inhabit, and how does contemporary moral philosophy stand to that morality? And in pursuing an answer to this question I was guided not only by Marx and Engels but also by John Anderson, who had urged that, if we were to understand social institutions and relationships, we should ask not what function or purpose they serve but to what conflicts they give expression. This suggested that both the morality and the moral philosophy of the present age are best understood as milieus of conflict, sites of disagreement. But those disagreements find significantly different expression in the arenas of philosophical debate on the one hand and in those of everyday moral and political practice on the other.

In philosophical debate utilitarianism and Kantianism are presented, with some rare and sophisticated exceptions, as incompatible and rival standpoints. To adhere to some version of one is to be at odds with every version of the other. But in many areas of the everyday life of modernity what we find instead is an oscillation between those two standpoints and a moral rhetoric designed to disguise that oscillation. So there are moments in which principles are laid down without qualification and moments in which exceptions to those principles are justified in the name of either the maximization of prosperity or the maintenance of public security. And it is in negotiating their way between such moments, both in private and in public life, that the characteristic skills of those who are socially and politically successful are exhibited. What we have then is a morality whose oscillations and contradictions show it to be in a state of disorder, but a kind of disorder that enables it to function well as the ideology of our present social, political, and economic order.

Yet although I had come to recognize this as a result of reflecting on the Marxist critique of morality, I had also had to acknowledge that within the communist movement there was to be found much the same oscillation between quasi-Kantian attitudes and a consequentialism that parodied utilitarianism, and this not only in the brutal and corrupting ethics of Stalinism but also in the ethics of Stalinism's Marxist critics. Marxism as a form of practice too often suffered from the same lack of moral resources as the social order that it aspired to replace, and this unsurprisingly, since it had been generated from within that social order. It was with the rise of the New Left in Britain, after the suppression of the Hungarian Rising of 1956, that the question of whether and how this defect in Marxist theory and practice could be remedied became urgent. But what were the resources needed to remedy it? I was able to answer this question only by considering further not only the issues posed by Kantianism and utilitarianism but also those raised by the disagreements between Thomists on the one hand and Ayer and Sartre on the other, concerning the nature and status of reasons for action. And to make progress with either of these sets of issues I had to look in a different direction, and my narrative has to move backwards in time.

TWO LINES OF THOUGHT ABOUT THE MEANING AND USE OF GOOD

Two opposed lines of thought about the meaning of the word *good* and its cognates had been developed in English-speaking philosophy since the 1930s. One of these finds its first formulation in Ayer's *Language, Truth and Logic* in 1936. To call something good or bad is to express one's feelings for or against it. To evaluate is to approve or disapprove. By the late 1940s Ayer was recommending C. L. Stevenson's better-developed version of this view, according to which uses of *good* have both an expressive and an imperative component. To say of something that it is good is both to commend it and to urge those whom one is addressing to do so as well. Stevenson recognized that the conventions governing many uses of *good* are such that it also commonly has a descriptive component. But insofar as this is so, the descriptive component on the one hand and the expressive and imperative elements on the other are distinguishable and disparate. The step beyond this was to be taken by R. M. Hare, who provided both a sketch of the logic of imperatives and an account of moral judgments that was in some respects Kantian, in others utilitarian.

I had found Ayer and Stevenson more persuasive than Hare, and from them I acquired both an insight and a problem. The insight was a corollary to their successful undermining of the intuitionism of Moore, Prichard, and Ross. Viewed in the light cast by Ayer and Stevenson, intuitionist moral philosophers turn out to be under the illusion that they are asserting moral truths when they are in fact doing no more than expressing their own individual feelings and attitudes. They suffer from a lack of self-knowledge. The problem was that this mistake by some English moral philosophers seemed to have its roots in the general moral culture of their time and place. For while, so far as I could judge, Ayer, Stevenson, and other expressivists had provided a compelling account of the characteristic *uses* to which moral judgments were now put in a particular culture, they had taken themselves to have provided an adequate account of the *meaning* of moral and evaluative sentences as such, whatever the culture. Yet the meaning of those sentences was such that they at least appeared to give expression to some impersonal standard of judgment to which appeal was being made. Meaning and use had, so it seemed, come apart, something on which the current philosophy of language shed no light. How might this have happened?

In asking this question, I had of course understood the significance of Ayer's and Stevenson's work very differently from the way in which they themselves understood it. The question that I therefore faced was: If moral judgments here and now are used, at least in large part, as Ayer and Stevenson say that they are, what else, in other social and cultural circumstances, might moral judgments and evaluative judgments be? Might there be or have been a condition from which they had degenerated to their present state? And what would that condition be? An answer to this question was suggested by quite another and deeply incompatible line of thought about the meaning and use of *good.*

This second line of thought began by taking seriously J. L. Austin's injunction to begin with lexicography, to accumulate a wide range of different types of examples of the relevant expressions. Those who do so find themselves also following Aristotle—and this is no accident. Austin's habits of thought were in several ways Aristotelian and certainly so in recognizing the multiplicity and the heterogeneity of our uses of *good, better, bad, worse,* and their cognates. We speak of bad kings and good jam, of a good day at the races and a bad holiday in Casablanca, of a good time to go on a spree and a bad way to do it, of someone's being good at tennis or good for nothing. And these are only a few examples of the variety that we need to catalogue. Austin himself took there to be an irreducible and inescapable heterogeneity here.[3] But Aristotle had identified a unity underlying that heterogeneity, and the clue to that unity was supplied by Peter Geach. In 1956 Geach had pointed out that *good* and *bad* are noun-dependent or noun-phrase-dependent adjectives and that *well* and *badly* are correspondingly verb-dependent adverbs.[4] What it is for an X to be good depends upon what an X is, so the criteria of goodness in a king are very different from those of goodness in jam. And what it is to X well depends upon what X-ing is, so the criteria by which someone who plays tennis is judged to have played well or badly are not the same as those by which someone who shoes horses is judged to do so well or badly. And so we take a first step toward answering the question: What makes these various uses of *good* more than puns?

Here we need to bear in mind the distinction between attributive and predicative uses of *good,* as W. D. Ross originally formulated it, together with Geach's thesis that *good* is essentially attributive, that to be good is always to be a good someone or something, and that predicative uses of *good* can be translated into attributive uses. We speak of "good parents" but also of "good burglars," of "the best athlete in the games" but also of "the best forger still at work." It matters therefore that we can always ask, "Is it good for someone to be a good parent?" and "Is it good for someone to be a good burglar?" and what we learned from Geach is that to ask these questions is to ask, "Is a good parent a good human being?" and "Is a good burglar a good human being?," questions that can be answered only by first answering the question "What is it to be a good human being?"

It is at this point that this line of thought has sometimes been thought to encounter insuperable difficulties. That there are criteria independent of our choices, feelings, and attitudes governing our applications of "good parent," "good burglar," or for that matter "good boxer" or "good violinist," is difficult to deny. For in each area, drawing on Aristotle's thesis that to be a good X is to excel in the activities characteristic of an X, we can say what it is to exhibit such excellence as parent, as burglar, as boxer, as violinist. But, many have urged, any analogy between goodness as attributed to these and goodness as attributed to human beings breaks down. There is, they argue, no set of activities characteristic of a human being, as there are activities characteristic of parents, burglars, boxers, and violinists. Hence it was to be argued by Hampshire and by Berlin, following Austin, that there is no such thing as *the* good life for human beings, no such thing as *the* human good.

To this it can be replied that there are indeed many different ways of leading a good human life, but that there are at least four sets of goods that are characteristically needed by every human individual if she or he is to flourish. First, without adequate nutrition, clothing, shelter, physical exercise, education, and opportunity to work no one is likely to be able to develop his or her powers—physical, intellectual, moral, aesthetic—adequately. Second, everyone benefits from affectionate support by, well-designed instruction from, and critical interaction with family, friends, and colleagues. Third, without an institutional framework that provides stability and security over time a variety of forms of association, exchange, and long-term planning are impossible. And fourth, if an individual is to become and sustain her- or himself as an independent rational agent, she or he needs powers of practical rationality, of self-knowledge, of communication, and of inquiry and understanding. Lives that are significantly defective in any one of these respects are judged worse, that is, less choiceworthy, than lives that are not. These goods are goods without which excellence in activity is often impossible, and so the key to our various uses of *good* with regard to them is a shared conception of excellence in activity, of what it is to live virtuously.

Thus on any version of this line of thought—and there are different versions of it, for example, Philippa Foot's naturalism and Iris Murdoch's Platonism—there are standards independent of our feelings, attitudes, and choices by which we may judge whether this or that is choiceworthy, whether this or that is good to choose, to do, to be, to have, to feel. And every version is in conflict with the view that our evaluative uses of *good*, unless in a linguistically degenerated culture, are no more than expressions of or determined by our feelings, attitudes, and choices.

This radical disagreement concerning how our uses of *good* are to be construed is of course closely related to the disagreement that I identified earlier concerning the nature of reasons for actions, one in which Thomists were at odds with Ayer and Sartre. What it means to say that, in giving a reason for doing this rather than that, we are identifying some good that will be achieved by doing this rather than that depends on whether we understand *good* in expressivist or in other terms. Only if our uses of *good* are governed by standards independent of our feelings, attitudes, and choices can something like the Thomistic account of reasons for action be justified. So how are the issues between these two incompatible and antagonistic lines of thought to be resolved?

HOW AT THE LEVEL OF THEORY THE DEBATE BETWEEN THE PROTAGONISTS OF THESE TWO LINES OF THOUGHT IS INTERMINABLE AND INCONCLUSIVE

Someone disposed to find credible the account of the condition of academic philosophy that I advanced earlier would, without knowing any of the facts about the subsequent debates concerning the use of *good*, predict that neither side would be able to provide conclusive arguments for its own view and against the other, except by its own standards. And so it turned out. For this disagreement was integrated into the longer and continuing quarrel between self-styled moral realists and self-styled moral antirealists, a disagreement in which the contending parties have enriched the statements of their rival positions by drawing on discussions of realism and antirealism in other areas. And, just as in those other areas, the debates between moral realists and moral antirealists have had no decisive outcome. Consider one theme of those debates.

On the expressivist view, when I assert that "doing such and such is bad," the meaning of the asserted sentence is such that it gives expression to the speaker's sentiments of disapproval. But suppose that someone says tentatively, "If doing such and such is bad, then so and so." Then, since no sentiments of disapproval are expressed, "Doing such and such is bad" as a constituent of this conditional must have a quite different meaning from that which it has when asserted. But if this is so, then inferences of the form "If doing such and such is bad, then so and so, but doing such and such is bad, therefore so and so" must be invalid, which is absurd. So the expressivist account of the meaning of such sentences must fail. It was Peter Geach who argued this thesis powerfully, thereafter referring to it as "the Frege point."[5]

To this Simon Blackburn replied by giving an admirably ingenious account of the relevant class of inferences,[6] a reply that was followed by a series of replies to the reply and replies to the replies to the reply by, among others, G. F. Schueler, Bob Hale, Mark van Roojen, Nicholas Unwin, Alan Thomas, and Mark Schroeder. At each stage in this still ongoing debate Blackburn and his allies reformulated their view in response to the most recent objections, and their success in so doing has made it clear that here we have one more example of an interminable controversy. The philosophical interest resides in the detail of the arguments. But what emerges from that often instructive detail is the large fact that, given the shared understanding of moral thought and practice presupposed by the two contending parties, and given their philosophical methods, neither party has the resources to defeat the other.

This is true more generally. Expressivists, whether followers of Alan Gibbard or Simon Blackburn or the earlier emotivist writers, have been able without notable difficulty to accommodate somehow or other every objection advanced against them. And a variety of antiexpressivists have been able equally easily to fend off the objections advanced against them. Each remains deeply convinced of the errors of the other. Both would regard it as intolerably frivolous to suggest that one should choose one's side by flipping a coin. But how then is one to decide?

HOW IT IS ONLY AT THE LEVEL OF PRACTICE THAT WE CAN BECOME ARISTOTELIANS

We need to begin again and to do so by returning to the social context in which we learned the use of *good* and its cognates. What we first had to learn was how to make the distinctions between what we desire and the choiceworthy, and between what pleases those others whom we desire to please and the choiceworthy. We characteristically and generally learn—or fail to learn—to make these distinctions, as we emerge through and from the family into the life of a variety of practices: such practices as those of housework and farmwork, of learning Latin and geometry, of building houses and making furniture, of playing soccer and playing in string quartets. What we can learn only in and through such practices is what the standards of excellence are in each type of activity and how our desires and feelings must be disciplined and transformed and our choices guided by the standards of excellence in each type of activity if we are to achieve such excellence and through it the goods internal to each type of practice.

So long as our desires have not been disciplined and transformed in the relevant ways, our uses of *good* and of cognate expressions will tend to be what expressivist moral philosophers have taken them to be, and our choices will give expression to our feelings and attitudes. Insofar as our desires have been disciplined and transformed in the relevant ways, our uses of *good* and of cognate expressions will be what Geach and others have argued them to be. So everything turns upon what we have been able to learn from the kind of practices in which we have engaged and on the nature of the particular moral culture or cultures in which we have participated. Understood in this light the philosophical quarrel between the two lines of thought that I sketched rests on a misunderstanding. It is not that we have two rival philosophical representations of one and the same subject matter but that we have two different subject matters, two different types of moral culture, an older one whose objectivist idioms and judgments are grossly misrepresented by expressivism, and one whose moral vocabulary exhibits just that blending of nonexpressivist meanings and expressivist uses that had forced itself on my attention a good deal earlier, a blending characteristic of the dominant moral culture of advanced modernity.

Consider now some further aspects of a practice-based understanding of goods, virtues, and rules. The identification of a variety of types of goods poses the question: What place should *we* give to each type of good in *our* lives? And it is no accident that this question is framed in terms of "we" and "our," rather than "I" and "mine." For this is a question that I can only hope to ask and answer with good reason if I ask and answer it in the company of trusted but critical others, others to whom I recognize that I am bound by certain unconditional commitments—commitments not to harm the innocent, to be truthful, to keep our promises, commitments that allow us to reason together without the distortions that arise from fears of force and fraud—and this for at least two reasons. First, it is only in and through such interaction with trusted but critical others that our practical reasoning is tested, so that our evaluations become less one-sided and partial and less liable to distortion by our not always conscious hopes and fears. Second, it is only insofar as we direct ourselves toward common goods, the common goods of family, neighborhood, school, clinic, workplace, and political community, that we are able to achieve our individual goods.

We learn what place in our individual and common lives to give to each of a variety of goods, that is, only through a discipline of learning, during which we discover what we have hitherto cared for too much and what too little and, as we correct our inclinations, discover also that our judgments are informed by an at first inchoate but gradually more and more determinate conception of a final good, of an end, one in the light of which every other good finds its due place, an end indeed final but not remote, one to which here and now our actions turn out to be increasingly directed as we learn to give no more and no less than their due to other goods.

This discovery of a directedness in ourselves toward a final end is initially a discovery of what is presupposed by our practice, as it issues in a transformation of ourselves through the development of habits of feeling, thought, choice, and action that are the virtues, habits without which—even if in partial and imperfect forms—we are unable to move toward being fully rational agents. Only secondarily, as we articulate at the level of theory the concepts and arguments presupposed by and informing our practice, are we able to recognize that we have had to become some sort of Aristotelian. I am not suggesting that in order to become an Aristotelian one first has to become virtuous—even a slender acquaintance with Aristotelians would be enough to dispose of that claim. I am saying that it is only through recognition at the level of practice of our need for the virtues, and through practical experience of how the exercise of the virtues stands to the achievement of goods, that a number of Aristotle's philosophical arguments become compelling.

To have become such an Aristotelian is to have found good reasons for rejecting both utilitarianism and Kantianism. What renders any form of consequentialism unacceptable is the discovery of the place that relationships structured by unconditional commitments must have in any life directed toward the achievement of common goods, commitments, it turns out, to the exceptionless, if sometimes complex, precepts of the natural law. What makes Kantian ethics unacceptable is not only that our regard for those precepts depends upon their enabling us to achieve our common goods but also that the Kantian conception of practical rationality is inadequate in just those respects in which it differs from Aristotelian *phronēsis* or Thomistic *prudentia*. Note, however, that these grounds for asserting that there are conclusive reasons for rejecting both utilitarian and Kantian ethics are Aristotelian grounds. Take away the Aristotelian premises from which this assertion is derived and it will cease to convince. Unsurprisingly, therefore, it lacks force precisely for those against whom it is directed, utilitarians and Kantians.

It is therefore of some importance that in arriving at a certain kind of Aristotelian standpoint I was not taking up one more theoretical position within the ongoing debates of contemporary moral philosophy. It is because I have been thought to have done just this that I have been unjustly accused of being one of the protagonists of so-called virtue ethics, something that the genuine protagonists of virtue ethics are happy to join me in denying. But what then is it to adopt this kind of Aristotelian standpoint? There are at least three aspects to such a change of view.

First, it enables one from a standpoint outside academic moral philosophy, that of an older tradition of moral practice, to understand why such moral philosophy was condemned to become what it has become, a scene of theoretical disputes between fruitlessly contending rival parties. The widespread loss of a shared practical grasp of the teleological structure of human nature and activity at the threshold of the modern world not only led to the theoretical fragmentation that I described in *After Virtue* but was itself the result of a prior loss of a shared mode of practical life. And there is no way to make the relevant concepts and arguments once more compelling except within some restored and contemporary version of just such a mode of practical life. Detach those concepts and arguments from the contexts of social practice from which and within which they draw their intelligibility and they too become mere debatable theoretical constructions.

Second, it is to adopt a standpoint that enables individuals, by situating themselves within such a mode of social practice, to make intelligible features of the narratives of their own lives and of the lives of others that will otherwise remain opaque, confused, disguised, or trivialized. A basic Aristotelian thesis is that only insofar as we understand our individual and common lives as potentially directed toward the achievement of goods and of *the* good through the exercise of the virtues are we able to identify the various types of frustration, misunderstanding, and failure by which our lives are marked.

Third, just as Aristotelian moral and political theory provides us with resources for interpreting and redirecting our practical lives, so too our practical experience provides us with reasons for criticizing and sometimes rejecting some of Aristotle's own concepts, theses, and arguments. We learn to identify that in Aristotle which derives from the limitations and prejudices of Athenian and Macedonian elites. So we develop Aristotle beyond Aristotle and in so doing may find—as I found—that our Aristotelianism has had to become that of Aquinas.

HOW FROM THE STANDPOINT OF ARISTOTELIAN PRACTICE CONTEMPORARY ACADEMIC MORAL PHILOSOPHY APPEARS DEFECTIVE AS A MODE OF INQUIRY

The conception of moral philosophy at which I had thus arrived put me at odds not only with the standpoint dominant in contemporary moral philosophy but also with the established analytic understanding of how philosophical inquiry should proceed. For on the view that I have found myself compelled to take, contemporary academic moral philosophy turns out to be seriously defective as a form of rational inquiry. How so?

First, the study of moral philosophy has become divorced from the study of morality or rather of moralities and by so doing has distanced itself from practice. We do not expect serious work in the philosophy of physics from students who have never studied physics or on the philosophy of law from students who have never studied law. But there is not even a hint of a suggestion that courses in social and cultural anthropology and in certain areas of sociology and psychology should be a prerequisite for graduate work in moral philosophy. (It was my great good fortune as a student at Manchester that I was required to take a course in anthropology with Max Gluckman and was driven by my resistance to Gluckman's views to an engagement with the work of very different anthropologists, such as Franz Steiner, and of such sociologists as Tom and Elizabeth Burns.) Yet without such courses no adequate sense of the varieties of moral possibility can be acquired. One remains imprisoned by one's upbringing. And the particular form that that imprisonment now takes is that of an inability to recognize, first, that the contemporary morality of advanced capitalist modernity is only one morality among many and second, that it is, as a morality of everyday life, in a state of disorder, a state of fragmentation, oscillation, and contradiction. So we should not be surprised when academic moral philosophers misconstrue their own subject matter.

It would not of course be sufficient to remedy this for students of moral philosophy to take courses in anthropology and sociology. A second necessary condition is a prior and continuing engagement with a variety of practices and a reflective grasp of what is involved in such engagement. Lacking such practical engagement and such reflection, there can be no adequate knowledge of the range and application of evaluative and prescriptive concepts. So we ought to require on the CVs of those who aspire to teaching or research appointments in moral philosophy accounts of their relevant experiences on farms and construction sites, in laboratories and studios, in soccer teams and string quartets, in political struggles and military engagements. And we do not.

A third respect in which academic moral philosophy fails as a discipline of inquiry is a result of the extraordinary pressure exerted to sustain the status quo. What is the penalty that threatens academics who do not conform to the established norms? It is that their writing will go unpublished and disregarded. And this threat is the more telling because of the intensive pressure to write, a pressure initially generated by two successive apprenticeships. The first is that of producing a PhD dissertation intended to be publishable in either article or book form by those at an age at which almost no one has as yet anything genuinely of interest to say, something easily confirmed by reading large numbers of recent dissertations in moral philosophy.

A second apprenticeship is devoted to the achievement of tenure or its equivalent. Once again the pressure to publish is intense, since the future career of a philosophy teacher will be determined almost exclusively by how much, on what, and where she or he publishes. The result is unsurprisingly a large quantity of publications, as well as an even larger quantity of unpublished writing. So far as moral philosophy is concerned, it is instructive to look at the proportion of articles submitted to articles published in one especially prestigious journal, *Ethics*. In 2006, the number of submissions was 321, and the number of articles accepted, all of them after revision, was 16. In 2007, the corresponding numbers were 334 and 16.

A high proportion of those rejected articles will later have been submitted to other journals, which either are devoted entirely to moral philosophy or contain articles on moral philosophy appearing alongside articles on epistemology, metaphysics, and other philosophical subdisciplines. The former class includes not only *Ethica, Ethical Perspectives, Ethics and Behavior, Ethics Today, Journal of Ethical Studies, Journal of Ethics, Journal of Value Enquiry*, and *Journal of Moral Philosophy* but also over thirty journals dedicated to business ethics, medical ethics, bioethics, and the like. The latter class includes journals published in Australia, Canada, Ireland, Norway, the United Kingdom, and the United States. (I am considering only the English-speaking world.) An inescapable conclusion emerges. In moral philosophy, as in other areas of philosophy, much of what is written must go unpublished and much of what is published must go unread. What function then is served by this cruel academic treadmill?

Its function is to inculcate the currently established conception of the tasks of moral philosophy and of its past history. It is to ensure that habits of mind are transmitted, so that students by and large follow their teachers in their assumptions about which few books and articles must or may be read and which may be safely ignored. It is to make certain that the young recognize whose arguments are to be taken seriously and whose disdained, when and about what to make jokes, and at whom and with whom it is permissible to sneer or condescend. It is to shape minds so that they are open to some ideas and closed to others. Academic moral philosophy is a conformist discipline, and habituation in writing what is well designed to secure the approval of those with established academic power is one principal means of producing and reinforcing that conformism.

EPILOGUE

Two salient thoughts emerge from this narrative. The first concerns the importance for the moral philosopher of living on the margins, intellectually as well as politically, a necessary condition for being able to see things as they are. The two standpoints without which I would have been unable to understand either modern morality or twentieth-century moral philosophy are those of Thomism and of Marxism, and I therefore owe a large and unpayable debt of gratitude to those who sustained and enriched those marginal movements of thought in the inhospitable intellectual climate of capitalist modernity, including Thomists as various as Maritain, Garrigou-Lagrange, De Koninck, and McInerny, and Marxists as various as Lukács, Goldmann, James, and Kidron. One way to make it highly improbable that you will enjoy outstanding academic success is to enter contemporary debates in moral philosophy as either a Thomist or a Marxist.

A second thought, perhaps in tension with the first, concerns the importance for the moral philosopher of nonetheless learning as much as she or he can from those at the academic center, those who have made definitive contributions to the ongoing debates of academic moral philosophy. For interestingly it is often they who supply the resources that one needs if one is to free oneself from the limitations of their standpoint. If one is to evaluate both the achievements and the defects of twentieth-century academic moral philosophy, it needs to be understood both from within and from a standpoint that is at once external and radically critical. It is such a standpoint that I have tried to define.

PART II

Challenging Contemporary Politics

ELEVEN

Breaking the Chains of Reason

"I am contending for the right of the living and against their being willed away by the manuscript-assumed authority of the dead."

—*Tom Paine*

I

There is not much enthusiasm abroad among intellectuals in our time for the day when the last king will be strangled with the entrails of the last priest. It is not just that the liberation of mankind has come to seem an impossibly Utopian enterprise. To most present-day British intellectuals the very concept of commitment to such a cause has become suspect. They are on the whole content with what they have; if they want anything else, it is more of the same sort of thing that they have already. An American

"Breaking the Chains of Reason," in *Out of Apathy*, ed. E. P. Thompson, 195–240 (Stevens & Sons, 1960).

sociologist has written of them that "never has an intellectual class found its society and its culture so much to its satisfaction," and has pictured our university teachers in a state of complacent delight, drinking port and reading Jane Austen. Remember the Spitalfield silk-weavers of the 1840s spending their Sunday leisure drinking porter and reading Tom Paine and you have a clue to how far and in what direction our society has travelled. The great-great-grandsons of the Spitalfield weavers are competing for scholarships to sit at the feet of the port-drinkers; their great-great-granddaughters are keen readers of those women's magazines in which the blue-eyed, fair-haired, six-foot-tall hero is increasingly likely to turn out to be an academic of some sort.

The sweet smell of the academic's social success helps to explain his unease when presented with images of radical change. He does not seek to be in any sense a prophet of hope; indeed the very notion seems to him pretentious and vulgar. Those prophets of hope, the great Marxist intellectuals, are treated as the authors of antique texts for commentary and refutation; the idea of "Left intellectuals" is such that when that glittering reflection of the contemporary intellectual scene, Mr. Anthony Crosland, wants to speak of them he has to guard himself by the qualification "if one may use the awful phrase." Small wonder then that when the contemporary intellectual's preoccupations are translated into terms of imaginative vision, he appears as one without hope. The repeated assurance of Mr. Butler that we can double our standard of living in the next twenty-five years if we only refrain from rocking the boat sounds very thin and unconvincing compared to the threats of what may happen to us if we don't. The increase in human powers which once seemed the very root of hope is now far more often a source of dread. The fantasies of Orwell, who was obsessed by the danger of the techniques of power getting into the hands of men of bad will, have only been outdone by the fantasies of Huxley, who sees just as dire consequences in the possibility of them getting into the hands of men of good will.

Yet fantasy here as always reflects life. If the intellectual has nightmares of a conformist future, he has only to wake up to find himself in a conformist present with the intellectuals conforming as hard as anyone else. The writers elevate Western values in *Encounter*. The scientists play their part at Harwell, Aldermaston and Porton. The teachers and the journalists purvey second-hand versions of the dominant ideas. It is in this conformist culture that power has become a means not to possibility but to a destruction of all possibility. That comparatively primitive technology which took us from gas-light to gas-chambers has been replaced by the achievement which took us from the disintegration of the atomic nucleus to the disintegration of Hiroshima and Nagasaki. Intellectual achievement hovers between the imagination and the reality of destruction.

It was not always so. We inherit from other times and places a series of images of the intellectual as rebel and critic: Condorcet, hiding from his executioners so that he may finish his *Sketch of the Progress of the Human Race*; Marx in the Reading Room at the British Museum, surviving on a pittance; Sartre playing his part in the Resistance. On the threshold of our society the intellectual appeared as liberator and revolutionary. But both before and after that eighteenth- and nineteenth-century stimulus to reason the intellectual has too often been a victim of the bureaucracies of the mind. Before there were those corporations of learning, the universities, providing a vital link between the powers of church and state. Since there have been the growing administrative tasks of industry and the civil service on the one hand, with the diffusion of ideas on the other through Press, television and schools, the universities once more providing an important link. Between the collapse of the older order and the rise of the new the intellectual achieved a short-lived independence during which he appeared as a voice of hope, speaking to men who might hear.

It is a mark of the conformism of contemporary intellectuals that not only do they not see themselves as able to speak in this way, but they are no longer able to conceive of there being an audience which might hear and respond. One component of the apathy of the intellectuals is a deep-seated belief in the apathy and conformism of the working class. Yet an addiction to I.T.V. is perhaps no more likely to reduce one to being an impotent spectator of life than is an habitual reading of *The Times* or the *Guardian*. The grooves of conformism are different for different social groups. What unites all those who live within them is that their lives are shaped and driven forward by events and decisions which are not of their own making. A lack of will to change this situation and an inability even to recognise it fully infect all classes in our society.

Where intellectuals are specifically concerned, an explanation may be looked for in terms of the specialisation of thought. The formal logician, the prehistorian, the neurologist and the poet all count as intellectuals: why should they have anything to say of outstanding social significance? Should this not be the province of yet another specialist, the sociologist or the political theorist? Part of the answer to this ought to start from the way in which what the sociologists and political theorists have to say today often seems as devoid of immediate political significance as the study of butterflies or Buddhism. But the core of the answer lies in the change in the characteristics of the intellectual. Among our intellectual ancestors, the thinkers of the eighteenth-century Enlightenment and their immediate heirs, it was taken for granted that to participate in intellectual life at all was to be committed to the ideas of reason and freedom and to the politics that could make these effective. What we have to ask about the intellectuals is not just what social pressures have driven them into their present unhappy state; but what has happened to emasculate their ideas and what in our culture has robbed the intellect of its social power. To ask this is not of course to ask a question that is only relevant to intellectuals; it is to ask what hinders intellectuals from contributing to a general breakthrough from apathy.

II

The inheritors of the Enlightenment are in their different ways Hegel and Marx. In their writings there is a ferment of concepts whose life derives from their close interrelationship, the concepts of reason, of freedom, of human nature and of history. "When individuals and nations have once got in their heads the abstract concept of full-blown liberty, there is nothing like it in its uncontrollable strength, just because it is the very essence of mind. . . ." So Hegel. His belief in the strength of this concept is not surprising in one who wrote in the shadow of the American and French Revolutions, above all in the shadow of the Tree of Liberty planted in his student days at Tübingen. Unlike all his successors in disillusionment with revolutionary politics from Wordsworth to Malraux, Hegel never came to think his youthful belief in freedom mistaken. Even when in old age he combined detestable political attitudes with bad logic in order to prove that the Prussian monarchy was an authentic embodiment of freedom, he would on every anniversary of the taking of the Bastille drink toasts with his students in commemoration of that great liberation. What survived every twist and turn of Hegel's career was the conviction that freedom is the core of human nature.

It is so because human action can only be understood in terms of such concepts as purpose and intention. To know what someone is doing is to know what ends he is pursuing, what possibilities he is realising. Human history is a series of developing purposes, in which through the exercise of reason in the overcoming of conflicts freedom is attained. To understand a particular episode is to place it within the context of that history. Men are understood not in terms of that which they have been but in terms of the intersection of what they have been and what they can be. Because possibility grows through conflicts of principle and purpose history is a dialectic of contradictions, intelligible not as natural events are or as a machine is but rather as a conversation or an argument is.

At every stage in human history the growth in reason and the growth in freedom are inseparable. Only in so far as reason guides action are men free to discern alternative possibilities and to frame purposes. Only in so far as the realm of freedom extends does reason have force against the non-rational. Without freedom reason operates only within limits, and so its constructions, however intricate, remain beyond those limits uncriticised, and, in so far as uncriticised, irrational. Without reason freedom becomes merely a lack of constraint which leaves the individual the plaything of all the forces which impinge upon and influence him, but of which he remains unconscious.

Post-Hegelian discussions of freedom have not often preserved this vital link between freedom and reason. The discussion has usually been carried on in terms of the contrast between negative freedom, belief in which is cherished by utilitarians, and positive freedom, belief in which was cherished by Victorian and post-Victorian idealists. Negative freedom is what I enjoy when I escape criticism by other people; positive freedom is what I enjoy when I am in that state which reason advises to be best calculated for my self-realisation. Both are ghosts of dead political philosophies which still haunt contemporary thinking. Both need to be exorcised. In the name of positive freedom men have been called free so long as they are being tyrannised over for their own good. In the name of negative freedom men have been called free when enclosed by ignorance and their natural situation, provided only that nobody else was actively coercing them. Certainly belief in negative freedom is less obviously vicious than belief in positive freedom, but so long as the choice is between these two, one can understand both why belief in freedom is not an active inspiration in much of our social life and why intellectuals have not felt that their vocation committed them to a devotion to freedom. For in both these concepts the interconnection between reason and freedom which is essential to the Hegelian concept is lost sight of.

Two other features of the Hegelian concept are also important. The first is the way in which the concept of freedom is firmly located in Hegel's overall historical scheme. Freedom is not something which at any given moment men either do or do not possess; it is always an achievement and always a task. The concrete content of freedom changes and enlarges from age to age; in the dialectical growth of human nature what was the freedom of the past may be the slavery of the present. Moreover, the tasks of freedom in any age are defined partly by the goal to be reached, partly by the obstacles to be overcome. It is this necessity of referring to what has to be overcome which makes "the negative" so important a notion to Hegel. The particular form of the negative which matters in this discussion is the alienation of man from himself which leads men to envisage as objective, impersonal and enslaving forces what are in fact creations of human consciousness and reason. God, the State, The Moral Law; these are but false objectifications by which we deceive and enslave ourselves. So at least the younger Hegel. The human task is to tear away the masks, to recognise our own faces behind them and so free ourselves from the domination of the mask.

To take the argument to this point is to feel the mounting irritation in most readers at this apparently abstract concern with expounding fragments of Hegel. Why, for the Absolute's sake, Hegel? The answer is that in Hegel's elucidation of the essential connections between the concept of human action and the concept of freedom and reason something is restored which is lost in the contemporary academic mind. The view that human activity can be reduced to patterns of response to the stimuli of conditioning, this is the view which is continually fed to us. And perhaps it is no accident that so many who want to eliminate from our concept of the human those features of it which are distinctively human have had no good words for Hegel. The antimetaphysical positivism of the American exponents of "rat psychology" joins hands with the Pavlovian determinism of the Stalinists. "The question of Hegel was settled long ago," snapped Zhdanov in 1947. "There is no reason whatever to pose it anew."

Not that there is not a peculiarly Hegelian way of betraying freedom and reason. Hegel's critics have pointed out that while Hegel was right to point to freedom and reason as essential possibilities of human nature, the translation of the possible into the actual is not to be achieved by making conceptual connections, but only by a transformation of human life. (This is a central point of Marx's criticism of Hegel.) But the mature Hegel retreats from the inadequacies of actual human life into the twin sophistries of the Absolute Idea and the Prussian monarchy. And Hegel's followers have too often fled into abstraction, so that they have seen the misleading character of our concepts, but failed to see that the distortion of our concepts cannot be corrected apart from correcting the distortion of our lives. When Marx wrote of the role of concepts in Hegel's *Logic* he spoke of them as "the money of the mind." What he had in view was the way in which we can be deluded into supposing that monetary transactions can occur independently of an actual transfer of goods. So we may wrongly suppose also that we can change our basic concepts, but not our lives. Because we are reasoning animals (even if we do not always reason well) the shape of our concepts shows in the outline of the shape of our lives.

Part of the reaction against Hegel and one effect of the reign of positivism has been that specialisation of the intellect which has been mentioned already. Not that the very growth of knowledge and especially of scientific knowledge would not have rendered specialisation necessary anyway. But it is not clear that specialisation had inevitably to be accompanied by a complete fragmentation of our culture. If there were only unity in our concept of human nature, for example, we should have at least a clue to the relations between the most diverse elements in our thinking. In past times some unity was given to our education by means of classical literature, history and ideals. The ancient world provided a backcloth for the modern. To learn the inner history of the modern academic is in part to write of the decline and fall of the ideals of a classical education.

III

"Absorbed in money making and in the peaceful warfare of competition, it [bourgeois society, that is] forgot that the shades of ancient Rome had sat beside its cradle." So Marx. But how did the bourgeoisie come to forget? For nascent bourgeois society the Greco-Roman world provided the mantle which human values wear, and this not only on the battlefields and amid the terror which brought that society into being, but also in its academic syllabuses. The prototype of all arts disciplines, as they exist in our universities today, is the Greats school at Oxford; and the Greats school in its inception was a study of a whole society, of the language, literature, history and philosophy of Greco-Roman culture. The small-scale in physical size of that culture, its relatively self-contained character, made it a suitable object for study. It was far enough away to be viewed dispassionately, near enough to provide a model for social behaviour. Lord Milner's young men building the modern empire, the Asquithian liberals—these in their own way echo Thucydides and Cicero.

But from very early on the school tends towards becoming a group of separate disciplines; the vision of a whole society—inaccurate as it may have been—is lost. As language and literature, history and philosophy, it becomes a model for the fragmented disciplines of modern civic universities. Sometimes when schools of English are founded in modern universities, Anglo-Saxon is deliberately introduced to parallel the linguistic demands of classical studies. And what happens in these fragmented disciplines in both older and newer universities is that a great many specimens of human culture are inspected without any connections being established which would bring out what it is anyway to be a part of human culture or society.

There is lacking any conception of the human as such, in terms of which relations between history and literature and philosophy might be established. So to do a course in one of these subjects is usually like going round a museum; the exhibits are there neatly labelled and you the spectator stand outside the case. But you can think of any connection between them and you only by imagining yourself dead and stuffed under the glass. For the alternative of seeing the exhibits as living, living as you are living, has never been opened to you by the demonstration of any vital connection between yourself and them. Such a connection could only be established by the concept of a common human nature. And to serve its purpose such a concept would have to be historical, have to be a means of showing the past growing into the present. Marxism possesses such a concept; why it has not been fruitful in British academic life we shall have to ask presently. But for the moment this is to rush ahead of the argument. What does matter is simply the divorce of arts subjects from the study of human society as such.

This lack of unity in arts subjects makes them all the more open to victimisation by administrative pressure. And administrative pressure in the university today exhibits that curious blend of the planned and the unplanned so characteristic of welfare capitalism.

On the one hand there is the pressure to produce more scientists and technologists and the consequent building programmes. On the other hand there is a general expansion in size of universities with very little, if any, thought as to what the purpose of arts faculties may be. The universities design their courses either to produce the kind of trained scientist that industry and the government demand or to produce the kind of arts graduate (I think here of the vast mass of those of middling ability, not of the few more distinguished) that nobody demands at all. The content of science courses is almost entirely non-problematic; how to get enough of the required subject-matter into three years teaching is the limit of the problem. The content of arts courses is almost entirely problematic; our only *firm* criterion is what has been done in the past.

In this situation the examination system and the tasks which it imposes become the limits of academic vision for many. About the ends of what one is doing no questions are asked, in the sciences because decisions about the ends have been taken by powers outside the universities, in the arts because there are no accepted and effective standards by which such decisions could be made. Thus all discussion is about means; the university teacher is turned into an administrator who has to accept a framework imposed from elsewhere—from industry and government in the sciences, from the past in the arts. And administrators are notoriously conservative; their criteria are, have to be, those of efficiency in producing *given* results. Theirs not to reason why, but only how.

So the universities have few answers to offer to their students when they ask why they should do what they do. They have to fall back on two extremes: either disciplined study is worth while just because of the sheer value of the experience-in-itself or it is a professional training which has as its end the getting of a certain sort of job or it combines these. The first answer which sounds idealistic is in fact cynical because everyone knows, although few admit, how few worthwhile intellectual experiences the mass of students encounter in a university career. (The best students are different here: but they would mostly achieve what they achieve anyway. One is sometimes tempted to think that the only students with whom the university teacher does not largely fail are those for whom he is really superfluous.) The second answer which sounds cynical is in fact idealistic, at least for arts students, because they are not in fact being trained to do anything except to teach others subjects which will land them in the same predicament. Unless, that is, they too, like the scientists, become the servants of the great corporations. The editor of *The Times Educational Supplement* has said recently that "it can still be maintained that the classics, for pure educational value, are outstanding amongst all other subjects. 'Greats' at Oxford, which is the crown of a classical education, still produces men and women with minds ideally prepared for work in the world. 'Why do you recruit firsts in Greats?' a former chairman of a great oil company was asked. 'Because they sell more oil' he replied."

What I have tried to depict in this section is an academic scene in which the breakdown of the admittedly inadequate norms of a classical education had left the academic world without any inner strength to resist the moulding pressures of industry and the state. The university assumes the shape of the social *status quo*. So does the university teacher. A product of the system which he now helps to administer, he can hardly avoid sharing the mood which I described in the first section of this essay. Himself without initiative or much room to manoeuvre, he becomes an admirable representative of conforming society. As the supporter of the dominant ideas in our culture he is gradually transformed into a trustworthy guardian of our society's ideology. The concepts of reason and freedom are not even a temptation to him.

To use the word ideology here may seem to give the discussion a quaint Continental flavour. European intellectuals have ideologies, are Croceans, Marxists, existentialists or whatever it is. We British, so the refrain runs, are less pretentious, less hospitable to these inflated general theories.

And this immediate reaction is of course one of the clues to our intellectual attitude, which needs to be characterised not just in terms of our various professed doctrines and theories, but in terms of the absence of general theories and unifying ideas. In particular, as I am going to repeat to the point of weariness, we lack any unifying concept of human possibility.

This is of course to say that the key point in our intellectual failure is in the human sciences. It is to what has happened to psychology, sociology and history that we need to turn. And now we need to pass beyond the patterns of administrative pressure. Certainly the human sciences too have been fragmented, becoming on the one hand abstract academic disciplines, as divided and divisive as any other disciplines, or on the other hand being turned into training schools for personnel managers and almoners. But the depth of our dilemma lies not in the way that they have been presented, but in what there has been to present. To approach this topic is to reach the heart of the matter.

IV

The dream which still haunts and informs the human sciences is the dream of mechanical explanation. Engels has narrated vividly how after 1848 with the death-knell of Hegelianism there was a revival of the mechanistic materialism of the eighteenth century. To do for society what Newton had done for nature was the revived hope. It looked back to the thought that Diderot had expressed when he spoke of "the complicated machine called society." It looked forward to the physiological laboratories of Germany and America where the anatomising of nerve-endings and the experimental study of reflexes was envisaged as a preliminary to the grand task of explaining human behaviour. What the psychologist looked for in the individual, the social scientist was to search for in the group. His task was to discover laws as simple as Newton's laws of motion, from which observed regularities in human conduct might be deduced and which would at one and the same time provide causal explanations of particular human actions and a basis for general and unifying theories. To explain, to predict, to control; to be able to see human behaviour as the outcome of physiological or environmental determinants; and to unify this understanding in a scheme as simple as Newton's: these have been the goals.

The assumption is of course that there is nothing distinctive in human behaviour which might render it unamenable to modes of explanation appropriate for understanding the behaviour of molecules or mainsprings or muscles or maggots. And with this assumption goes another, that the mode of understanding human beings resembles the mode of understanding natural objects in that to understand is to control, or at least is to take the first steps towards controlling. For to understand is to give causal explanations; to explain an event causally is to state under what given conditions the event occurs and under what conditions it does not occur; and to state this is to tell us what we have to contrive if we wish to produce this type of event. So to understand is to be in a position to manipulate. To carry through this programme would be to acquire possession of that power the exercise of which is depicted in *Brave New World* and *1984*.

The central paradox of this mechanistic view of human life is well brought out by the third of Marx's Theses on Feuerbach:

> The materialist doctrine that men are products of circumstances and upbringing, and that, therefore, changed men are products of other circumstances and changed upbringing, forgets that it is men that change circumstances and that the educator must himself be educated. Hence, this doctrine necessarily arrives at dividing society into two parts, of which one is superior to society....

That is, if we think of society as a machine and recognise that we are part of society, then to discover the mechanics of social change is to discover those laws of which we are the victims as much as anyone else. If on the other hand we think of knowledge of the mechanics of society as affording us levels of change, we at once have to think of ourselves as outside the machine, operating it, as a part "superior to society." In other words, to conceive of ourselves as acting to change society is at once to recognise the inapplicability of the machine model to ourselves; the machine model will do to explain how we come to be modelled and acted upon, but not how we act. And we can only apply the mechanistic type of explanation to this by making an arbitrary distinction between them and ourselves.

That the mechanistic type of explanation must therefore break down we can see. That it did break down in practice was revealed simply by its failure to yield results except in limited small-scale contexts. But the project of an overall mechanical explanation of human life continued to dominate the human sciences. For such alternative approaches to human nature as are considered receive their definition in terms of the breakdown of that project. So much is this so that those features of human life which render it unamenable to mechanistic explanation still fail to receive their due. Such features, which I have already connected with the notion of activity, are twofold. First, human activity is never to be equated with physical movements. Physical movements are certainly susceptible of mechanistic explanations. And every human action involves physical movement. But to understand the physical movement is not to approach understanding the human action. The same physical movements involved in signing my name may be the bearers of quite different actions. The same physical movements may be involved in endorsing a cheque, signing a peace treaty or putting my name to a proposal of marriage. What differentiates these are the socially recognised conventions, the rules, in virtue of which the movement is taken as signifying this or that. So that I cannot explain the action except with reference to established rules and meanings. A society constituted by such an ability to communicate presupposes, but cannot be explained in terms of, physical movement.

More than this, as Engels pointed out, mechanical explanations are unhistorical. A machine runs or breaks down; it has no historical development. To explain a particular human action is to place it in relation to the circumstances out of which it arose and the goal which the agent sought. Stages in a mechanical operation can be explained in terms of preceding and following sequences of events. But they have no goals and they do not respond to circumstance by means of understanding. They simply follow out predetermined paths.

The insight that human activity is intelligible and explicable only in a social and only in an historical context is lost sight of, not only in the dream of a general mechanistic theory of human behaviour, but also in the various intellectual adaptations to the breakdown of that dream. The first and most striking of these adaptations is social and psychological science as it actually exists amongst us. The assumption behind it is that what went wrong with the dream was not its mechanistic character, but the *a priori* character of its generality. What we need is to amass particular studies of particular cases. From these we shall derive low-level generalisations and correlations; the study remains causal, mechanistic and manipulative, but it is accepted that as yet we cannot ascend to the simplicity of an overall theory. This entails that our studies are essentially statistical and out of social and historical context. The study of man in nature gives way to the study of delinquents in a Chicago suburb. "Twenty-five years ago and earlier," wrote Bernard Berelson, an American social psychologist, in 1956—

> prominent writers as part of their general concern with the nature and functioning of society, learnedly studied public opinion not "for itself" but in broad historical, theoretical and philosophical terms and wrote treatises. Today, teams of technicians do research projects on specific subjects and report findings. Twenty years ago the study of public opinion was part of scholarship. Today it is part of science.

The equation of science with the study of social phenomena out of social context is what is striking. This equation leads on to two other fallacies.

The first is that significant generalisations can arise out of material collected without any general principles of significance. I think here of a recent volume of statistical information about contemporary British social life from which you can learn how many people in our society spend their holidays in caravans, but not how many own shares. The second fallacy is that the use of formal, mathematical devices might make other than trivial at the level of generalisation what is trivial at the level of the particular case. The human sciences are haunted in any case by the view that what is less complex is necessarily more comprehensible than what is more complex; that understanding technologically primitive societies is therefore a step towards understanding technologically complex ones, and that understanding the nervous system is a task prior to understanding thought. This misses the point that you may not be able to comprehend the goals for which men in the primitive society strive unless you look beyond it to the more advanced; and you certainly cannot hope to even embark upon the project of explaining thought in terms of the nervous system until you understand thought sufficiently to know what it is you are hoping to explain by your neurophysiology. The point which I am making was made by Marx against some of Darwin's disciples. Marx first agreed with them in rejecting that one-sided teleology which wants to explain an earlier stage only as a preliminary to a later one; but he then rejected their mechanistic assumption that the earlier can be made sense of without the later, but not the later without the earlier (and for "earlier" and "later" one could also read here "simple" and "complex") in the bold statement that "the anatomy of man is a key to the anatomy of the ape."

To ignore this is necessarily to condemn the human sciences to become a collection of particular observations and cases without any overall unity or significance. Dignified by the name of empiricism it can then become the received doctrine that this is how the human sciences should be. Academic standards of objectivity and impartiality are invoked to show how admirable our lack of standards of importance is. But even among those who take up this attitude there are divisions of standpoint. There are those who hold that the limited and particularising nature of the human sciences at the moment merely reflects a temporary phase in their development. To such sociologists as Lundberg or Lazarsfeld the only misleading feature of the attempt to assimilate the human sciences to physics is that expectations were pitched too high too soon. The human sciences still await their Newton. We continue to collect data and to hope. There is, however, another possible response, and one as much in vogue in British circles as that which I have just indicated is in American. This is the doctrine that the limited and particularising nature of the human sciences, as we have them, is due not to the slowness of our progress nor to the fact that we searched for the wrong sort of general theory, but to the fact that the concept of any general theory or overall understanding of society is nonsensical. For any general theory of society will be an overall theory of the historical development of society. To advance such a theory is to fall into what Professor Karl Popper has called "Historicism" and castigated as the original sin of the modern intellect.

I have in this essay criticised the contemporary human sciences as non-historical, atomistic, content with limited, contextless, low-level generalisations, and unable to discern or construct theories of overall social structure. These are for Professor Popper precisely the features which any well-constructed human science would have to have. He thus provides a splendid rationalisation for the contemporary sociologist. The most interesting feature of the arguments of Popper's social philosophy is that they systematically persuade when they do persuade (and the incense which so many acolytes burn at his shrine is evidence of how often that is) by presenting us with pairs of what are alleged to be exclusive and exhaustive alternatives. One alternative is then exhibited as fallacious in its logic and destructive in its moral consequences. This involves us in a vindication of the other. If these false alternatives were merely Popper's they would not be so important to discuss; but, as I have already remarked, Popper's thought in many ways systematises and represents the assumptions of the age.

The most obvious of these dichotomies is that which allows us only to be *either* historicists *or* without any overall view of history. Popper defines historicism as the belief in unconditional trends in history. He ascribes such a belief to the error of supposing that an historical process can be explained solely in terms of a law or laws without adding a statement of the initiating conditions from which the process commenced. Clearly if anyone supposed this he would both be committed to a belief in "absolute trends" and be in gross error. But who has ever believed this? Certainly neither Hegel nor Marx. To bring Marx into the picture is to make clear at once how Popper is involved both in historical and logical error. For Marx both believed in the possibility of overall theorising about history and did not believe in "absolute trends." Knowledge of the trends that are dominant is for Marx an instrument for changing them. So his belief that he has uncovered "the economic law of motion of capitalist society" is not a belief in an absolute trend, but a trend whose continuance is contingent on a variety of factors including our activity. It is interesting here that the error of which Popper believes Marx to be guilty, namely that of treating historical processes as if they were explicable in the same way as physical events were, is one which Marx himself indicted. But Marx goes on to explain human history in a different way, beginning with the family of concepts which belong to what he called "practical consciousness": the concepts of intention, deliberation and desire, those concepts which are essential to understanding men as agents and not as mere passive reflexes of non-human forces. Then Marx asks what the limiting factors upon human agency are in every age and finds these in the basic economic relationships which are built into particular modes of production. Human history is the successive liberation of possibility as economic limitation of this kind is removed. In each age the economic relationships mean that the rules in accordance with which social and economic life are carried on are different and differ with the mode of production. In each age the character of the rules is determined by the relationships between men which are involved in that particular mode of production, and these relationships are not between individuals but between groupings of men, who are united by their common economic and social role, and divided from other groupings by the antagonisms of economic and social interest. So—"all history is the history of class struggle." This is not a generalisation built up from instances, so much as a framework without which we should not be able to identify our instances; yet also a framework which could not be elaborated without detailed empirical study. We see its growth not just in Marx, but also in historians like Michelet and Taine.

The relevant feature of Marxism for the present argument is the way in which the economic basis appears as a limiting and conditioning of human actions, but not as an exhaustive explanation of its dynamic. This enables us to see how Marxism cannot be labelled "historicist" in Popper's sense. And this is important to my whole argument, both because of my own Marxist approach, and because it exposes the misleading character of the choice which Popper's alternatives offer us.

The second false dichotomy in Popper's thought is that expounded in terms of what Popper calls "methodological individualism." This is the doctrine that groups are to be understood as collections of individuals and that individuals are concrete while societies are abstract. "The army" is an abstract concept; "the soldier" is a concrete one. An army is a collection of soldiers. The vice to which "methodological individualism" is opposed is "holism," the view that social groups can and ought to be viewed as more than, or other than, just a collection of their members. This is supposed to involve us in a belief in the reality of fictions and abstractions. *Either* we take Popper's nominalist view *or* we fly to super-empirical entities. Once again the choice posed is utterly misleading. What is important is that no individual can be characterised except in terms applicable to other individuals. To characterise a given individual by any predicate at all is to exhibit that individual as a member of a class. (This is, of course, to use the word "class" in the logicians', not the sociologists', sense of the word. Many logicians have made the point, including Hegel.) Moreover, of classes many things may be said which cannot be said of individuals; one consequence of this is that no class can be characterised by referring only to the individuals who compose it. You cannot characterise an army by referring to the soldiers who belong to it. For to do that you have to identify them as soldiers; and to do that is already to bring in the concept of an army. For a soldier just is an individual who belongs to an army. Thus we see that the characterisation of individuals and of classes has to go together. Essentially these are not two separate tasks. What Popper no doubt fears, and fears rightly, is a belief in social groups and historical trends as states existing apart from individuals, of which individuals are but the playthings. Popper is right to stress that there is no history and no society which is not the history or the society of concrete individuals; but equally there are no individuals who exist apart from their history or apart from their society. So that to insist on the latter truth also is to realise that we do not have to choose between "methodological individualism" and a vicious, supra-empirical "holism."

The third false dichotomy is presented by the alternatives that *either* we must be illegitimately partisan in the social sciences *or*, and this is Popper's view, we can be concerned only with means and not with ends. The fallacies in this thesis are twofold. It assumes a possible total separation of means and ends in social life. This only needs to be stated for its dubiety to become evident. What is more immediately important is that Popper's thesis is self-refuting. For to assert that our concern can only be with the means and to add that the result of that concern can only be limited and particular statements of social correlation is already to be partisan. An example of what Popper takes to be a genuine discovery of the social sciences is that "You cannot have full employment without inflation" (the rider "in our type of economy" is not added). If such limited discoveries are all that we can hope for from the social sciences, it follows that we cannot hope to transform society as such; all that we can hope to change are particular features of social life. To adopt this view of the means available for social change is to commit oneself to the view that the only feasible ends of social policy are limited reformist ones, and that revolutionary ends are never feasible. To be committed to this is to be partisan in the most radical way. Popper again presents us with a false choice, and one that depends of course on the other false alternatives which he presents. In all of them he mirrors so aptly the actual condition of the social sciences that we can understand the almost religious consolation which his views offer to social scientists. What might have otherwise appeared to them as a lamentable incoherence and impotence appears now as necessary and unavoidable. More than this it appears praiseworthy, for Popper is apt to insist that historicism is the doctrine of totalitarianism. So that not to share his condemnation of it is not merely to be mistaken, but also to be wicked. Thus the practitioner of the social sciences who cannot transcend their present condition finds his state not only a necessary but even a virtuous one.

This is perhaps a point at which to recover the general thread of the argument. I have argued that the human sciences have been dominated by the conceptual ideal of laying bare the clockwork of human nature. For this ideal has shaped the thought both of those who have accepted it and of those who have rejected it. Those who have rejected it have accepted it as the only form in which the ideal of a general understanding of society might be formed; and so in rejecting it they have rejected the concept of any such general understanding. Or else they have accepted the mechanistic ideal as the paradigm of rational explanation; and in rejecting it they have fallen back upon treating human life as irrational and inexplicable. We can merely record and amass our records; or we have to point to irrational and incomprehensible forces. The dilemma thus presented arises from a failure to see the point of Hegel and Marx; and this failure is endemic not just in the minds of our sociologists but in the life of our society.

Surely, however, it will be replied, I have not allowed for the variety of positions taken up in non-Marxist sociology. Within the scope of this essay I am necessarily concerned to indicate and outline a position rather than to argue for it exhaustively. But it may help to underline the point which I am trying to make to append to this section something on the work of two very different sociologists who are in their own way submerged by the situation which I am trying to describe. Both are contemporaries.

The first contemporary at whom I want to look is Talcott Parsons, because in Parsons' massive work on *The Social System* some of the basic patterns of non-Marxist sociology are revealed. I almost in this last sentence said "bourgeois sociology" and if I had done so I would have not only been classifying the social order to which Parsons' work belongs. For Parsons begins by recalling that early bourgeois thinker, Hobbes, and he explicitly states his problem in terms reminiscent of Hobbes. We begin with individuals and their desires at one pole and we ask how social order is created at the other. Parsons is about three hundred years more sophisticated than Hobbes in his psychology; the elaborate devices of the theory of "socialization" replace the simple Hobbesian psychology of the fear of death and the desire to dominate. But, as with Hobbes, society and the individual are counterposed and the task is to explain how the individuals are brought into a state where social equilibrium is maintained. With Parsons we are back in a mechanistic theory designed to explain order and stability. It is no wonder that Parsons finds it difficult to provide plausible speculations for social disorder. He can explain stability; but how does change arise? Parsons' work is therefore profoundly nonhistorical and this is perhaps also a consequence of his attempt to discuss the life of social groups in a general, comparative, timeless way. More than this, his starting point in the motivation of the individual and the reasons why the individual has come to share the values of his society pushes into the background all questions about the hierarchy of power-relations and the political and social institutions which embody them. Both history and politics become marginal to society in Parsons' social theory; and when Parsons does write, as he has done, directly on political and historical questions, he notoriously abandons his own concepts and has even been accused of Marxist ideas.

The contemporary sociologist whom I want to compare with Parsons is that fierce critic of Parsons and hero of radicalism, C. Wright Mills. Wright Mills might be thought to be close to my own position on a superficial reading. "Freedom" and "reason" are for him key words and he has criticised these tendencies in sociology which are criticised in this essay. But Wright Mills' position seems to start far away from Parsons and end close to him. Where for Parsons the institutions of power were marginal, for Wright Mills they are central. Whether it is the internal development of American society that is in question or the approach of another world war Parsons is concerned to locate the effective decision-makers, and why they are who they are and where they are. Yet Wright Mills still has to stress the autonomous character of contemporary social processes.

Great and rational organisations—in brief, bureaucracies—have indeed increased, but the substantive reason of the individual has not. Caught in the limited milieux of their everyday lives, ordinary men often cannot reason about the great structures—rational and irrational—of which their milieux are subordinate parts. Accordingly they often carry out a series of apparently rational actions without any ideas of the ends they serve, and there is the increasing suspicion that those at the top as well—like Tolstoy's generals—only pretend they know.

When social scientists, such as Wright Mills himself, discern what is happening, what are they to do? Wright Mills' only answer is that they must speak both to those at the top and to "ordinary men," but on Wright Mills' own showing those at the top are unlikely to want to hear and ordinary men are unlikely to be able to hear. If Parsons showed us a social equilibrium in which individuals are wholly absorbed, Wright Mills shows us a machine in which individuals are trapped.

There is no picture in Wright Mills of the resistances that men can and do offer to such pressures, no conception of the Hegelian "negative" with all of what Hegel called its "patience, labour and suffering." The only independent power in human life that Wright Mills can see is the independent reason of social scientists of integrity. This kind of misconception rests not just on factual error; it rests above all on the image of human nature with which the social scientist approaches the evidence. That Parsons from the political Right and Wright Mills from the political Left should both be submerged by the determinist image of man is testimony to its continuing strength; that Wright Mills should be so conscious of this in Parsons and so unconscious of this in himself is even more impressive testimony on the same point.

We are now in a position to frame the fundamental dilemma with which the human sciences confront us. Psychologists, sociologists and the rest, they offer us two possibilities so far as large-scale human change is concerned, so far as man's control of his own life is concerned. Either men can discern the laws which govern social development or they cannot. If they can, then they must avow that their own behaviour is subject to those laws and consequently they must admit that they have discovered themselves to be not agents, but victims, part of a social process which occurs independently of human mind, feeling or will. If they cannot discern such laws, then they are necessarily helpless, for they have no instruments of change in their hands. So that in any case human agency is bound to be ineffective. Of course, so far as small-scale adaptive changes are concerned, it may be otherwise. All sociologists leave room for reformist manoeuvre.

The important characteristic of this dilemma is that it separates understanding and action. Understanding and the lack of it are both a condition of inaction. At the heart of the concept of explanation there is the insight that we could not ever be in a position to assert that one event is the cause of another, unless we could produce the second event by means of the first and avert the second event by averting the first. Unless our activity was effective in bringing about changes we could not give causal explanations; how odd then that the concept of causal explanations should underpin a thesis which culminates in the conclusion that our activity must necessarily be impotent.

Those who swallow the oddness of this and indeed live so inside the dilemma that they cannot hope to see it as a dilemma must therefore see men either as rational subjects in an irrational world (they can frame concepts of social explanation, but cannot find application for them) or as objects in an irrational world (they can find explanations, but discover that they too are among the explained). It is scarcely surprising then that the human sciences reflect and reinforce the prevailing apathy and conformism of the intellectuals. In the first section of this essay I pointed to the fact of this conformity; in the second it was contrasted with the intellectual and moral hope offered by the intellectuals of the Enlightenment and by Hegel and Marx. In the third section I argued that the traditional educational norms of our culture now offered no source of strength to withstand the prevailing mood and I argued that we lacked any proper concept of human nature. Now we have seen why. In one sense, at this point in the essay, the ideology of the age has already been unveiled. At the heart of the theorising of those self-appointed therapists of our culture, the social scientists, we find precisely those ideas necessary to define and to buttress our intellectual malaise. As Herzen remarked of some of their predecessors, they see themselves as the doctors of a sick society, whereas they are in fact symptoms of its disorder.

V

Diseases know no frontiers. This is as true of intellectual as of physical disorders. If it were not so we might treat the human sciences as an infected area which could be quarantined off, rather as anxious but misinformed middle-class parents in the 1930s hoped to shelter their children from Marxism by forbidding them to go to the LSE In fact, however, there is no discipline which is not touched by our present condition. Yet the vast quantity of detailed, specialised, hard-working study by means of which academic disciplines endure is apt to conceal this. For the numerous tasks to hand distract from attention to that total picture, without a possibility of which the individual tasks would no longer have any point. And where any sort of total picture does begin to emerge from the individual pieces of research it seems to be just a consequence of the research, something whose acceptance is as inevitable as is the result of a chemical analysis or the dating of a document.

What picture in fact emerges? One in which the absence of a central concept of human nature and the non-historical features of the social sciences continually invade other disciplines. It might be thought paradoxical that this should be above all true of history. After all, contemporary history is strikingly different from liberal history. The descent from the Whig view of English history as freedom broadening down from precedent to precedent to H. A. L. Fisher's boast of being unable to discern any purpose or pattern in historical sequence is a tale of the past. Whatever the disciples of Namier have brought into historical studies, they have brought a realism about power and a cynicism about ideals which is a change from the Whigs. All that one wonders is whether having caught the Whigs bathing they are not now merely wearing their clothes turned inside out. For history has now become the history of the arrangements of power. The Namierite attention to the day-to-day events of the rise and fall of politicians in the reign of George III, for example, works on the assumption that it is almost a work of nature that there are positions which are positions of power and influence and positions which are not. Given the ladders up and down which our rulers ascend and descend, their climbing can easily enough be described. But is it adequately described if we never ask how the ladders come to be there?

This attention to the individual cases of powerholding, power-gaining and power-losing may appear superficially to underline the activity of individuals. But because it does not raise questions of context it in fact presents the individual as hemmed in by social circumstance, always responding to external pressure and never a fully autonomous and responsible individual. Consider, for example, a recent account of the Peterloo Massacre. The government had to keep public order and rely on local information. They never willed it. The local magistrates faced what they understandably—in the context of time and place—took to be a seditious uprising. The troops were under orders from the magistrates. No individual is responsible; and since the story contains nothing but the doings of individuals there is no responsibility to be ascribed. The system in which such things happen is accepted as a framework to the story in such a way that it never appears inside the narrative as a culprit. There are no culprits. When the readers of such histories report to us that ideals and aspirations have no historical leverage and that what matters is power, the reply should be that the powerlessness of ideals is written into the methodology of this sort of history from the outset.

This is the other side of the sociological coin. We have seen how Popper's rejection of the equation of social science with history reflects in sociology. Now we see what it reflects in history. With history and sociology in this state it would be strange if political theory were not similarly placed. What should we deduce that the state of political theory would have in these circumstances to be? If it reckoned with the actual state of the human sciences and history, it would have to see social development as a self-making process or tradition since men cannot consciously or rationally move it. The role of reason in this development would at best be that of understanding or recording after the event. What reason could not hope to do would be to prescribe before the event. Since it would be an illusion to suppose that reason might do this, political rationalists would be not just intellectually mistaken but politically and morally dangerous. Since political activity cannot be rationally guided, how shall it take form? The only possible answer is that it should be adaptive, a matter of knowing how to secure the safe passage of the institutions we inherit into changing circumstances with the least possible derangement and disturbance. If we were to ask for a political theory to be tailor-made to fit the state of the social sciences and history, this would have to be its content. But a tailor has anticipated our needle and already done the job and the clothes are being worn. For this is none other than the political theory of Michael Oakeshott, a theory which has certainly the merit of being self-confirming, since it is so splendidly adapted to the prevailing climate. It is almost superfluous to point to the profoundly conservative and anti-revolutionary nature of this theory.

If creative, rational human activity has disappeared from the intellectual scene so thoroughly, why has it done so? The answer which I am approaching is that our social life and our intellectual vision reinforce each other. Our social life is one in which human activity is rendered uncreative and sterile. We live in a society of grooves and ladders, a society of predetermined lives. But this is a society created out of human activity and which human activity could abolish. Yet it cannot be simply reasoned out of existence; reasoning can give direction to human activity, can make it effective. But there must be human activity to be informed and directed. Where is it? It is there wherever those whose lives are most made and imposed upon them, the working people in the industrial and in the colonial centres, revolt against the conditions of their life. Cut off from those revolts, and over-impressed by the reports which sociological explorers have brought back from the proletarian jungle, the intellectuals see the working class as being the most helpless, inactive group of all. They come from a mechanically moulded and conditioned way of life and they describe what they see in mechanised and deterministic terms. Then their own concepts blind them and those to whom they speak to there being any alternative possibilities. The vices of our lives and the errors of our concepts combine to keep both in being.

How great the intellectual pressures are may perhaps best be grasped by looking at the typical distortions to which genuinely independent thought in our culture is subjected. Probably the two greatest thinkers of our age were Freud and Wittgenstein, both of them conscious inhabitants of a fallen world who had lived through the collapse of the Austro-Hungarian empire. Both of them thought against the intellectual climate of their time. What is interesting is the way in which each has been domesticated and rendered harmless by the spreading abroad of versions of their theorising from which all the bite has been removed.

Freud was in revolt against the mechanistic climate of the age. That he was so has been concealed by most of his expositors, not least by himself. He abandoned neuro-physiology and the search for causes of neurotic and psychotic disorders in order to connect them with motives and desires. He invented a technique whereby one could become conscious of unconscious motives and thereby free oneself from their compulsive hold. He saw in the rational comprehension of desire the path to freedom. We can free ourselves from the infantile demands which oppress, and remake ourselves. We can pass from super-ego morality to the morality of the ego-ideal. As to the content of this ideal Freud stops short; honesty, reasonableness, a care for people—having prescribed a practice of life dominated by these he does not ask how such a life could be realised against the weight of our social institutions. This, then, becomes the vulnerable point at which his interpreters are able to rewrite him back into an adaptive and deterministic setting. At the level of therapy the ideal, especially among American neo-Freudians, becomes one of "adjustment," of fitting the individual into a social niche. At the level of theory the explanation of unconscious motivation becomes not a prelude to freedom but a prelude to explaining away social dissatisfaction as neurotic. We tread the path here from the important to the trivial, from Freud to Kingsley Amis.

When the Nazis burnt Freud's books they testified to the essential anti-Fascism of his stress on rationality and freedom. The next stage is that of Koestler's novel *Arrival and Departure* where the hero discovers the roots of his anti-Fascist activity in repressed guilt at a forgotten injury which he had done to his brother in childhood. But at least Koestler's hero goes on as an anti-Fascist. With Amis in his Fabian Society pamphlet on *Socialism and the Intellectuals* the watering down and misunderstanding of Freud reaches its climax. Politics is a matter of temperament; love of the established pulls you to the Right and hate of it to the Left. "And behind that again lies perhaps your relations with your parents". No hint is here that those whose adult politics are merely patterned after their relationship with their parents need to be freed and can be freed. No hint is here that one might free oneself through social action.

Or take the case of Wittgenstein. Wittgenstein is a philosopher about whom it is hard to write without distortion. His own thoroughness, patience and integrity mean that he never elaborated views easy enough to be fitted into neat summaries. If I pick out from his thought just one theme it will indicate again the type of intellectual pressure that is in question. A variety of tangles in philosophy have arisen around the view that we are able to talk about our experiences because words are names for specific experiences with which they have become associated. I know what "red" or "pain" means because I have seen red lights or felt pain and the words and the experiences have come to be marks which remind me of these experiences. Against this view Wittgenstein argued that what matters is the *use* to which an experience can be put in the context of human activity, its role, point, or purpose. Consider a word like "cow." Norman Malcolm, expounding Wittgenstein, has commented on an imagined case where a man utters a certain sound every time that a cow appears, and said that "we need to ask, what makes the latter sound a word, and what makes it the word for *cow*? Is there no difficulty here? Is it sufficient that the sound is uttered when and only when a cow is present? Of course not. The sound might refer to anything or nothing." That is, it need not be a word any more than if I suffered from a nervous tick of the head every time that I saw a cow, my movement of my head would be a word. Malcolm then says of the sound in question,

> What is necessary is that it should be playing a part in various activities, in calling, fetching, counting cows, distinguishing cows from other things and pictures of cows from pictures of other things. If the word has no place in activities ("language-games") of this sort, then it isn't a word for cow. To be sure I can sit in my chair and talk about cows and not be engaged in any of these activities—but what makes my words *refer* to cows is the fact that I have already mastered these activities: they lie in the background.

This supposition makes it clear how for Wittgenstein language is essentially social, essentially a matter of human activity and not at all to be understood mechanistically. It recalls Marx's assertion that "language is practical consciousness. . . ."

Yet in many accounts of Wittgenstein from both hostile and sympathetic viewpoints everything has been turned upside down. Wittgenstein set out to elucidate "ordinary language"; he is represented as having tried to argue from it. Instead of the purposive concept of "use" we get the naturalistic concept of "usage." The philosopher's task is not that of understanding the standards for success in language-using: it is the bleakly conservative one of recording and classifying how we all talk anyway. Language is not something that men do and make, it becomes merely a part of the given and made environment. This sort of reinterpretation fences round Wittgenstein's thought just at the point at which it might help us to break through the prevailing miasma.

Thus in every field there has come into its own an intellectual conservatism protected against change by the alleged impossibility of change. The villain of the piece, it ought to be clear by now, is not that scapegoat so often invoked, positivism. Positivism, with its narrowed view of rationality, its acceptance of physics as the paradigm of intellectual activity, its nominalism, its atomism, its lack of hospitality to all general views of the world—positivism with all these merely recorded after the event what the intellectual landscape of our culture had become. Those who could not bear to hear what it reported fled often not from an alien force but from the mirror-image of their own minds.

VI

This, then, is the ideology of apathy and conformism. It provides the ideal climate in which to disarm the intellectual and transform him into an educational technician who can safely be charged with training the social administrators of the established order. How are we to break its hold upon us? Many of the fallacies in it have been exhibited in the course of the argument, and the Hegelian and Marxist alternative has appeared to point the context from time to time. But how are we to live out that alternative in both our thinking and our action? Not by manipulation of people so that they will move in some direction that we desire, but by helping them to move where they desire. The goal is not happiness, or satisfaction, but freedom. And freedom has to be both means and end. The mechanistic separation of means and ends is suitable enough for human manipulation, not for human liberation.

This entails a decisive break with utilitarianism. Marxists have in the past crippled themselves intellectually by adapting even their Marxism to a determinist, mechanistic mould and consequently to a utilitarian mould. I think here of the career of Georg Lukács. Lukács faced the dilemmas of bourgeois sociology as they are classically presented in the work of Max Weber and found a solution in the work of Hegel and Marx. He participated in the Hungarian Soviets of 1919 and was Minister of Education in Bela Kun's government. Then when he expounded Marxism in 1923 he came up against the mechanistic attitude of the Right-wing Soviet Marxists. He recanted and allowed that he had underestimated the objective weight of historical determination and overestimated human possibility. Weighed down by the specious arguments of determinism he lived through the era of objective necessity. We must do the lesser evil for the greater good; we must use the means for that end; we must pull the levers at the trials of Bukharin, Radek and the rest to move on the machine of Soviet society. Then in 1956 when Nagy broke through the smoke-screen of Stalinist ways of thinking, Lukács again became Minister of Education. He vindicated his philosophical work in his life.

In the social-democratic tradition, too, utilitarianism has dominated and with it mechanistic modes of thought. And social democracy has been quite self-conscious in its Benthamite approach.

What Benthamite utilitarianism lacked, as J. S. Mill saw at once, and what liberalism by becoming utilitarian came to lack, was any critique of satisfaction. The ultimate criterion is "happiness" and "happiness" is simply that state in which people are getting what they avowedly want. There is no scope within the terms of utilitarianism for criticising their preferences. So that one seems condemned if one remains within the terms of Benthamism to say that people are satisfied if they get what they think they want. And if one attempts to emerge from those confines and says that one knows what people really want (that is, in the long run, if they only had the relevant experiences) better than they do themselves, one seems bound to adopt policies which will necessarily compel and coerce people. The second course is a violation of negative freedom, the first an abdication to all the unconscious pressures which mould popular taste, and to those who are able to contrive and control such pressures. And it is the first course that classical utilitarianism adopts as its own.

It is thus the case that utilitarianism can become an instrument for removing immediate dissatisfactions rather than a doctrine of genuine reform and that it easily becomes an instrument for contriving people's good rather than for activating people themselves. J. S. Mill's characteristic doctrines on happiness and liberty point to what is absent in Benthamism rather than succeed in repairing the gaps. What matters is that the utilitarian spirit accords exactly with the changing purposes of capitalism. Dickens has remarked through the characters of Gradgrind and Bounderby how early capitalism found application for utilitarian themes; it has less often been remarked how easily the utilitarian spirit wears a Fabian dress and appears as the maximiser of common interests in the promotion of pleasure and the diminution of pain. At two points utilitarianism informs Fabianism: by setting in front of all men the common goal of the greatest happiness of the greatest number (in itself a harmless and humane slogan) it encourages the belief that there is a common interest in society. So that what is needed is an adjustment of interests. Whereas Marxists differ from Fabians in asserting that in class-divided society there is a fundamental conflict of interests; and that there can be no reconciliation of these interests. Again utilitarianism offers to Fabianism the idea that it is the group of intelligent and benevolent administrators (whose native wit and training have provided them with the relevant knowledge which the masses lack) who will contrive this adjustment of interests for society.

This is precisely in the spirit of welfare capitalism. Profoundly as the interests of different groups under capitalism are divided, it remains the case that there is a need for this clash to be concealed, for the mask of common interest to be worn. Thus demands for social insurance, health services and educational opportunity up to a certain limited point can express militant dissatisfaction with capitalism and yet be skilfully tamed by the capitalist administrative machine. Bismarck was a pioneer here and the Fabian tradition is uncomfortably close to Bismarck.

The breakthrough comes from awakening what Marx called self-activity. The dissatisfaction with the established order, which is that awakening, appears spontaneously at many points in our society. But it is too often allowed to die or is discouraged; or—if sufficiently militant a specimen of working-class activity—receives direct hostility. Our deep need is instead to provide all the growing points of human activity against the present social order with coherent theoretical expression, so that they may be rationally guided and effective. What is necessary for the intellectual is to accept his responsibilities for this both in the working-class movement and to those for whom he is professionally responsible.

Anyone who has taught in a university since the war has seen three phases of student life. There was the ex-service generation, for whom many of the causes and motives of the thirties remained alive. Their maturity and experience have been remarked on often enough. What gave to that maturity its edge was a sense of the enormous possibilities that the war had opened up, possibilities which were gradually to disappear in the Cold War climate. The next generation were essentially the children of war and Cold War, their younger days surrounded by consciousness of shortage and uncertainty, their adolescence presented with the newly made careerism of welfare capitalism. They were the nonpolitical, the non-anything, the universities' gift to Lord Hailsham. For they were conservatives in the profound sense that they accepted the environment as *given*: all that they had to do was to find a suitably sheltered niche. But this started to change as the fifties wore on and it ended in 1956 not with a whimper but a bang. The twin crimes of Suez and Hungary, the premeditated crime of nuclear warfare, and moreover the apparent deadness and dull cynicism of official politicians in the face of these things—these launched students along with other adolescents into the world of political questions.

Of political questions, not of political answers. All that tremendous adolescent energy, which the very rawness of the emotion involved makes so impressive, is still looking for intellectual satisfaction at the political level. If no coherent answers are found, then as the student generations pass on they will become all the more frustrated and disillusioned for having been so hopeful and awakened in the past. And this is what the reactionaries hope for. "I was a socialist when I was young, too." The unspoken completion of this—"How good to grow middle-aged, conservative and self-satisfied like me"—points to the danger: the silting up of the poetry of adolescence into the prose of bourgeois middle age. All the pressures are there: the need to get a job, to succeed in it, to bring up a family, to pay for a house. Not to succumb to these the feeling and the questioning must find a theory and a way of life which will transmute the poetry of adolescence into continuous life-long activity.

Two images have been with me throughout the writing of this essay. Between them they seem to show the alternative paths for the intellectual.

The one is of J. M. Keynes, the other of Leon Trotsky. Both were obviously men of attractive personality and great natural gifts. The one the intellectual guardian of the established order, providing new policies and theories of manipulation to keep our society in what he took to be economic trim, and making a personal fortune in the process. The other, outcast as a revolutionary from Russia both under the Tsar and under Stalin, providing throughout his life a defence of human activity, of the powers of conscious and rational human effort. I think of them at the end, Keynes with his peerage, Trotsky with an icepick in his skull. They are the twin lives between which intellectual choice in our society lies.

VII

The philosophers have continued to interpret the world differently; the point remains, to change it.

TWELVE

The *Theses on Feuerbach*

A Road Not Taken

When we reread Marx nowadays, that reading has to address two salient and related features of our recent experience. The internal collapse of the Communist state apparatus in so many countries has left behind a variety of groups in those countries struggling to attain or rather to reattain the standpoint of civil society. At the same time the distinctively contemporary social theorizing of our own political culture, theorizing which gives a voice to the now dominant forms of power, either asserts or presupposes that the standpoint of civil society cannot be transcended. What then was and is the standpoint of civil society?

The expression 'civil society' and its cognates in other European languages had first been used to translate Aristotle's '*koinōnia politikē*'. But by the early nineteenth century it had come to be used in a variety of very

"The *Theses on Feuerbach*: A Road Not Taken," in *Artifacts, Representations and Social Practice: Essays for Marx Wartofsky*, eds. Carol C. Gould and Robert S. Cohen, 277–90 (Springer, 1994).

different ways and Hegel, who learned it from Adam Ferguson, adopted it to name those social, economic and legal relationships into which individuals enter in order to satisfy their needs, forming by so doing "a system of complete interdependence wherein the livelihood, happiness and legal status of one human being is interwoven with the livelihood, happiness and rights of all" (*Rechtsphilosophie* 183). The individual from the standpoint of civil society is to be distinguished from and contrasted with the set of social relationships into which she or he has chosen to enter. Those relationships, often understood as contractual, are on the one hand a means to the attainment of each individual's ends and on the other a system so constructed that by entering it each individual becomes a means for the attainment by other individuals of their ends. Among the needs generated by such a system therefore is one for the protection of individuals from being so used by others as a means that their pursuit of their own ends becomes frustrating rather than fulfilling. Hence appeals to moral and legal norms affording such protection have an important function within civil society. The central conceptions informing thought within civil society about human relationships are therefore those of utility, of contract and of individual rights. And the moral philosophy which gives expression to the standpoint of civil society consists of a continuing debate about those concepts and how they are to be applied.

Up to 1844 Marx had engaged in a philosophical debate with Hegel, with the Left Hegelians and with Feuerbach about the nature of civil society, its relationship to the state and to religion, and the inadequacy of the criticism of civil society by its critics so far. The subtitle of *The Holy Family* summarizes his enterprise: 'a Critique of Critical Critique'. In 1845 Marx and Engels together embarked on a new project in the course of first writing and then abandoning the manuscript of *The German Ideology*, that of offering an historical and analytical account of the genesis and dynamic of modern capitalist economies. What were Marx's reasons for thus turning away from philosophical enquiry? When I speak of a turning away from philosophical enquiry I am not of course denying that Marx's later historical and economic analyses are themselves informed by philosophical presuppositions. That would be absurd. But philosophy is no longer the object of his enquiries and the questions which he poses are generally not philosophical questions.

Lucio Colletti has remarked on how few of Marx's later writings advert to this change by giving us "the reasons, philosophical as well as practical, which had induced Marx to give up philosophy after his break with Hegel and Feuerbach", citing the short text to which Engels later gave the title 'Theses on Feuerbach', the *Preface* to *A Contribution to the Critique of Political Economy* published in 1859 and the *Postface* to the second edition of the first volume of *Capital*.[1] But the latter two were written a very considerable time later from what had become Marx's mature standpoint. Only in the first of these do we have a genuinely transitional text.

Colletti's own diagnosis of the change focuses upon Marx's critique of Hegel, in which Marx had worked through Hegel's conceptions of dialectic and of the state to the point at which their empty abstractions and incoherences had led him to reject them. And Colletti understands Marx's next stage as one that had progressed beyond the limitations of those conceptions. I want instead to suggest that the important question is not so much why Marx rejected Hegel and Feuerbach as why, in rejecting them, he rejected philosophy, and moreover that, by rejecting philosophy, at a stage at which his philosophical enquires were still incomplete and were still informed by mistakes inherited from his philosophical predecessors, Marx allowed his later work to be distorted by presuppositions which were in key respects infected by philosophical error.

Marx's *Theses on Feuerbach*, on this view, are in part a successful, but in part an unsuccessful attempt to identify what is involved in transcending the standpoint of civil society. In distinguishing the success from the failure I cannot but presuppose some particular interpretation of the text and there is no interpretation which is not contentious. But I shall bypass the scholarly disputes, because within the space of this paper any adequate treatment of them would be impossible. And in so doing I shall also fail to acknowledge scholarly debts. Informed readers will notice, for example, that I take for granted George L. Kline's thesis that Marx did not have a materialist ontology and that the word '*Materiell*' has, in *The Theses on Feuerbach* as elsewhere, to be construed with care; and that I presuppose the truth of Carol Gould's account of Marx's ontology of individuals-in-relation and its Aristotelian antecedents.[2] But they and a number of unacknowledged others cannot be held responsible for an interpretation that I assert rather than argue.

My approach will be to identify and to comment upon six central assertions expressed in Marx's eleven theses. The first of these is that the standpoint of civil society cannot be transcended, and its limitations adequately understood and criticized, by theory alone, that is, by theory divorced from practice, but only by a particular kind of practice, practice informed by a particular kind of theory rooted in that same practice. The philosophers have hitherto tried to understand, but their understanding was not guided by the aim of transforming the social and natural world in the requisite way. The eleventh thesis does not tell philosophers to abandon the attempt to understand; it tells them to direct their tasks of understanding towards the achievement of a particular *telos*. What *telos*?

It is the *telos* of some form of what Marx in the first thesis calls *objective* activity, taking over this expression from Fichte and Hegel. Objective activity is activity in which the end or aim of the activity is such that by making that end their own individuals are able to achieve something of universal worth embodied in some particular form of practice through cooperation with other such individuals. The relationships required by this type of end are such that each individual's achievement is both of *the* end and of what has become her or his own end. Practices whose activity can be thus characterized stand in sharp contrast to the practical life of civil society. It is a contrast which is best expressed in Aristotelian rather than in Hegelian terms.

In activities governed by the norms of civil society there are no ends except those which are understood to be the goals of some particular individual or individuals, dictated by the desires of those individuals, and no goods are recognized except those involved in the satisfaction of the wants and needs of individuals. Because there are many goods which individuals can achieve only by cooperative attention to the goods of others, civil society recognizes as common goods those goods which are pursued in common by individuals. But the only available conception of a common good is one constructed from and reducible to conceptions of the goods pursued by various individuals in their attempts to satisfy their desires.

By contrast the ends of any type of practice involving what Marx calls objective activity are characterizable antecedently to and independently of any characterization of the desires of the particular individuals who happen to engage in it. Individuals discover in the ends of any such practice goods common to all who engage in it, goods internal to and specific to that particular type of practice, which they can make their own only by allowing their participation in the activity to effect a transformation in the desires which they initially brought with them to the activity. Thus in the course of doing whatever has to be done to achieve those goods, they also transform themselves through what is at once a change in their desires and an acquisition of those intellectual and moral virtues and those intellectual, physical and imaginative skills necessary to achieve the goods of that particular practice. So, as Marx puts it in the third thesis, there comes about a "coincidence of the changing of circumstances and of human activity of self-changing".

Yet at once it is plain that there are at least two objections to construing Marx in this way. First and most obviously on this construal Marx is presented as if he had made a distinction which is expressed in an Aristotelian vocabulary, a vocabulary which he did not in fact use and some of whose presuppositions he had rejected. The conception of a type of practice teleologically ordered to the achievement of a or the common good may, it will be said, be at home in an Aristotelian or Thomistic perspective, but it is alien to Marx's. To this I respond by agreeing in part: what I have ascribed to Marx is indeed not what Marx said. Nonetheless I am contending that, if Marx had done the work of spelling out in detail the key distinction which the argument of the *Theses on Feuerbach* needs, he would have been compelled to articulate it in something very like Aristotelian terms. Hegel's idiom is just not adequate to the task.

To this a second objection must be that what Marx says is far too compressed and elliptical to support this kind of interpretation. Those interpreters who have elucidated the theses by drawing on Marx's other writings have at least had the evidence of those other writings to offer. To this I reply that, if we understand the theses as on the one hand marking a significant break with what Marx had done hitherto, and on the other pointing in a direction which Marx did not in fact take, then reliance on his other writings may itself be misleading. What we should be looking for is an attempt to articulate, in terms that are not deformed either by the errors of Hegel or by those of Feuerbach, an effective rejection of civil society. So our first question should be: what was it that, on Marx's view, rendered any rejection of civil society in either Hegelian or Feuerbachian terms ineffective?

Marx's rejection of all Hegelianism, and more especially of that of the Left Hegelians, was in important part a rejection of purely theoretical enquiry as an instrument of social change. What the Left Hegelians had characteristically supposed was that to exhibit the incoherences of the principles embodied in the social and political *status quo*, thereby exposing its irrationality, was by itself to have made an important and effective contribution to bringing about its downfall. We should not be harsh in condemning their error. After all we have over a century and a half of experience which they lacked, an experience of modern social orders not merely surviving the exposure of the incoherence of their governing principles, but even in some cases seeming to flourish because of that incoherence. The modern state, for example, behaves part of the time towards those subjected to it as if it were no more than a giant, monopolistic utility company and part of the time as if it were the sacred guardian of all that is most to be valued. In the one capacity it requires us to fill in the appropriate forms in triplicate. In the other it periodically demands that we die for it. This deep incoherence in the modern state is not a secret, but the fact that it is plain for everyone to see of itself does nothing at all to undermine the modern state. And Marx was perhaps the first to recognize how very little the exposure of incoherence generally achieves.

Other aspects of Marx's critique of Hegelian philosophy he shared with and had indeed learned from Feuerbach. By the time that he wrote the theses, he needed to take great care to distinguish his own positions from some of those of the later Feuerbach.[3] Feuerbach after all had already written in *Principles of the Philosophy of the Future*, published in 1843, that "The road taken so far by speculative philosophy from the abstract to the concrete, from the ideal to the real . . . will never arrive at true objective reality", but only at a reification of philosophy's abstractions, and that "The transition from the ideal to the real takes place only in practical philosophy." This seems to anticipate Marx. How then is Marx's position in the theses to be differentiated?

Marx in the theses makes one of the main heads of his criticism of Feuerbach a charge that Feuerbach's critique of religion had been inadequate. Feuerbach had understood religion as a distorted expression of human sentiment, one in which truths about love were expressed in a disguised form, one in which the true relationships of subject and predicate were inverted. Philosophy was to pierce through this disguise and by setting out the relevant truths in rational form dispel supernaturalist illusions. But Feuerbach then went on to announce what he took to be his discovery that philosophy also by its abstractions generates illusions. Marx's criticism of Feuerbach on religion is therefore perhaps best read as a prologue to Marx's criticism of Feuerbach on philosophy.

Marx's criticism of Feuerbach on religion had two parts. First he complained that Feuerbach, while understanding, in Marx's view correctly, that religion has to be wholly explained in terms of its secular basis, does not then ask what it was in "the cleavages and self-contradictions" (the fourth thesis) in that basis which had engendered illusion, and how that secular basis would have to be transformed so that it was no longer liable to engender illusion. Secondly Marx contended that Feuerbach had not analyzed "the religious sentiment" adequately as a social product, since Feuerbach's explanation of it terminates at the point at which he analyses it psychologically as a sentiment of individuals, rather than as a mode of expression characteristic of a particular type of social order (the eighth thesis). What matters to Marx here is the particular conception of the individual upon which Feuerbach relies. Feuerbach does not understand about that conception, first that it too is among those conceptions which are defective because abstract, and secondly that it belongs to the conceptual scheme of one particular type of social order.

If we apply Marx's criticisms of Feuerbach's account of religion as distortion to Feuerbach's later account of philosophy as distortion, what then is it that Marx is saying? He is asserting, first that philosophy has its secular basis in a particular type of social order, that informed by the standpoint of civil society, and secondly that, if we suppose that in understanding philosophical enquiry and argument as the activity of individuals, and that by giving an account of the secular basis of that activity as the activity of individuals, we have successfully moved from the abstract to the concrete, then we shall be deceiving ourselves. Marx's use of the notion of abstraction has of course often been criticized. Surely, it has been said, all concepts, all uses of language, involve abstraction, and therefore it cannot be a criticism of any particular concept or conception that it is abstract. But this criticism misses the point, something that has also been often said, but which still bears repeating. In Marx's semitechnical Hegelian usage, to abstract is always to frame a concept in a way which deprives it of the contextual connections in which alone it is at home and therefore to present it as having application independently of the relevant set of contexts. It always in consequence involves conceptual error and misunderstanding. We should perhaps note in passing that Marx's use of this notion of abstraction is often Wittgensteinian rather than Hegelian.

What then is it about the concept of the individual, as deployed by Feuerbach, which renders it abstract, and what is it about that abstraction which enables it to play its part in the thinking and acting characteristic of civil society? An answer to this latter question itself supplies an answer to the former. We already noticed that all transactions in civil society are understood to be between individuals and sets of individuals and that those individuals are only contingently related through their own acts of will to the social circumstances and the social relationships which they happen at any particular moment to inhabit. It may be of course that an individual finds her or himself entangled in certain social relationships without having willed this to be the case. But that she or he continues in them is, except when force or fraud are at work (the force and fraud which the legal and moral protections of civil society are designed to prevent), her or his own doing. Everything that comes about is understood to be either an intended or an unintended consequence of the actions of one or more individuals. The human individual must therefore be viewed in abstraction from her or his social relationships and the human essence must be specifiable by reference only to properties possessed by individuals apart from and in independence of their social relationships.

What is important is to recognize that it is this conception of the individual which is actually embodied not just in the thought, but also in the activities characteristic of civil society. To regard individuals as distinct and apart from their social relationships is a mistake of theory, but not only a theoretical mistake. It is a mistake embodied in institutionalized social life. And it is therefore a mistake which cannot be corrected merely by better theoretical analysis. Better theoretical analysis is of course necessary and in the sixth thesis Marx indicates what kind of theoretical account is required. The human essence is not given by considering the properties of individuals in isolation. "In its reality it is the ensemble of social relations". And of course what Marx means by "*the* ensemble" in this aphoristic utterance is not entirely clear. What is clear is that human beings who genuinely understand what they essentially are will have to understand themselves in terms of their actual and potential social relationships and embody that understanding in their actions as well as in their theories.

In civil society however there has to be a contradiction, a cleavage between how human beings really and essentially are and how they understand themselves to be. This "cleavage and self-contradiction", whereby civil society is a social order in which human beings are generally deprived of a true understanding of themselves and their relationships, is the source of the illusions diagnosed by Feuerbach. Even though these are philosophical illusions, whether about religion or about philosophy itself, they can have no philosophical cure. Here Marx becomes anti-Wittgensteinian. The only remedy for such illusions is an alternative form of practice of just that kind which we have already seen to be incompatible with the standpoint of civil society. Why so?

Civil society is characterized not only by its abstract individualism, but by a particular way of envisaging the relationship between all theory, including social theory, and practice. The adequacy of a theory to its objects is conceived of as a matter of the conformity of "thought objects" to "sensuous objects" (the first thesis). On this view we are to correct "abstract thinking" by our contemplation of the sense-experience afforded by the physical and social world. From the point of view of what Marx calls Feuerbach's "contemplative materialism" what contemplation of the social world reveals are "single individuals" and their agglomeration in civil society (the ninth thesis). Theoretical investigation leads to the materialist conclusion that these individuals are what they are because of their circumstances and their upbringing. Human beings are then taken to be a product of causal agencies over which they have had no control.

The social theorist who has arrived at this conclusion has by so doing completed the work of elaborating an adequate theory. Now she or he has to understand her or himself as about to embark on a second distinct task, that of applying this theory in order to effect change. But in so envisaging their task theorists have, characteristically without recognizing it, made the sharpest of distinctions between: how they understand themselves and how they understand those who are the subjects of their enquiries. They understand those whose actions and experiences are to be explained by their theory as the wholly determined products of circumstance and upbringing. Their biological and social inheritance makes them what they are, independently of and antecedently to their own reasoning and willing, which are no more than products of that inheritance. By contrast such theorists understand themselves as rational agents, able to and aspiring to embody their intentions in the natural and social world. They understand others in terms of a determinist theory. They understood themselves in terms of a rational voluntarism. Marx put this in the third thesis by saying that "The materialist doctrine concerning the changing of circumstances and upbringing forgets that circumstances are changed by men and that it is essential to educate the educator himself. This doctrine must, therefore, divide society into two parts, one of which is superior to society." What do we need to learn from these remarks?

A first lesson concerns the relationship between the autonomy of theory and the social order of civil society. Marx had already identified the autonomy of theoretical enquiry as characteristic of civil society. Now he adds to that as also distinctive of civil society the self-conception of the theorist as an autonomous agent and as therefore in her or his own understanding always a potential legislator for and on behalf of others. Marx here suggests what was misleading in an antithesis which was later to dominate a good deal of discussion of Marxism, that between the view that theoretical enquiries inescapably function within and as part of economic and social formations and the rival view that theoretical enquiries can be autonomous and independent of the social contexts inhabited by theorists. Marx however identifies one particular kind of autonomy and independence of theory as themselves characteristic of and inseparable from a particular type of social order.

Secondly Marx, in asserting that such autonomous social theory cannot but envisage human beings in two incompatible ways, on the one hand as products of objective social and natural circumstances and on the other as rational agents, identified a continuing *aporia* for all modern social theory. It has not been uncommon in this century for social theorists to announce that they have solved the problem thus posed, among them Parsons, Sartre, Habermas and most recently Bourdieu. But various as their solutions are, they have all been solutions from *within* theory. Even Bourdieu, whom Loïc J. D. Wacquant has recently congratulated on "the inclusion, at the heart of a theory of practice, of a theory of theoretical practice" relates theory primarily to the practice of the scientific enquirer, that is, of the theorist.[4] But Marx's point, I take it, was that no solution from within theory or even from within the practice of theorists is possible. It is only from the standpoint of social practice of a very different kind, one prior to both enquiry and theory, that a solution will be possible. What kind of practice might that be? It cannot be the kind of practice envisaged by those concerned to reform the institutions of civil society, without however abandoning its basic beliefs. For Marx had identified and found reason to reject the hierarchical structure of that type of reformist theory and practice. Those who without abandoning the standpoint of civil society take themselves to know in advance what needs to be done to effect needed change are those who take themselves to be therefore entitled to manage that change. Others are to be the passive recipients of what they as managers effect. This hierarchical division between managers and managed is thus legitimated by the superior knowledge imputed to themselves by the managing reformers, who have cast themselves in the role of educator. Marx almost certainly had foremost in mind Robert Owen, whom he had described in the Paris manuscripts as the author of "an abstract philosophical philanthropy". Owen was to have numerous successors in the subsequent history of socialism, among them both Lenin (at least on occasion) and Beatrice and Sidney Webb.

Notice that in the sixth thesis we once again confront the problem of interpreting what Marx expressed only in compressed and elliptical terms. What is it about the social educator's possession of theory that is taken to legitimate the educator's superior role? It must surely be that the educator takes her or himself not only to know more, but also to know best, that the educator takes her or himself to know what is genuinely good for others, something that they do not themselves know. Hence educators suppose themselves to be entitled to impose upon others *their* conception of the good. Marx contrasts the activity of this type of educator in respect of knowledge of the good with the activity involved in quite another kind of practice, one such that those engaged in it transform themselves and educate themselves through their own self-transformative activity, coming to understand their good as the good internal to that activity. Here again the elucidation of Marx's anti-Hegelian and anti-Feuerbachian thesis has had to be in Aristotelian terms. But this elucidation could scarcely be justified, if it proved impossible to cite any relevant example of just such a form of practice, one which would *both* be entitled to be called 'revolutionary' (the first and third theses) *and* be adequately characterizable only by an Aristotelian reference to the goods internal to it.

We find just such an example in the account given by Edward Thompson in *The Making of the English Working Class* of the communal life of the hand-loom weavers of Lancashire and Yorkshire before and during the greatest prosperity of those weaving communities at the end of the eighteenth and the beginning of the nineteenth century.[5] At its best the hand-loom weaver's way of life sustained his family's independence and his own self-reliance. Honesty and integrity were highly valued and what Thompson calls the "rhythm of work and leisure" allowed the cultivation of gardens, the learning of arithmetic and geometry, the reading and the composition of poetry. What the hand-loom weavers hoped to, but failed to sustain was "a community of independent small producers, exchanging their products without the distortions of masters and middlemen."[6] At their best they embodied in their practice a particular conception of human good, of virtues, of duties to each other and of the subordinate place of technical skills in human life, but one which they themselves had no theory to articulate. By so doing they had, to the extent that it was possible, placed themselves outside civil society. And a theory which had successfully articulated their practice and which had been formulated so that its dependence on that practice was evident would have supplied just the kind of example of the relationship of theory to practice which the argument expressed in the theses on Feuerbach so badly needs.

What made the practice of the hand-loom weavers revolutionary? It was the degree to which, in order to sustain their mode of life, they had to reject what those who spoke and acted from the standpoint of civil society regarded as the economic and technological triumphs of the age. So Thompson relates how capitalist progress in the end "transformed the weavers into confirmed 'physical force' Chartists . . ."[7] Marx himself had experience of the militancy of weavers in the insurrection of the Silesian weavers of the Eulengebirge in 1844. But he seems not to have understood the form of life from which that militancy arose, and so later failed to understand that while proletarianization makes it necessary for workers to resist, it also tends to deprive workers of those forms of practice through which they can discover conceptions of a good and of virtues adequate to the moral needs of resistance. Yet in the theses on Feuerbach Marx came very close to formulating just the distinctions which might have enabled him to understand this. But to have expressed those distinctions clearly and to have developed their implications would perhaps have left Marx unable to define his relationship to the large-scale revolutionary changes which he had identified as imminent, tied instead to what he took to be already defeated forms of past life. Marx therefore may have had the alternatives either of rejecting philosophy or else of depriving himself of the possibility of immediate effective participation in great events. And perhaps this is why he rejected philosophy.

Some of Marx's thoughts in the theses do of course reappear in his later writings. But with his rejection of philosophy in 1845 he lost the opportunity to develop those thoughts systematically and to understand their implications for the relationship of theory to practice. In so doing he left behind him unfinished philosophical business and, when, later on, philosophy was revived within Marxism, it was typically either as the dialectical and historical materialism of Plekhanov, which emerged from Engels' misunderstanding of Marx's relationship to Feuerbach, or as the rational voluntarism of the young Lukács, in which Lukács revived strains in Marx's thought whose fullest expression had been in the Paris manuscripts of 1844. But this opposition, between on the one hand the philosophy of Engels and Plekhanov and on the other that of the young Lukács, revived in a new version, or rather in a series of new versions, one of the antitheses already put seriously in question by Marx himself in the theses on Feuerbach. Each party in these subsequent debates had an excellent diagnosis of the errors of its opponents. The partisans of the younger Lukács understood very well that if human beings were the products of circumstance and upbringing, in the terms propounded by Engels and Plekhanov, then the kind of revolutionary agency through which the limitations of circumstance and upbringing could be transcended became unintelligible. The partisans of Engels and Plekhanov understood equally well that if the possibilities of revolutionary agency were what the Lukács of *Geschichte und Klassenbewusstsein* and of *Lenin* took them to be, then the nature of the historical determination of social and economic orders became quite unclear. In an early review of the former book Ernst Bloch predicted of the Bolsheviks that "Some of them will say that Marx had not placed Hegel on his feet so that Lukács can put Marx back on his head."[8] Both the Bolsheviks who did so and Lukács himself were in different ways victims of this same misleading metaphor and with it of a philosophical inheritance which prevented both parties from understanding the significance of Marx's theses on Feuerbach.

This failure is peculiarly evident in two aspects of the history of moral philosophy within Marxism. One is the degree to which, when Marxists have been forced into moral debate, they have had to fall back upon the resources already provided by the moral philosophy of civil society, so that the contending parties merely repeat what had been already said earlier and better by the protagonists of that moral philosophy. So Kautsky in one way and Trotsky in another repeated theses of Benthamite utilitarianism, while theorists as different as Bernstein and Guevara echoed Kant. But even more significant is a second aspect of Marxist moral thinking.

From Marx and Engels onwards Marxists have generally supposed that an historical and sociological understanding of moral concepts and precepts as articulated within practices was incompatible with an appeal to objective standards of goodness, rightness and virtue, standards independent of the interests and attitudes of those engaged in such practices. And Marxists of course have not been alone in so supposing. But here once again there is a false antithesis. What the objectivity of moral and other evaluative standards amounts to is to be understood only from within the context of and in terms of the structure of certain types of historically developed practice, in which the initial interests of those engaged in such practices are transformed through their activities into an interest in conforming to the standards of excellence required by those practices, so that the goods internal to them may be achieved. These are types of practice socially marginalized by the self-aggrandizing and self-protective attitudes and activities characteristic of developing capitalism, types of practice alien to the standpoint of civil society. But they are the types of practice within which moral thinking is put to the relevant practical tests and achieves objectivity. It is only in such contexts that the question of "whether objective truth can be attributed to human thinking" can be answered in respect of moral thought, and this question is not one "of theory, but is a practical question" (the second thesis), answered by members of fishing crews and farming cooperatives and string quartets, just as by eighteenth century handloom weavers and their medieval and ancient predecessors, only through and by reference to forms of practice which precede the theory that they so badly need. Only in and through such practices can the standpoint of civil society be transcended.

We still therefore need to take serious account of the insights of the theses on Feuerbach, if we are to be able to take a road forward which Marx himself did not take. I have noted how Marx was unable to develop his own insights in the theses. But the important thing now about the errors that resulted is not so much that they were Marx's errors, as that for so many of us they were *our* errors and the defeat of Marxism has been *our* defeat. But Marxism was not defeated, and we were not defeated, by the protagonists of the standpoint of civil society, who now mistakenly congratulate themselves on the collapse of Communist rule in so many states. Marxism was self-defeated and we too, Marxists and ex-Marxists and post-Marxists of various kinds, were the agents of our own defeats, in key part through our inability to learn in time some of the lessons of the theses on Feuerbach. The point is, however, first to understand this and then to start out all over again.

THIRTEEN

Politics, Philosophy and the Common Good

I am grateful to the editors of *Studi Perugini* for their invitation to contribute an introductory essay to this issue. But how should I respond? I have already elsewhere recounted how I found my way into the themes that have preoccupied me.[1] And to summarize over again theses and arguments from my books would be less than helpful. Philosophy in abbreviated summary is no longer philosophy. How then to proceed? What may be useful is to confront some misunderstandings of my work, especially those that concern its political implications. Hilary Putnam, for example, has asserted that my point of view is one which, by its attitude to alternative ways of life, tends to immunize institutionalized oppression from criticism.[2] And several commentators have mistakenly assimilated my views to those of contempo-

First published in English as "Politics, Philosophy and the Common Good," *The MacIntyre Reader*, ed. Kelvin Knight, 235–52 (Notre Dame, IN: University of Notre Dame Press, 1998). Originally published in Italian translation as "Politica, filosofia e bene comune," *Studi Perugini* 3 (1997), 9–30.

rary communitarianism. One principal aim of this present paper is therefore to dispel such misunderstandings. (For an accurate and perceptive discussion of my political views see Kelvin Knight, 'Revolutionary Aristotelianism'.) But I can only explain the full extent of my differences from communitarianism in the context of a diagnosis of the defects of the dominant politics of contemporary society. To this larger task I therefore turn first.

1. PHILOSOPHY AND THE EXCLUSIONS OF CONTEMPORARY POLITICS

How should the relationship of philosophy to politics and politics to philosophy be understood? Every complex form of social life embodies some answer to this question and the societies of advanced Western modernity are no exception. A central feature of those societies is the exceptional degree of compartmentalization imposed by their structures, so that the norms governing activities in any one area are specific to that area. As individuals move between home, school, workplace, the activities of leisure, the arenas of politics, bureaucratized encounters with government, and church or synagogue or mosque, they find themselves cast in different roles and required to express different and even sometimes incompatible attitudes. And, to the degree that one is at home in this kind of society, one will have to have acquired, not only the skills necessary for effectiveness in each of one's roles in each area, but an ability to move between areas and to adapt to the norms of different contexts. Someone who, for example, insists upon observing the same ethics of truthful disclosure in every sphere of life, holding her or himself and others accountable for their deceptions in the same way, whether it is a matter of conversation within the family, the pledges of politicians, the presentation of products by advertisers in the marketplace, or the information given to patients by physicians, will acquire a reputation not for integrity, but for social ineptitude. A compartmentalized society imposes a fragmented ethics.[3]

Unsurprisingly contemporary philosophical enquiry and contemporary politics both exhibit the marks of this compartmentalization. Each has become a specialized and professionalized area of activity, with its own specific idioms and genres, its own forms of apprenticeship, its own methods of protecting itself from anything that would put the form of its activities seriously in question. Consider how much that philosophers now write is addressed exclusively to other philosophers through the medium of the professional journal or how the teaching of philosophy has increasingly become the teaching of that philosophy that will enable those who receive it to become, if they wish, professional academic philosophers. Philosophical activity involves reflection upon concepts, theses and arguments that are central to the activities, attitudes, choices and conflicts of everyday life. But the outcome of such philosophical reflection cannot any longer play a significant part in reconstituting those activities and attitudes, in directing those choices or resolving those conflicts, just because of the barriers imposed by compartmentalization.

Just as philosophy has thereby been rendered unpolitical, so politics has been rendered unphilosophical. The rhetoric of political life sometimes suggests otherwise, but there is a large gap between that rhetoric and the types of argument that are practically effective in contemporary politics. The modern state is a large, complex and often ramshackle set of interlocking institutions, combining none too coherently the ethos of a public utility company with inflated claims to embody ideals of liberty and justice. Politics is the sphere in which the relationship of the state's subjects to the various facets of the state's activity is organized, so that the activities of those subjects do not in any fundamental way disrupt or subvert that relationship. Voters in liberal democracies are in some sense free to vote for whom and what they choose, but their votes will not be effective unless they are cast for one of those alternatives defined for them by the political elites. Conventional politics sets limits to practical possibility, limits that are characteristically presupposed by its modes of discourse, rather than explicitly articulated. It is therefore important in and to the political sphere that there should not occur extended argumentative debate of a kind that would make issues about these limits explicit and therefore matter for further debate. And one means of achieving this is to proscribe appeals to first principles. So in practice those who appeal in the course of political discussion to the will of God or the natural law or the greatest happiness of the greatest number or the categorical imperative will be heard only as adding rhetorical embellishments to their presentation, not as engaging in serious argument. When on occasion some set of issues from outside politics, as it is now normally understood, issues such as those raised in the United States by the civil rights movement, or by controversies over abortion, seems to make some reference to first principles inescapable, the task of the professionals of political life is to contain and domesticate those issues, so that any political appeal *to* first principles does not become a philosophical debate *about* first principles. And their success in achieving this exemplifies the degree to which politics has been successfully insulated from philosophy and philosophy from politics.

Politically the societies of advanced Western modernity are oligarchies disguised as liberal democracies. The large majority of those who inhabit them are excluded from membership in the elites that determine the range of alternatives between which voters are permitted to choose. And the most fundamental issues are excluded from that range of alternatives. An example of just such an issue is that presented by the threat of the imminent disappearance of the family or household farm and with it of a way of life the history of which has been integral to the history of the virtues from ancient times onwards. Good farming has required for its sustenance, and has in turn sustained, virtues that are central to all human life, and not just to farming.

Of course farming households have often failed to exhibit those virtues and farming societies have sometimes been mean-spirited and oppressive. But good farming has itself provided the standards by which bad farming and bad farmers are to be judged, through the way in which it has at its best fostered virtues of independence, virtues of cooperation in contributing to larger human enterprises and virtues of regard for the relationship of human beings to land that has been entrusted to their care. The destruction of the way of life of the household farm has therefore great significance for all of us and powerful statements of that significance—from Andrew Lytle to Wendell Berry—have not been lacking. Yet these statements have had no effective political impact, and this not because they have been heard within the political arena and then rejected. They have gone politically unheard. Why so?

There are of course issues that do receive recurrent attention within the political arena that are relevant to this final transformation of family farming into multinational agribusiness: taxes, tariffs, farm subsidies, interest rates, bankruptcy laws. What is remarkable is that, although under each of these headings multifarious issues are decided by bureaucrats, or debated by legislators, or lumped together with others in party programs for parliamentary elections, there has been nowhere in the entire political process where the members of modern political societies have been invited to confront systematically the question: 'What do we take the significance of this transformation to be and should we or should we not acquiesce in this loss of a whole way of life?' Questions about the value of ways of life, let alone the provision of practically effective answers to such questions, are excluded from the arenas of political debate and decision-making, even though answers to them are delivered by default, since among the effects of modern governmental decisions is their impact upon different ways of life, an impact that promotes some—the way of life of the fashionably hedonistic consumer, for example—and undermines others.

So far I have drawn attention to three salient features of the politics of the modern state: the unphilosophical nature of that politics and with it the exclusion from politics of philosophical questions concerning politics; the closely related exclusion from political debate and decision-making of substantive issues concerning ways of life; and the fact that the activities of government are such that they are not in their effects neutral between ways of life, but undermine some and promote others. To these three features it is important to add a fourth. Political debate, whether in electoral campaigns, in legislatures or in governmental bureaucracies is rarely systematic or in any depth. It is not directed by canons of enquiry or committed to following through the implications of arguments. It is instead sporadic, apt to be more responsive to immediate concerns than to the longer term, carried through by those who are both swayed by and themselves make use of rhetorical modes of self-presentation, and open to the solicitations of the rich and the powerful. Political debate, that is, is generally and characteristically the antithesis of serious intellectual enquiry.

This fourth salient feature of contemporary politics marks the frustration of the political hopes of the Enlightenment and especially of Kant. Enlightenment, on Kant's view, consists in thinking for oneself and not in thinking as directed by the authority of some other. To achieve independence in one's thinking is to make what Kant called public use of one's reasoning, that use which the scholar makes before the whole reading public ('An Answer to the Question: What is Enlightenment?'). Foucault pointed out that the verb that Kant uses here—*räsonieren*—is characteristically used by him to refer to reasoning that pursues the goals internal to reasoning: truth, theoretical and practical adequacy, and the like. Those to whom such reasoning is presented are invited to evaluate it not from the standpoint of this or that interest or purpose, but from the impersonal standpoint of reason as such. And it was Kant's hope that the modes of thought embodied in scholarly enquiry, publication and debate, modes which exemplified just such invitations to rational evaluation, would spread from the arts and sciences to religion and thereafter to the framing of legislation and the activities of government. But this of course is not what has happened.

What we have instead in contemporary society are on the one hand a set of small-scale academic publics—scientific, historical, literary—within which the rational discourse of enquiry is carried on more or less in accordance with Kant's ideals, publics however whose discourse has no practical effect on the conduct of political life, and on the other those areas of public life in which politically effective decisions are taken and policies implemented, areas from whose discourse for the most part systematic, rational enquiry is excluded, and in which decisions and policies emerge from a strange *mélange* of arguments, debating points and the influence of money and other forms of established power. What is lacking in modern political societies is any type of institutional arena in which plain persons—neither engaged in academic pursuits nor professionals of the political life—are able to engage together in systematic reasoned debate, designed to arrive at a rationally well-founded common mind on how to answer questions about the relationship of politics to the claims of rival and alternative ways of life, each with its own conception of the virtues and of the common good. And it is perhaps in terms of the idiom of the common good that these issues raised by contemporary politics are best formulated.

For, if this account of contemporary politics is in outline correct, then we now inhabit a social order whose institutional heterogeneity and diversity of interests is such that no place is left any longer for a politics of the common good. What we have instead is a politics from whose agendas enquiry concerning the nature of that politics has been excluded, a politics thereby protected from perceptions of its own exclusions and limitations. Enquiry into the nature of the common good of political society has become therefore crucial for understanding contemporary politics. For until we know how to think about the common good, we will not know how to evaluate the significance of those exclusions and limitations.

2. RIVAL CONCEPTIONS OF THE COMMON GOOD

The notion of the common good has been used in so many different ways and for so many different purposes that some preliminary considerations are in order. First, we may justifiably speak of a common good in characterizing the ends of a variety of very different types of human association. The members of a family, the members of a fishing crew and the members of an investment club, the students, teachers and administrators of a school and the scientists at work in a laboratory all share aims in such a way that a common good can be identified as the end of their shared activities. Secondly, among these there are cases in which the common good of an association is no more than the summing of the goods pursued by individuals as members of that association, just because the association itself is no more than an instrument employed by those individuals to achieve their individual ends. So it is, for example, with an investment club, by means of which individuals are able to avail themselves of investment opportunities requiring capital sums larger than any one of them possesses. Participation in and support for such associations is therefore rational only so long as and insofar as it provides a more efficient method of achieving their individual ends than would alternative types of activity open to them.

There are also however kinds of association such that the good of the association cannot be constructed out of what were the goods of its individual members, antecedently to and independently of their membership in it. In these cases the good of the whole cannot be arrived at by summing the goods of the parts. Such are those goods not only achieved by means of cooperative activity and shared understanding of their significance, but in key part constituted by cooperative activity and shared understanding of their significance, goods such as the excellence in cooperative activity achieved by fishing crews and by string quartets, by farming households and by teams of research scientists. Excellence in activity is of course often a means to goods other than and beyond that excellence, goods of types as various as the production of food and the making of reputations. But it is central to our understanding of a wide range of practices that excellence in the relevant kinds of activity is recognized as among the goods internal to those practices.

The achievement of excellence in activity characteristically requires the acquisition of skills, but without virtues skills lack the direction that their exercise requires, if excellence is to be achieved. So it is characteristic of such practices that engaging in them provides a practical education into the virtues. And for individuals who are so educated or are in the course of being so educated two questions arise inescapably, questions that may never be explicitly formulated, but which nonetheless receive answers in the way in which individuals live out their lives. For each individual the question arises: what place should the goods of each of the practices in which I am engaged have in my life? The goods of our productive activities in the workplace, the goods of ongoing family life, the goods of musical or athletic or scientific activity, what place should each have in my life, if my life as a whole is to be excellent? Yet any individual who attempts to answer this question pertinaciously must soon discover that it is not a question that she or he can ask and answer by her or himself and for her or himself, apart from those others together with whom she or he is engaged in the activities of practices. So the questions have to be posed: what place should the goods of each of the practices in which *we* are engaged have in *our* common life? What is the best way of life for *our* community?

These questions can only be answered by elaborating a conception of the common good of a kind of community in which each individual's achievement of her or his own good is inseparable both from achieving the shared goods of practices and from contributing to the common good of the community as a whole. According to this conception of the common good the identification of my good, of how it is best for me to direct my life, is inseparable from the identification of the common good of the community, of how it is best for that community to direct its life. Such a form of community is by its nature political, that is to say, it is constituted by a type of practice through which other types of practice are ordered, so that individuals may direct themselves towards what is best for them and for the community.

It is important to observe that, although this type of political society—let us recognize that in it which is Aristotelian by calling it a *polis*—does indeed require a high degree of shared culture by those who participate in it, it is not itself constituted by that shared culture and is very different from those political societies whose essential bonds are the bonds of a shared cultural tradition. A polis is at least as different from the political society of a *Volk* as either is from that of a liberal democracy. A *polis* is indeed impossible, unless its citizens share at least one language—they may well share more than one—and unless they also share modes of deliberation, formal and informal, and a large degree of common understanding of practices and institutions. And such a common understanding is generally derived from some particular inherited cultural tradition. But these requirements have to serve the ends of a society in which individuals are always able to put in question through communal deliberation what has hitherto by custom and tradition been taken for granted both about their own good and the good of the community. A *polis* is always, potentially or actually, a society of rational enquiry, of self-scrutiny. The bonds of a *Volk* by contrast are prerational and nonrational. The philosophers of the *Volk* are Herder and Heidegger, not Aristotle.

Enough has now been said for it to be possible to sketch the part that different conceptions of the common good play in different types of political justification. Political justifications are those arguments advanced to show why we, as members of some particular political society, should or should not accept as having legitimate authority over us the commands uttered by someone claiming executive authority over or in that society or the laws uttered by someone or some body claiming legislative authority over or in that society. Consider now the part played by different conceptions of the common good in different types of political justification.

There is, for example, the claim that political authority is justified insofar as it provides a secure social order within which individuals may pursue their own particular ends, whatever they are. Individuals need to cooperate, both in order to pursue their own particular ends effectively and in order to sustain the security of the social order. But all such cooperation is a means to their individual ends. The conception of the common good invoked in this type of justification of political authority is such that the common good is arrived at by summing individual goods. It is a conception at once individualist and minimalist. And justifications which employ it have this important political characteristic: that to the extent that they are believed in a political society, that political society is endangered by them, and this for two reasons.

First, if this is the justification for the acceptance of political authority, then rational individuals will attempt to share fully in the benefits provided by political authority, while making as small a contribution as possible to its costs. It will be rational to be a 'free rider', so long as one can avoid whatever penalties are imposed by political authority for free riding. Secondly, it will correspondingly be contrary to rationality, thus understood, to accept an undue share of the costs of sustaining political authority. But no political authority can be sustained over any extended period of time, unless some of those subject to it are prepared to pay an undue share of those costs and this in the most striking way, since the sustaining of political authority requires that some of those subject to it should be prepared, if necessary, to die for the sake of the security of the political and social order: soldiers, police officers, firefighters.

It follows that no political society can have a reasonable expectation of surviving, let alone flourishing, unless a significant proportion of its members are unconvinced that the only justification for accepting and upholding political society and political authority is individualist and minimalist. Only if they believe that there is some other and stronger type of connection between their own ends and purposes and the flourishing of their political society do they have good reason to be willing, if necessary, to die for the sake of that flourishing. And indeed, only if they believe that there is just such another and stronger type of connection, do they have sufficient reason to resist the temptation to act as 'free riders' on occasions in which they could do so without penalty.

An individualist and minimalist conception of the common good is then too weak to provide adequate justification for the kind of allegiance that a political society must have from its members, if it is to flourish. And any political society whose members hold themselves and one another to account in respect of the rational justification of their actions, including their collective political decision-making, will have to be one in which rational argument can sustain the claim that their practices and institutions exhibit a connection between the goods of individuals and the common good sufficient to afford a justification for their political allegiance. But we must not picture this connection between individual goods and the common good as something that might exist apart from and independently of the rational activity of the members of that society in enquiring and arguing about the nature of their goods. For it is a connection constituted by practically rational activity. Practical rationality is a property of individuals-in-their-social-relationships rather than of individuals-as-such. To be practically rational I must learn what my good is in different types of situation and I can only achieve that through interaction with others in which I learn from those others and they from me. Our primary shared and common good is found in that activity of communal learning through which we together become able to order goods, both in our individual lives and in the political society. Such practical learning is a kind of learning that takes place in and through activity, and in and through reflection upon that activity, in the course of both communal and individual deliberation.

When I speak of practical learning and practical enquiry, I refer to that type of learning and enquiry that takes place in the course of asking and answering practical deliberative questions about some subject matter, whenever there is a serious attempt to answer those questions as adequately as possible and to diagnose and to remedy whatever has been defective in one's past answers. Practical learning and enquiry are therefore features of various kinds of activity. It is found among farmers and fishing crews, in the work of households and in the practice of crafts. What is learned does not have to be formulated explicitly in words, although it may be so formulated. But it cannot take place without some significant transformation of activity. And where deliberation is integral to some type of activity, as it is to any politics of the common good, practical enquiry will be embodied in that type of reflective deliberation to which rational participants in such a politics are committed. Indeed politics will be that practical activity which affords the best opportunity for the exercise of our rational powers, an opportunity afforded only by political societies to whose decision-making widely shared rational deliberation is central, societies which extend practical rationality from the farm and the fishing fleet, the household and the craft workplace, to its political assemblies. It follows that no *Volk* can be such a society. It also follows that, if the political characteristics of advanced Western modernity are as I suggested earlier, and if, as I am now suggesting, claims to political allegiance can be justified only where there is the common good of communal political learning, then modern states cannot advance any justifiable claim to the allegiance of their members, and this because they are the political expression of societies of deformed and fragmented practical rationality, in which politics, far from being an area of activity in and through which other activities are rationally ordered, is itself one more compartmentalized sphere from which there has been excluded the possibility of asking those questions that most need to be asked.

3. LIBERALISM AND COMMUNITARIANISM

Political philosophy in our culture is an academic and not a political activity. There are of course important parallels between the discussions in each sphere. Issues of rights, of utility, of legitimate authority and the like are central to both and in both the same principles are on occasion invoked and attacked. Yet it is only rarely, due to some quite unusual conjunction of circumstances, that something said in political philosophy has any effect on something done in politics. And even when it appears that this has happened, it is always wise to ask whether whatever it was that was done in politics would not have been done anyway, no matter what had been said in political philosophy.

It is therefore one thing to criticize liberalism as a philosophical theory and quite another thing to engage in conflict with contemporary liberal politics. It is true that contemporary liberal politics owes a good deal to past theorizing. For the formative periods of liberalism in the eighteenth and nineteenth centuries were periods in which the relationships of philosophy and politics were other than and closer than they are now. But the actualities of contemporary liberal politics—and I use the word 'liberal' inclusively here, so that it covers the whole spectrum of liberalisms from that of American self-styled conservatives to that of European self-styled social democrats—are not only in crucial respects different from the politics hoped for by the great prophetic theorists of eighteenth- and nineteenth-century liberalism but also at odds with the guiding principles of contemporary liberal theory. It is therefore not at all impossible to elaborate positions that are plainly incompatible with at least some versions of liberal theory, but nonetheless quite at home in the realities of contemporary liberal politics. Just this, I want to suggest, is the case with the theses of the movement that is identified by the name 'communitarianism'.

The principal exponents of communitarianism have defined their own positions by contrast with some central theses advanced by liberal theorists. Where liberal theorists have emphasized rights, communitarians have stressed relationships. Where liberal theorists have appealed to what they take to be universal and impersonal principles, communitarians have argued for the importance of particular ties to particular groups and individuals. And where liberal theorists have characteristically held that it is for each individual to arrive at her or his own conception of her or his good, communitarians have been anxious both to establish the existence of irreducibly social goods and to argue that a failure to achieve such goods will result in a defective social order.

It is easy to frame each of these two positions so that it not only contrasts with, but is set in sharp opposition to the other. And liberal critics of communitarianism have usually presented matters in this way. But there are certainly some versions of liberal theory and some formulations of communitarian positions which are such that the two are not only not in opposition to each other, but neatly complement one another. Communitarianism from this latter point of view is a diagnosis of certain weaknesses in liberalism, not a rejection of it. And consequently it is unsurprising that just as liberal theorists disagree among themselves about their own positions, so too they disagree about the implications of communitarianism. Yet the outcome of these debates at the level of theory may not be of great significance. For at the level of contemporary political actuality the key issues have already been settled. What is it about contemporary politics that makes this so?

Modern states retain the allegiance of those heterogeneous, overlapping and sometimes competing social groups to which their subjects belong by negotiating temporary settlements with those groups, whenever failure to achieve settlement with them would exact too high a price for the state to pay. But, in so doing, those engaged in government and in politics have to adopt a range of varying and sometimes incompatible stances, appealing to different and sometimes incompatible values, here giving market considerations an overriding value, there denying them this weight, here accepting governmental responsibility for this or that aspect of social life, there disowning it, here expressing respect for custom and tradition, there flouting them in the name of modernization. Modern government, that is to say, needs and has a ragbag of assorted values, from which it can select in an *ad hoc* way what will serve its purposes in this or that particular situation with this or that particular group. So it shows different faces and speaks with different and often enough incompatible voices in different types of situation. It is therefore no accident that contemporary politics is a politics of recurrently broken promises or that successful contemporary politicians are so often open to charges of flagrant inconsistency. A willingness to break promises and to shift positions has become, not a liability, but one aspect of what in the social life of modernity is accounted the chief of the virtues, adaptability.

The values defended by liberalism are of course among those indispensable to the governments of advanced modernity. Even those who flout them must pay lip service to them. But the values of communitarianism are also to be found in the state's ragbag of values and they were there long before the name 'communitarianism' was given to them. So alongside the commitments of modern governments to universal principles that safeguard rights and confer liberties, there are the commitments of the same governments to uphold family ties and the solidarities of a variety of groups. And alongside the commitments of modern governments to extending the scope of market economies, there are a variety of commitments to sustain institutions whose workings are inimical to market relationships. What happens when in some particular situation one set of commitments conflicts with another? The answer is that there is no higher-order set of principles to which appeal can be made to resolve such conflicts. There are instead outcomes determined by shifting coalitions of interest and power within the limits set by and for those elites who determine—although not at all at will—the range of choices confronting governments.

So in the politics of modern government communitarian values coexist, sometimes uneasily, sometimes quite happily, with liberal values and it is only at those extremes of the political spectrum at which consistent adherence to principle entails political impotence that allegiance to liberalism is allowed to entail the rejection of communitarianism or vice versa. A communitarian politics is at home within the contemporary institutional framework imposed by the state and the market and, just because it is thus at home, its conception of the common good is limited by that framework. Communitarians are apt to place great emphasis on their rejection of any merely individualist conception of the common good. But the communitarian conception of the common good is not at all that of a kind of community of political learning and enquiry participation in which it is necessary for individuals to discover what their individual and common goods are. Indeed in every statement by the protagonists of communitarianism that I have read the precise nature of the communitarian view of the relationship between the community, the common good and individual goods remains elusive. And that it should remain elusive is perhaps a condition of communitarians accommodating themselves, as they have in some cases so notably done, to the realities of contemporary politics.

4. THE POLITICS OF LOCAL COMMUNITY

My arguments so far have resulted largely, if not entirely in negative conclusions. How are we to move beyond these? Any more adequate account of political community and authority will have to begin from a somewhat fuller account of political justification.

Political reflection is a relative latecomer on the human scene. And, when it does emerge, it must inevitably at first be local reflection, reflection upon local political structures, as these have developed through some particular social and cultural tradition, and moreover reflection guided by and limited by the conceptual and argumentative resources of that same tradition. As such reflection develops into philosophy, it continues debates and enquiries that are framed in terms that are in crucial ways specific to its own tradition—consider the differences between Confucian political reflection, the discussions in the *Mahabharata* and the political philosophies of Plato and Aristotle—but the questions that are thus framed in local terms are understood to have universal import and the answers supplied to those questions in local terms give expression to universal claims.

It could not be otherwise. For there is no culture whose inhabitants treat their own norms and their own conceptions of the human good as having merely local significance and local authority. Anthropologists, historians and philosophers may sometimes be relativists, but those about whom they write never are. So that when philosophers come to evaluate those norms and those conceptions, they confront the task of evaluating them as norms for which it is claimed that it would be right and best for all human beings to live by them and as adequate conceptions of the human good, and not of the Greek, or the Indian, or the Chinese good. So local philosophies, each with its own specific conceptual and argumentative resources, its own conception of reason, must pose such questions as: What are *the* norms appropriate for human beings as such? What is the human good? What is reason as such? And these turn out to be political as well as philosophical questions.

For every political and social order embodies and gives expression to an ordering of different human goods and therefore also embodies and gives expression to some particular conception of the human good. Hence when philosophers enquire about goods and the good, and most of all when they enquire about the common good of political society, and about what kind of political society it is in which human beings can best come to an understanding of their good, they necessarily put to the question the political order of their own society.

Correspondingly, when the representatives of the political order claim authority for their legislative, executive and judicial acts, they can now justify their claims only by showing that the exercise of their political authority accords with norms that serve the common good and the human good. There are indeed types of political justification that antedate the rise of philosophy, but the rise of philosophy transforms the nature and standards of political justification, by opening up questions to which political authority must either respond or discredit itself. Among these questions one is central: under what conditions are individuals able to learn about their individual and common goods, so that questions about the justification of political authority can be asked and answered through rational enquiry and debate? What form of social and political life makes this possible?

It will have three sets of characteristics. First, it will be a type of community whose members generally and characteristically recognize that obedience to those standards that Aquinas identified as the precepts of the natural law is necessary, if they are to learn from and with each other what their individual and common goods are.[4] In such a society the authority of positive law, promulgated by whatever means the community adopts, will derive from its conformity to the precepts of the natural law and from the acknowledgment of that conformity by plain persons. And plain persons will thereby exhibit their understanding that truthfulness, respect for, patience with and care for the needs of others, and the faithful keeping of promises, are required of us, just because without relationships governed by these norms they will not be able to learn what they most need to learn. But strict observance of these norms of a kind that involves a practical understanding of their point and purpose, rather than a mere fetishism of rules, requires the cultivation and exercise of the virtues of prudence, temperateness, courage and justice. So the life of such a society will embody to some significant extent a shared practical understanding of the relationships between goods, rules and virtues, an understanding that may or may not be articulated at the level of theory, but that will be embodied in and presupposed by the way in which immediate practical questions receive answers in actions.

This type of shared understanding is one familiar to most of us in a variety of local social contexts. We rely on it in many of the everyday enterprises of family and household life, in schools, in neighborhoods, in parishes, on farms, in fishing crews and in other workplaces, and, that is to say, in all those practices and projects in which immediate decision-making has to presuppose rationally justifiable answers to such questions as 'How does my good relate to the good of others engaged in this enterprise?' and 'How does the good to be achieved through this enterprise relate to the other goods of my and their lives?' Where that understanding is absent, is indeed excluded, is in the activities that have come to be labeled 'politics' in the contemporary meaning of that term. So paradoxically the life of so-called politics is now one from which the possibility of rational political justification is excluded, while in many local contexts that possibility remains open. Reflection on why this is so directs our attention to a second set of characteristics that a society must possess, if it is to be one in which individuals are able through practice to learn about their individual and common goods.

Such societies must be small-scale and, so far as possible, as self-sufficient as they need to be to protect themselves from the destructive incursions of the state and the wider market economy. They need to be small-scale, so that, whenever necessary, those who hold political office can be put to the question by the citizens and the citizens put to the question by those who hold political office in the course of extended deliberative debate in which there is widespread participation and from which no one from whom something might be learned is excluded – that is, from which no one is excluded. The aim of this deliberative participation is to arrive at a common mind and the formal constitutional procedures of decision-making will be designed to serve this end. Once again I am not describing something alien to everyday experience. This is a kind of deliberative participation familiar in many local enterprises through which local community is realized. What is less familiar is the claim that these local arenas are now the only places where political community can be constructed, a political community very much at odds with the politics of the nation-state.

Two aspects of the difference between them should be stressed. First, the politics of small-scale local community politics cannot be a separate compartmentalized, specialized area of activity, as it is for the politics of advanced modernity. More generally, the forms of compartmentalization characteristic of advanced modernity are inimical to the flourishing of local community. The activities of local communities will indeed be differentiated into different spheres, those of the family, of the workplace and of the parish, for example. But the relationship between the goods of each set of activities is such that in each much the same virtues are required and in each the same vices are all too apt to be disclosed, so that an individual is not fragmented into her or his separate roles, but is able to succeed or fail in ordering the goods of her or his life into a unified whole and to be judged by others in respect of that success or failure. One and the same set of individuals and groups will encounter each other in the context of a number of very different types of activity, moving between one sphere and another, so that individuals cannot avoid being judged for what they are. And in politics especially individuals show themselves as deserving the confidence of others as holders of political office by the integrity of their own pursuit of both their own good and the common good in a variety of spheres, and especially those of the home and the workplace, as well as in their specifically political abilities. Where adaptability is now the key virtue of the dominant and conventional forms of politics, integrity is the key virtue of the politics of local community.

Once again the difference from the politics of the modern state is striking. For this latter is a politics in which the techniques of self-presentation, the techniques of advertisement in the market place, are characteristically used to project images behind which candidates for public office can conceal aspects of their reality. The candidate has become to some degree a fictional construction, a figure constructed by public relations experts, speech-writers, manipulators of opinion and cosmetic artists, very much as a film star is or used to be. The problem here is not only that of the gap between image and reality. It is that the ambitious candidate tends all too often to become whatever an effective image requires her or him to become.

We have then identified two sets of characteristics that must be possessed by any society in which there is a possibility of rational political justification, and with it of rational politics: first, it must have a large degree of shared understanding of goods, virtues, and rules and, secondly, it must be a relatively small-scale society whose relationships are not deformed by compartmentalization. But there is also a third set of conditions to be satisfied. The deliberative and other social relationships of such a society are systematically violated by some of the most notable effects of large-scale so-called free market economies.[5] Such economies are misnamed 'free markets'. They in fact ruthlessly impose market conditions that forcibly deprive many workers of productive work, that condemn parts of the labor force in metropolitan countries and whole societies in less developed areas to irremediable economic deprivation, that enlarge inequalities and divisions of wealth and income, so organizing societies into competing and antagonistic interests. And under such conditions inequality of wealth ensures inequality in access to the sources of both economic and political power.

Genuinely free markets are always local and small-scale markets in whose exchanges producers can choose to participate or not. And societies with genuinely free markets will be societies of small producers—the family farm is very much at home in such societies—in which no one is denied the possibility of the kind of productive work without which they cannot take their place in those relationships through which the common good is realized. Such societies can never of course aspire to achieve the levels of economic and technological development of advanced modernity. But from the standpoint of those who give their allegiance to such societies the price to be paid for limitless development would involve a renunciation of their common good. Indeed the conception of the common good presupposed by large-scale so-called free market economies is necessarily an individualist one, although the 'individuals' are sometimes corporate entities. So that the conflict between the kind of local community that I have been characterizing and the international and national economic order is at the level of practice, as well as that of theory, a conflict between rival conceptions of the common good.

5. A RESPONSE TO SOME MISUNDERSTANDINGS AND OBJECTIONS

We are now in a position to understand better what it is that makes some types of social relationship oppressive. Some measure of inequality—it must not be too large—is not necessarily oppressive. And that some people rather than others should exercise power through political office is not necessarily a mark of oppression. What is always oppressive is any form of social relationship that denies to those who participate in it the possibility of the kind of learning from each other about the nature of their common good that can issue in socially transformative action. It is this that makes relationships between slave-owners and slaves oppressive and it is no accident that defenders of slavery from Aristotle to the apologists for slavery in the American South have felt compelled to assert what is plainly false, that their slaves do not possess the capacity for rational learning. And so it is too with certain other forms of oppression. The justification of the oppression of women has characteristically represented them as inferior to men in rationality. The justification of European imperialist annexations of territory has characteristically represented its native inhabitants as lacking the rational powers to develop it.

Although I have not drawn attention to it, the argument that has led us to this point is one that has drawn systematically on the conceptual and argumentative resources of a Thomistic Aristotelianism. But while it is important to notice this, it is also important to notice how much of this account of political community and political justification is at odds with Aristotle himself, and not only because it rejects his exclusions of women and slaves from citizenship. For Aristotle believed falsely that the life of productive labor of a farmer, for example, was incompatible with the political life.[6] And here he needs to be corrected, on the basis of his own principles, by drawing upon another tradition, one also stemming from the ancient world, that agrarianism, to which I referred earlier—its charter document is Xenophon's *Oeconomicus*—which has understood that the virtues of the farmer and of the fisherman are the same virtues needed in the politics of small-scale community. And some of the positions for which I have contended in this paper constitute just such a correction. But still more is needed by way of correction, and a philosopher who can provide much of what we need at this point is Marx, Marx himself, that is, rather than those Marxist systems that have been apt to obscure Marx. The questions that we now need to put of Marx's texts are significantly different from those most often posed in the past, whether by those participating in or by those opposed to the movements of social democracy and communism.[7] And they are questions—about the relationship, for example, of the ineradicable defects of the so-called free market economy to the nature of social activity— answers to which are badly needed by any form of Aristotelianism that aspires to contemporary relevance.

It is one of the marks of a community of enquiry and learning that, while it cannot but begin from the standpoint of its own cultural and social tradition, what it is able to learn, in order to sustain itself, includes knowing how to identify its own incoherences and errors and how then to draw upon the resources of other alien and rival traditions in order to correct these. And Hilary Putnam's misinterpretation of the political content of my positions can now be seen to derive not only from failing to understand what they imply about oppression, but also from resolutely ignoring what I have written about the relationships between different and rival traditions of enquiry. Nonetheless there is a much more plausible objection to my positions than Putnam's that is closely related to his.

I have asserted not only that the kind of small-scale political community that deserves our rational allegiance will characteristically have a high degree of shared cultural inheritance, but also that its life will have to be informed by a large measure of agreement not only on its common good, but on human goods in general. And not only liberals may find this alarming. For this may seem at first glance to be a kind of community that could have no room for individuals or groups who do not share the prevailing view of human goods. But this is a mistake, and not only because nothing that I have said precludes the existence within such a political society of individuals and groups who hold and are recognized to hold radically dissenting views on fundamental issues. What will be important to such a society, if it holds the kind of view of the human good and the common good that I have outlined, will be to ask what can be learned from such dissenters. It will therefore be crucial not only to tolerate dissent, but to enter into rational conversation with it and to cultivate as a political virtue not merely a passive tolerance, but an active and enquiring attitude towards radically dissenting views, a virtue notably absent from the dominant politics of the present. This is a lesson to be learned from our own Christian past. For among the worst failures of Christianity has been the inability of Christian societies, except on the rarest of occasions, to listen to and learn from the dissenting Jewish communities in their midst, an inability that has been both a consequence and a cause of the poisonous corruption of Christianity by anti-Semitism.

A very different accusation that has been and will be leveled against my political positions is that I am recommending a politics of Utopian ineffectiveness. It is impossible, so such critics will say, to change anything worth changing in the modern world except by engaging in the conventional politics of the nation-state, since too many of the problems of local communities are inextricably bound up with national and international issues. This objection moves from true premises to a false conclusion. Any worthwhile politics of local community will certainly have to concern itself in a variety of ways with the impact upon it of the nation-state and of national and international markets. It will from time to time need to secure resources from them, but only, so far as is possible, at a price acceptable by the local community. It will from time to time have to concern itself with the conflicts between and within nation-states, sometimes aligning itself with this or that contending party in order to assist in defeating such politically destructive forces as those of imperialism or National Socialism or Stalinist communism. But it will always also have to be wary and antagonistic in all its dealings with the politics of the state and the market economy, wherever possible challenging their protagonists to provide the kind of justification for their authority that they cannot in fact supply.

For the state and the market economy are so structured as to subvert and undermine the politics of local community. Between the one politics and the other there can only be continuing conflict.

To this it may be replied in turn that these responses to misinterpretations and objections are much too brief to be convincing to those who advance them. Indeed they are. In this paper all that I have attempted is to state rather than to defend a set of positions, and even so to state them only in outline. Those statements provide, I hope, a starting-point for further debate and enquiry and this in at least three areas. First, the diagnosis of the ills of contemporary politics needs to be extended and deepened. Secondly, it is important to note that the conflict between the politics of local community and the dominant modes of contemporary politics is not only a conflict between rival conceptions of the common good. It is also a conflict between alternative understandings of practical rationality and we need a better philosophical account of what is at stake in this conflict than has hitherto been provided. And finally it is important to examine instructive examples of the politics of local community in a variety of social and cultural contexts, so as to learn better what makes such politics effective or ineffective. There is both philosophical and political work to be done.

FOURTEEN

How Aristotelianism Can Become Revolutionary

If we listen to much contemporary discussion of ethics, we might conclude that ethics is principally or only a matter of arguments. Yet Aristotle says that rational argument in the areas of politics and morals will be ineffective with those who lack adequate character formation. And, if this is true, as it is, we need to know more about what adequate character formation would be for us here now. Aristotle also remarked that it is impossible to teach ethics and politics to the young, not only because their passions are insufficiently controlled, but also because they have not yet had sufficient practical experience. Yet we know that it is often true of adults too that they lack the kinds of experience from which they are able to learn. And so the question that I need to address is 'What is the relationship between character formation, being able to learn from experience, and being

"How Aristotelianism Can Become Revolutionary: Ethics, Resistance, and Utopia," *Philosophy of Management* 7, no. 1 (2008): 3–7.

open to political and moral argument?' Aquinas says that we only learn adequately when we are on the way to becoming self-teachers. So we can reformulate our question as: 'What kinds of experience might those be as a result of which we can become self-teachers about politics and morals? What kinds of experience might those be that enable us to achieve the character formation necessary for this?'

In *After Virtue* and elsewhere I focused attention on the relationships between practices and institutions, on the types of practice in which a kind of learning goes on that enables us to identify and pursue individual and common goods, and on the ways in which institutions that provide the social framework for practices may sustain and reinforce that learning, but may also undermine, subvert, and corrupt it. It is clear that in our present culture learning how to ask Aristotelian questions at the level of practice, let alone formulating Aristotelian answers, is difficult precisely because of the institutional structures within which most contemporary practices are carried on. Consider four characteristics of such structures. In our everyday lives we recurrently find our activities compartmentalised. Our lives are divided between different spheres, each with its own roles and its own set of norms. So in the course of a single day someone may move from their role in the home as, say, parent or sibling to their role in some particular kind of workplace, and later on to dealing in quite another capacity with some government or private agency, with, say lawyers or social workers, and later still return to their role in the home. As they enter each different sphere of activity they find themselves cast in some different role that requires that they satisfy some different set of expectations. So day after day our lives are compartmentalised into distinct areas to the norms of each of which we are expected to adapt, so that adaptability itself, social malleability, has become an important social characteristic. The problem, however, with this kind of compartmentalisation is that the point of such Aristotelian questions as 'What would it be for my life *as a whole* to be a flourishing life?' and 'What is my good *qua* human being and not just *qua* role-player in this or that type of situation?' disappears from view, so that such questions no longer get asked or become very difficult to ask.

The questions substituted for them are 'What do I feel about my life?' and 'Am I happy or unhappy?', questions about psychological states. And one consequence of this is that we now have in academic life a growing happiness industry. Recent research concerning happiness is problematic in more than one way. Some of its findings need unusually careful scrutiny. So, for example, the discovery that most Danes take themselves to be happy with their lives looks very different when it is discovered that most Danes have very low expectations. More importantly, what matters is not so much whether people do or do not feel happy about their lives as whether they do or do not have good reason to feel happy about them. And most importantly of all, this focus on psychological states once again gets in the way of asking the Aristotelian questions.

A second feature of our institutionalised cultural life that is inimical to asking Aristotelian questions concerns our habits of character formation from childhood onwards. Part of what we need to learn as children and adolescents is how to distinguish between those of our desires that are desires for genuine goods from those that are not. Failures in making this distinction both distort our character formation and lead to the frustration of those desires that are most important for our human flourishing. But we inhabit a social order in which a will to satisfy those desires that will enable the economy to work as effectively as possible has become central to our way of life, a way of life for which it is crucial that human beings desire what the economy needs them to desire. What the economy needs is that people should become responsive to its needs rather than to their own, and so it presents to them as overridingly desirable those goals of consumption and goals of ambition, pursuit of which will serve the economy's purposes. Desires to achieve these goals, when they become central to our lives and to our self-evaluations, prevent us from becoming self-critical about our desires and so prevent the asking of Aristotelian questions about character and desire.

A third example is closely related to the first two. It is not just that our lives are compartmentalised, and it is not just that we are continually seduced and solicited by desires that are corrupting, it is also that we live under conditions of gross inequality—inequality of money, inequality of power, inequality of regard—and it is an undeniable fact that even the most successful examples of growth in the present globalising economy generate further inequalities. Aristotle pointed out long ago that a rational polity is one that cannot tolerate too great inequalities, because where there are such, citizens cannot deliberate together rationally. They are too divided by their sectional interests, so that they lose sight of their common good. The poor are driven to defend themselves, in order to meet even their basic needs, and cannot learn how to rule. The rich are concerned with accumulation and self-advancement and cannot learn how to be ruled. Therefore a precondition for a rational polity is a radical reduction of inequality. And, so long as that is not achieved, the questions that Aristotle poses about what it is to have a rational polity remain questions for which it is difficult to get a hearing, let alone answer.

For a fourth example I go to Aquinas's development of Aristotle's thought. It is not just that our lives are compartmentalised, that we are continually having our desires solicited and distorted, and that we suffer from the effects of gross inequalities, it is also the case that the nature of the rule of law, something necessary for adequate human relationships in any society, in ours is systematically misunderstood and misrepresented. There was an important moment in our past history when the protagonists of the modern state first claimed for it an unqualified autonomy in respect of law, that is, claimed that the state should have the last word on what law is. By so doing, the modern state and its protagonists set themselves against Aristotle's and Aquinas's conception of natural justice and of the natural law as having an authority prior to and independent of the authority of any state. What we need to have learned from Aristotle and Aquinas is that it is only insofar as our social relationships are structured by the precepts of the natural law, only insofar as we acknowledge the authority of the natural law, that we are able to engage together in rational deliberation aimed at the common good. For only conformity to those precepts enables us to trust each other and to listen to each other as rational agents, rather than as agents of money or of power. It is those precepts that enable us to act on the basis of compelling arguments, rather than as a result of being threatened or seduced or charmed. But when the modern state was born, the rule of law was taken to be the rule of positive rather than natural law, and positive law was taken to be whatever the modern state takes it to be. And nowadays, since the modern state has become so well integrated with the market, it is in fact the state-and-the-market that is our lawmaker. So the formulation of Aristotelian questions about our present social order involves a critique not only of compartmentalisation, desire, and inequality, but also of law. What kind of critique?

No theoretical critique by itself will provide what we need, no matter how insightful, right-minded, or scholarly. And this for a reason that we have already noticed, that argument by itself, even sound argument, is ineffective upon those who have not had the kind of experiences from which they can learn. So what kind of experiences are needed in our social order, if we are to be able to learn what we need to learn about ethics and politics, in order to transform that order? Everything turns on the kind of projects in which plain people may get involved. Here I can give only one example, but there are of course many others. From time to time it becomes possible in some local community either to bring into being a new school or to remake some existing school, so that it can provide an education for the children of that community. When such an opportunity arises, it is sometimes possible for parents, teachers, and other interested members of the community to become involved and to participate in discussion and decision-making. By so doing they become unable to avoid such questions as 'What kind of school do we want to construct for our children?' and 'What do we want our children to learn?' This latter question, however, cannot be answered unless we also ask not only 'What do we take the goods of childhood to be?' and 'How through achieving the goods of childhood can our children be prepared to achieve later on the goods of adult life?' but also 'What are the virtues of teachers, children, and parents?'

All of these are recognisably Aristotelian questions, practical questions that will be well answered only if we answer them in the light of what we have learned from Aristotle and Aquinas, but also in the light of things that we now know, that Aristotle and Aquinas perhaps did not know, about how children have to be taught if their needs are to be met. One of the things that we now know is that children become unteachable if they are too hungry. So the question 'How do you make sure that the children in your school are not going to be too hungry?' becomes an educational question. We also know that children are generally unable to learn well in school unless they enjoy a stable family life. And therefore the question 'How can we produce effective schooling?' is also the question 'How can we provide the bases for an effective family life, by providing for the kind of stability in employment and the kind of income that will enable parents and teachers to bring up their and our children well?' We cannot therefore set ourselves to create an adequate school, let alone a good one, unless we also set ourselves to make and sustain a society in which jobs are not abolished in the name of growth, in which income is perennially uncertain, or in which both parents have to work so hard in order to achieve an adequate minimum income that they are unable to give the time that they need to their children. In other words, once you begin to map out what is involved in the project of bringing this kind of school into being, you will have to raise at the level of everyday practice a much wider range of political and moral questions about human goods.

When you do so—and we can observe this happening in many places in the world—and when you try to secure the resources that you need in order to educate children, you find almost immediately that you encounter the systematic resistance of the representatives of the larger social and economic structures. The word 'resistance' in my title may have been taken to refer to the resistance that, for example, trade unions offer to attacks on their members' wages and working conditions. And that resistance is certainly not irrelevant to my thesis. But the resistance with which I am primarily concerned is the resistance of the established order, of the representatives of the established patterns of power, to any attempt to ask and answer Aristotelian questions at the level of practice. As you and I encounter the resistance elicited by any systematic attempt to achieve central human goods, we learn how to define what we are politically. It is this kind of project and this kind of encounter that provide the experience and the character formation that enable us to learn, to learn at the level of everyday practice, what our good consists in, in concrete and particular terms. We also become able to learn why, when we try to achieve the human good, there is going to be entrenched resistance to it.

What you will be told by those who represent established power is that the kind of institutions that you are trying to create and sustain are simply not possible, that you are unrealistic, a Utopian. And it is important to respond by saying 'Yes, that is exactly what we are'. This Utopianism of those who force Aristotelian questions upon the social order is a Utopianism of the present, not a Utopianism of the future. Utopianisms of the future have been and are misleading and corrupting, because they are always apt to and almost invariably do result in a sacrifice of the present to some imaginary glorious future, one to be brought about by the sacrifice of the present. But the present is what we are and have, and a refusal to sacrifice it has to be accompanied by an insistence that the range of present possibilities is always far greater than the established order is able to allow for. We need therefore to acquire a transformative political imagination, one that opens up opportunities for people to do kinds of things that they hitherto had not believed that they were capable of doing. And this can happen when someone becomes involved for the first time in community organisations and actions, when parents become involved in some community that sustains their children's school in the inner city, or when unorganised workers struggle to create a union, or when immigrants find themselves involved in forms of communal enterprise that enable them to resist attempts to treat them as no more than a disposable labour force. It is in these contexts of everyday conflict that the accusation of Utopianism becomes important, since it is in such contexts that the achievement of human goods often takes new and unpredicted forms, for which the existing social order hitherto afforded no space. But such new forms of practice and new relationships between institutions and practices often desperately need to be able to draw on what we have learned from past forms of community.

It is here that the importance of empirical studies of past and present relationships between institutions and practices in particular contexts becomes evident, studies such as Ron Beadle's recent admirable study of the circus both as practice and as institution. What matters is that such empirical studies should provide occasions for further learning, so that what is learned can be put to use in the kind of projects that I have been describing. So we badly need good empirical studies of both success and failure in creating forms of schooling that enable children, their parents, and their teachers to achieve forms of good not otherwise achievable, just as we need good empirical studies of many other kinds of experience that illuminate the relationships of practices and institutions to each other and to the human good.

Instructive examples can be found in the history of the practices and institutions of fishing crews and fishing communities in various parts of the world. I think particularly about the history that I know best, that of fishing crews in the northeastern United States, but much the same story can be told of other places. Almost everywhere fishing crews are now suffering badly, as a result of overfishing, as a result of forces that make it difficult to survive, unless you participate in large-scale factory fisheries, that is, in the kind of capitalist fishing that has no place for the traditional fishing crew. Yet we also need to remember that capitalist prosperity could be bad for fishing crews too.

Fishing has always been hard and dangerous work, and those who take on this work often do so initially for purely economic reasons. They need the wages and they have no other way to get them. But they soon discover that their lives and their livelihood now depend on other people, in whom they have to put their trust, and that those other people depend on them not only to do their work well—often boring, fatiguing work—but also expect them to be prepared to risk their lives on occasion to save other crew members. Moreover, although fishing boats are always competing with each other, everyone knows that if another boat is in danger, you have to go to its aid, if at all possible. So in the life of a fishing crew common goods—of the crew, of the fishing fleet, of the fishing community—are achieved only through the exercise of virtues, both cardinal virtues, such as the courage of endurance and risk-taking, and virtues of acknowledged dependence. And over long periods of varying prosperity a way of life, a tradition of the virtues, has been developed in many fishing communities. But then, not too long ago in New England, modern technology brought about a dramatic change. It became possible to fly tuna from New England to Japan, so that it arrived in prime condition. And the price of tuna in Japan was such that a quite new kind of prosperity—riches by the standards of the past—became possible. And of course it was good that this was so. But with the prospect of becoming rich, competitiveness intensified, the costs of going to the aid of others were weighed against the benefits of successful competition, and the solidarities of fishing crews and fishing communities were threatened and sometimes weakened. In fact, the norms and values of the community were upheld, and virtues that had sustained individuals and communities in New England through bad economic times also sustained them through their prosperity, but the lesson for the rest of us is clear.

The practice of the virtues, conceived as Aristotle and Aquinas conceived them, is difficult to reconcile with functioning well in the present economic order, whether it is a time of hardship or a time of prosperity. It is of this kind of episode that we need good empirical studies, histories of past success and failure in the life of the virtues, histories of those experiences from which, as we engage in our present projects, we need to learn. That learning develops still further as the projects that challenge the limitations of the existing order move forward. And such projects are important, not only because and insofar as they are informed by a desire to achieve the human good, both individual goods and common goods, but also because they bring into being types of community through which we are liberated from compartmentalisation, from distorted desires, from inequalities, and from the lawlessness of the present order.

They are important too because within them we discover the indispensability of the virtue of hope, a virtue that directs us beyond the facts of our present situation, whatever it is. Lenin urged us not to bow down before the tyranny of the established fact, before established conventional opinions about what is possible and what is not. And St. Paul and St. Thomas Aquinas tell us how there is always more to be hoped for in any and every situation than the empirical facts seem to show. It is insofar as we are able to find through the virtues a mode of social life in which practical rationality is informed by shared hope that we will know that we have begun to learn what we need to learn.

FIFTEEN

The Irrelevance of Ethics

At the end of Plato's *Phaedrus* Socrates addresses a prayer to Pan and other local gods, a prayer that concludes: 'May I think him rich who is wise; and of gold may I have only as much of it as a temperate man might bear and carry with him'. Plato's thought is this: that we may measure ourselves and our activities *either* by the standards of wisdom and temperateness, the standards of the virtues, *or* by the standards of money, but that we cannot do both. We have to choose between them. Yet we here now inhabit a culture in which on the one hand the truth of Plato's thought is recurrently confirmed, while on the other our dominant economic institutions and our business schools continue to present themselves rhetorically as fostering and often attaining excellence by both standards.

From time to time however it becomes impossible to avoid acknowledging that there is a problem. So it has been strikingly in the period following the large-scale economic disasters that the capitalism of advanced

"The Irrelevance of Ethics," in *Virtue and Economy: Essays on Morality and Markets*, eds. Andrius Bielskis and Kelvin Knight, 7–21 (Burlington, VT: Ashgate, 2016).

modernity recently brought on itself and on the peoples of the world. It matters a good deal how we formulate those questions, since, if they are badly posed, we will misdirect our enquiries. And misdirected enquiries will lead to conclusions that are not just false, but that may confirm us in some of the modes of thought and action that generated the disasters. So it has been, I shall suggest, with much recent discussion of ethics and business activity, especially discussion of the place of ethics in business education.

The presupposition of such discussion has been that individuals who went astray in their judgements and actions often did so only because they had failed to pay sufficient heed to what the standards of the virtues enjoin and so had been morally misguided as to what standards should have guided them in their money-making activities. On this view it is not that there is anything about the activity of money-making as such that it is difficult to reconcile with the injunctions of the virtues. It is just that too often morally inadequate or misguided individuals have not understood what was required of them, if they were both to make money successfully and to conform to what the virtues require. What is missing in such individuals, so it is claimed, is an ethical dimension. And, if we are to have fewer such individuals in future, we must, it is concluded, provide for more strenuous teaching of ethics as part of a business education, perhaps indeed of education in general.

Ethics has of course been in vogue for quite some time: medical ethics, legal ethics, journalistic ethics, the ethics of this and of that. Whenever there is serious malpractice, the cry goes up: Bring on the teachers of ethics! So courses, programmes, academic appointments, centres, have multiplied. There is now money to be made in ethics, even if not all that much. Here I shall speak only of the teaching of ethics designed to be relevant to business, arguing first that such teaching, like the academic teaching of ethics in general, has little or nothing to do with the formation of moral character and is ineffective as an instrument of moral transformation, and secondly that, in the case of business ethics, its teaching is a dangerous distraction from enquiry into the nature and causes of what *is* morally flawed in our economic institutions and activities.

Begin from some facts about the teaching of ethics. First, there is no hard evidence of any kind that the teaching of ethics in academic courses has any effect whatsoever on the subsequent conduct of students in such courses. Of course absence of evidence leaves open the possibility that such teaching is morally effective, although we do need to note that, even if it were the case that students who attended business schools in which the teaching of ethics was given special attention were found to behave better subsequently than the graduates of other business schools, this might be only because students of better moral character choose to attend business schools which attend to the teaching of ethics.

We should however note that we do possess one piece of indirect evidence about the effects of the academic teaching of ethics, albeit evidence about its teachers, not its students. Eric Schwitzgebel and Joshua Rust have recently canvassed and reported on the moral evaluations of teachers of ethics by their colleagues in university and college philosophy departments. Their finding is that those colleagues 'do not tend to see ethicists, in general, as particularly well-behaved. Indeed a substantial minority of non-ethicists asserted that ethicists on average behave morally worse than non-ethicists'.[1] Given this, we should not be too surprised if the teaching of ethics turns out to fail as a remedy for bad behaviour. But we have a much better reason for not being surprised at this. Everything that we already know of moral character should have suggested that attendance at courses on ethics, no matter how good the teacher, is bound to be ineffective. Why?

Begin with the record of those notable, although not too numerous institutions that have had significant success in taking young people who have gone badly wrong and redirecting them into participation in constructive activities and worthwhile ways of life, some of them prisons for juvenile offenders or reform schools, some of them tough boarding schools, some of them providing the kind of basic training that the United States Marine Corps affords its recruits.

Uniformly such institutions succeed by subjecting the young to rigorous discipline, introducing them to testing activities in which they have to depend on others and become such that others can depend on them, learning a mode of common life, learning some trade, and always incurring penalties, if they fail to learn, until they have learned at last that failing to learn is itself the worst penalty.

What such imposed discipline achieves, if successful, is a radical transformation of attitudes and habits, a transformation without which those who need it would be unable to hear, let alone to be persuaded by, arguments about how it is best for them to live. And we have only to say this to be reminded that it has already been said by Aristotle in Book X of the *Nicomachean Ethics*. In order to attend to and learn from arguments, we must first have certain predispositions of character, formed by right training and habituation (1179b2–31). This is why in the modern world of business ethics, although it is just those who lack the relevant character formation who most need a moral education, it is they who will be least able to benefit from academic courses in ethics. What then *are* the habits that we need to acquire, if we are to act as morally responsible agents?

Let me select just four. I begin not from Aristotle, but from D. W. Winnicott, whose psychoanalytic understanding of the influence of mothers on very young children has still not been surpassed.[2] What Winnicott taught us is that mothers of such children have to find a mean between a too strict and a too indulgent regime. The outcome of an over strict regime is apt to be a child who is too compliant, too deferential to authorities and too yielding to circumstance, while the outcome of a too indulgent regime is apt to be a child insufficiently able to distinguish realities from the projections of her or his fantasies. And in our subsequent lives we need to strengthen those character traits that enable us to chart a way between, on the one hand, unrealistic confidence in ourselves and in our powers and, on the other, an overestimation of obstacles and difficulties. So a first mark of moral character is a tempered realism about oneself, one's powers, one's self-knowledge.

Those traits are closely related to dispositions that Aristotle identified in his discussion of the virtue of courage, dispositions that are a second mark of the morally responsible agent. The courageous human being, on Aristotle's account, strikes a mean between rashness and cowardice. She or he is able to assess impending dangers accurately, to identify the resources available to confront those dangers, and to judge which risks it is reasonable to take and which are foolhardy, whether those risks are to her or himself or to others. But in any case the courageous agent puts her or himself on the line. If things go wrong, she or he will be among those who lose out. And this trait is in turn related to a third mark of morally responsible agents. Their care for and commitment to particular others is not at the expense of their care for and commitment to themselves. And their care for and commitment to themselves is not at the expense of their care for and commitment to particular others. They are neither self-sacrificing altruists nor self-indulging egoists. What they have understood is that the achievement of their own good is inseparable from their achievement of some set of common goods, common goods shared with those others whom they encounter or on whom their lives impact in their various activities.

A fourth characteristic of those with developed moral character is neither to focus on the present at the expense of the future nor on the future at the expense of the present. This involves understanding oneself as responsible not just for this or that set of actions, but for living out and for having lived out one's life well or badly. It is to know which projects are to be persisted in, even when they are going badly, and which are to be set aside. It is to prefer honourable failure to dishonest success and to know what to do next when one fails. It is to understand the importance of contributing to projects that began before one was born and that will flourish long after one's death. It is to know to what history one belongs.

There are of course other significant marks of moral character, but attention to these four is instructive when we consider what is demanded of those at work in the financial sector who trade in securities and currency, either on behalf of their firm's clients or for their firm itself, that is, what personality traits seem indispensable for success as a trader. Begin with self-confidence. Adam Smith remarked that 'The chance of gain is by every man more or less overvalued and the chance of loss by most men undervalued'.[3] Traders, in order to be successful, need to communicate to their clients, to their employers, and most of all to themselves that their abilities and resourcefulness are such that gain can be confidently expected from their activities. And reports of how traders behave both when engaged hour after hour in complex and testing transactions and afterwards when celebrating success suggest that self-questioning and self-doubt are states of mind that traders cannot afford to entertain. Studies by social psychologists provide persuasive evidence that it is those of us who have mildly depressive personalities who are most likely to see things as they are. It is difficult not to conclude that by contrast an ability to see things—including oneself—as more promising than they are is an essential ingredient in trading success. And here then is a first respect in which the possession of a trait that is the mark of an agent with well developed moral character is generally incompatible with success as a trader. Traders have to be too self-confident and therefore lacking in self-knowledge.

Turn now to risk-taking. Traders want to be able to calculate risk accurately and they want to distribute risk, so that as much of it as possible is borne by other people. Their wish to calculate risk accurately is in itself admirable. But it has very often misled overconfident traders into believing that they could get from a formula what can only be supplied by good judgement. And this belief has been powerful enough to allow them to rely on formulas provided by others, formulas too often understood only imperfectly. In such cases bad judgement or at least an incapacity for good judgement has worn the mask of mathematical sophistication. One result of this has been that a wish to transfer as much risk as possible to others has been accompanied by either an inability or an unwillingness to explain either to those others or to oneself the nature and extent of the risk that is being taken on. So traders are apt to fail as risk-takers, unable to distinguish adequately between rashness, cowardice and courage, and they fail not because they fall short of their own professional standards, but just because and insofar as they conform to those standards.

A third salient characteristic of traders is the line that they draw between those others whom they take into account when making professional decisions and those others whose fate they believe that they can safely ignore. On one side of that line are the traders themselves, the firm that employs them, most of their firm's clients, and those on whose goodwill they may have to rely in future. On the other side lies everyone else, including those who are the victims of collateral damage resulting from transactions in the financial markets. Speaking of the effects of the market crises of the 1990s on those who were both socially and geographically remote from those markets, the Governor of the Bank of England, Mervyn King, noted that 'In Korea unemployment tripled. In Indonesia several years of economic growth were wiped out leading to political instability and similar results have been visible in other parts of Asia as well as Latin America'.[4] Yet, if such effects were remembered at all by analysts or traders during the next decade, it was only as contributions to the data that enabled them to assign probabilities to the various possible outcomes on which they were placing wagers. And it is clear that only by putting the larger human costs of transactions in the financial markets out of mind that traders are able to function as they do, with their own severely limited versions of cost-benefit analysis. So their understanding of the relationship of their professional actions to the common goods that they share with others is inevitably and radically defective.

Fourthly, the focus of traders has to be almost exclusively on the present and the near future. They are held strictly to account for short term successes and failures under conditions of extreme competitiveness in which immediate responsiveness to changing prices is required of them. Their effectiveness is always under scrutiny and their annual self-reviews and reviews by their managers, reviews that determine the size of their income, define their professional time horizons. Thought of and for the longer term is professionally precluded.

Compare then point by point what on the one hand is required for the formation of moral character in respect of self-confidence and self-knowledge, in respect of risk-taking, in respect of regard for the relationships of the self to multifarious others, and in respect of time horizons, and on the other how traders are shaped by their professional norms. It is at once obvious that the differences are such that, were we successfully to impose on someone the kind of discipline that issues in the formation of genuine moral character, we would have disqualified that someone from success as a trader and, most probably from employment as a trader. We have thus arrived at a second conclusion much stronger than our first. Our first conclusion was that we have no reason to believe that the teaching of courses in ethics effects any significant moral transformation in those subjected to them. Our second conclusion is that, just as the successful training of a boxer will destroy his prospects as a violinist, so the inculcation of qualities of moral character is no way to prepare someone for a rewarding career in the financial sector. Ethics is not just irrelevant. It is a probably insuperable disadvantage.

To understand this conclusion it is important to note what I am *not* saying. I am not saying that traders are or are apt to be 'bad' people by any conventional standards. My conclusion holds of traders who are meticulous in their performance of their duties to their clients and their firms, who abstain scrupulously from bad professional behaviour. It is indeed because of and not in spite of their being good in this way that they fail by the standards that I have identified as the standards of moral character. So it is easy to imagine as a vigorous rejoinder a complaint that I have simply not understood what ethics is or should be. And it would turn out if the quarrel resulting from this complaint were pursued that what divides me—and more importantly Aristotle and Aquinas—from the complainants is the view that each of us takes of human flourishing.

Note too that my thesis is not only about traders. It is true that trading is only one among several types of activity in the financial sector. Investors, analysts, quants, managers of different kinds, all are unlike traders in various ways. But all of them are able to function as they do only because and insofar as traders function as they do. So that it is the financial sector as a whole that is from the Thomistic Aristotelian point of view a school of bad character, while from the point of view of those at work in it, it is, if rightly conducted, a benevolent engine of growth, productive of goods conferred on very many people by a globalised and globalizing economy. How then did this conflict in points of view occur? The answer that I propose provides a third reason for regarding the standard teaching of ethics as irrelevant to the problems presented by the financial sector. It is that those concerned with ethics in the last two hundred years, from whatever standpoint, became insufficiently concerned with money and those engaging with money became insufficiently concerned with ethics. What ethics became as a result and what the management of money became as a result are such that we no longer know how to connect them. The most that we can hope to do is first, to understand the limitations of our present moral and intellectual condition, and then to ask how we can best live and act in that condition.

In the thinking of the Enlightenment it took a long time for the divorce between ethics and concerns with money to become as complete as it is today. Political economy was the offspring of moral philosophy and Adam Smith after all wrote both *The Theory of the Moral Sentiments* and *The Wealth of Nations*. But the former is now read in one set of courses by one set of students, while the latter is generally read only selectively—how seldom do we hear Smith quoted as saying that 'People of the same trade seldom meet together, even for merriment and diversion, but the conversation ends in a conspiracy against the public . . . '—and, when it is read, it is by a very different set of students in other courses.[5] John Stuart

Mill wrote both *Utilitarianism* and the *Principles of Political Economy*, but, while many students still read the former, very, very few now read the latter. My point is not just that post-Enlightenment academic ethics has gone one way and academic economics another, but that this divide is one symptom of a condition such that no one knows how to educate our culture into thinking coherently about money. So what *is* the problem set by the way we think about money? How do we think about money?

In at least four ways. The first provides a simple-minded starting-point, although it is of course the starting-point of Aristotle and Aquinas. The value of money is by them and by many of us much of the time taken to be no more and no less than the value of the goods which can be exchanged for it, so that we have no good reason to want money except insofar as we want particular goods. A second way of thinking about money moves us one small step further. Given that I have money, I can exchange it for a number of different kinds of goods. Money affords me indefinitely more choices and choice is itself a good. So I seem to have after all some reason to want money independently of my wanting this or that particular set of goods. But what kind of a good then is choice? It is certainly not an unqualified good.

When individuals as rational agents have a tolerably clear grasp of what individual and common goods they and others need to pursue, if they are to flourish as human beings, then the choices between alternative possibilities that they make will be for the most part choices of genuine goods and money will be important, although only as opening up possibilities for achieving such goods. Goods will still be the measure of money. But, when individuals lack such a grasp, they may find their choices framed for them and imposed on them by others and by others whose interest is primarily in getting them to spend money, so that what are presented in the market as goods are designed to elicit predictable consumer responses. And for those who make those seductive presentations money has now become the measure of goods. Goods are to be made and supplied, just insofar as they can be turned into money. And this is only the beginning of an inversion of the relationship between money and goods.

We have then moved from a first stage in which money is valued only because and insofar as it is translatable into goods to a second in which it is also valued because it extends the range of possibilities in the choice of goods, and from this to the beginning of a third stage in which the relationships of goods to money become more complex and various. What lies beyond this is not only increasing complexity and variety, but a movement towards money becoming the measure of all things, including itself.

It is crucial to this final stage that money is made not just from the exchange of goods for money, but also from the exchange of money for money, as, for example, in currency transactions. And in due time trading in derivatives and in derivatives of derivatives will distance those at work in the financial sector more and more from the uses of money in everyday life. The outcome is that how individuals fare in the world increasingly depends upon a complex and often badly understood set of relationships to money, to the money that they have, that they owe, that they save or fail to save, that they are owed. To do well in this monetary world requires just that kind of self-confidence in the getting and the spending of money which we noted earlier as informing the activities of traders, a self-confidence that characteristically disguises from those who have it the fragility and vulnerability of the economic and monetary relationships that constitute their world. Consider just one example of the irrationality of that world.

One thing that money procures is deference and deference is procured not by spending money, but simply by having it. With deference of this kind money has become the measure of a human being. What this reflects are the gross inequalities that have emerged, so that even the rich have become dwarfed into ordinariness by the superrich. Peter Drucker, the best apologist that the capitalist corporation has ever had, argued 30 years ago that the most highly paid executives of such corporations could reasonably be paid 20 times the average wage of their workers. In the year 2000 in the United Kingdom such executives received 47 times the average wage, while by 2009 the multiple was 81, while in the United States in 2008 the multiple was 319. So money generated a new kind of hierarchy, a hierarchy of patent absurdities—for you have to be a fool to believe that you should be paid that amount of money—yet absurdities that are treated with great solemnity. We are not supposed to laugh at the foolishness of the rich.

Note that in describing these developments I have been talking for the most part not about money itself, let alone about the network of economic relationships in which money plays its part, but only about how we think about money. Note too that in identifying these various stages in the development of how we think about money I have not suggested that at later stages we leave behind the earlier stages. My thesis has been that in thinking about money, that in trying to understand the place of money in our lives, our thought has become not only increasingly complex, but also increasingly incoherent, so that at one end of a spectrum experts move comfortably without thinking about it from one stance to another, while at the other end of that spectrum many plain people caught up in the nexus of wages, prices, taxes, pension funds, mortgages and investments are rightly uneasy about money and view it as one more great Incomprehensible. Remember how I began from Plato's thought that we can measure ourselves by the standard of the virtues *or* by the standard of money, but that allegiance to the first set of standards precludes allegiance to the second. Yet we now inhabit a society in which, whether we like it or not, we find ourselves on a great many occasions measured by the standards of money and in consequence afflicted by either the incoherence or the incomprehensibility of our thought about money. What then can be said to those of us in this condition from the standpoint of a Thomistic Aristotelian understanding of the virtues?

Part of the problem is that, in the period in which a Thomistic concern with the virtues still did extend to the economic realm its focus was principally on questions concerning the legitimacy or otherwise of usury and that from the sixteenth century onwards those who attempted to follow Aquinas in defending the prohibition of usury underwent defeat after defeat, both in intellectual debate and in the economic practices of the age. In Benjamin Nelson's narrative of these defeats the last unhappy and defeated defender of that prohibition in the 1820s was William Cobbett's wild and engaging friend, Father Jeremiah O'Callaghan, against whom an official of the Irish diocese of Cloyne and Ross argued and rightly that, were the Catholic clergy in general to adopt O'Callaghan's view, they 'would, by now opposing a deep rooted and general custom, fall into contempt and be despised upon all questions'.[6] With that apparently final defeat it became difficult to spell out what, in its Thomistic or any other version, the tradition of the virtues requires of us, when we are engaged in economic transactions.

It is not that a need to understand those requirements did not continue to be felt. The concept of a just wage and of what justice requires in the way of relationships between employers and workers remained central to Catholic and especially Thomistic social teaching. But if we remember that, when Leo XIII published *Rerum Novarum* in 1891, it was two years after Georg Simmel had published the first of his essays on money and only nine years before his definitive *Philosophie des Geldes* appeared, we at once become aware of the lack of communication between those for whom Aristotelian and Thomistic thought about the virtues is central and those, like Simmel, who had recognised what money had become and of the need to think about it in quite new ways. They inhabited and still often inhabit quite different moral cultures.

That this is so received striking confirmation 30 or 40 years later in the sad history of the distributivist movement in England. Both Belloc and Chesterton were deeply engaged with the politics of their time, but had become disillusioned with the politics and economics of all the British political parties. Each rejected both capitalism and socialism. Each had searching questions about the place of money in our lives. But neither Belloc nor Chesterton understood quite how much was presupposed by their distributivist stance. That radical understanding was supplied by the Dominican Father Vincent McNabb, someone whose thinking was deeply Thomistic.

What McNabb recognised was that the concepts of just wages and just exchanges, of the proper relationships of workers to their work and to the products of their work, of the proper relationship of the household to the work place and of both to the arenas of politics, as understood by the distributivists, were so much at odds with the norms governing the British political, economic and monetary system of the 1930s that what was implied by distributivist doctrine was a total withdrawal from that system.

McNabb's conception of that withdrawal entailed that each household should become as far as possible self-sufficient, responsible for producing its own food. In so concluding he not only confirms my thesis about the distance between these two worlds, the world of the theory and practice of the virtues, as Aquinas understood them, and the world in which money exercises its magical power and influence, but provides a *reductio ad absurdum* of the view that we can simply withdraw from or reject that latter world. It is, like it or not, the world in which we now have to live.

It may perhaps seem that the third of my conclusions warrants a pessimism even more radical than its first formulation suggested. My first conclusion, I should remind you, was that we have no good reason to believe that the teaching of ethics through academic courses can be effective in bringing about moral transformations. My second conclusion was that an effective education into the virtues would in fact disqualify one for a successful career in the financial sector. And my third conclusion has been that the present content of even an ethics of the virtues is such and the ways in which we think about money are such that we are generally at a loss when we try to connect them. What I have also shown, I believe, is that this has been at times markedly true of the Thomistic Aristotelian conception of the virtues, as understood by some of its best exponents. So what are we, especially those of us who are committed to that tradition, now to do? How are we to make ethics relevant? We have to begin all over again.

What we need to do first is to redescribe the nexus of economic and financial relationships in the vocabulary of the virtues, drawing upon the resources provided both by economists and by Simmel on the one hand and by the thinkers of the Thomistic Aristotelian tradition on the other. And part of what our description has to capture is the double aspect of the globalising economy and its financial sector, so that we understand it both as an engine of growth and as such a source of benefits, but equally as a perpetrator of great harms and continuing injustices. The apologists for globalisation too often treat it as by its essential nature only a source of benefits, only accidentally and incidentally a source of harms, harms that could be prevented by vigilant regulatory agencies. The critics of globalisation sometimes talk as though there is somewhere offstage some alternative to the globalisating economy that we now have, a set of possible economic structures that would be free from the evils of globalisation. The truth is that we have no alternative to the globalising economy as it now is and that its propensities for good and for harm cannot be split apart. To be for or against globalisation is in some ways like being for or against the weather.

Yet, unlike the weather, it is a human work, although one which it is all too easy to treat as a set of impersonal forces representable by the equations of the economists' blackboards. Even Karl Marx in his preface to the first volume of *Capital* could write that:

> here individuals are dealt with only in so far as they are the personification of economic categories ... My standpoint ... can less than any other make the individual responsible for relations whose creature he socially remains, however much he may subjectively raise himself above them.[7]

Marx thus, like so many others, supposed that, if individuals in their social and economic roles act out their parts with systematic regularity, they cannot be called to account as responsible moral agents for what they do. But this is a mistake. For at key points the system can be successfully resisted and even changed. And a first condition of its being so resisted, of knowing when and how to resist it, is that its workings are understood in moral terms. So to understand it, we have to describe those workings in terms of such vices as those of injustice, intemperateness and imprudence. What is it to be an unjust agent? It is not simply to violate the canons of a just distribution of goods. It is to do so because one is a certain kind of person with a misconception of one's good and wrongly directed desires. Aristotle takes the vice that is the counterpart of the virtue of justice to be *pleonexia*, an expression that Nietzsche translated as *Mehrundmehrwollhaben*. (The only better translation, as I have suggested elsewhere, would perhaps have been '*Mehrundmehrundmehrundmehr ... wollhaben*'.) This is indeed the vice that informs the financial sector of the globalising economy: growth both for the sake of growth and at the service of and as an expression of acquisitiveness.

To be economically and financially unjust, intemperate and imprudent is to deny others their due in the interests of increasing one's own gains. The principal expression of such vices in the economic life of the past 30 years has been the unjust infliction of debt. And this has not been an accidental or incidental aspect of the system. To understand why begin where Karl Marx began, with the appropriation of surplus value. Surplus value is the difference between what the labour of productive workers earns in wages and what capitalists receive for the products of that labour. It is only because capitalists are able to appropriate that difference—their profits—and to invest it in their businesses that capitalism is a growth economy. Successful capitalists maximise their profit-taking and to do so they must keep their costs as low as possible. The owners of capital and those who manage their enterprises always therefore have a compelling reason to keep wages low. But, insofar as they succeed, they create a recurrent problem for themselves. For workers are also consumers and capitalism requires consumers with the purchasing power to buy the products that are brought to market. So there is a tension between a need to keep wages low and a need to keep consumption high.

In the course of its history capitalism has solved the problems generated by this tension in various ways. But in the last 20 years its most important solution has been the extension of credit and the infliction of debt. Capitalism legitimates itself to those who are not large owners of capital by portraying itself as the instrument of both past and future growth, by its seductive promises as well as by its often spectacular achievements. And when, as in the United States in the last 20 years the achievement of growth has been remarkable, but the wages of very many have remained stagnant or even fallen, then the legitimation of capitalism to those who have not shared in the benefits of growth has become more and more a matter of promises not yet kept. But promises of future reward are insubstantial things. So the strategy has been to bring future consumption, future prosperity into the present by dramatic extensions of credit, including credit to those hitherto judged not creditworthy. And by this there *was* achieved for a time an equally dramatic increase in purchasing power, so for a moment the problems arising from the appropriation of surplus value were resolved.

The extension of credit took a number of forms and each of them influenced consumers in how they think about money and in how they think about themselves. The different forms wear different faces: credit cards, gold, platinum, and platinum plus cards, cards that earn airline points, free nights in hotels; mortgages that promised to transform improvident renters into prudent homebuyers, building equity in their homes over 10, 20, 30 years; student loans either from banks or government, not repayable until you graduate; multifarious services provided by governments that borrow money in order to provide them and to win elections because they provide them. So the message is: you may not as yet have enough money to make yourselves and others happy, by getting an education, by providing your family with a home, by taking a vacation from your treadmill of a job, but you do and will have enough money for us to make you a loan and for you somehow or other to repay it.

One of the crafts highly valued by all these lending agencies is a form of writing for nonreaders, the writing of legalese in small print that is not meant to be read or, if read, understood. And this bizarre use of the written word is accompanied by the blandishments of the spoken word and the visual presentations of the advertiser, designed to assure as many of us as possible that we are unproblematically creditworthy. This vast expansion of credit was accompanied by a distribution of risk that exposed to the possibility of ruin millions of people quite unaware that they had been thus exposed. And so, when capitalism once again fatally overextended itself, massive credit was transformed into even more massive debt, into loss of jobs and loss of wages, into bankruptcies of firms and foreclosures of homes, into one sort of ruin for Ireland, another for Iceland and a third for California and Illinois, into savage cuts in welfare, laid off teachers, children, already educationally deprived, deprived still further. It is not just that capitalism, as always, imposes the costs of growth and of lack of growth on those least able to bear them. It is that much of this debt is unjust and unjust in at least three ways.

First there are those—especially, but not only children—who are paying the costs of money having been borrowed which they never borrowed. Secondly, a large number of those who did borrow were either misinformed or miseducated about the nature and extent of the risk to which they were being exposed. And thirdly those who were the engineers of this debt and who had already benefited quite disproportionately from the extension of credit have been to an extraordinary degree allowed to exempt themselves from the consequences of their delinquent actions. And these injustices are not accidental or peripheral phenomena. The imposition of unjust debt is a symptom of the moral condition of the economic system of advanced modernity and is in its most basic forms an expression of the vices of intemperateness, injustice and imprudence. Until it is described in these terms it has been underdescribed and misdescribed.

It is not that there is an economic system whose relationships can first be described and elucidated in purely economic terms and then evaluated by moralists from some external standpoint. It is that the relationships that are constitutive of the economic system are from the outset norm-governed moral relationships, relationships of trust or lack of trust, of prudence or imprudence, of appropriate or inappropriate risk-taking, of candour or deception, relationships in which individual and common goods are at stake, and we have not grasped those relationships adequately, if we have understood them in nonmoral terms, as most economists continue to understand them. We need instead to interpret them as Marx, that almost, but not quite moralist, interpreted them and as Aristotle and Aquinas would have interpreted them. Remember that I began this simple-minded moral account of the economy—and in these matters it is important to remain simple-minded—with Marx's identification of surplus value. From this starting-point what we need to do is bring Aquinas and Marx together, both in characterising the relationship between the appropriation of surplus value and the infliction of unjust debt and in formulating the principles that should inform our attitude to such debt.

Begin with the latter. We need at least three kinds of principle, one set concerned with issues of desert, one with responsible risk-taking, and one to do with setting limits to the burdens of debt. Let me sketch examples of each. Desert is an issue when the consequences of debt are inflicted on those who played no part in incurring that debt. Among those who undeservedly suffer from those consequences are, as I have already noticed, large numbers of children. And our first political and economic responsibility in every situation is to the children of our society. So child care, child nutrition, child health, education: these must be insulated, as far as possible, from the effects of public and private debt. And, that is to say, family life must be protected.

A second set of principles enjoin that those who expose others to risk in the financial markets must spell out in public in advance the risks that they are distributing, in terms that are intelligible to those whom they are putting at risk. And when there are bad consequences of risk-taking in the financial markets, the consequences for those who made the relevant decisions must be made as bad as they are for the worst off amongst their victims. Thirdly, limits must be set to the burdens imposed by debt on individual and family lives, so that those burdens are not disproportionate. And this will involve in many situations a required forgiveness of debt, amnesty, years of jubilee.

Those principles have of course implications for the kinds of regulation that should be imposed on financial markets. But debates over regulation commonly have as their aim the prevention of further large-scale crises. By contrast the kind of principle that I have sketched is intended primarily to identify and to respond to the moral dimensions of the *normal* workings of our economic and financial arrangements. To which it will be retorted that these principles, as I have sketched them, are much too abstract and general for this purpose. That is, of course, true. And therefore the next urgent task is to spell them out in adequate and concrete detail, noting that to do so will be impossible without major incursions into economic theory, since the social structures of an economy informed by such principles would be very different from those of either a wholly free market economy or of the state-and-market economies of present day Europe. It would be a type of economy in which, among other things, deference to wealth would be recognised as a vice.

Yet spelling out such principles in appropriate detail would still be of little moment, unless and until they were acted upon in resistance to the continuing imposition of unjust debt. It would only be with such action that our thinking about the virtues and our thinking about money would finally have been reconnected. And it is only with such a reconnection that ethics will once again become relevant.

SIXTEEN

Four—or More?— Political Aristotles

The four political Aristotles whom I will discuss are Aristotle himself, Aristotle as understood in the thirteenth century by Aquinas, Aristotle as understood by some sixteenth-century renaissance Aristotelians, and the Aristotle of the present day, object of scholarly enquiry, subject of a huge and, even as we speak, ever-growing number of dissertations, invoked politically from time to time by protagonists of several alternative and rival points of view. So my first remarks are about Aristotle himself or rather about his text. I note immediately that a high proportion of the statements that scholarly commentators make about that text fall into one of two classes. Either they are presented as obvious truths, and so are scarcely worth repeating, or they are much disputed claims, only to be asserted if

"Four—or More?—Political Aristotles," in *Virtue Ethics and Contemporary Aristotelianism: Modernity, Conflict and Politics*, eds. Andrius Bielskis, Eleni Leontsini, and Kelvin Knight, 11–24 (New York: Bloomsbury, 2020).

backed up by extensive interpretative argument. So what is someone to do if, as now, they need to provide a brief but accurate portrait of Aristotle as a political figure in less than five pages, so that what they say will unavoidably be highly contestable but shamelessly unargued? If they are shameless enough, they will simply proceed with the task. As I do now.

I

I begin by juxtaposing two aspects of Aristotle. He famously asserted that the human being is by nature a political animal (*Politics,* I.2.1253a2–3); an animal, that is, whose well-being requires citizenship in a *polis*. But he himself resided for part of his life in Macedonia, which was not a *polis,* and for an even longer period in Athens, where he was a *metic,* a resident alien and not a citizen. And his friends and allies among the Macedonian elite imposed on Greece a form of rule quite other than that of a *polis*. Yet, on Aristotle's view, someone without a *polis* must be either a beast or a god, and evidently Aristotle did not think himself to be either of these. What he did think of himself as was an enquirer, someone exemplifying another universal human trait, the desire to understand. So, as such an enquirer, how might he have conceived his political role and function? When Aristotle returned to Athens in 335, no longer a member of the Academy, but a teacher and researcher, presiding over other teachers and researchers at the Lyceum, he was nearly fifty years old. What political role would Aristotle have expected a man of his achievements and that age to play?

The relevant texts are from Book VII of the *Politics* and Book X of the *Nicomachean Ethics*. In the former, Aristotle dissents from Plato's view that soldiers should be one kind of person and rulers another. They should be the same people, but at different times in their lives, since 'younger men have *dynamis*, but older men have *phronēsis*' (*Politics* VII.8.1329a14–16). Aristotle thus seems to have envisaged the political life as proceeding through stages, beginning with a period of military service, then a period of undertaking those tasks of personal and political decision-making through which *phronēsis* is acquired—the *phronēsis* required for 'deliberation about what is expedient and judgment about what is just' (*Politics* VII.9.1329a4–5)—and finally the stage of holding those high offices in which *phronēsis* is exercised as a ruler. But if this is so, something has been left out, for in his discussion of political education at the close of the *Nicomachean Ethics* Aristotle makes it clear that for the acquisition of political *phronēsis* deliberative experience, although necessary, is not sufficient, since 'if anyone wants to become adept in a *technē* or in *theōria,* he must go to the universal' (*NE* X.9.1180b20–22). How is he to do that? What has been left out is just what Aristotle intended to supply in his teaching at the Lyceum. His political role and function is that of the educator, and that role can only be discharged by two different kinds of attention to the formation of moral habits.

First, attempts to instruct will be fruitless unless the students have already developed to some significant degree those moral and intellectual habits without which political learning cannot take place. Lacking such habits, the student will be guided by passions and immune to argument (*NE* X.9.1179b26–9). Second, the aim of instruction is to produce legislators who will know how to design, enact and administer laws that will inculcate those same habits, so that citizens may learn how to rule and how to be ruled for the common good of the *polis* (*NE* II.1.1103b3–6). Such political education does of course require more than good habits. It also requires a degree and kind of experience that is inevitably wanting in the young, but also missing from those whose upbringing has resulted in an inability to learn from experience (*NE* I.3.1095a2–6). Notice that these remarks all come from the *Nicomachean Ethics,* not the *Politics,* something not surprising if we follow Richard Bodéüs in understanding the former as just as much a political discourse as the latter.

Bodéüs's claims in *Le philosophe et la cité* are of course contentious.[1] But I do not think that his critics have shown him to be mistaken in what he asserts, only in what he denies, in his giving too exclusively a political account of Aristotle's intentions. What critics have rightly emphasized— Sparshott is an excellent example[2]—is not only that Aristotle's concern with moral and intellectual habits extends beyond the political, but also that, unless we give due weight to this, we shall not understand Aristotle's conception of politics. The good of the citizen *qua* citizen is the common good of the city. But the good of the citizen *qua* human being is more and other than his good *qua* citizen. And the moral and intellectual habits, the virtues, that the citizen needs are human virtues. Aristotle insists that the virtue of the citizen is not the same as the virtue of the human being, that one can be a good citizen without being a good human being (*Politics* III.4.1276b35–1277a5 and III.4.1277a12–25). But he also says that, when rule is exercised over free human beings, 'the good citizen must have the understanding and the ability to rule and to be ruled and this is the virtue of a citizen' (*Politics* III.4.1277b12–15). Yet one cannot have the understanding and ability to rule without *phronēsis*, and one cannot have *phronēsis* without also having the moral virtues, the virtues of the human being as such.

What then is the relationship between the achievement, together with one's fellow citizens, of the good of the *polis*, and the achievement by each citizen as an individual of his own final good as a human being? Aristotle poses this question in Book VII of the *Politics*, when he discusses the disagreement between those who hold that the best life for a human being is the life of political practice and those who hold, to the contrary, that it is the life devoted to philosophical enquiry. Aristotle's response is to argue that this is a badly framed set of alternatives. The activities of *dianoia* and *theōria,* the activities of philosophical enquiry, are as much or even more a part of the life of practice as are political activities (*Politics* VII.3.1325a16–1325b23). The plain inference is that the political life is by itself an incomplete life for a human being. It is indeed through developing and exercising the virtues in the life of the *polis* that we become rightly disposed and directed towards the achievement of our final end, but we will be politically in error if we believe that, or act as if it were the case that, there is not more to each life than politics. We will also of course be in error if we suppose that the pursuit of our ultimate end can, except in some exceptional cases, be an alternative to the pursuit of the ends of political life.

If so, one conclusion follows for us as interpreters and teachers. The *Nicomachean Ethics* and the *Politics* have to be taught together or not at all. Yet academic practice is such—and has been such for a very long time—that almost always the *Nicomachean Ethics* is taught in courses in moral philosophy to one set of students and the *Politics* in courses in political theory to quite another. The presupposition of such practice is that ethics is one thing, politics quite another, and that questions about the relationship between the two are to be raised only after each has been studied largely in isolation from the other. The lesson to be learnt is that the organization of the curriculum always has intellectual and sometimes moral and political presuppositions. And, if I am right, the presuppositions of our modern curriculum are and have been anti-Aristotelian. So that to teach students to read Aristotle's texts as they should be read is to teach against the cultural grain.

It is important that the thesis that the *Nicomachean Ethics* and the *Politics* must be read together can be held without a commitment to Bodéüs's interpretation of Aristotle's purposes. It was urged upon us in a 1984 article by A. W. H. Adkins, whose compellingly argued contention was that 'the relationship of *ergon* to *aretē* and *eudaimonia*, and the importance of all three to Aristotle's ethical and political thought' can only be understood when the *Ethics* and the *Politics* are read together.[3] Adkins laid particular emphasis on the relationship between the *ergon* of a ruler and the *ergon* of a human being, and in this I would want to follow him. Why so? For two different and contrasting reasons.

First, there is the place that this relationship has in Aristotle's instructive accounts of what he takes to be cases of political failure, for example in what he says about Sparta and in his analysis of the danger to democratic constitutions posed by the characteristic democratic conception of freedom. The Spartans prized and praised virtue, but their almost exclusively military conception, or rather misconception, of the virtues resulted in a lack of ability to manage their own affairs. 'They find it necessary to undertake large wars, but there is never any money in the public treasury' (*Politics* II.9.1271b11–13), something to be remarked not only of the Spartans but also of contemporary, far from Laconic Americans. On Aristotle's view, it is because they—certainly the Spartans, and perhaps also the Americans—are defective in respect of the human *ergon* that they are defective in respect of the *ergon* of a ruler.

At first sight, a very different case is that of those democrats who undermine democratic constitutions because of their democratic misconception of liberty. On that democratic view, 'to be free is to do whatever one wants' (*Politics* V.9.1310a31–32); it is to be free from external interference that may frustrate one's desires. But, on Aristotle's view, this is a misconception of freedom. To be constrained by respect for the constitution is not to be unfree, but to live in security. Democracies thus become the victims of demagogues, and the bad political outcomes for both victims and victimizers have their source in failures to discipline and transform their desires. Once again, it is because rulers are defective in respect of the human *ergon* that they are defective in respect of the *ergon* of a ruler.

That human beings *qua* human beings, *qua* rational animals, have a distinctive *ergon* is then, so Adkins reminds us, a thesis indispensable for any genuinely Aristotelian politics and ethics. Yet just here is the great difficulty that Aristotle creates for himself. As Adkins puts it, it was Aristotle's view that 'in the case of other things that have *erga*, not all of them perform those *erga* excellently: not all sculptors are as good as Phidias, not all eyes have 20/20 vision. But all can and must perform the *ergon* to some extent . . . However in the case of the *ergon* of man (*anthrōpos*), the function can be discharged, the task performed, by only a small fraction of mankind'.[4] And this suggests that Aristotle confronted a dilemma that he failed to recognize.

Let me therefore put it to Aristotle, albeit posthumously, that, if he continues to assert that only 'a limited number of adult male Greeks with a leisured way of life', as Adkins puts it, are capable of pursuing and achieving the ends of political activity, then he will have to accept that his use of *ergon*, his conception of *ergon*, is incoherent and so put in question the central theses of his ethics and politics. But, if he reforms his use of *ergon*, so that it is no longer incoherent, then women, productive workers, such as farmers, slaves and barbarians can no longer be excluded from the ranks of citizens. And there is no third way. Modern followers of Aristotle have of course often argued—I have been one of them—that these exclusions can be excised from Aristotle's political theory without damage to its overall structure. Here I am suggesting something much stronger, that, unless they are excised, the foundations of that theory are put seriously in question. I have used the verb 'suggest': for clearly further argument is needed, although some of it is supplied by Adkins in his article. Here all that I can do is to take note of Aristotle's dilemma and move on.

II

The movement is one of sixteen centuries, from fourth century BCE to thirteenth century CE. And at once an obvious question is posed. Must it not be absurd to try to find application for Aristotle's theory of the *polis* to the empire, or the kingdoms, duchies and city-states of thirteenth-century Western Europe? The events that led to the disappearance of the *polis* were after all set on foot in Aristotle's lifetime by his nasty pupil, Alexander, and the history of political change that separates Aristotle from his thirteenth-century followers surely makes any genuinely Aristotelian politics impossible and his theory irrelevant. R. G. Collingwood made the point once and for all: 'Can you say that the *Republic* gives one account of "the nature of the State" and the *Leviathan* another? No; because Plato's "State" is the Greek *polis,* and Hobbes's is the absolutist State of the seventeenth century'.[5] And Collingwood's argument seems to hold as compellingly of Aristotle and Aquinas as it does of Plato and Hobbes. Is there any reply to it?

I begin by putting on one side Aquinas's *De Regimine Principum*, a puzzling text in a number of ways, as well as the unfinished commentary on the *Politics,* and what I have to say about Aquinas will focus largely, although not entirely, on his mature judgements in the *Summa Theologiae*. One of Aquinas's intentions in writing the *Summa* was to instruct those whose role it might be to give moral and political advice either to rulers or to ruled or to both, and also to those who were the teachers of those called upon to fill such advisory roles. There are two ways to read the *Summa*. One is to begin at the beginning and work through the text question by question until one reaches, not the end, but the point at which Aquinas broke off, leaving it to be finished by his Dominican colleagues. The other, which is pertinent to my present purposes, is to begin from one or more of the practical conclusions in the Second Part of the Second Part, that is, from the answers that he was providing to questions posed by his morally and politically puzzled contemporaries. Then we read backwards, first in order to identify the premises from which Aquinas had derived his conclusions, next in order to discover the justifications that he had advanced for taking those premises to be true, and so we proceed until we arrive at the relevant first principles, whether principles of natural reason concerning the moral and the political or revealed truths. If we read the text in this way, we learn something interesting about Aquinas's use of Aristotle. What Aquinas is doing is drawing upon Aristotle's concepts, theses and arguments—and also of course upon those of others, most notably of

Augustine—in order to construct answers to thirteenth-century questions, some of which Aristotle himself could not have asked.

Aquinas's most important debts to Aristotle are in respect of his conception of human agency. Note at once that the problems that I posed earlier about Aristotle's use of *ergon* do not arise over Aquinas's use of *opus*, William of Moerbeke's translation of *ergon*. Every human being, in Aquinas's view, is actually or potentially capable of that exercise of reason which is the human *opus* (*Sententia libri ethicorum* I, lect. 10, 122–6). And in exercising their practical reason in their everyday lives, human agents always presuppose some answer to the questions 'What is my final end?' and 'To what ends should my actions here and now be directed, if I am to be directed towards that final end?' Reflection upon those questions at once makes it plain that, whatever ends they are or should be pursuing, their progress towards them depends upon their relationships to and interactions with others, those with whom they share the lives of the family, workplace and political society, and together with whom they engage in a variety of projects. So agents come to pose questions not only about their individual goods but also about those common goods that they share with others and about the parts that the achievement of those common goods inescapably play in the achievement of their individual goods. It is in asking and answering those questions about common goods that they show themselves to be not only rational animals but also political animals.

What qualities must we have, if we are to act with others in achieving our and their common good? To answer this question, we must first consider what kinds of relationships we need to have with them. Aquinas contends that those relationships must be structured by their and our acknowledgement of the authority of law. But whose law and which law? A central political and legal problem for Western Europe in the thirteenth century was that of competing jurisdictions, of rival authorities and of rival claimants to authority. What falls to the church courts to decide and what to the secular courts? Within the church, who is accountable to the local bishop and who only to the pope? How is the administration of the king's law to take account of the courts in which local feudal landowners preside? Is this or that university to be subject to the authority of the city council, of the bishop, of the king or of the pope? Does customary law have the force of law? A prerequisite for giving an answer to these questions that is not dictated by the present distribution of power is that we are able to appeal to a shared conception of law. It is Aquinas's contention that we are able to appeal to such a conception, because we already possess such a conception, often without knowing that we do so.

What then is law? Aquinas's answer is that the precepts of law are precepts of reason directed towards the common good and promulgated by someone with the authority to promulgate them (*Summa Theologiae* Ia-IIae q. 90). And each of us as a rational agent is potentially aware of the authority of those precepts without conformity to which we will be unable to deliberate rationally with those others with whom we share common goods and so be unable to achieve those common goods. For, if we are to be able to deliberate rationally with others, both we and they must be able to evaluate each other's practical reasoning as reasoning and respond to it as rational agents rather than trying to get our own way by force or the threat of force or deceit and fraud. But this is possible only if both we and they speak to each other truthfully, abstain from doing each other bodily harm, respect each other's legitimate property, keep our promises to each other, and so on. And to obey such injunctions and rules is to conform to the precepts of the natural law.

What the natural law provides is therefore twofold. It tells us what our relationships to others must be, if we are to be able to deliberate rationally with them about how to achieve their and our goods. And it provides a standard by which we may pass judgement on the various systems of positive law enacted in various societies, including our own. But practical knowledge of the natural law involves more than an ability to identify its precepts. It involves knowing how to judge which precepts are relevant in this or that set of circumstances and how to apply those precepts to particular cases, especially to difficult cases. What do we need if we are to be capable of this kind of knowing how? We need the virtue of *phronēsis*, Latinized as *prudentia*, defined as Aristotle defined it, that habit of mind and action that directs us towards our individual and common goods through the contingent particularities of our situation. But, and here again Aquinas follows Aristotle, no one can have the virtue of *prudentia* unless she or he has the other moral virtues to a significant degree. Aquinas recognizes that our moral development is characteristically uneven, so that someone who is generally just may still be inadequately courageous or temperate, but without a certain degree of courage, justice and temperateness, we will also be lacking in practical judgement, in *prudentia*.

For Aquinas, therefore, unlike some of our contemporaries, an ethics and politics of rules is not to be contrasted with an ethics and politics of virtues. Without the virtues we would be inept in our application of rules. And without rules, our understanding of the virtues would be incomplete, since the rules set limits to the kinds of action through which our good can be achieved. Consider the relationship of rules to virtues in the decision-making of legislators. It might seem that, since, as Aristotle and Aquinas agree, the aim of rulers is to legislate so that those who are ruled may become good, whatever the natural law enjoins should be enacted as positive law. But this is a mistake. Enacting prohibitions of certain types of bad act may well make matters worse rather than better: 'imperfect human beings, unable to tolerate such precepts, would break out into even worse evils' (*Summa Theologiae* Ia-IIae q. 96 a. 2). What the ruler has to judge is the effect of this particular legislation as moral education on this particular population and such judgement requires the exercise of the virtue of *prudentia*.

What I have been trying to bring out is the way in which and the extent to which Aquinas puts Aristotle's conceptions of the deliberative rationality of the agent and of the virtue of *phronēsis* to work in discussions of political problems of the thirteenth century, so that it becomes clear that the charge of anachronism fails. I could have tried to meet this charge in other ways, by for example showing how Aquinas is able to find thirteenth-century applications for Aristotle's conceptions of justice, courage and temperateness, so spelling out those conceptions further. Had I pursued this line of argument systematically, it would have involved the claim that Aristotle's conceptions of deliberative rationality and of the virtues, although first advanced in the fourth century, are not only fourth-century conceptions but also conceptions that have so far withstood criticism from many standpoints in many times and places. To do so however would be to divert me from taking note of what is more relevant to my present purpose, namely, that Aquinas was only one of a number of Aristotelian writers on politics in the high and the late-middle ages, and that some of these were in some respects more faithful to Aristotle than he was. Here I take note of only one, Nicole Oresme, fourteenth-century translator of both the *Nicomachean Ethics* and the *Politics* into French.

Of him Jean Dunbabin wrote: 'When he misinterprets Aristotle, it is not because medieval political preconceptions blur his understanding, but because it suits his book to do so.[6] She cites as an example Oresme's use of Aristotle's teaching that priestly offices ought not to be held by farmers or craftsmen to attack the Dominicans and the Franciscans for admitting to their ranks just such people. Oresme, as an aristocratic humanist, invokes Aristotle as an authority against the Dominican and Thomistic tradition, a tradition that as political and moral theory had no great influence beyond the Dominican order until the sixteenth century, when it was infused with new life by Francisco de Vitoria. For Vitoria, Aristotle's texts play a crucial part in his incisive critique of Spanish claims to exercise rightful authority over the indigenous inhabitants of the Americas. That critique was carried further by Bartolomé de las Casas, Dominican and bishop of Chiapas, in his insistence that the Spaniards were wholly without justification in making war upon and enslaving those inhabitants. In the great disputation on these matters at Valladolid in 1550, conducted before an audience of jurists, theologians and members of the royal council, Las Casas's antagonist was another aristocratic humanist, Juan Ginés de Sepúlveda, whose arguments against Las Casas invoked Aristotle's doctrine of the natural slave. So in these debates, two rival and antagonistic Aristotles confronted one another. We should note that Sepúlveda was, unlike Las Casas, a distinguished Aristotle scholar, at home with Aristotle's Greek and translator of several of Aristotle's works into Latin, including the *Politics*. He belongs to, even if a minor figure among, those renaissance Aristotelians for whom Aristotle is at once a fourth- and a sixteenth-century figure, a contemporary of both Demosthenes and Machiavelli.

III

A full history of the Aristotelianism of the Renaissance and more particularly of the moral and political Aristotelianism of that period still has to be written. When it is, it will be deeply indebted to such path-breaking scholarship as that of Charles B. Schmitt and a number of others.[7] But until it is, all generalizations have to be cautious. Yet some common themes are plainly of the first importance, especially when they appear in Aristotelian thinking in very different political contexts. Consider two contemporaries, the Englishman John Case (1539/46–99), who taught at Oxford, and the Sienese Francesco Piccolomini (1523–1607), who taught at Padua. Case published commentaries on several of Aristotle's works, including the *Nicomachean Ethics* and the *Politics*, while Piccolomini was the author of a treatise, *Universa philosophia de moribus*, in which, although he occasionally disagrees with Aristotle, his overall project is to present an Aristotelian account of the virtues.[8] I begin with Piccolomini.

He addressed his book to the senators of the Venetian republic, urging upon them that sound instruction of Venetian young men concerning the virtues was necessary for the flourishing of the Venetian or any other republic. Virtue is that which renders a human being fit for *imperium* (X.110), and philosophical teaching about the virtues has an indispensable part in making the young virtuous. Such teaching is not of course the only thing necessary. Natural endowments and good habits are also essential. 'Nature forms appropriately what belongs to the body, habituation corrects desire, education forms reasoning' (X.33). What kind of education? 'The mistress of this education is civil philosophy: by forming prudence it prescribes laws to particular inclinations' (X.33). How then does philosophy carry out this task? It supplies a theoretical knowledge of the human good that enables the student of philosophy in particular situations to judge whether or not it would further the achievement of that good, if he were to act on this particular inclination. Prudence is just applied philosophy, and generally, although not necessarily, the lack of a philosophical education will be a source of imperfect prudence, especially of the kind of prudence required to manage the affairs of the Venetian republic.

The difference from Aristotle is striking, although unperceived by Piccolomini. Aristotle did indeed hold that a theoretical knowledge of the human good can and should inform practice on certain occasions, as I suggested earlier in this chapter and as I have argued elsewhere.[9] But, in order to make good use of this theoretical knowledge, one must already possess the virtue of prudence. The acquisition of prudence, on Aristotle's account, does not itself require theoretical study. An action is virtuous when it is the kind of action that a *phronimos* would perform in that particular type of situation, when the agent, knowing that what he does is the just or courageous or temperate thing to do, does it just because this is what justice or courage or temperateness requires, and when in so acting the agent acts from a settled and stable disposition (*NE* II.5.1105a31–33). To become prudent and virtuous, one needs teachers who both by example and by instruction will train one so that one becomes disposed to respond appropriately in each particular set of circumstances, while still unable to explain why one acts as one does, let alone to provide a theoretical account. At this stage what matters about one's teachers—older family members, friends, athletic trainers, whoever—is their possession of prudence and other moral virtues, and not their aptitude for theory.

With Piccolomini, by contrast, the key role is that of the philosopher as teacher, the philosopher as servant of the Venetian republic, playing a badly needed part in the life of that republic. Venice was, on Piccolomini's view, an example of that mixed form of government that Aristotle had commended, a city whose senators already exhibit the virtues that are needed for the political life. It never seems to have occurred to him either that Aristotle would have taken sixteenth-century Venice to be the type of commercial oligarchy that embodies a drastic misunderstanding of the point and purpose of a *polis* or that, if Venice's senators—who had not been educated in philosophy—already exhibited the virtues, his claims about the need for a philosophical education were put in question. Yet none of this makes his bold claim that it is through learning moral and political philosophy that one becomes prudent less interesting, especially because it is not only his claim, but one to be found in the writings of other renaissance Aristotelians.

In 1585, the Oxford University Press published its first book, John Case's *Speculum quaestionum moralium, in Universam Ethicen Aristotelis*, a detailed exposition of and commentary upon the *Nicomachean Ethics*. Case's preface addressed the students of both Oxford and Cambridge, telling them that moral philosophy is 'the norm of *mores*, the mistress of the virtues, the *gnōmon* of life, the rule of actions'. What then is the relationship between moral philosophy and *phronēsis, prudentia*? We are not simply to identify them, as we may be tempted to do, since 'moral philosophy treats these goods in terms of *genus*, *prudentia* in terms of *species*' (lib. VI, cap.5). The philosopher supplies the agent with a set of generalizations. The prudent agent applies them to particular types of situation. As with Piccolomini, prudence is taken to be applied moral philosophy. And, again as with Piccolomini, the university teacher of moral philosophy has been assigned an indispensable social and political role.

To anyone who cites Aristotle—as Shakespeare did (*Troilus and Cressida* II, ii, 16)—in order to argue that the students of such teachers are too young to benefit morally from their instruction, Case has two replies. The first is that what matters is not being young in years but being immature. The second is a response to the objection that, if a boy can obey the precepts of virtue, as on Case's view he can, then it must be that the precepts of virtue can be obeyed without prudence. Not so, says Case. Prudence must be already in the boy, even if inchoately (lib. VI, cap.13). So, contrary to Aristotle, the teaching of moral philosophy to the young can be effective by moving the young from inchoate prudence to the exercise of that heroic and general prudence which it is the end of moral education to inculcate. Why does this matter politically? In his unpublished *Apologia academiarum*[10] Case declared that 'without universities and men educated in letters great empires are nothing other than dens of wolves and tyrants: So that, just as with Piccolomini, the teacher of Aristotelian moral philosophy is portrayed as an indispensable servant of the renaissance state.

It is important in more than one way that the Aristotle whose texts were given this kind of political importance, whether in Venice or in England, was of course Aristotle misunderstood. How typical this type of misunderstanding was certainly needs further enquiry. Yet, if the teaching of Aristotle was to win the regard and approval of those for whom the most urgent question was whether or not that teaching would foster respect for established authority, whether in Venice or in England, perhaps the only acceptable Aristotle was the Aristotle of Piccolomini and Case. And those of us who identify ourselves as Aristotelians can take comfort in this, that, when that Aristotle was not too long afterwards rejected as a political and moral teacher, the philosopher who was rejected was not in fact Aristotle, but an impostor.

IV

For two hundred years, from the early seventeenth to the early nineteenth century, no one made anything much of Aristotle, politically or otherwise. But then two things began to happen. Classical philology gradually provided better texts than anyone had had since Aristotle's ancient editors. And scholars provided commentaries of ever-increasing linguistic, historical and philosophical sophistication. A privileged minority of German, British and French schoolboys—and a few determined and intense girls—learnt at school and as undergraduates to be at home in classical Greek, even in Aristotle's crabbed Greek, in numbers that would have amazed their medieval and renaissance predecessors. And even the linguistically deprived Greekless students in moral philosophy and political theory classes found and find themselves provided with translation after translation. So it might seem that the twentieth and twenty-first centuries must be the age of Aristotle finally being understood, rescued from medieval and renaissance disagreement and partisanship by the objectivity of classical scholarship and by the excellence of historical and philosophical commentary. The objectivity and the excellence are real enough. But so too is the continuing depth of disagreement and partisanship. So that ours has become yet another age of a multiplicity of Aristotles, political and otherwise.

There is a foreshadowing of this in the nineteenth century, when Aristotle is invoked as a predecessor by thinkers of quite different philosophical and political views. Mill in *On Liberty* refers to Aristotle as a judicious utilitarian and, since this is what he took himself to be, this is more than a compliment. Marx remarkably often cites and praises Aristotle as having prepared the way for his own thought, and Heinz Lubasz[11] and Patricia Springborg[12] have brought out just how far Aristotle's influence on Marx extended. T. H. Green believed himself to be developing Aristotle's view in his discussion of the relationship of duties to rights, saying of Aristotle that he 'regards the state (*polis*) as a society of which the life is maintained by what its members do for the sake of maintaining it . . . and which in that sense imposes duties; and at the same time as a society from which its members derive the ability . . . to fulfil their several functions and which in that sense confers rights'.[13] And A. C. Bradley argued in 1880 that, just because the ideals of modern civilization are so different from those of the

Greek city, the spirit of Aristotle's conception of the Greek city is a valuable corrective to the errors and defects of modernity.[14] Aristotle thus retains his place in our recent and contemporary conversations.

Yet at this point, we cannot avoid asking whether what this narrative has provided are four—or more—perspectives on Aristotle, four—or more—different uses to which Aristotle can legitimately be put or, instead, four—or more—Aristotles. With all the gains provided by twentieth-century translation and commentary, questions of this kind remain to vex us, so that I cannot avoid returning to the account of Aristotle that I presented in the introductory section of this chapter, noting that each of its main contentions is an answer to a still disputed question. I begin with my assertion that Aristotle's exclusions of women and others from the political life rendered his use and understanding of the concept of the specific *ergon* of human beings incoherent, and that therefore a consistent Aristotelianism would require their excision from his political philosophy. Susan Moller Okin, whose scathingly effective feminist critiques made her untimely death even more lamentable than it would otherwise have been, argued that those exclusions cannot be excised from Aristotle's thought, unless we reject some of his central metaphysical concepts, notably that of form, since these too presuppose the inferiority of women. One does not have to be an antifeminist to disagree with Okin, as the example of Charlotte Witt shows. My point is simply that, in arguing as I did and do, I was and am taking up a position on a still highly disputed terrain.

Second, consider my claim that the *Politics* and the *Nicomachean Ethics* should be read together or not at all and set beside it what Carnes Lord has written in his 'Introduction': 'It is probably best to assume that the *Politics* was composed by Aristotle as an independent work intended to be intelligible in its own terms without depending essentially on the ethical writings'.[15] So here again extensive argument is needed, but there is no reason to believe that it would, no matter how skillfully deployed, secure agreement. The same is true of a third claim that I made, when I presented as Aristotle's view the thesis that the philosophical life, the life that culminates in the achievement of *theōria*, is the completion of the political life and not an alternative to it. A very different view is argued powerfully by Richard Kraut. 'On my reading, Aristotle holds that there are two good ways of answering the question "What is happiness?" According to the best of these two answers, happiness consists in just one good, the virtuous exercise of the theoretical part of reason . . . . According to the second best answer, happiness consists in virtuous practical activity',[16] and Kraut goes on to speak of these as the best life and the second best life.

I am, as of now, convinced of two things: first, that I will not be justified in continuing to hold the positions that I do, unless I am able to supply adequate argumentative responses to such arguments as those of Okin, Lord, Kraut and all those others whose positions are incompatible with mine *and*, second, that I can in fact supply such a response. But I would be foolish to suppose that by making it, I will secure agreement, if only because those with whom I disagree share those convictions with respect to their positions. How then should we proceed? Immediately, by reminding ourselves of how wide and deep the disagreements are, some of them wide-ranging and systematic, others concerning the translation of particular passages, yet others to do with both of these. As an example of the latter, I think of my own disagreements with the author of one of the more impressive late twentieth-century books about Aristotle's politics, Fred D. Miller, Jr., in which Miller ascribes to Aristotle the thesis that 'that constitution is best according to nature which is unqualifiedly just and which guarantees the rights of its citizens according to this standard',[17] so making of Aristotle a precursor of modern theorists of rights.

The case for this thesis could not be made better than Miller makes it. Yet quite a number of us remain unconvinced. What do we quarrel with? In part, it is Miller's broad claim about the place that a Hohfeldian notion of a claim right has in Aristotle's thought; in part it is Miller's translations of such expressions as '*to dikaion*', '*to hautou*' and '*exousia*'. But these are closely related. Miller says, for example, that 'one important use of "*to dikaion*" is to refer to a right in the sense of a just claim' and he goes on to give examples of what he takes to be such uses. One problem for me is that in modern English, the expression 'right' never has the same sense as the expression 'just claim'. A right may well be cited in order to show that a particular claim is just. But just claims can have other grounds. So, if we translate '*to dikaion*' to mean 'just claim', this is enough to show that it cannot be translated by 'right' and the grounds that Aristotle might give for asserting that some particular claim is just would certainly not include the citation of some right. So Miller and I would translate such passages as

NE 1132a24–29 very differently. Do I think that in saying this I have given someone who takes Miller's view sufficient reason for changing her or his mind? Of course not. Yet this is only one among a set of apparently unresolvable disagreements, and no single political Aristotle emerges from contemporary debates, but rather a figure presented in very different guises. Tell me merely that you are an Aristotelian and I will not as yet know what you are telling me.

V

How then should we think about this condition that we find ourselves in? Very much, I suggest, as we already think about medieval and renaissance Aristotelians. With such figures as Aquinas and Oresme, Piccolomini and Case, we distinguish, so far as we can, between what they found in Aristotle's texts as they encountered them and what they brought to those texts as interpreters, and we further distinguish, so far as we can, between what they brought to those texts that was influenced by their culture and what they brought to those texts that was peculiarly their own. In putting these distinctions to work, we have to recognize that Aristotle's texts, even when we have learnt more from the philologists than was possible for our medieval and renaissance predecessors, underdetermine their interpretation at significant points. Learning to think about ourselves in this light is not an alternative to developing further and defending further the various accounts of Aristotle as a political thinker that some of us have advanced. But, if we do not so learn, we may be in danger of becoming the victims of our own unrecognized presuppositions.

SEVENTEEN

Two Kinds of Political Reasoning

I

It is for me a peculiar pleasure to give this lecture *here*. A special importance attaches to universities part of whose central mission is to provide education and enquiry for those for whom this is more of an adventure than it is for standard student populations, for those who may be the first members of their family ever to enter a university, for those who have the courage to risk failure in order to achieve success. Those of us who have the good fortune to aid this mission even in small ways, whether directly or indirectly, are thereby privileged.

What I am presenting in this lecture is a research project which is still in its early stages. That project, at once philosophical and sociological,

"Two Kinds of Political Reasoning," paper presented at Centre for Contemporary Aristotelian Studies in Ethics and Politics, London Metropolitan University, 2010.

is concerned with the relationships between desire and practical reasoning, relationships that have a number of dimensions, one of them political. Since the tradition within which I work is that of a Thomistic Aristotelianism, one task that I need to carry through is that of sketching—and at the moment no more than sketching—what it would be to engage with contemporary politics in a manner at least consonant with what Aristotle and Aquinas say. And of course the first danger here is that of falling into absurdity. For any attempt to move too quickly or too easily from political descriptions and prescriptions framed either in the ancient Greece of the fourth century BC or the medieval France of the thirteenth century AD to descriptions and prescriptions relevant to our modern condition is bound not just to fail, but to result in anachronistic irrelevance.

How then to proceed? I am able to keep in mind the sharp contrast between contemporary political preoccupations and those that found expression in the writings of Aristotle and Aquinas by contrasting two kinds of practical reasoning, one first identified and described only in the twentieth century and one that, although still informing the judgments and actions of some of us, was recognized and identified by Aristotle and Aquinas.

What I contrast are two forms of shared deliberation. By shared deliberation I mean any type of rational debate in which through reasoned argument members of some group, institution, or organization arrive at effective decisions about what they or those authorized to act in their name should do in some particular area. The kinds of group that I have in mind are diverse: families, schools, trade unions, theatre companies, cities, political societies. The subject-matter of such deliberation is the rank ordering and distribution of those goods that are the common concern of members of the group.

To speak of a rank ordering of goods is to pose questions about which goods are to be preferred to which, either more generally or on this or that particular occasion. Are we to prefer increased leisure over increased productivity or vice versa? Do we choose to have limitations on freedom in order to secure an egalitarian society or do we choose instead to have freedoms that generate inequality? Are we to invest in string quartets and jazz bands or in soccer clubs and sporting arenas? To speak of the distribution of goods is to pose questions about *whose* claims for scarce resources are to be given priority. How do we rank the needs of the young against those of the old? What should be allocated to active productive workers and what to the sick or disabled? How should we reward those whose activities are necessary for the community's flourishing in special ways, school teachers, physicians, nurses, circus clowns, as contrasted with productive workers in farms and factories?

The difference between the two forms of shared deliberation through which we can arrive at answers to such questions can be framed initially either as a difference in the concepts presupposed and put to work in each type of deliberation or as a difference in the norm-governed social relationships of the members of the group. But these turn out to be one and the same. To presuppose and put to work certain types of concept in one's shared deliberations with others just is to stand in a certain kind of norm-governed relationship to those others. So that it does not matter from which we begin and I choose arbitrarily to begin from the conceptual differences.

Consider first those groups in which the goal of shared deliberation is the resolution of conflicts between those with competing interests. Such groups are divided into two or more subgroups, each with a strong and settled preference for an ordering of goods and an allocation of scarce resources that is incompatible with the strong and settled preferences of the members of the other contending subgroups. How the members of each subgroup determined what their preferences are is generally and characteristically irrelevant to the members of the other subgroups. Each has to treat the preferences of the others as given. Deliberations between such subgroups, or more often between their representatives, takes the form of bargaining and skill in shared deliberation is skill in conducting negotiations in bargaining situations, skill exhibited in good judgment as to what concessions will be sufficiently attractive to the other rival bargaining parties for them to be prepared to offer in return just those concessions that are most attractive to you and to your group. What the outcome of such bargaining is will therefore depend both on what resources each group brings to the bargaining table, that is on what and how much that others want they are able to offer to those others, and on the bargaining skills of the negotiators for each group. But no degree of skill will avail, if the group has nothing relevant to offer, if, that is to say, it is powerless.

Powerlessness however is not in the least a disqualification for effective participation is the other kind of shared deliberation that I want to consider. For here the attempt is to identify what—here and now and in concrete terms—the common good of this or that particular group is. But to be able to contribute to determining what the common good of one's group is does not in the least depend on what resources one brings to the discussion, other than resources of character and mind. What then is it that we mean when we speak of common goods, contrasting them with both individual goods and public goods? What it is good and best for an individual to do here and now is what will contribute most to her or his flourishing *qua* individual. But individuals, in order to achieve this or that individual good, often need to cooperate with other individuals who are each of them engaged in trying to achieve *their* individual goods. Individuals need such public goods as highways and street lighting and police forces, if they are to have the ordered environment that they need to pursue their individual goals. And one agency, sometimes the only agency, through which those public goods that are a necessary means for individuals to achieve their individual goods may be provided is government. But the public goods thus provided must not be confused with what Aristotle and especially Aquinas taught us to call common goods.

Common goods are more than a means to achieving and are not reducible to individual goods. A common good is always the good of some institution, organization, or other group, so that we may speak of the common goods of family, of workplace, of school or clinic, of orchestra or scientific research team, and sometimes of political society. A common good is something that can be achieved and enjoyed by individuals only *qua* family member, *qua* worker, *qua* teacher or student, *qua* citizen, and so on, and to determine what must be done here and now to achieve the good, the flourishing, of this particular family in these particular circumstances or that particular political society in those particular circumstances requires characteristically that individuals who belong to the group, or at least some of them, deliberate together as to what is now to be done or left undone, as to how goods are to be ordered and allocated on this particular occasion, if the common good is to be achieved. In political societies of course the achievement of the common good characteristically involves the achievement of certain public goods.

When I remarked earlier that relative powerlessness does not disqualify one from participation in this kind of shared deliberation, I did not mean to imply that the distribution of power within such groups plays no part in determining the course of the reasoning about common goods that their members engage in. For, if inequalities of power result in the exclusion from deliberation of some members of the group whose voices need to be heard if the common good is to be identified and attained, what will ensue will be only the appearance, but not the reality of effective deliberation aimed at achieving the common good. So too, if inequalities of power result in undue deference to some participants' arguments rather than to those of others, what will ensue will be once again the mere appearance of shared rational deliberation.

What the relevant equalities or inequalities of power are varies of course with the type of institution or organization. Which voices have to be heard, which points of view have to be taken into consideration, are not the same in families, in workplaces, in schools, in orchestras, in political societies. What does have to be the same, if common goods are to be achieved, is a widely shared high degree of regard for the common good and involving a recognition by individuals that their individual good is to be achieved only through the achievement of the common good. And this shared motivation is thus significantly different from the motivation of those engaged in maximizing their own preference satisfaction through negotiation and bargaining. How then do these two very different types of reasoning differ in the kind of shared deliberation in which they engage?

II

Happily we already possess an excellent account of the norms of rationality that govern deliberation among those concerned to maximize the satisfaction of their own preferences and the preferences of the like-minded. It is the account advanced by rational decision theorists and game theorists. Rational decision theory identifies the norms that each of us must respect in ordering our own individual preferences, if we are to make those decisions that we will subsequently have the least reason to regret, given those preferences. Game theory identifies the norms that we must each of us respect in bargaining with others, if we are to arrive at those agreements that we will subsequently have the least reason to regret, given those same preferences. Taken together those norms are constitutive of one conception of what practical rationality is, a conception that has been notably influential among economists and political scientists. But, if we are to understand what it is to act in accordance with this conception, when it is embodied in some form of our common life, we need to take note of two additional characteristics.

The first is that, in cases where there are more than two subgroups which are engaged in deliberative bargaining, it is often rational for one such subgroup to enter into either a short-term or a long term alliance with some other subgroup, in order to maximize their joint bargaining power on particular issues where the interests of the two overlap or coincide. About the formation and stability or instability of such coalitions we know a good deal as a result of the by now classical work of William Riker and his successors.

A second characteristic is the way in which moral considerations may enter into this type of practical reasoning. Such considerations may well play a part in the process by which individuals or groups determine what the ordering of their preferences is on this or that issue. Nothing in rational decision theory precludes individuals or sets of individuals from having among their preferences, perhaps as their strongest preference, a preference that such and such a morally desirable state of affairs should be realized. And it is a crude misunderstanding of rational decision theory and of those transactions of which it gives an accurate account to suppose that individuals as understood by rational decision theorists are necessarily self-interested. Moreover individuals engaged in this type of deliberation who share their moral preferences with others so engaged, whether as partners or as opponents, may agree, consistently with the norms of decision theory and game theory, to bargain only under certain moral constraints.

Yet what force moral considerations have in such deliberations depends entirely on the relative strengths of the various preferences of the participants in deliberation. Those preferences provide the only inputs to this kind of deliberative reasoning. There is no shared or sharable standard, moral or otherwise, external to those preferences by reference to which they might be evaluated. To be rational just is to maximize preference satisfaction, whatever one's preferences happen to be.

By contrast for those whose shared deliberations aim at the achievement of some common good our knowledge of goods is independent of our expressions of preferences and such knowledge provides standards by which preferences are to be evaluated. Preferences that direct us away either from our own individual goods or from common goods are taken to be expressions of imperfectly ordered passions and desires and practical rationality requires of us that we should habituate ourselves, so that our preferences become preferences for the appropriate goods. Of what it is to reason as such an agent does we once again already have the outline of an account, that provided by Aristotle and Aquinas in what they say about deliberative excellence and the practical syllogism.

There are of course rival interpretations of the relevant texts. And I claim no more for my version as an interpretation than that it is as consistent with those texts as any of its rivals. What I do claim for it is that it captures accurately the practical reasoning employed by those aiming through shared deliberation to achieve some common good.[1] Such reasoners argue from at least one of each of two kinds of premise to a conclusion that is an action or a set of actions. The first kind of premise expresses a judgment that such and such is the good to be aimed at here and now. The second identifies that in the immediate circumstances which makes that good attainable. So in one of Aristotle's examples someone proceeds from the assertion of the premises 'Dry food is good for every human being' and 'This food is dry and I am a human being' to the conclusion that is the action of eating it (*Nicomachean Ethics* 1147a5–7). Such premises supply the answer to a question that it always makes sense to pose to an agent after she or he has acted: 'What was the good of your doing that then and there?' What an agent provides in giving such an answer by citing her or his reasoning is both an explanation and a justification, successful or unsuccessful.

For it to be a successful justification the good that it identifies as the good aimed at must not only be a genuine good, but it must also be *the* good to be aimed at in these particular circumstances by this kind of agent, a good such that there was no other good that this particular agent in these particular circumstances had a better reason to aim at. So a first stage in shared deliberation has to be a survey of the range of different goods that, given the present situation and the resources of this particular group, might now be attained, including among those goods the prevention or minimization of impending evils. And a second stage must be the rank ordering of those goods, so that it becomes clear either that there is better reason to aim here and now at this particular good rather than any other, or that there is more than one such good and that it is a matter of rational indifference which we attempt to achieve.

Note that in both stages the characterization of the present situation and of the group's resources plays a crucial part. And note too that the agents' desires never of themselves provide a reason for action. That an agent in reasoning and acting is in fact motivated by a desire for some particular good and thereby desires the attainment of whatever good will here and now contribute to the achievement of that good is what makes that agent's reasoning *practical* reasoning, is what makes it the case that her or his reasoning issues in action. But allusion to this presupposed motivating desire has no place in the reasoning itself. And, as with practical reasoning whose end is the achievement of individual goods, so it is too with practical reasoning whose end is the common good.

Consider a family in which, the three children having reached a certain age, the question is whether or not the mother should now take a job, perhaps part-time, perhaps full-time. The benefits of increased family income, of the intellectual stimulus of the job to the mother, the impact of her absence on the children, and on aunts and neighbors who may have to assume new responsibilities, the fatigue that may result from the job, all these are relevant to the issue of how the common good of the family will best be served. The good of each individual member of the family is involved, but also how the mother's decision will affect the relationships between family members, relationships informed to greater or lesser degree both by an unpretentious justice that gives to each family member her or his due and by a cheerful commitment of each family member to care for each other. It is in the enjoyment of those relationships, in both contributing to them and being sustained by them, that the common good of a family is to be found. What such relationships exclude is that family members should each seek in their relationships with other family members to maximize their own preference satisfaction, substituting for argument that presupposes a shared allegiance to their common good argument designed to secure those outcomes that are most agreeable to each individual *qua* individual, rather than *qua* family member.

It is not of course that individual family members are precluded from bargaining and negotiating with each other. But such bargaining and negotiation, if it is not to corrode family relationships, has to be constrained by an overriding regard for the common good of the family, the flourishing of the family. And this point can be generalized. The social relationships among those who are participants in deliberation about the achievement of some common good are not only different from, but incompatible with the social relationships of those whose norms of practical rationality are those of rational decision theory and game theory. We have distinguished not just two kinds of practical reasoning, but two different modes of social life.

To this large claim there will be immediately at least two objections. The first is that by choosing the family as an example of the type of group whose activities are or can be directed to its common good I have made things too easy for myself. That the flourishing of families requires their members not to act towards each other as rational decision theory and game theory dictate might be true without this holding more generally of groups whose members share some common good. To which a first reply must be an unargued claim that a multiplication of different examples will in fact confirm this generalization. And I shall make a modest beginning to such a multiplication later in this paper. A second objection is that by speaking of families in terms of norms of justice and commitment to caring I have taken a wholly unrealistic and distortingly idealized view of families. This objection is based on a misunderstanding. What I have identified are the norms to which family members are committed by allegiance to the common good of the family. That most, even perhaps all families exemplify those norms only more or less imperfectly is of course true, but not to the point.

III

I have so far spoken of two kinds of shared deliberation. But each of these in some contexts becomes a form of shared political deliberation, of political reasoning. So let me consider the political aspect of each in turn. I begin from the politics of the modern liberal democratic state, which has as a principal function the resolution of conflicts between the representatives of rival and contending interests, economic, ideological, and social.

The institutions to which the representatives of such interests address themselves are characteristically one or more of the political parties, in the hope that the parties in return for financial and electoral support will become protagonists for their particular interests. Parties thus become coalitions of interest groups, characteristically defining their basic stance in terms that will allow for the coexistence within the party of the representatives of a variety of often very different interests.

Within parties bargaining and negotiation therefore have to take place as to which items in the party program are to be given greater priority and which lesser. And here a major consideration has to be the known preferences of probable voters. For only by satisfying those preferences can a party hope to win elections and become a governing party. A political party is therefore an arena within which debates on the program that is to be presented at an election are about how to satisfy *both* the preferences of those members of interest groups who provide the party with its support and membership *and* the preferences of the voters who will decide the election, a complex exercise in the maximization of preference satisfaction.

To think politically in this way is to reason in accordance with the norms of decision theory and game theory. It is to reason about the rank ordering and allocation of goods, and what counts as a good is whatever happens to be taken to be a good by those whose preferences must be taken into account in the calculations of those engaged in building coalitions and attempting to win elections. And the preferences thus weighed are the preferences of individuals, some of them translated in—given Arrow's theorem—not always satisfactory ways into the group interest of this or that contending faction and many more of them expressed in elections precisely as the preferences of individuals whose right to vote is a right of individual adults *qua* individual adults.

So my claim is that reasoning in accordance with the norms of decision theory and game theory is *the* dominant form, even if not the only form, of political reasoning in the societies of advanced liberal modernity. It is very much to the point that, insofar as one thinks about politics in this way, one thinks of politics in economic terms. Parties that compete for the allegiance of voters, by promising to satisfy their preferences more adequately than any rival will, in some salient respects resemble corporations that compete for the allegiance of consumers by promising to satisfy *their* preferences more adequately than any rival will. And it is not difficult therefore to be equally at home in the arenas of politics and in the marketplace. What fosters success in both realms is economic growth, growth in the availability of those resources that will enable this interest group or that party or that firm to outbid its rivals.

So it is an almost unquestioned presupposition of such political thinking that economic growth is a very great good, and that consumption is to be encouraged not only for the present satisfaction that it affords, but also as a stimulus to future economic growth, and that, whatever good reasons there may be in favor of engaging in actions that do not conduce to economic growth, there may always be good reason to question the devotion of resources to such activities. Thus whatever good reasons there may be for investing in, say, art or education or intellectual enquiry, there may always be a case to be made against such investment, if it does not conduce to economic growth.

Consider now by contrast some ways in which shared deliberation aimed at the achievement of common goods may become political reasoning. The activity in which the common good of a family is most obviously realized is in the education of children, an education that at its best—and even the best of us are not at our best all the time—provides children with what they need rather than what they want, without damaging their spontaneity or their questioning. But the provision of such an education generally lies well beyond the powers and resources of a single family. So there is a common good for families in each particular area in having a flourishing school, or schools in their neighborhood, schools whose participants—parents, teachers, students, janitors, maintenance staff—all have as their common good the flourishing of that particular school. But where are they to find the resources—the building, the well-trained teachers, the playgrounds, the child-friendly janitors and maintenance staff? It is in answering this question that politics begins. And parents can only bring up children well, if at least one of them is in full-time employment with not too long working hours and wages adequate for bringing up a family. But to achieve these often requires not only trade union militancy, but once again a politics of local and beyond local government. So what would it be to engage in such a politics?

IV

There have been some notable cases in the modern world from the seventeenth century onwards in which a politics of the common good was able to achieve its ends in a small scale political society in which regard for that common good informed the activities of a sufficiently large number of its members, so that the common goods of family, of workplace, of school, clinic, and the like, were achieved and enjoyed in and through the achievement of the larger common good of the political society as a whole. Examples of such political societies have flourished in very different environments. Consider four such: the Jesuit-led Guarani Indian settlements in seventeenth and eighteenth century Paraguay, comprising in their final period over 21,000 families—the first Communist societies in the modern world; the kibbutzim, the autonomous collective farm communities founded by Jewish settlers in British-ruled Palestine in the nineteen thirties; the state of Kerala in Southern India after the electoral victory of the Communist Party of India (Marxist) in 1957, when a program was implemented, whereby slower rates of economic growth and high rates of taxation combined to sustain a just distribution of basic social goods, resulting in widespread literacy, education, good health, life expectancy, and political participation; and the successful farming and fishing cooperatives in Glencolmcille in the Co. Donegal in Ireland between the nineteen sixties and nineteen eighties.

The very different political and economic structures in these four cases all turned out to be compatible with a widespread regard for the achievement and enjoyment of the common goods of family, schools, workplaces, and of the political society itself. And all of them flourished for significant periods of time. It is at once obvious however that what they have in common renders them atypical. They are or were all relatively small-scale, and even the exception, Kerala, in 1951 had a population of only 13.5 million. They are or were all either economically self-sufficient or so situated that the acquisition of the needed economic resources was relatively unproblematic. They are or were all morally and religiously homogeneous or else in the case of the exception, once again Kerala, with a long history of peaceful pluralism. And none of them are or were afflicted by gross inequalities of wealth or power, except, once again in Kerala, where diminishing the power of the landowners was an essential ingredient of Kerala's communal achievements. But, that is to say, they are or were all of them atypical of the larger political societies of modernity, characterized as those generally are by large populations, large-scale institutions, integration into, dependence upon, and vulnerability to global markets, lack of religious and moral consensus, and gross inequalities of wealth and power. So, it might well be concluded, although, I believe, mistakenly that in these four political societies what justifies us in understanding their modes of political reasoning and their ordering of goods in Thomistic Aristotelian terms is just that which makes them irrelevant as models for political practice in contemporary societies.

Yet the concept of the common good of political society is not so easily to be set aside. For care for the common goods of families, work places, schools, and other local institutions not only requires political engagement aimed at providing the resources that all of these need and a systematic and aggressive critique of all those policies of the larger political society that would deny them those resources, but also recurrent political struggle in the larger society for the control of those resources, so that the conclusions arrived at thorough the shared deliberation of those participating in the lives of families, workplaces, schools, and the like *can* effectively determine how the resources that they obtain are to be used.

And what the examples of political achievement that I have cited— and numerous others—teach us is that the achievement of such relatively small-scale political institutions *can* be successful in a variety of different forms, all involving the achievement of some degree of independence from the modern state and from its centralizing tendencies. Such independence has three dimensions. It requires powers of local political self-determination, local control over the resources needed for the flourishing of families, workplaces, schools, and the like, and leadership that makes itself locally accountable. But how are these to be achieved? To this question I want to give two answers that are at first sight very different, but that are, so I shall argue, complementary.

The first is this: the only way to construct and sustain local institutions and local societies within which a politics of the common good is at home in the circumstances of modern societies is for those dedicated to the common good of those local groups to engage at whatever level is necessary, local, regional, national, in the liberal democratic politics of interest and bargaining and compromise in a piecemeal way. It is often only through campaigning in those terms and by those means for trade union goals, for better schools, for better provision of medical services and the like that resources can become available, that local control can be achieved. And therefore it is from time to time necessary for those committed to a politics of the common good to make conditional and qualified alliances with this or that interest group or coalition of interest groups or political party. Opposition to the dominant political modes of advanced modernity does not preclude, but often requires participation in its politics, participation designed in the end to be subversive of just those modes. But what form should such participation take?

V

I shall delay an answer to this question in order first to consider an objection that any Thomistic Aristotelian might advance against what I have said so far about the politics of common goods. For I must seem to have ignored almost completely the importance of what Aristotle and Aquinas say about the relationship of the life of the virtues to political activity. After all both Aristotle and Aquinas insist that the end and purpose of law and of law-governed institutions, their proper effect, is to make human beings good and to do so by inculcating the virtues. And they also agree that the achievement of common goods is possible only in and through the exercise of the virtues. So what is the relationship of these claims about the virtues to the account that I have given so far of what it is to reason productively with a view to determining and achieving the common good?

In that account my references to the virtues have so far been brief and incidental. I spoke at one point of the need for those aiming at the common good to order their passions and desires, so that they become motivated by desire for the common good. And this ordering certainly requires training in and exercise of the virtues. I also spoke of the need to rank order goods and whether such rank ordering is done well or badly also depends upon how the virtues are exercised. And finally in sketching what it is for the members of a family to aim at their common good I noted that their relationship must be informed by justice. But to carry the argument any further I must now say a good deal more about the political exercise of the cardinal virtues.

When Aristotle and Aquinas remark that the end of political actions is to make human beings good, this sounds much less moralistic in Aristotle's Greek or Aquinas's Latin than it does in contemporary English. To be good, as Aristotle and Aquinas understand it, is to be good at achieving those goods that characteristically and generally enable human beings to flourish. The virtues are those qualities in which we need to excel, if we are to achieve those goods. And without the virtues we are unable to rank order goods in importance either generally or for each of us here and now in this or that particular set of circumstances. So to have an adequate conception of what it would be for this or that individual to have lived her or his life well is to be able to say what it would be for her or him to have made good virtue-informed choices between alternative courses of action, so that she or he was directed beyond the various finite goods of her or his life towards that ultimate good which provides the measure of those finite goods, which is presupposed in the evaluation of those goods.

Yet the ordering of goods in each of our lives is of course something that we cannot achieve on our own, but only in and through relationships with others, those relationships through which common goods are achieved, family relationships, work relationships, political relationships and, since it is only in and through political relationships that many of our other goods are to be achieved ethics is for both Aristotle and Aquinas a part of politics. So the key to the moral life is a political understanding of the virtues.

What would it be to translate such an understanding into contemporary terms? We learn, on a Thomistic Aristotelian view, to understand the virtues in two ways: first through training in and exercise of the virtues, so that we ourselves become agents whose habitual responses in feeling, judgment, and action are such that we not only act as we should, but would not want to act otherwise; and secondly as those whose activities are recurrently frustrated by vices that misdirect action, whether our own or those of others. Good judgment acquired through exercise of the virtues is an indispensable prologue to this second kind of learning, for not only do we find it much easier to recognize the vices of others than our own, but even our judgments about their vices will be distorted and inadequate, if our own standpoint is not that of an agent committed to judging her or himself by the standards of the virtues. Nonetheless it may be instructive for my present argument to begin from the second, by asking what, in contemporary terms, are the key political vices.

Aquinas's scheme of virtues and vices classifies a number of virtues that Aristotle treats as distinct as parts or aspects of the four cardinal virtues. So I should consider in turn, if I were to follow his account, the vices that mark the characters of those who are lacking in courage, temperateness, justice, and prudence. Here I will restrict myself to examples of failure in courage and temperateness. The vices that are the counterparts of courage are rashness and cowardice. Cowards risk too little. The rash risk too much. Questions of which risks it is right to take and how to take them are at the heart of political life and political risk-taking can go wrong in at least three ways. It can result from underestimations of the potential harms and dangers to the risk-taker or to others. It can result from an over or underestimation of the goods to be achieved or the evils averted through this or that particular act of risk-taking. Or it can result from ineptitude in acting as the situation requires. Consider in this light as examples of political virtue in respect of risk-taking the four examples that I cited earlier.

The seventeenth century Guarani Indians faced a choice between on the one hand a certain fate of enslavement by Spanish settlers, hard labor, and early death, and an unknown and certainly hazardous collective future under the proto-Leninist leadership of Father Antonio Ruiz de Montoya and his fellow Jesuits. The early founders of the kibbutzim both had a vision of a future for European Jews that was at odds with more than one influential competing vision and an estimate of the possibilities of agricultural settlements in Palestine that was at odds with other estimates. The local leadership of the Communist Party of India (Marxists) in Kerala in 1957 had to steer a difficult path between doing too much to placate the opposition of the Indian central government and of the landowning classes and doing too little to transform the condition of the poor. The small farmers of southwest Donegal and their children in the nineteen sixties had to decide between a hitherto unknown life of collective and cooperative farming and fishing that would sustain them as an Irish speaking community and emigration to join earlier generations of emigrants with much higher incomes in English-speaking Chicago.

What needs to be emphasized is twofold: that in each case the judgments made were based on a reasonable but tough-minded estimate of the risks involved in the key choices and that the leadership who provided these estimates knew how to act decisively and effectively in carrying through the initial and subsequent phases of the project. The sound practical reasoning about the common good of those leaders and their shared deliberation with those whom they led were crucial. And what was required of both, in order to be effectively courageous, was therefore not only courage itself, but also prudence, the virtue of practical intelligence.

When we turn to the political vices that are the counterpart of the virtue of temperateness, the lessons to be learned are remarkably similar. Those vices consist in undisciplined wanting, in excessive desire or inadequate desire. Those who desire too little, who are happy with what little they are given, are unable to embark on great enterprises. Those who desire too much require to be satisfied too soon and are consumed by their own desire, so that it dictates to them rather than motivates them. The first defect results in political passivity, the second in unbridled acquisitiveness and so in political and economic misdirection. It is noteworthy that in all four of my examples those who participated in the enterprises set themselves large goals that could not be quickly accomplished. Their desires had to be such as to allow them to be patient and to make them persistent, characteristics that, on Aquinas's account, are marks of courage. So temperateness and courage complement one another. And, if we follow Aquinas further, we need to note that both virtues are possible only for those who are also to a significant degree just and that no one can be just, courageous, or temperate without also being prudent, for to be prudent is to know how to reason well practically and politically.

It is prudence that needs to be exercised in deciding when and how, in the interests of a politics of common goods, to go beyond the contexts of local community in the interests of constructing local community and to participate in the regional and national politics of coalitions, bargaining, and compromise in order to gain or keep resources and local control. What such participation must be informed and constrained by is an identification of the political and economic vices embodied in the dominant structures of regional, national, and global enterprises. And here the events of the last two years have done much of my work for me: the irrational risk taking of some, the political passivity of others, and the unbridled acquisitiveness of those in the financial sector are not just defects of individuals, but are the inescapable outcome of the institutional structures, roles, and goals of the dominant polity. It is on these that any critique of the failure of contemporary political orders not directed towards the common good would have to focus. And participation in the politics of such orders by anyone whose allegiance is to common goods has therefore two aspects. It has indeed to be directed towards the achievement of resources and of decentralized control for the local community, but it must also provide the basis for a critique of the larger society by the standards of the political virtues, virtues which are not just local, but human.

VI

On a Thomistic Aristotelian view of the relationship of the virtues to practical reasoning anyone who aspires to be a good practical reasoner, anyone whose goal is both the determination and the achievement of common goods, must learn to exercise the virtue of prudence and, since prudence is impossible without the exercise of the other moral virtues, good practical reasoning and significantly developed moral character are inseparable. But for those who take the aim of practical reasoning to be, one way or another, the maximization of preference satisfaction, this is certainly not the case.

From the standpoint of the norms of decision theory and game theory practical rationality is one thing and morality another. There have indeed been theorists who have tried to derive the prescriptions of morality from those of decision theory and game theory, but—and I cannot argue this here—I take them to have failed. Indeed I take the employment of decision theory and game theory *in limited contexts* to be compatible with almost any moral standpoint, including that of Thomistic Aristotelianism and even the treatment of the norms of decision theory and game theory as definitive of practical rationality is compatible with a number of moral standpoints. What matters for my present argument is that such an understanding of practical rationality can find no place for any substantive conception of the common good. The expression 'the common good' may 'indeed find a place in the political rhetoric of those whose conception of practical rationality is of this kind. But all that can be referred to by it are some set of public goods, reducible to and a means to the achievement of individual goods. Any use of this expression intended to mean what Thomistic Aristotelians mean by it must appear from this point of view to be grounded in philosophical error and expressive of political obfuscation and illusion.

It turns out then that what I initially identified as two contrasting types of practical reasoning, each at home within a different set of social relationships, do in fact presuppose not just different, but incompatible ways of understanding the political and social world. The next tasks are therefore twofold, first to develop in detail what I have only here sketched in outline, the content of each of the two conflicting views, and secondly to identify further the several points at which they are in philosophical disagreement or political conflict and to ask by what standards the arguments on each side are to be evaluated. But these, perhaps happily, are tasks for other occasions.

EIGHTEEN

Happiness

I

Announcements by kings of Bhutan rarely reverberate beyond the kingdom's borders. But, when the fourth king, on assuming power in 1972, declared that his government would take as its goal not the maximization of the Gross National Product, but the maximization of the Gross National Happiness, he provided political reasoning and political rhetoric with a new and growingly influential concept. It is true that most of those who have made use of this concept have paid scant attention to the detail of what the king said, ignoring the Buddhist strains in the king's conception of happiness. Had they done so, it might have been a little less easy than it has been to give happiness the place that it has had in recent political discussions. Why has it been so easy? For two reasons.

The first is the important place that a certain conception of happiness now has in our everyday thought and speech. As customers enter a local

"Happiness," paper presented at Centre for Contemporary Aristotelian Studies in Ethics and Politics, London Metropolitan University, 2010.

department store, a poster tells them that 'Our goal is to make you happy'. And the king of Bhutan and the directors of JCPenney are joined by a host of advertisers, lovers, authors of self-help books, therapists, and politicians promising happiness, while those to whom such promises are made often feel uneasy, anxious, and even sometimes indignant, if they fail to be happy. For unhappiness can now be thought of as a kind of failure. So unhappiness can become a guilty secret, happiness a proud boast. And, given all this, it is easy to understand why the proposal to make the maximization of the happiness of its citizens the goal of the state should have persuaded so many. But a second line of thought pointed in the same direction.

In 1991 Martin Seligman, a psychologist at the University of Pennsylvania justly notable for his theory of 'learned helplessness', laid the basis for the movement known as 'Positive Psychology' by publishing *Learned Optimism: How to Change Your Mind and Your Life*. One effect was a remarkable growth in studies of happiness and related topics by experimental and social psychologists, with a multiplication of interesting findings. Ed Diener and his colleagues had already been at work on the relationship between income levels and happiness.[1] Other research identified relationships between happiness and aging, happiness and marital status, happiness and satisfaction with work, and the like. Daniel Kahneman and Daniel Gilbert both provided strong evidence about how bad we generally are at predicting what will make us happy. And some different measures of happiness were devised.[2] One outcome was the construction of the World Data Base of Happiness at Erasmus University in Rotterdam.

Enter the economists, whose contribution has been to show both how happiness studies can contribute to a more sophisticated understanding of what it is to maximize preference satisfaction and what the relationship might be between economic and social institutional arrangements and the achievement of happiness.[3] This kind of work was made possible by those who had showed how measurements of happiness deriving from one source could be compared with measurements of happiness deriving from another. So, for example, in the United Kingdom it was recently the case that an increase of salary of one thousand pounds on average increases happiness by 0.0007 points on a seven point scale, while seeing one's friends more often increases one's happiness by 0.161 points on the same scale (reported appropriately enough in the *Financial Times*, August 28, 2010).

What has been noteworthy about this enterprise is the degree to which the study of happiness has become a joint enterprise of psychologists, sociologists, and economists, who constantly cross-reference each others' work. It is then of the first importance that, when they use the word 'happiness' and its cognates, they should all mean much the same thing by it. Do they? And do they mean by it what the advertisers, the therapists, the politicians, and the everyday language-users mean by it?

At first sight we may seem to have a considerable problem. Different researchers offer different definitions of happiness. Some researchers define happiness in one way in one paper, in another in another. Different and rival measures of happiness have been proposed and employed. Yet a careful reading of the literature suggests that all these are attempts to grasp one and the same notion, the very notion that is at home in everyday thought and language. It is a notion captured by the sociologist, Ruut Veenhoven, Professor of Happiness Studies at Erasmus University and Director of the World Data Base, when he declared that "In my fifty years of researching the subject the definition of happiness hasn't changed. It's a subjective appreciation of life," and by Richard Layard, economic advisor to the United Kingdom's New Labour government from 1997 to 2001, when he wrote that "by happiness I mean feeling good—enjoying life and wanting the feeling to be maintained."[4] Let us spell out what they were saying a little further.

When people speak of happiness, as they understand it and as they take others to understand it, they refer to a psychological state, a state of being pleased with, contented with, satisfied with some aspect of one's life—one's marriage and family life, one's financial circumstances, one's work—or with one's life as a whole. And it is not just that one finds life as a whole or in this or that respect agreeable, but that one finds the thoughts and feelings that one has in contemplating it agreeable. So if one is happy, one wants to go on being happy, and, if one is unhappy, one wants to become happy. Happiness is something that everyone wants. Might I take myself to be happy, when in fact I am not? This plainly seems to be possible. I may perhaps have discontents that I refuse to acknowledge, insisting to myself and to others that I am perfectly happy, deceiving myself and also perhaps them. But by and large the best evidence that someone is happy is that they say that they are without manifest insincerity and give no evidence to the contrary. And it is on this assumption that almost all of our contemporaries proceed in their everyday lives and that social scientific researchers into happiness proceed. Both parties are happy with a rough and ready conception of happiness. But ought they to be? The most notable recent attempt to show that they should not be is that by the analytic philosopher, Fred Feldman, in his *What Is This Thing Called Happiness?*

Feldman allows that "'happy' is used loosely and vaguely in ordinary English"—he might have added that the same is true of its cognates in ordinary Danish or French—and he argues that 'happy' does not have multiple senses, a thesis to which we shall need to pay attention later.[5] So that, when he advances his own account of happiness, he does not purport to tell us how the word 'happiness' is used. What he is telling us is what happiness really is. How then does he proceed? He does so by first examining and rejecting accounts given by other philosophers and then advancing his own account as one not open to the objections that he takes to be fatal to those earlier views. What are the views that he rejects?

They include the thesis that happiness consists in a preponderance of pleasant sensations over painful ones, a view that he associates with Bentham, Mill, and Sidgwick, Daniel Kahneman's theory of objective happiness, Wayne Davis's claim that happiness consists in a certain kind of desire satisfaction, and the contention of a number of philosophers that happiness consists in being satisfied with one's life as a whole. In each case Feldman advances one or more counter-examples, cases where someone would not be accounted happy by the standards of the theory that he is examining, but who, on Feldman's view, plainly is happy. In so proceeding Feldman provides us with an example of contemporary analytic philosophy at its rigorous best. He then proceeds to advance and defend his own view and the core of that view is also the core of the contemporary everyday view and of the researchers' view. It is that to be happy is to be pleased that such and such, to take pleasure in the fact that such and such. It is to have a particular attitude towards whatever it is that pleases. And a parallel account can be given of unhappiness. Oddly however Feldman then goes on to deny that to have this attitude involves having certain *feelings* characteristic of the happy. For there certainly are such feelings. He does so because he believes that he can envisage an admittedly unusual type of case in which someone has the attitude and lacks the feelings from which he concludes that the feelings "are not essential constitutive elements of happiness."[6]

Feldman can be faulted on two counts here. The first is his assumption that there is a concept of happiness that can be elucidated by identifying its essential constitutive elements. But, when our contemporaries speak about happiness what they have in mind is not a concept for the application of which there are necessary and sufficient conditions, but rather a cluster of characteristic properties widely, even if not universally shared by those who are pleased that such and such or pleased about such and such. Such properties include being pleased about various aspects of one's life, feeling pleased about them, not having important unsatisfied desires, and being contented with one's life continuing to be as it is now. Some speakers, if asked what they mean by 'happiness' may emphasize some of these properties, others others. But there is a sufficiently large degree of overlap, a sufficient degree of agreement, for there to be a genuinely shared concept. What they do not have in mind are a set of necessary and sufficient conditions. To this Feldman would certainly retort that my point is irrelevant. For, as I noted earlier, he is not concerned with the meaning of the word 'happiness' in everyday English. But this is where I become puzzled. For with concepts such as happiness every concept is somebody's concept. Every concept has to be located in some linguistic and social context. But Feldman seems to believe—I apologize, if I have misunderstood him—that there is such a thing as *the* concept of happiness.

I therefore put aside Feldman's further development of his account of that concept and turn back to the rough and ready account of Ruut Veenhoven. (Happiness, on Feldman's account, occurs in moments of time, atoms of happiness. "I will say that a person is *intrinsically attitudinally pleased* to some degree about some state of affairs, p, if and only if he is pleased about p to that degree for its own sake . . . Every atom of happiness is an attribution of occurrent *intrinsic* attitudinal pleasure or displeasure to a person, at a time, to a degree, in a specific propositional object."[7] And Feldman goes on to discuss how such atoms are aggregated over intervals of time, over a whole life, and with respect to some particular domain.) Happiness on that account, I have already noted, is a psychological state of which individuals are generally well aware, the state of being pleased or satisfied or contented with their life as a whole or with some aspect of their life. Happiness precludes grave apprehensions and fears. It generally involves positive feelings. It is a state of freedom from affliction by unsatisfied desires. It comes in degrees, as does unhappiness. And everyone wants to be happy with as much of their life as possible. Different individuals in avowing or ascribing happiness may lay stress on different aspects of happiness. But they agree—and here individuals in their everyday lives and researchers are at one—in judging happiness, so understood, to be good, perhaps the good, something with which Feldman too agrees. And it is of course because happiness is so widely judged to be good that the concept of happiness is politically important. It matters therefore politically as well as in other ways whether happiness as such is in fact good.

II

Begin by considering the nature of verbs that we use in avowing and ascribing happiness or lack of happiness so conceived. We say that we are contented with, pleased by, satisfied that such and such or that we are pained by, displeased with, unhappy because so and so. The 'with', the 'by', the 'that', and the 'because' are important, for such verbs, as Feldman emphasizes, express attitudes towards something or other. They have intentional objects. And those objects are such that it always makes sense to ask about them whether they do or do not give us good reason for being and feeling happy or unhappy in the way and to the degree that we are. What then is it to have good reason for being and feeling happy?

First, the relevant object must be what the individual has good reason for taking it to be. If I am happy because I passed some examination, then I only have good reason to be happy, if I have good reason to believe that I did in fact pass that examination. If I am pleased because the wheat harvest is going to be unusually good, then I only have good reason to be pleased, if I have good reason to believe that optimistic predictions about that harvest are warranted. Secondly, the object must be such that it contributes somehow or other, directly or indirectly, either to my good or to the good of those about whom I care. For someone to have good reason for being and feeling unhappy, the first of these conditions holds and the second also, if it is rewritten so that, where the word 'good' appears, the words 'harm or loss' are substituted. And of course I can have good reason for being happy, but not *that* happy, and good reason for being unhappy, but not *that* unhappy. Having noted this, we are now in a position to make a first attempt to answer the question: Is it good to be happy?

Consider the example of a teacher with two very different students. One consistently does mediocre work with great cheerfulness, although quite capable of work of a higher standard. He views his hard working contemporaries with some contempt and prides himself on doing just enough to get by. He does only what he enjoys doing and is very pleased with himself and his life. The other student is hard working and always does well, but she is continually anxious, haunted by the thought that she could have done better. The one is a lazy, but happy wastrel, the other an unhappy perfectionist. The teacher's duty plainly is, so far as possible, to make the happy student unhappy, the unhappy student happy.

This suggests a first thesis, that it is good to be happy if one has good reason to be happy, and good to be unhappy if and only if one has good reason to be unhappy. Someone may ask: Why in the first case should we say 'if' and in the second 'if and only if'? I began by speaking of those ascriptions and avowals of happiness and unhappiness that are expressed by verbs that take intentional objects, where we are speaking of states in which we are pleased or pained by or with something or other, that or because something or other. But there are also states of happiness or unhappiness that involve no intentional object. I wake up in the morning feeling unaccountably happy, not happy about this or happy that so and so, just happy. Or I wake up in the morning feeling low and depressed, unaware of any reason for so feeling. It is evidently better to wake up happy rather than depressed, so that it would as evidently be a mistake to assert that it is good to be and feel happy only if I have good reason to do so.

Is it the case then that any consideration of reasons is irrelevant to such states of cheerfulness, contentment, and the like, or of depressed and unhappy feelings—let us call them moods—where we have no particular reason for feeling as we do? The answer is 'No'. Imagine someone whose mood is one of happy tranquility. She has no particular reason for feeling at peace with herself and everyone else. She just does. Then a friend calls with appalling news. Someone very dear to her has died in peculiarly distressing circumstances. It matters now that she has the best of reasons for not continuing to feel happily tranquil and, if she did continue so to feel, we would be inclined to diagnose some psychological disorder. And so it would be too with someone feeling far from cheerful who unexpectedly receives extraordinarily good news and is not cheered up by it. From such cases we rightly conclude that it is bad to feel happy when one has good reason to be unhappy and vice versa.

We can now formulate the generalization that holds of the very different types of case that we have surveyed. It is always good to be unhappy when one has good reason to be unhappy and always bad to be happy when one has good reason to be unhappy. And this conclusion seems to put us dramatically at odds with the widespread folk belief that happiness is an unqualified good and the endorsement of that belief by so many researchers. But does it? Someone might argue that those who respond to survey questions by saying that they are happy, either with their lives as a whole or with their financial or marital or other circumstances, are telling us that their lives or their financial circumstances or their marital circumstances give them good reason for being and feeling happy. Their answers presuppose, even when they do not spell out explicitly, a particular evaluation of their reasons for happiness or unhappiness. But, even if this is so, a question still remains. What reason, if any, do we have for supposing that they not only are happy and have their own reasons for being happy, but that those reasons are sufficiently good reasons?

Some notable empirical research suggests an answer. For some three decades before 2006 Danes ranked first among European nationalities in respect of self-avowed happiness, more than two thirds of them regularly reporting, according to the Eurobarometer Survey, that they were very satisfied with their lives, while for most countries the proportion so reporting is less than a third. In 2006 an enquiry into why this was so yielded an explanation. Danish culture is a culture of low expectations.[8] Danes, so it turns out, expect less from life than do, for example, Finns or Swedes and because of this are more satisfied with their lives. And we should note that Danes have a high divorce rate and relatively low life expectancy. So the question is raised: Do Danes expect too little from their lives? And this is a type of question that we need to ask not just about Danes, but about everyone. For, if people are happy only because their expectations are too low or are otherwise misguided, then they do not have good reason to be happy.

Those whose expectations are too low are those who believe that to hope for any large and significant change for the better in their circumstances is unrealistic, including those who fear that any change would be for the worse. What matters of course is whether their lack of hope and their fears are or are not well grounded. And, until we know this, we do not know how to evaluate what they say about their own happiness or unhappiness. More importantly they themselves do not know whether their happiness—or unhappiness—is illusory, until they know this. And this is not the only way in which expectations are involved in our judgments about our own happiness. We may be pleased with our present condition either because it is how we want our lives to be or because, although it is not particularly pleasing, it is a stage in a progress towards what we take to be a desirable condition. Expectations concerning the future are often an ingredient in present happiness and, when they are, we only have good reason to be happy, if those expectations are well founded.

Consider now another source of mistakes about whether or not we have good reason to be happy. The nineteenth century socialist, Ferdinand Lassalle, spoke of "the damned wantlessness of the poor." He referred to the state of those who had been so ground down by their poverty and consequent hardships that they remained aware only of their own most basic everyday needs and no longer had a desire for anything beyond these. In asserting that this can be among the effects of extreme poverty Lassalle was quite right. But it is not only among the very poor that a loss of desire can be found. Those who have been disappointed too often, those who have learned from experience to be grateful for small satisfactions and to expect nothing more, and those who suffer from fatigue or boredom or depression may all have diminished desires and be far too easily satisfied. So once again, if we are to evaluate what people say about their happiness or unhappiness, there is something else about which we need to know, the state of their present desires, what the range of those desires is, how strong they are, and how far they are recognized and acknowledged.

My claim is this: that both ascriptions and avowals of happiness and unhappiness, whether in the course of everyday life and conversation, or in answer to survey questions, or in interviews with researchers, always need to be interpreted and that such interpretation requires knowledge of the expectations and desires of those whose happiness is in question. It requires too a sensitivity to their vocabulary and to the nuances of the sentences that they employ. Asked, for example, about my feelings about my job, I may say that I am satisfied with it, meaning either that I am quite content with it or instead that I am satisfied, even if barely so. Christensen and her coauthors showed themselves admirably aware of this in their careful discussion of the Danish word '*tilfreds*', which may be translated either 'contented' or 'satisfied'. They were right to conclude that in this case nothing turns on the choice of translation. But this is not always so. Indeed an adequate enquiry into happiness would do well at least as a precaution to start by cataloguing for a number of languages the differences in meaning between 'is pleased by', 'is contented with', 'is glad that', 'is satisfied by', 'rejoices that', and so on.

Another complexity badly needs to be introduced at this point. Among the states of affairs with which we may be pleased or displeased are those which consist in our being pleased or displeased. I hear that someone whom I dislike has suffered a misfortune and in a moment of *schadenfreude* I take pleasure in this and am at once pained that I should do so. Or perhaps I am pained by some malicious remark and am pleased that I am pained. Mill asserted that it is better—and for Mill this means more pleasing—to be Socrates dissatisfied than a fool satisfied. Why does it matter that we can and do make such higher order judgments? Consider some group who up till now have failed to recognize just how bad their situation is and so have been unwilling to mobilize their energies to remedy it. But, now that they have recognized the truth about their situation, they are cheerfully setting about their new tasks. In one respect they are a good deal less content than they were. In another they are much happier about themselves. It would be a foolish mistake to ask whether they are happier or less happy than they were *simpliciter*. And it would be equally foolish to ask the same question about many groups that are in transitions that involve new kinds of moral and political self-awareness.

III

Are we now in a position to evaluate the recurrently influential proposal that the central aim of governments should be to make their citizens happy and that it is by their success or failure in this respect that they are to be judged? We need first to carry our enquiry into the concept of happiness a little further and to do so by comparing the dominant contemporary conception of happiness with an older conception. Consider one common use of words translatable by 'happy' in classical Latin. "Happy (*felix*) he who is able to investigate the causes of things," said Lucretius. "Happy (*beatus*) he who, far from business affairs works his family fields with his own oxen," said Horace. They were not speaking about the feelings of the scientist or the ploughman, but congratulating them on having good reason to think well of themselves. So what is it to be in a state in which one is justified in thinking well of oneself and one's life? Aristotle had earlier given an answer to this question and his medieval followers use the same words as Lucretius and Horace to name that state, *felix* and *felicitas*, *beatus* and *beatitudo*, both in medieval and later English translated as 'happy' and 'happiness', while *beatus* and *beatitudo* with their theological connotation are also translated by 'blessed' and 'blessedness'.

Two Aristotelian theses inform their use of these words and their concept of happiness more generally. First to be happy is to engage in certain worthwhile kinds of activity. It is to lead a certain kind of life. What kind of a life? One in which one's physical, moral, aesthetic, and intellectual powers are developed and educated. To educate them is to direct their exercise towards the achievement of that which it is good and best for human beings qua rational animals to achieve. 'Happiness' is not primarily the name of a state of mind. But states of mind are not irrelevant to happiness. For a second Aristotelian thesis is this: that what you enjoy, what you take pleasure in, depends upon what sort of person you are. And, insofar as you have those qualities of mind and character that are the distinctive excellences of human beings, you will enjoy just those types of activity that constitute the life of happiness for rational animals. It is because human beings are animals that the education of their biologically given feelings is important. It is because they are rational that it matters to them whether or not they have good reasons for feeling as they do. So, on this account of happiness, what matters first and foremost is whether or not they have good reasons to feel happy.

By calling this account of happiness Aristotelian I may be thought to suggest that it is no more than a philosopher's theory about happiness. But Aristotle understood his task as a philosopher to be that of identifying and elucidating the concepts embodied in and presupposed by the utterances and activities of nonphilosophical plain persons. And I take it that those of his medieval and postmedieval followers who endorsed these two theses about happiness were claiming that and were correct in claiming that happiness thus conceived was a concept informing the judgments and activities of many, at least, of their nonphilosophical contemporaries. Certainly a good deal of ordinary English—and Irish and French and Polish—usage was in the past consistent with this claim. And this conception of happiness is still to be found long after the peculiarly modern conception of happiness as a state of mind, of happiness as the state of feeling good about oneself and one's life has become dominant. J. S. Mill is an interesting transitional case.

On the one hand Mill treats happiness as a balance of pleasure over pain, pleasure and pain as psychological states, and actions and states as better or worse depending on how pleasant or painful they and their consequences are. On the other he declares that it is better to be Socrates dissatisfied than a fool satisfied. These two positions cannot be held consistently and Richard Layard chides Mill for what Layard supposes to be the error of thinking that some pleasures are better than others. But Mill's error is more interesting than that. Indeed Mill's errors are commonly more interesting than other people's truths. For Mill was much closer to an Aristotelian view of these matters than commentators usually recognize. (He called Aristotle "a moderate utilitarian" and that was also what he considered himself to be.) But he tried to find a basis for his own often Aristotelian ethics in a psychology derived from Hartley and Bentham with inevitably incongruous results. So that the lesson to be learned from Mill concerns the incompatibility of any psychological state conception of happiness, such as Hartley's or that of Hartley's twenty-first century heirs, and any version of Aristotle's view.

We are then confronted with two rival views of how happiness is to be conceived, the distinctively modern and the Aristotelian. (I am not implying that there are only two.) It is not just that they are incompatible, but that the criticism of the first points us immediately towards the second. My earlier criticism of the modern view issued in the complex thesis that it is generally, if not quite always, good to be and feel happy, in the sense of 'happy' given to it by the modern view, if and insofar as one has good reason to be and feel happy, and that it is good to be and feel unhappy when one has good reason to be and feel unhappy. But not only does this thesis follow from the Aristotelian view, the Aristotelian account includes an account of those goods that supply us with the relevant sets of good reasons. And the key point of difference between the two views is perhaps this, that on the Aristotelian view to be happy is to lead a life directed towards the achievement of the good and the best, so that without an independent account of the human good our account of happiness will be incomplete, while on the modern view happiness just is the human good and to know in what one's happiness consists is to know everything that needs to be known about goods and the good.

IV

We are now in a better position to evaluate the claim that the maximization of happiness, as understood both by happiness researchers and by most of our contemporaries should be the aim of governments. One premise for any such evaluation is that citizens should, so far as possible, have true beliefs about and a correct understanding of both their own economic, political, social, and moral condition and that of relevant others. For without such beliefs and understanding they cannot, as we noticed earlier, have good reasons for being and feeling happy—or unhappy. This premise is itself already a source of difficulties. For it has been strenuously asserted that you can be either intelligent and clearheaded in your view of the world or happy, but not both. So Flaubert in a letter of 1846 remarked that "to be stupid, selfish, and have good health are three requirements of happiness, though, if stupidity is lacking, all is lost." And, nearer to our own time Charles de Gaulle, asked by an imprudent enquirer if he was happy, replied "I am not stupid." Is it then true that we can be intelligent and clearheaded or happy, but not both?

For this there is some evidence. Social psychologists have reported that those of us who are mildly depressive are significantly more likely to see things as they are than are normally cheerful individuals.[9] Their conclusion was anticipated by Adam Smith, who argued that "in time of sickness or low spirits" we take a realistic view of the satisfactions afforded to the great and the rich by their possessions and powers, but that in times of cheerful good health we are victims of illusions fostered by our imagination. "And it is well", adds Smith, "that nature imposes on us in this manner. It is this deception which rouses and keeps in continued motion the industry of mankind."[10] Economic growth, on Smith's view, is generated by shared illusions that sustain and are sustained by feelings of cheerfulness about ourselves and our prospects. So why should we want ourselves or others to be undeceived?

To answer this question we have to ask what it is to be politically and economically clearheaded, politically and economically undeceived. And interestingly part of the answer refers us to just those conditions that have to be satisfied if we are to have good reason for being and feeling happy or unhappy. We have to be aware of not only what our present condition is, but also of what alternatives there are to that condition, and we have to have well-grounded expectations about what the political and economic outcomes would be, if we were to choose one of these alternatives rather than others. It may seem almost too obvious to remark that a prerequisite for such awareness is a grasp of the relevant concepts and of the different ways in which one may think about such things, but in fact this thought is where evaluation of the proposal that the aim of governments should be to maximize happiness has to begin. For evidently the proposal that happiness, understood in one particular way should be the aim of government is a proposal that happiness, so conceived, should become a key notion in the thought and judgments both of those who govern and those who are governed. But we have already identified grounds for believing that happiness, so understood is often a state of illusion, since it is possible to be happy only because of unnecessarily low expectations, lack of awareness of alternative possibilities, diminished desires, and lack of an adequate understanding of one's present condition. Yet this is not all. Let me consider three further lines of thought, each of which puts in question the project of achieving happiness, so understood.

First, there is the important place that unhappiness has in our lives. To care about something or to love somebody is to make oneself vulnerable to loss, to the unhappiness of grief. To make oneself invulnerable to grief would be to render oneself incapable of caring or loving. To make choices under conditions of radical uncertainty is to make oneself vulnerable to future regret, to the unhappiness of knowing that one's own choices had harmed oneself or others. But to make oneself invulnerable to such regret would be to have a life without creative and courageous risk taking. To have a realistic view of the dangers and harms that are at hand sometimes involves learning to live with fear and fear is not a happy state. But a life without fears would be a life marked either by irresponsible bravado or by excessive and crippling caution. The catalogue could continue. Anxiety, indignation, anger, and disgust all play a part in good lives. And none of these are happy states.

To this someone might reply that just because some kinds of unhappiness are integral to human life, it is all the more important to render as much as possible of human life happy. But to say this would be to miss the point that in some lives of achievement the unhappiness may be integral to the achievement. Caring desperately about doing just what is needed, impatience with oneself on occasions when one fails to get things quite right, apprehension about the loss of what is culturally valuable, all these may be inseparable from certain kinds of insight, conflict, and struggle. Neither Wittgenstein's nor Rothko's were notably happy lives, but without their unhappiness I do not think that they could have been Wittgenstein and Rothko. Or consider the testimony of Hans Keilson, physician, psychoanalyst, novelist, who looks back to his parents, who were murdered in Auschwitz, as the basis of his life and adds "Sadness is the basis of my life."[11] So it may be better for some of us, for our projects, and for those with whom we interact, that we should be from time to time quite seriously unhappy.

A second line of thought begins from Aristotle's insight, of which we took preliminary note earlier, that pleasure supervenes upon completed activity, upon doing this or that well (*Nicomachean Ethics* 1179b31–33). We enjoy activities as disparate as playing cricket, climbing a mountain face, solving a set of mathematical equations, catching a fish, planting a garden, reading Aristotle. In each case the enjoyment is specific to the type of activity. It is not that there is a state called 'enjoyment' to the achievement of which solving equations and climbing mountains are alternative means. Pleasures, as Aristotle puts it, come in different kinds. But, if this is so, there are two difficulties confronting any attempt to treat happiness as such as an end. For the question will inescapably arise, 'What kind of happiness?' And here not only the happiness of individuals, but that of local societies is in question. The happiness of a prosperous, but isolated farming community is one thing, the happiness of a city neighborhood where workers in the textile and fashion trades live side by side with police officers, firefighters, and school teachers quite another.

A second difficulty is that, if Aristotle's point is well-taken, happiness—understood as the state of being pleased at or by some aspect of one's life—is not to be achieved, whether by individuals or groups, by aiming at happiness, but only by aiming at some other end. Happiness, so understood, cannot be an end, and, if we take it to be an end, only frustration, so it seems, can result. To which it will be replied, "That cannot be so. I have been working hard and want an evening of enjoyment and relaxation. I know what I enjoy and so with a friend I play a game of chess, then go to see a revival of *Les Enfants du Paradis*, and then eat an excellent Italian dinner. So by these means—and I could have chosen alternative means—I achieve my end. I enjoy myself." In response we need to modify our thesis, by distinguishing cases where we engage in activities, only or primarily so as to enjoy them, from cases where we engage in activities because we have good reason to do so, independently of whether or not we enjoy them, although we may indeed enjoy engaging in them. The former type of activity has a special place in our lives, even if a subordinate one. Subtract it from our lives altogether, as sometimes we need to do or are forced to do, and those lives would be seriously impoverished. But such activities get their significance from the contrast with the rest of our lives, the contrast with those activities that we have good reason to engage in, quite apart from any enjoyment that may ensue. So that once again it is clear that happiness, understood as a state of mind in which one is pleased with one's life, could not be an overall goal either for individuals or for groups.

This conclusion is yet further reinforced by another set of considerations drawn from Aristotle. What we are pleased by differs from individual to individual and depends upon the moral and intellectual qualities, the virtues and vices, of each individual (*Nicomachean Ethics* 1176a10–29). What pleases the greedy and the acquisitive, what makes them happy—in the sense of 'happiness' that we are discussing—is not what make the just or the generous happy. It follows that if anyone makes the general happiness their goal, we must ask whether a society in which gross inequalities in educational opportunity are tolerated or even welcomed has any good reason to feel pleased with itself and whether it would not be better for such a society to be generally unhappy about its shared life. If Aristotle is right this question will be answered very differently by those whose moral and intellectual qualities are such that they care about the common good and those for whom all goods are the goods of individuals, no matter how wide or narrow the scope of their benevolence.

V

Taken together these three lines of thought enable us to formulate some political conclusions. Suppose that someone has a care for the common good of her or his family, her or his school, her or his workplace, her or his political society. By what would she or he be pleased, by what displeased, as parent, aunt, or sibling, as teacher or student or janitor, as skilled worker or apprentice or manager, as citizen? Since justice is the principal virtue needed to achieve the common good, a first answer is that such a one would be pleased by and would have good reason to be pleased by just social relations, displeased by unjust social relations. What in advanced countries is the most flagrant example of unjust social relations? It is the massive inequality in the distribution of educational opportunity to children who are all equally deserving, an inequality often closely related to inequalities in income, in employment opportunities, and in health care, an inequality that is the source of many other inequalities.

What then should we make of a political society, such as our own, in which on the one hand there is this kind of injustice, and no apparent prospect of putting an end to it, and on the other a relatively high proportion of citizens who declare themselves to be happy? Are we to infer that those citizens are all of them heartless and uncaring? That would be a foolish inference. What the argument so far suggests is that we should not only look to what they have learned to take for granted, to their limited conceptions of the alternatives to their society's present condition, to their low expectations both for themselves and others, but also to the relationship between these and the ways in which they think about happiness. It matters that the dominant conception of happiness is that it is a property of individuals *qua* individuals, rather than of individuals *qua* family members, *qua* students or teachers, *qua* skilled workers and trade unionists, *qua* members of their local community, *qua* citizens. For to think realistically of oneself in one's various social relationships requires a recognition that the overall condition of one's society in respect of justice and injustice—and not only of these—often gives one the best of reasons for being and feeling happy or unhappy. And it is impossible to care for the common good without such a recognition. So what we are entitled to conclude is that a politics in which happiness, as now generally understood, is taken to be the goal of government is incompatible with a politics of the common good and that, insofar as political thinking is informed by that conception of happiness, it prevents due weight being given to any adequate conception of the common good. Happiness, that is to say, functions as an ideological concept, serving the purposes of the *status quo*.

I have been tediously careful on each occasion, when speaking of happiness, to make it clear to which of the two conceptions of happiness that I have identified I was then referring and this because the two are not just different, but rivals, and unsurprisingly since a conception of politics in terms of the common good and a *eudaimonistic* conception of happiness belong together. To engage in a politics of the common good is to share in the enterprise of constructing forms of community in which citizens develop their physical, intellectual, moral, and aesthetic powers, so that they achieve their own individual and common goods. And of course 'happiness' ('*eudaimonia*', '*felicitas*', '*beatitudo*') is a name of that state in which individuals are perfecting or have perfected their lives and are directed towards or have achieved their final good. Such individuals may indeed be said to aim at happiness, but happiness is in no sense, on this Aristotelian view, the aim of government. That is to educate citizens so that they acquire those qualities of mind and character that enable them to act prudently, courageously, justly, and temperately and to legislate so that the common good is achieved. It follows that within strictly political discourse there is no place for any notion of happiness. But this conclusion may seem to have unfortunate practical implications for participants in contemporary politics whose aim is to achieve the common good.

If it is true, as it is, that many of our fellow citizens have learned from the dominant culture to think about their own lives in terms of their happiness and unhappiness, a tendency powerfully reinforced by much contemporary political rhetoric, then what hope can there be for a politics that invites them to look in quite another direction? The answer perhaps is that everything turns on where such a politics begins. For one of its starting-points has to be a practical and political critique of the rhetoric of happiness, so that promises of happiness, stated or implied, are exposed as the false promises that they are. What rhetoric do we need instead? That is a topic for another paper.

NINETEEN

Political Rhetoric in a Fractured Society

In the first of these papers I identified two kinds of political reasoning, one designed to achieve the maximization of individual preferences in liberal democratic societies, the other to identify and achieve the common goods of families and local communities. But it became clear that the achievement of such common goods would be impossible in contemporary conditions, unless those whose politics is a politics of the common good also engage in the liberal democratic politics of their larger societies, in order to secure the resources needed by families and local communities. And such engagement requires, although it is not restricted to, effective public speech and reasoning about the common good in the larger political arenas of our society. One initial difficulty is that the expression 'the

---

"Political Rhetoric in a Fractured Society," paper presented at Centre for Contemporary Aristotelian Studies in Ethics and Politics, London Metropolitan University, 2011.

common good' is often used or rather misused in contemporary political debate, perhaps to refer to certain public goods or to what is in the interest of a majority of individuals, rather than as the good of some institution or group that is not reducible to the goods of individuals. But I shall put this practical difficulty on one side in order to pose the problem: How is it possible to reason and speak effectively about common goods in a political culture to which the concept of a common good is alien? What kind of rhetoric do we need?

I

As an Aristotelian, I begin with Aristotle, but in this case only because it is instructive to recognize how little help we can expect from him in answering these questions. Scholars have recognized a number of ways in which Aristotle in the *Rhetoric* presents views that seem to be at odds with what he says in the *Topics* and in the *Nicomachean Ethics*, concerning for example, his conceptions of argument and proof and his accounts of particular virtues. One partial explanation is that Aristotle was concerned that orators should make their appeals to audiences only on the basis of beliefs about argument and proof and about the virtues which they and their audiences share and that therefore he put on one side those aspects of his own views that were not widely shared. Be that as it may, it is clear that one of the background assumptions of the *Rhetoric* is that the orators whom he is instructing are expected to take for granted and to exploit a remarkable degree of agreement in the background beliefs, evaluations, and passions shared by them and their audiences. The art of the orator is to know how to appeal to and evoke those beliefs, evaluations, and passions, so that the audience accompanies the orator step by step on his route to the conclusion at which he wants them to arrive.

This is not all that orator and audience must share. Speech making, as Aristotle understands it, takes place in political assemblies and law courts where the alternatives between which the audience has to decide are well defined and unproblematic. An orator may have to win over an initially hostile or sceptical audience. But his speech is well devised just insofar as it makes his audience aware of grounds and attitudes that they already have, but do not as yet recognize that they have, for judging otherwise than as they initially do. And what was true of ancient Greek orators and audiences was true of their Roman and later successors. Successful modern oratory too—I think of Churchill in 1940—requires occasions for decision between well defined alternatives, convictions, and passions shared by orator and audience, and the art of using language to guide that audience towards the orator's desired conclusion. But what then are the possibilities of effective political speech on occasions when those conditions are not satisfied? What are the possibilities of effective political speech designed not to appeal to an established consensus, but instead to put in question the shared assumptions of the conventional politics of the present from the standpoint of a politics of the common good?

Our present political culture has three characteristics that make it difficult to address questions concerning the common good. One is the narrowness and the limitations of the ways in which the alternatives between which political choices are made are formulated and presented, whether in elections or in parliamentary debates or in the decision making of those in power. And since the focus of that culture is on elections, parliamentary debates, and governmental decisions this same narrowness and these same limitations constrain discussion in the media and everyday political conversations. What counts as realistic and moderate, what counts as extreme and utopian, are so defined that any radical alternative to the present is ruled out before debate begins. Hence arises both an urgent need for and the difficulty of finding forums in which the terms of current political debate can be challenged.

A second characteristic of the dominant political culture is the nature of the moral consensus that is the counterpart to its political agreements. The two concepts through which that consensus is principally articulated are those of *rights* and of *the maximization of utility*, so that moral argument is characteristically a weighing of right against right, or of utility against utility or of right against utility. But since there is no incontestable way of rank ordering claims to rights, no incontestable way of measuring utilities, and no standard at all for deciding between rights claims and utility claims moral argument is characteristically inconclusive. And if in the arenas of such moral argument the claims of the common good were to be advanced, they would either go unheard or would be translated into claims about rights or utility.

A third salient characteristic of the contemporary political culture is its limited notions of political and economic responsibility and accountability. These derive from more than one source. In part they are the expression of a widely shared attitude towards economic systems and structures such that economic outcomes are to a remarkable extent regarded as the effect of impersonal forces for which individuals can be held responsible only in a very limited way. Those limits are defined legally and bureaucratically and the resulting social relationships are ones between individuals and corporations, so that no one is taken to have responsibility for achieving or failing to achieve the common good.

To pose questions about these three characteristics is to recognize how far we have distanced ourselves from the orators of the ancient world and from their later heirs. We are raising questions that they could not have raised and we cannot rely, as they did, upon an evaluative and normative consensus. As importantly, our aim has to be very different from theirs. For our primary aim has to be to get those to whom and with whom we speak to pursue answers to questions that they have not hitherto asked and to be dissatisfied with the conventional answers to those questions. The ancient orators were able to identify some particular conclusion that they wished their audience to reach and asked themselves from what premises they should invite that audience to begin. We have instead to identify a set of questions that we want those with whom we speak to make their own and therefore we have to discover what might provoke them into posing those questions. And, because we have different rhetorical ends, we will have to make use of different rhetorical means. So how should we proceed?

II

We need to develop both an argument and a narrative. The argument concerns how responsibility is to be assigned for the unjust and divisive outcomes of the workings of our economy and our politics. The narrative is a story of particular individuals and groups, tracing the effects of the activities of some upon the lives of others. Both argument and narrative involve issues of accountability and responsibility. It is therefore very much to the point that in our political culture, for reasons to which I alluded earlier, notions of accountability and responsibility that are treated as unproblematic in other contexts are seldom put to work in our discussions of economic and financial agents. I begin then from what are well established conceptions of intention and causality. We have all learned to distinguish, and rightly, between the intended consequences of someone's action, and the foreseeable, but unintended consequences. For the latter an agent may or may not be held responsible, depending upon the nature of the case.

Let me begin with two uncontroversial examples. Someone who has the responsibility for grading examination papers may happen to know of one candidate that, if he passes the examination, he will celebrate by getting horribly drunk, doing himself and others possibly serious harm. But this harm the examiner must put out of his mind. His intention in grading the papers must be only to give each candidate the deserved grade, whatever the consequences. Contrast with this the type of case discussed by Elizabeth Anscombe in *Intention*, sections 23–26, in which someone is pumping water in order to replenish a house's water supply. At some point he learns that someone else has introduced poison into the water supply, so that, if he continues pumping, the members of the household will be poisoned. Suppose that he does continue pumping and justifies his action by saying that his intention was simply to fill up the water tank and that the incidental poisoning of the water was no concern of his. He poisoned the household unintentionally. The reply will surely be, and rightly, that his knowledge of the consequences of his actions is sufficient to show that his poisoning of the household was not unintentional. It could not but inform his intentions.

We therefore need to be able to distinguish those cases in which an agent should not take foreseen, but unintended consequences into account from those in which an agent should be held accountable not only for intended, but also for foreseen and indeed foreseeable consequences. Necessary conditions for assigning a case to the former class are that the good to be achieved by excluding attention to the unintended, but foreseeable consequences is a significant good, that that good cannot be achieved without such exclusion, and that the foreseeable evils are not of a disproportionate kind. Each of these conditions needs spelling out in detail. But, even without doing so, we can see how the application of these conditions to particular cases is likely to be contestable. What is to count as a significant good? What is a disproportionate evil? Which consequences are genuinely foreseeable?

Consider as a further example that of those engaged in waging a just war who are well aware that inevitably, as a consequence of their actions, innocent bystanders will be injured and killed. Their aim is both to mount effective military actions and to limit, as far as possible, the harm to such innocent bystanders. So they have to determine how much harm would be disproportionate and how reliable their means for predicting the kind and degree of harm are. Twentieth century military history provides us with many examples of the discussion of those questions, both before and after the event. By contrast twentieth century economic history is remarkably sparse in its provision of such examples. And this is because of a failure to pose, let alone answer the question: For what effects of her or his economic effects should someone be held responsible? The responsibility to which I refer is responsibility first of all to those on whom, one way or another, one's economic activities impact and then to the other members of one's political society. It is a more fundamental notion than that of legal responsibility. How then should we set about answering this question?

We need first to note that in a globalizing economy the range of effects of economic mistakes and failures is far wider than it was in earlier economies. Market failure in Japan or the United States can result in unemployment in Korea or Latin America. Commodities trading in the metropolitan centers can issue in rising food prices and subsequent hunger in Africa. Everyone knows this, but almost nobody asks for which foreseeable effects of their actions, if any, should such traders be held responsible, at least until those times when the capitalist system as a whole enters a state of crisis. And then there is unsystematic outcry, often expressed as indignation that those responsible for that particular crisis have not been held legally accountable for their acts and omissions. But the laws and regulations governing market transactions are designed by and large to enable, not to prohibit economic activity and in consequence not only are prosecutions relatively rare, but, when penalties are exacted, they are treated by those on whom they fall as among those costs of doing business which they hope to pass on to others. The law therefore is of little help to us in assigning economic and financial responsibility. This is work yet to be done.

It may be useful therefore to begin in an elementary way by cataloguing the various types of attitude and activity that led to the most recent crisis and by so doing to identify some of the prime movers of economic failure. This will be a boring exercise, because by now there are all too many books and articles that have already done this. But this is part of the point. I am merely reminding you of what any tolerably well informed person already knows and the question is going to be: Why does this common knowledge issue in so little action? Why does it not inform our moral and political thinking to any great extent? I proceed then to the work of cataloguing. The first item—the order is temporal—is the consistently growing use of leverage since the 1980s and the consequent astonishing disproportion between the capital held by many corporations, especially banks, and the debt for which they are or one day may be liable. A corporation borrows money to buy some asset. It then uses that asset as security to borrow further money to buy some further asset, and so on—indefinitely. For the moment we need say no more, except to notice the bearing on successful—or unsuccessful leverage of the relationship between asset prices and interest rates.

A second type of activity dates from the late 1990s when J. P. Morgan and American International Group's Financial Products department developed new forms of those complex derivatives that were to become known as Collateralised Debt Obligations, derivatives that, as they developed further, involved those who invested in them in a degree of risk and a kind of risk for which there was no precedent in the financial markets. The paradox was that the initial intention of the devisers had been to manage risk in predictable and controllable ways. And what made both the original construction of such derivatives and their later development possible was a mathematical sophistication in the use of models, whose first great victory as long ago as 1973 had been the equations for the pricing of stock options discovered by Fischer Black and Myron Scholes and by Robert Merton. By the 1990s reliance by traders on the activities of quants, the applied mathematicians of the stock market, whether those traders themselves understood the mathematics or not, was such that reliance on models and formulas for the estimation of risk had become a salient feature of trading. And that reliance had a significant part in generating an inadequate understanding of risk. Add to these the activities of those in the United States and Ireland who acted as if there was an ever expanding housing market and encouraged imprudent risk taking by home owners and investment in subprime mortgages by investors.

All these activities would not however have had the kinds and degrees of effect that they had without the actions or inactions of five other groups. The first is composed of those lawyers who enabled investment bankers and others to circumvent the intentions embodied in much existing regulation, so that the major agents of economic disaster were not at any legal risk. (It is important to recognize that, had none of the criminal activities exposed during the crisis occurred, the dimensions of the crisis would have been exactly what they were.) A second group are those in central banks responsible for monetary policy, while a third consists of those political office holders and bureaucrats responsible for devising and administering the regulation of financial markets. Fourthly we have the governments and the directors of the central banks who determined how much of the cost of rescuing financial institutions from disaster should be borne in the first instance by governments and then by those on whom governments chose to impose those costs. And last, but far from least, are those academic economists who provided theoretical justification for the major actors before the event and theoretical exculpation after it.

Here then we have a motley array of individual and corporate actors, investment bankers, money managers and traders, central bankers, applied mathematicians, professors of economics, lawyers, holders of government office, regulators, and bureaucrats of other kinds who jointly set on foot those causal chains that issued in not just one, but a number of related catastrophes. Whom do we find suffering the effects at the other ends of those chains? Among others, but most notably, an extraordinarily large number of children, although that number seldom includes the children of the agents of the catastrophe. In what ways do children suffer the consequences and pay the costs? Through parental unemployment and consequent poverty, through foreclosures on their homes and consequent homelessness, and through savage cuts by national and local governments in educational provision. Let me attend only to the last.

Educational opportunity is already unequally distributed in countries such as the USA and the UK. In times of economic stringency far larger numbers of children suffer from a pared down curriculum—music and the arts in general are always among the first to be eliminated—from inadequate numbers of teachers, from low quality teachers, from lack of equipment, from decaying school buildings. So at the most crucial stage in their lives they are deprived of what they need, if they are to develop their full powers as human beings and as citizens. That is to say, the costs of financial crisis are borne by those who least deserve to bear them and are least able to bear them.

So should we as a society hold those who initiated the causal chain individually and collectively responsible for those who suffer from its effects? Evidently we do not in fact do so and what is taken to be the justification for not doing so is equally evident. For in order to hold them responsible it seems that we would have to show that either they intended the remoter effects of their actions or that, even although they did not intend them, they foresaw them and that their scale is such that they could not be dismissed as mere collateral damage. Now plainly they did not intend them. And it may at first seem equally plain that they did not in fact foresee them. For those academic economists who did foresee the crisis were uniformly treated with scorn both by their fellow economists and by the international financial community. As early as 2005, when Raghuram Rajan of the International Monetary Fund argued to an audience of central bankers that the system of rewards to bankers for taking risks with the money of others at no risk to themselves was liable to produce a "full-blown financial crisis," he was at once denounced by Larry Summers as a Luddite. And in Ireland, for example, the warnings of a coming crisis by Morgan Kelly of University College Dublin were treated with what amounted to contempt. Yet what matters here is that a number of such economists and also a small number of money managers did foresee the crisis. So the interesting question is: What was it that made the crisis foreseeable by them and not by others?

Dirk Bezemer has argued compellingly that what those who foresaw the crisis shared was attention to various aspects of the flow of funds between the financial sector and the rest of the economy, more especially to the way in which growing financial asset markets could not but be matched by a growing burden of debt, so that at a certain foreseeable point that debt became unsustainable.[1] And Bezemer has also pointed out that the official forecasting models in the USA, the UK, and the OECD took no account of these changing relationships between the financial sector and the rest of the economy.[2] What we had then was an economic and financial culture in which the goals pursued by individuals as they lived out their roles were such and the attention focused on those goals was such that they could not allow themselves either to become aware of what the remoter consequences of their actions might be or to entertain the thought that their economic presuppositions might be mistaken. This was—and is—a culture not only of deception, but also of self-deception, and what makes it worthwhile to study the work of those such as Rajan and Kelly, who understood what was going on while it was going on, is the evidence that they provide that it was possible not to be thus self-deceived.

Does the fact that financial markets turn out to be systematic generators of self-deception and illusion to any degree exculpate? In answering this question the behavior of some of the major agents of catastrophe after the event, when the effects of their actions are plain to see, is significant. For by and large investment bankers have been extraordinarily resistant to the imposition of the kind and degree of regulation that might prevent another crisis of the same kind. And academic economists have been equally resistant to the thought that their discipline failed both them and us on matters of the highest importance. More generally almost no one in such circles has taken the thought seriously that anyone who is going to impose significant risk on others, without the consent of those others, has a minimal duty to those others to provide them in advance with all relevant information about the kind and degree of that risk, including worst case scenarios, and about how, if at all, they might be able to protect themselves. So we find an unwillingness to accept responsibility for the future which is a counterpart to an inability to acknowledge responsibility for the past.

What this evidence shows, I suggest, is this, that those who caused the crisis and its effects were responsible just insofar as that crisis and its effects were foreseeable, but unforeseen because of their collusion in their own self-deception. The ethos of the culture of the financial markets, and perhaps also of a certain kind of academic economics, is such that it makes many of those who inhabit it unable to acknowledge let alone to act upon some of their duties to others, and those who inhabit that culture have been de-moralized. This failure to accept and acknowledge responsibility is matched by the absence of in the wider moral culture of recognition by others of this failure. Whence this absence? It is a symptom of the poverty of the shared morality of our culture that it lacks the conceptual and argumentative resources needed to characterize the moral relationships between those who are the agents of economic and financial crises and those who suffer most from its effects. This is why any attempt to characterize the moral condition of those agents in the arenas of contemporary public debate is likely to be rhetorically ineffective. What then should we do? The answer is to construct our economic and political narrative, a narrative of tragic self-deception, and to begin from the effects, not from the causes, to begin with the children, not with the bankers, traders, and economists, to begin with the common good of families and local societies, not with the meager resources of contemporary morality.

III

The principle of subsidiarity tells us that in that hierarchy of institutions in which families have the lowest place and the governing institutions of political society the highest things go well when, so far as possible, what is lower governs itself and achieves its own goods, rather than having those functions usurped by some higher authority. A counterpart to that principle tells us that, when some institution lower in the hierarchy, such as the family, cannot supply something necessary for its flourishing, then that something must be supplied by some higher governing authority. So the common good of families cannot generally be achieved unless their children are able to move towards achieving such development of their physical, intellectual, aesthetic, and moral powers as will enable them to function well as rational adults in their particular culture. But this can rarely, if ever, be achieved by any one family on its own. What is needed can only be supplied by good schools and good teachers. And good schools and good teachers can only be provided by local, regional, or national government, either directly through schemes of public education, including the education and training of teachers, or indirectly through private institutions that satisfy public standards.

It is therefore for the common good of the family that children should have a good education. But this is also for the common good of political society, since the worse the education of children is the worse their politics will be, when they grow up. Good citizens need to have had a shared education through which they have become participants in those ongoing conversations about the fabric of everyday life which provide the background to political discourse. They need a shared understanding of the history of their society, a shared sense of the imaginative possibilities of their common language, a shared recognition of what the sciences have to tell us about ourselves and our place in nature. For without these they will not be able as adults to define the issues that will inevitably divide them as citizens, let alone to work their way through those political conflicts constructively. They will not be able to identify, let alone to achieve the common good.

It follows that for any politics of the common good in the contemporary world a first priority, perhaps *the* first priority, must be the provision in each local community of what children need, so that what has to be sacrosanct, uncuttable in our budgets, is the most adequate financial provision that we can afford to make for our children's educational needs and for those other needs—such as the need for a hot breakfast—which have to be met if children are to be educable. This would put a constraint on economic and financial policies comparable to the constraints imposed by other types of necessary public expenditure and it would involve taxation with radically redistributive effects. But such expenditure on children and on their schools and teachers would also function as an economic stimulus. And it would have as a counterpart a series of measures designed to ensure that whatever risk taking is permitted in the markets, it is not such as to inflict the costs of bad financial judgment on children.

This thought returns us to issues of rhetoric. If we have identified correctly the policies that a regard for the common good requires, with respect to the treatment of children, we can now ask why in our society children are so often treated with so flagrant a disregard for the claims of the common good. And our answer should take the form of an enriched narrative in which we are able to characterize more fully just what it is that those who through deception and self-deception unjustifiably expose others to economic risk have to ignore, have to put out of mind, if they are to continue to proceed as they do. It is no accident that for them any substantial conception of common goods has to be rejected and excluded.

Their reply to the case that I have tried to make will be at another level. They will argue, they do argue that the policies to which an economics and a politics of the common good commits us are not economically viable. And of course nothing that I have said so far shows them to be mistaken. So I here take note of a set of questions not yet answered. First any government that allows no inroads to be made on its expenditures on education will have to forego some other types of expenditure. Notably it will not be able to pay debts incurred by banks as a result of taking on too much risk and, if it is to have a stable economy, it will have to prevent its bankers from taking on such risk. This will involve a kind and degree of regulation unacceptable to many of those at work in the financial sector. More than this it will involve a restructuring of the relationships between the financial sector and the rest of the economy, a restructuring that will produce lower rates of growth than would otherwise occur. How are these things to be done?

A second set of questions have to do with the nature and content of the education that is to be provided, since, when I speak of protecting education from cuts in expenditure, I am not committed to endorsing the presently established patterns of expenditure. And a third set concerns the relationship between investment in education and economic growth. So, if I put these crucial questions on one side, even for the moment, I am asking a good deal. But my immediate task has to be that of clarifying further my claim that an ethics and politics of the common good can be given an effective rhetorical voice.

IV

We need to present, I have suggested, both an argument and a narrative. Both need to be introduced as answers to a question, the question of why our children are deprived of the resources that they need, if the common goods of their families, their schools, and their local societies are to be achieved. The argument that I have advanced is one in which the conclusions may be understood as following from the conjunction of two distinct sets of premises, one concerning the workings of the economic and financial system, the other derived from an account of what the achievement of the common good requires. But to interpret my argument in this way would be to misunderstand it. For on this interpretation the economic is one thing, the moral quite another.

What I am contending is that the actions that constitute the workings of our economic and financial system have not yet been adequately characterized as actions until their bearing on the common good, direct or indirect, has been identified. Of any action whatsoever we can and should ask at what good it aims and what goods or evils are foreseeably among its consequences. And, until we have answered both these questions, we have not yet determined what kind of action it is, we have not yet made it fully intelligible that someone should so act. So someone who directs his rifle fire towards a target on a firing range does not perform the same action either as someone who directs it towards a human target or as someone who closes his eyes and directs it at random. Each of these actions is directed towards something taken to be good by the agent and those goods are very different goods.[3] There is no action that consists simply in firing a rifle. And there is no action that consists simply in engaging in some type of transaction in a market. Markets exist for the sake of and are justified only insofar as they contribute to the achievement of common goods. But the various agents engaged in market transactions aim at achieving very different types of good, so performing different types of action, some of them incompatible with the good of the market and, consequently, with what justice requires in market transactions. And, since unjust transactions frustrate the achievement of common goods, market transactions have not yet been adequately characterized until they have been characterized as just or unjust, both to those parties engaged in the transaction and to those others for whom this particular transaction has or will have significant consequences.

The criteria of injustice in market transactions have to do both with the motives of those who engage in them and with both the intended and foreseeable outcomes and of such transactions. So far as motivation is concerned, we should agree with Aristotle and Aquinas that *pleonexia, avaritia,* a will to self-aggrandisement, marks the unjust human being, and that incentives that reward successful self-aggrandisement are marks of an unjust organization. So far as outcomes are concerned, unjust outcomes are marked by unfair distributions of costs and benefits that result in unjustifiable inequalities, such as the gross inequalities in respect of income and wealth that were and are found in most advanced societies both before the onset of the present crisis and since the beginnings of recovery.

What we need most of all then is a transformation of argument into narrative by constructing a moral history of recent capitalism in which the actions of those agents who brought about the crisis are identified and adequately characterized in terms of justice and injustice, that is to say, in terms of the common good. It will be a history that begins in the years of the expansion of credit and debt before the crisis and ends as the effects of the crisis work themselves out in countless families and schools long after the crisis is supposed to be over. It will begin, as we have already noted, with the actions of bankers, traders, economists, and others and end with the deprivations of children. And it will trace the causal chains that run from the former to the latter in such a way as to make the assignment of responsibility unambiguous. It will in this respect not be like the history now taught in our schools. The rhetorical task for anyone committed to the achievement of the common good is to find a way of recounting that history that will enable others—as many of them as possible—to recognize that history as their own and as the history of themselves, their families, and their communities. How is this to be done?

It will be done only by making explicit and spelling out further questions that many plain people try to ask, yet have difficulty in formulating, as they have difficulty in identifying those to whom their questions should be addressed. What the political spokespersons of the state and the market commonly do is to answer questions that those plain people have not posed, while leaving unanswered the questions to which they need answers. Consider four such questions. The first is: What must my children learn here and now, if they are not later to be at a disadvantage as reflective and concerned citizens? The second is: What is the difference between the teaching that they now receive and the teaching that they would have to receive, if they were to learn what they need to learn? The third is: What are the causes of them failing to receive the education that they need to receive?

And the fourth and final question is: What must we do, locally, regionally, nationally, globally, if we are to prevent those causes from having the effects that they do? The lack of any coherent narrative that proposes answers to these questions is the counterpart to the failures of radical politics.

Note that, when parents and teachers do begin to ask and pursue answers to those questions in this or that particular situation, they already exhibit a concern for the common good of their families and for the common good of their local community. They give evidence of a grasp of concepts for which they may not as yet have the right words. They are asking, without perhaps realizing it, to what ends their own and their children's learning and other activities should be directed. For many of them of course the attitudes and commitments that find expression in such questions will be at odds with attitudes and commitments in other parts of their compartmentalized lives. And so they will be putting themselves to the question as well as those others whom they are addressing. The moral history of our economic lives needs to be written so that it provides answers to those four questions, so that our rhetorical task has to be with constructing a narrative that elicits questions from those who hear it, a narrative that transforms its audience into questioners. If the narrative is such that their questions are rightly framed, those who are put to the question, the defenders of the established political and economic order, will find themselves part of a conversation that they have been trying to avoid for quite some time, part of debates structured as debates on disputed questions were structured in medieval universities. For ours has to become a politics of rival narratives and of disputed questions. It is through these that our arguments can be communicated.

TWENTY

Common Goods, Modern States, Rights, and—Maritain

The first parts of this paper are elementary expositions of positions that will be presupposed or alluded to in the arguments of later sections that concern Maritain's thought. The reader is asked not to feel insulted by being subjected to these initial, all too familiar accounts. This paper is designed to define issues and to set an agenda rather than as a defence of the positions that I take.

1. SOME ARISTOTELIAN THOUGHTS

Aristotle uses the expression 'common good' rarely. But later conceptions of the common good owe a great deal to two of his central claims: that there is such a thing as the good of the political society, the *polis*, which is prior to and not reducible to the goods of individuals (*NE* I, 1094b7–10), and that

"Common Goods, Modern States, Rights, and—Maritain," paper presented at Centre for Contemporary Aristotelian Studies in Ethics and Politics, London Metropolitan University, 2011.

individuals can only function well as human beings through membership of and participation in the life of the *polis* (*Politics* I, 1253a18–28). They achieve their individual goods, which are other than and more than their goods qua citizens, only through having lived the life of and achieved the good of a citizen. To excel in exercising the faculty of guiding a city (*politikē dunamis*) requires high virtue, unsurprisingly since the good at which its exercise aims is the achievement of justice, which is for the common advantage (*Politics* III,1282b14–18). The rule of law is necessary, but not sufficient for the achievement of justice, which requires just legislators and administrators.

The aim of good legislators is to educate citizens into the exercise of the virtues (*NE* II,1103b2–6), those excellences without which they will be unable to achieve either their own goods or the common good of the political society. Here we have to be careful to avoid the moralistic flavor which the word 'virtue' and its cognates have acquired in modern English. Virtues, *aretai*, are just those qualities that enable one to live well as a human being. A good regime is one that has regard to, that aims to achieve the common good, *to koinon agathon* (*Politics* III,1284b3–7). Such a regime excludes (i) tyranny; (ii) rule by this or that section of the community in its own interest; (iii) rule that presupposes that the relationships and aims of political societies are either those of a military order, as at Sparta (*Politics* II, 1269a29–1271b19), or of a commercial enterprise (*Politics* III,1280a34–1280b11); and (iv) rule by the kind of democrat who believes that to be free is to do whatever one wants (*Politics* V,1310a 31–32).

Aristotle himself of course believed that participation in political society thus conceived was possible only for male Greeks and not for those of them who were productive workers, whether slave or free. But, as A. W. H. Adkins argued, these exclusions are incompatible with Aristotle's central claims about the *ergon* and the *aretē* of human beings and they result in the incoherence of what he says about women and about natural slaves.[1] The project therefore of a political Aristotelianism without Aristotle's exclusions is a possible one. This is one of Aquinas's projects.

2. AQUINAS'S CONCEPTION OF COMMON GOODS

What I present as Aquinas's theses and arguments are his mature positions, as set out in the *Summa Theologiae*. These are in important respects different from and constitute a rejection of the political views advanced in the *De Regimine Principum*.

Human beings, as Aquinas understands them, are parts of a number of wholes: of the household and family, of political society, of the universe. The good of a whole is the end of each of its parts and each individual qua family member, qua member of political society, qua being with this specific nature achieves her or his good only in and through achieving these various ends as well as her or his individual ultimate end which is more and other than these (*Summa Theologiae* IIa-IIae q. 47 a. 10, q. 58 a. 9). Angels too (*Quaestiones disputatae de spiritualibus creaturis*, a. 8), indeed members of every species, are by their natures directed towards the end of the universe in being directed towards their own good. There is therefore a common good of political society (*Summa Contra Gentiles* III, 80) and the common good of the household and family is such that, insofar as it is achieved, it contributes to the common good of political society (*Summa Theologiae* q. 90 a. 3).

The precepts of law are directed to the common good and therefore also to the common happiness or beatitude (90 a. 2). The precepts of the natural law, like the precepts of law in general, are precepts of reason (90 a. 1), which is to say both that one cannot fully understand them without also understanding that one has good reason to obey them and that, insofar as we are rational, we can distinguish between precepts that deserve our obedience just because obedience to them conduces to the achievement of our common good and precepts presented to us by the powerful under the guise of law, which in fact lack the force and authority of law. The good at which law aims is, as both Aristotle and scripture have said, justice (96, a. 4; IIa-IIae 57 a. 12, q. 58) and more widely a civic education into the virtues (Ia-IIae 92, art.1). So to have a care for the common good of family and household or of political society is to have a care for both a just ordering of those institutions, in which each individual receives her or his due, and for the justice of transactions between individuals and between individuals and institutions. If we ask 'Why should we be just?', the short answer is that it is only in and through just relationships that we are able to achieve not only the common goods of family and household, of political society, and of other forms of association, but also our own individual goods. Yet here it is important to understand that, in order to achieve my own individual good I have to become just, that is I have to learn to care for the common good for its own sake and not because, through caring for it, I achieve my own individual good.

Just positive laws are framed to meet the needs, among them the changing needs, of the whole community over time. They may not therefore always capture what is needed in particular cases in exceptional circumstances (96, art.1). And, while the aim of legislators in framing laws is to prescribe a way of life in which education into the virtues takes place, the laws themselves should not be aimed at prohibiting every moral evil, since the effect of such laws is apt to be to make human beings less and not more virtuous, which would be contrary to the common good. The precepts of positive law that have been framed in accordance with the natural law are of two kinds, those that hold for all societies in all times and places and those that are framed with an eye to the particular circumstances of this or that time and place (100, art.8). Precepts that do not accord with the natural law do not command our obedience as rational agents. It may on occasion be prudent to obey them, but it is not unjust to disobey and justice and reason sometimes require us to disobey.

The rule of a tyrant is "wholly corrupt" (95, art.4) and incompatible with the rule of law. Aquinas follows Aristotle in holding that there are various forms of legitimate government. And he follows both Aristotle and scripture in holding that the best form of government is a "benign mixture" of kingship, aristocracy, and democracy, democracy because it belongs to the people to elect the rulers (IIa-IIae 105, art.1). For "to order something to the common good is the business of the whole community or of someone acting on behalf of the whole community" (Ia-IIae 90, art.3). And law can be made only by the whole community or by someone authorized by the whole community.

In the thirteenth century—and not only then—Aquinas in advancing such views was a political eccentric. The political background that he took for granted was one of various political forms—kingdoms, city states, feudal lordships, diocesan administrations, monastic houses—and of contested jurisdictions: the king's laws against local customary law, the king's courts against the courts of rival feudal landowners, the authority of bishops against that of the superiors of religious orders, the claims of city councils against the claims of local landowners, of civil law against canon law, of pope against Holy Roman Emperor. What an understanding of the different kinds of law provides are resources for judging between rival claimants to authority over one. In particular the precepts of the natural law and of justice rightly conceived provide standards for evaluating political claims advanced both by secular rulers and by church authorities. And just as we can appeal against the decrees of secular rulers to church authorities, so we can in many areas appeal against both to the verdict of practical reason.

3. THE MODERN STATE

A first difficulty in being a political Thomist in the modern world is that in our world competing authorities and disputed jurisdictions are rare and exceptional. Between the thirteenth and the seventeenth century there emerges a type of state in which power and authority are centralized, in which the state claims and often moves close to achieving a monopoly in the use of violence, and in which the state recognizes no possibility of an appeal from the verdicts of its highest organs. There is a single system of law enforced within the well-defined boundaries of each state. The state determines who is subject to its authority and it requires loyalty from its subjects. The state has an exclusive right to tax and characteristically controls a central bank. It functions through hierarchically structured administrative bureaucracies. It is essential to the modern state that religion has a subordinate place in the lives of its subjects, that there is no appeal beyond the state to the church.

It has been up to the state to decide how far the state's powers should extend. And states have generally made provision for education and welfare, have regulated and sometimes provided health services, while regulating transport, communications, and financial institutions and controlling travel across frontiers. States conduct censuses, register births, marriages, and deaths, and retain the right, even when they do not exercise it, to conscript its subjects for military service. States conduct covert operations. Politicians who on being elected to public office say that they will shrink the powers of the state and cut its expenditures characteristically enlarge those powers and increase those expenditures. A recurrent problem for those who by authority of the state wield the power of the state is how to justify that authority and their uses of that power.

The most compelling and influential solution to that problem has four parts. First is the claim that the authority and power of the state are justified by the benefits conferred by the state, sometimes in the Hobbesian form of a contrast between the law and order of states and the horrors of statelessness, sometimes in advanced societies by cataloguing the resources that the state makes available to its subjects. Secondly, it is claimed that the relationship between the state and its subjects is contractual. Once again there is a Hobbesian version according to which consent to the terms of that contract is implicit and a less startling version according to which subjects give their consent to the authority and power of the state by participating in the democratic processes through which governments are elected. This latter claim is sometimes presented in conjunction with a third and stronger form of justification, according to which the authority and power of democratic governments give expression to the political choices of the electorate voiced through voting. It is by voting as they do that plain persons authorize the actions of government and of the apparatus of the state more generally.

What then of states where either there is not universal adult suffrage or where conditions for genuinely free elections, including the rule of law and freedom of expression, do not exist? Individuals in such states have been denied rights that belong to them as individuals, independently of and prior to the enactments of positive law, such rights as the natural rights to life, liberty, and the pursuit of happiness of the American Declaration of Independence or the *Rights of Man* catalogued by Saint-Just for the Jacobins. And states which have recognized such rights are taken to be legitimated in part at least by that recognition.

Finally the problem of the relationship of the state to its subjects takes on a new complexity when it is not just the state but the-state-and-the-market, the state as a locus of both political and economic power that those subjects confront.

4. THE SOCIAL TEACHING OF THE CATHOLIC CHURCH

The modern social teaching of the Catholic Church as explicit doctrine dates from the encyclical letter *Rerum Novarum* of Pope Leo XIII in 1892, modern in that it addressed peculiarly modern issues of the poverty of wage earners and of the unemployed in industrial societies, but not only modern, since it presupposes both Aquinas's conception of justice and the precepts of scripture. It is important that what Leo XIII presented as authoritative teaching already informed the practice of bishops and priests in some parts of the world. Cardinal Manning, for example, had given unstinted support to the dockers' strike of 1889, joining with such working class leaders as Tom Mann. That strike was the single most important episode in the growth of trade unionism in England among unskilled and semi-skilled workers and support for independent and militant trade unions was a crucial aspect of Catholic social teaching. But, since working men and women have a right to work and to work that should be meaningful, the goals which they should set themselves extend beyond trade union activity. What trade unions must strive for is a just wage, a wage that can support a flourishing family life, good hours of work and safe conditions of work, and just provision for health and old age. And plain people should be active participants in the politics designed to achieve these aims.

What are at stake in achieving or failing to achieve these are the common goods of at least three forms of association, those of families, those of workplaces, and those of political societies. The principle of subsidiarity enjoins that societies should be so organized that families are able, so far as possible, to provide for themselves, and, where they are not able to provide for themselves, local authorities should make the necessary provision. Only insofar as they are inadequate should central government function as the provider of last resort, which often enough it has to do. Notably required is the protection, nurture, and education of children from conception until entry into the adult world. (Hence the peculiar scandal of crimes of child abuse!)

As Catholic social teaching has been presented by national conferences of Catholic Bishops in the last half century three problems have become evident. First it is uniformly taken for granted that the structures and procedures of the modern state in its liberal democratic forms are such that through them the common good of political society can be achieved. The tension between the need to identify and to achieve common goods through active participation by plain persons in local grass roots politics and the imposition upon local societies of the party politics of national government is very occasionally noticed, but nothing beyond this. The fact that the modern democratic system requires that the vast majority of citizens should be politically passive, except at elections when the only choices that they are allowed to make are between alternatives selected for them by political elites goes unnoticed. The bishops have in general regressed from the distributist positions of G. K. Chesterton, who understood the evils of great concentrations of either political or economic power in the modern state.

Secondly, for understandable reasons the bishops have often for a time focused almost exclusively on this or that particular issue in this or that particular political situation. And for equally understandable reasons they have often presented Catholic social teaching on such particular issues detached from its philosophical and theological presuppositions, hoping thereby not to endanger political cooperation with those who do not share those presuppositions. The problem is that some of the central contentions of Catholic moral and social teaching are only fully intelligible in the light of those presuppositions. So the prohibition of abortion is an integral part of a larger conception of families and children detached from which it is bound to appear less intelligible than it is. So the hospitable concern for immigrants, including illegal immigrants, is grounded in a conception of the part that hospitality to strangers plays in the achievement of *our* common good, detached from which it must appear as arbitrary benevolence. The effect of this detachment is even more obvious, when we consider another notable aspect of the bishops' recent teaching.

Among the many things that justice requires, on a Catholic and on a Thomist view, is that various individuals and groups should be accorded certain rights, most often through the enactments of positive law. The justification for recognizing those rights is that without such recognition just relationships and the common good cannot be achieved and that it is only through striving to achieve these that we can each of us achieve our own individual goods. On a distinctively modern conception of natural or human rights however the reason for recognizing many rights is that individuals already have rights just in virtue of being human individuals, a claim supported by a number of arguments all of which are contestable, indeed on my own view unsound. It is not just that the adherents of these two views differ in their accounts of how claims to rights are to be justified. They also differ in their catalogue of fundamental rights.

When however the bishops detach their teaching about rights from its theological and philosophical presuppositions, they tend to assimilate their view of rights to modern liberal views of human rights and often take themselves to have thereby discovered common ground for political and economic action. So there is now a shared rhetoric of human rights so influential that the present United Kingdom Home Secretary has made it one of the defining characteristics of terrorists, that they do not believe in human rights. Someone should introduce her to Jeremy Bentham.

Present day Catholic social teaching therefore is problematic in three respects: in its failure to put the powers of the modern state in question, in its treatment of single issue politics, and in its capitulation to the rhetoric of human rights. We might note in passing that their recurrent condemnations of the sometimes naïve Neo-Marxism of liberation theology, like their predecessors' condemnations of atheistic communism, justified as both sets of condemnations have been, have prevented the Vatican's theologians from learning from Marxism what they badly needed and need to learn. We should also note that Catholic social teaching as communicated through both the theory and the practice of the Catholic Worker movement is often free from the defects of the bishops' presentations.

5. JACQUES MARITAIN (1882-1973)

The political importance of Maritain is that he made what he took to be a Thomistic case both for the modern state as an institution through whose structures and procedures the common good of political society can be realized and for a conception of human rights which assimilates a Thomistic understanding of what justice requires to a modern liberal democratic understanding of human rights. If Maritain's projects were successful, then the doubts that I have suggested about what I take to be problematic in the most influential versions of Catholic social teaching are unjustified. It will be my claim that they do not succeed. Maritain's political thought developed through three stages. In the first which lasted from just before the First World War until 1926 the chief influence on Maritain was that of Charles Maurras. In the second which lasted from around 1931 perhaps until the Second World War the chief influence was that of Emmanuel

Mounier. The third period from 1944 to 1952 is one in which political activity as French ambassador to the Vatican and as president of the French delegation to UNESCO was accompanied and followed by the publication of the two books which define Maritain's mature political thought, *The Person and the Common Good* (1947) and *Man and the State* (1951). In all three periods Maritain's primary work and achievement was as a Thomistic philosopher, in dialogue and controversy with other Thomists and nothing that I say about his political arguments and stances should be read as incompatible with admiration for his philosophical achievements.

6. MARITAIN, MAURRAS, MOUNIER, AND THE UNITED NATIONS

Charles Maurras (1868–1952) was the most gifted enemy from the right of French republicanism and democracy. As such he would in any case have had a sympathetic hearing from those considerable sections of the conservative French Catholic bourgeoisie, who until the First World War had never fully accepted the Third Republic and who rejected Catholic social teaching. But Maurras's positive doctrines also attracted them. For he and the extreme right-wing movement that he cofounded, *L'Action Française*, wished to restore in large measure the Catholic France of the past, putting primary and secondary education under the control of the Catholic Church. Why so? Not at all because he was a Catholic. Maurras was by conviction a Comtean positivist, an atheist, who as a Comtean believed that ordinary people, being less than rational, needed the guidance and the motivation of religious belief, so that they might understand themselves as inhabiting a social and political order in which it was right and natural that they should be ruled from above. On Maurras's view what the French needed were those Catholic beliefs and practices through which the traditions of the French prerepublican past had been transmitted.

At the core of Maurras's politics was his conviction that the common good of the French could not be achieved in a republic in which the different political parties represented different and rival sectional interests and nobody represented the common good. A restoration of the French monarchy was required in which the care of the common good would be the responsibility of the monarch and his advisers. Maritain for a time endorsed Maurras's critique of the politics and the political parties of the Third Republic and, although he was never persuaded by Maurras's monarchism, he agreed that the central problem of French politics was that of how the common good was to be identified and achieved. That concern remained with him after he broke with Maurras and *L'Action Française* in 1926, a result of its condemnation by Pius XI, and in a remarkably short space of time moved from being a Catholic of the more or less extreme Right to being at least in conversation with the Catholic Left. The new influence on his thinking was that of Emmanuel Mounier.

Mounier, a student of Bergson's student Jacques Chevalier, had been open to a wide range of influences, both Catholic and other, and had in consequence become persuaded that all the major political movements of the twentieth century misconceived human nature in their theory and deformed human beings in their practice. The concept that had eluded them was that of the human person as one whose spiritual and moral possibilities can only be realized through certain kinds of social relationship, among which the relationships of family life, of the workplace as a place of meaningful work, of friendship, and of a political community that shares this recognition of family, of work, and of friendship are of the first importance. It was in these terms that Mounier framed his criticisms not only of fascism and communism, but also of the politics of bourgeois individualism. In 1934 he published his *Manifeste au service du personnalisme*. By this time Maritain had already separated himself from Mounier's politics. But the concept of the person was from then on central to his thinking.

It is worth noting that in his political writings Maritain never acknowledged his debts to either Maurras or Mounier, although here is not the place to ask why. But his conceptions both of the common good and of the person had in fact been detached from the theoretical and practical contexts in which he had first encountered them and therefore had to find a place within a new framework, a framework that also had to accommodate the lessons that Maritain took himself to have learned from his political and other experiences between 1940 and 1950. In 1940, when France was defeated, the Maritains were in the United States and Maritain remained there until late in 1944, when, as I noticed earlier, De Gaulle's provisional government appointed him ambassador to the Vatican. It was through his subsequent work for France in UNESCO that he played a small part in formulating and became committed to the Universal Declaration of Human Rights adopted by the General Assembly of the United Nations in December 1948. So to the concepts of the common good and of the person there was added that of a universal human right. Add to this that Maritain took no part in the conflicts in postwar France over the form that the Fourth Republic should take, conflicts in which rival conceptions of and attitudes towards the common good were at stake, but in practice identified himself, although not uncritically, with American democracy. In 1948 the Maritains left France and Maritain took up an appointment at Princeton in the Fall of that year.

The problem had thus been set for Maritain: How can the concepts of a person, of the common good, and of a universal human right be understood within the framework of Maritain's Thomistic philosophy, so that they can inform the political practice of a modern liberal democratic state, such as the United States?

7. THE PERSON AND THE COMMON GOOD

In 1947 Maritain put together some of his lectures and essays from 1939 onwards and published them in English translation as *The Person and the Common Good*. Four theses are central to Maritain's overall argument. The first contrasts the individuality of a human being with her or his personality: "In each of us, individuality, being that which excludes from oneself all that other men are, could be described as the narrowness of the ego, forever threatened and forever eager *to grasp for itself*."[2] Personality "signifies interiority to self." It is that in us which "requires the communications of knowledge and love."[3] A second thesis relates the vocation of persons to goods that transcend the common good of political society. Each person is directed towards a final good that belongs to the order of eternal goods and the service of the common good must not interfere with, but contribute to the attainment of that final good. Yet persons, because of their concern for others, must be concerned with the common good of political society which includes "roads, ports, schools, etc.," fiscal health and military power, "just laws, good customs and wise institutions," the nation's cultural heritage and the integration of virtues, liberty, material prosperity, and "friendship, happiness, virtue and heroism in the individual lives of its members."[4]

A third thesis concerns the relationship of the concept of a person to that of the common good: "There is a correlation between this notion of the *person* as a social unit and the notion of the *common good* as the end of the social whole. They imply one another."[5] Neither has priority over the other and neither can be fully spelled out without reference to the other. The common good is common because it is a good communicated to and received by persons. Fourthly and finally Maritain draws political conclusions. Bourgeois liberalism must be rejected because it conceives of all goods as goods of individuals and so misconceives the common good as a sum of individual goods. Communism in reacting against bourgeois individualism subordinates the individual to society and the state, so that once again the common good is misunderstood. Authoritarian dictatorships suppose that society can be organized for its good from above and so do not recognize the part that persons must play in achieving their own individual and common goods. So we should reject these three types of regime. What is it that we should strive for instead? Maritain's answer is set out in *Man and the State*.

8. MAN, THE STATE, AND THE COMMON GOOD

The lectures which were published as *Man and the State* were delivered at the University of Chicago in 1949. He had already settled in Princeton, where he would live until 1960. The political institutions that he presupposes in his lectures are those of American constitutional democracy and the questions that he frames concern how those institutions must be structured and understood, if the political common good and a proper respect for persons is to be achieved. Maritain seems to have been anxious to secure as much common ground with his Chicago audience as possible and, although he presents his views as Thomistic, he generally argues from what he takes to be widely shared premises. I shall focus on what he says about the political common good and on what he says about rights.

A people compose a body politic and the common good of a body politic "demands a network of authority and power" and therefore "a special agency endowed with uppermost power, for the sake of justice and law. The State is that uppermost political agency," a means to the body politic's ends.[6] The common good is characterized using exactly the same words that were used in *The Person and the Common Good*.[7] The common good will be realized only in political societies in which moral constraints are imposed on the choice of political means (chapter III) and it is only in democracies that the right moral constraints will be imposed. The state is in permanent danger of violating those constraints and no institutional protection will always be effective. But politics is a rough business in which coercive force has a necessary place and, just as Machiavellianism is a vice, so is the "fear of soiling ourselves" by dealing with the harsher political realities.[8] The citizenry must be united in their allegiance to democracy and the range of permitted political disagreements must be consistent with this underlying agreement. The educational system will be designed to produce belief in democratic principles. For every one of these theses Maritain has arguments and a fair treatment of *Man and the State* would require us to engage with these arguments and with his always interesting discussions of a number of topics that I have left unmentioned. Moreover it would be quite wrong to present Maritain as wholly uncritical of the workings of American democracy. His friendship with Saul Alinsky is strong evidence to the contrary. But Maritain invites criticism as much for what he left unsaid as for his theses and arguments. So let me draw attention to what went unsaid in three major areas.

The first is the relationship between the contemporary state and the market economy. In the sixty years since Maritain wrote that relationship has become increasingly complex at both national and international levels. But even so it is notable that Maritain devotes only two pages to the place of social and economic issues in politics, where he briefly summarizes Catholic social teaching.[9] About the following two questions, for example, he has nothing to say: Is the distribution of economic power in modern liberal democracies such as to exclude the relatively powerless from participating in setting the agendas for political discussion and from getting a hearing for any view that is unacceptable to the relatively powerful? And is the distribution of educational resources in some of those democracies such that many of the children of the economically less well off fail to receive the kind of education needed for effective participation in political debate?

A second area where he has nothing to say is that which concerns the centralization of power, authority, and political debate in the modern state and the relationship of grass roots political discussion and activity to the achievement of the political common good. Maritain never asks what kind of institutions are needed at local, regional, and national levels, if there is to be ongoing debate at local levels which is a genuine expression of the concerns and claims of plain persons and if the conclusions of those debates are to have an effective influence at regional and national levels. Thirdly, he does not reckon with anything like the range of different and incompatible moral and religious outlooks that are found within many modern states and so never asks whether a modern liberal democracy can have enough of a common moral and political mind for government to function as the kind of educator in the virtues that Aristotle and Aquinas described. It was in part because Maritain provided no answers to these questions that he also failed to address five issues that are crucial for any attempt to translate Aristotle's and Aquinas's account of the political common good into contemporary terms.

First, the most obvious differences between modern states and the kinds of political society that Aristotle and Aquinas had in mind are differences in size and scale. Moreover those societies in various parts of the modern world in which some degree of regard for the common good has been embodied—the kinds of cooperative enterprise to which I have referred in earlier papers—have all been relatively small scale. Add to that the contentions by anthropologists about the numerical limits on our abilities to keep track of and give weight in our own reasoning to the intentions and actions of others (R. I. M. Dunbar for one view, H. Russell Bernard and Peter Killworth for another) and the evidence provided by Elinor Ostrom[10] that prudent cooperative use of shared resources for the common good, in which everyone participates, has to be small scale and it becomes close to incontrovertible that societies on the scale of most contemporary nation states cannot have a politics informed by any strong Aristotelian or Thomistic conception of the common good.

The politics of the common good is then primarily a politics of local community. For such a politics a second type of issue arises, that of the relationship between the common goods of families and households and the common good of the political society. Questions of employment and wages, of housing, of schools, and of transport and communications are of key importance for both and so is that of how these questions are to be dealt with justly, effectively, and in a way that preserves the independence and decision-making powers of families. So the question of what the well-being of families in contemporary societies is is a crucial political question. Any systematic attempt to answer it makes it impossible to avoid engaging with a third issue.

Maritain's characterizations of the common good are highly general and, given his purposes, understandably so. But those purposes distance him from the local and particular realities of politics. The problem for those committed to a politics of the common good is that of how to translate those generalities into concrete and particular terms, so that a set of goals are identified, the achievement of which would constitute the achievement of their common good by this or that particular community with its particular resources in its particular circumstances. To identify those goals would be to provide a set of major premises for the shared political reasoning of the members of that political society. A precondition for them to arrive at such an identification is that they are able to agree—an agreement characteristically expressed in their everyday practice rather than in theorizing—in a rough and ready way on their rank ordering of goods. And their agreement must extend further, if they are to reason together not only about ends, but also about means. For, if they are to arrive at conclusions about what actions to take in order to achieve the proximate ends of the common good, they will have to agree in their understanding of what law and justice require, since it is only through relationships governed by the precepts of the natural law and informed by justice that common goods can be achieved.

Such agreements are necessary, but not sufficient for those engaging in the kind of shared political reasoning needed to inform activity aimed at the common good. They also need to have shared in an education concerning the history, geography, social structure, and political economy of their own and other societies, so that they know how to make relevant and accurate judgments about the situation in which they find themselves, about what has to be changed in that situation, and about the alternative ways in which such change can be achieved. For, unless everyone from every sector of the political society has shared in such an education, there will be those who will be excluded from or disabled in political enquiry, debate, and decision making. A fourth set of issues therefore for anyone committed to a politics of the common good concerns how such an education, education that is a preparation for engaging in practical reasoning, is to be provided for every citizen.

To pursue any or all of these issues is to take us in a direction very different from that taken by Maritain. Just how different becomes even clearer, if we turn to questions concerning rights and the Universal Declaration of Human Rights of 1948. In order to approach those questions I need first to consider some different kinds of reason for acting in this or that particular way, reasons that may be advanced as a sufficient justification for so acting.

9. REASONS, JUSTIFICATIONS, AND RIGHTS

Example One: Someone asks why I uphold the right of every citizen to participate in political debate, including debate on setting the agenda for debate. I reply: Because only thus can the common good of this political society be identified, let alone achieved. If pressed further, I justify my assertion by showing in what ways the denial of this equal right may prevent the common good from being correctly identified. If pressed still further by being asked why it matters whether or not the common good is correctly identified, I justify my claim by spelling out the connection between the common good and the individual goods of myself and my interrogator. At this point practical justification terminates, although skeptical philosophers may express doubts of a very different kind.

Example Two: You and I, while on a mission of some importance to us—if we succeed in it, it will benefit ourselves and some others considerably—come across some helpless individual or group in urgent need. Unless we act to help them now, they will die from their injuries, starve to death, be kidnapped by slave traders. One of us says: We must act to help them now and begins to act. The other asks: Why? For what reason? The only appropriate response is: If you need a reason for so acting, you have already missed the point. And the same is true of someone who does agree to respond to urgent need, but only after calculating, after weighing the costs and benefits. What is the difference between someone for whom all questions of justification are irrelevant in such situations and someone who in such situations still asks for a justification? The former acts and acts immediately as the virtues of justice, generosity, and compassion require, the latter lacks those virtues in important respects. Is there a rational justification for valuing, inculcating, and exercising those virtues? There is indeed. It is that without those virtues we are unable to achieve either our individual or our common goods. But it is one of the marks of the virtuous to recognize when justification is required and when it is irrelevant.

Consider now a different kind of irrelevance, the irrelevance of the concept of a universal human right to both these examples. Suppose that in the first example someone were to say that every citizen has an equal right to participate in political debate, including debate on setting the agendas for debate, *because* there is a universal human right to do so. What reason with what kind of weight has been adduced? Will anyone not disposed for other reasons to hold that every citizen should have such a right have been given a reason with something more than rhetorical force? I think not. Suppose now that in the second example someone similarly intervenes by trying to justify aid to those in urgent need by citing some alleged universal human right. Such a one will make the same mistake as the individual who pauses to calculate. In that type of situation no justification is needed and all justification is irrelevant.

From these two examples therefore I draw a general thesis. Whenever an alleged universal human right is cited in justification of some action or policy, either it provides the wrong kind of justification or it attempts to justify what needs no justification. Why then did Maritain think otherwise?

10. MARITAIN AND THE UNIVERSAL DECLARATION OF HUMAN RIGHTS

The thirty articles of the Declaration make a number of very different claims that need to be supported by different kinds of argument. In a few cases it is difficult to give any determinate meaning to an article (e.g., Article 30 which states that "Everyone is entitled to a social and international order in which the rights and freedoms set forth in this Declaration can be fully realized") and nowhere are any key terms defined. Yet in many articles the substitution of 'should have a right to' for 'has a right to' yields an intelligible and justified claim. I shall not ask here why the delegates to the United Nations would have rejected this substitution, but only why Maritain did. Maritain made his reason quite clear. He took it that the acknowledgment of rights that are prior to and independent of the enactments of positive law was an acknowledgment of law that is prior to and independent of the enactments of positive law, indeed an implicit acknowledgment, first of the authority of the precepts of the natural law, as understood by Aquinas, and then as a corollary of the *jus gentium*.

Maritain knew that many of the United Nations delegates rejected anything like Aquinas's account of the natural law, but he saw in their assent to the Declaration an agreement with the content of important Thomistic claims, even by those whose justification of that assent involved an appeal to Enlightenment philosophies, such as those of Rousseau and Kant, which Maritain rejected. What he counterposed to those philosophies was not a set of arguments, but a claim—which he confidently ascribes to Aquinas—that knowledge of the precepts of the natural law "is not rational knowledge, but knowledge *through inclination*. That kind of knowledge is not clear knowledge through concepts and conceptual judgments; it is obscure, unsystematic, vital knowledge by connaturality or congeniality" in which intellect "consults and listens to" something other than itself.[11] What should we say to this?

Maritain is of course right both in asserting that and in ascribing to Aquinas the view that practical knowledge of the precepts of the natural law is not a matter of first recognizing the truth of the first principle of practical reason and then reasoning from it. The first principle of practical reasoning is presupposed by the reasoning expressed in our activity and much of that reasoning is never made explicit. Indeed the relatively inarticulate may and often do exhibit in their practice a remarkable grasp of what it is to act as practical reason requires in particular situations and yet be unable to spell out those requirements. But what matters is that they can be spelled out. And when they are fully spelled out reference will have to be made to those *inclinationes*, those directednesses towards different kinds of good, that we discover in ourselves and in other human agents.

But nothing in the relevant texts of Aquinas (especially *Summa Theologiae* Ia-IIae q. 94 a. 2) suggests, let alone says that there is a nonrational apprehension of the precepts of the natural law of the kind described by Maritain. And I find it difficult to understand Maritain's thesis except as a misunderstanding of the practical rationality of the inarticulate.

It is of course true that the text of article 2 of question 94 has been interpreted in a number of importantly different and incompatible ways. My own account of the rationality of willing conformity to the precepts of the natural law is to be found in 'Intractable Moral Disagreements' (in L. S. Cunningham, ed. *Intractable Disputes about the Natural Law*, University of Notre Dame Press, 2009, where there are essays by critics who take a different view, notably Jean Porter. Still other views have been defended by Germaine Grisez and John Finnis and by Ralph McInerny. None provide support for Maritain's thesis). My conclusion is therefore that Maritain's defense of the conception of human rights in the Declaration is inadequately argued, even if the difficulties that I have with that conception could be overcome. And it may be that this inadequacy is rooted in a more fundamental mistake, one concerning Maritain's view of the common good and the human person. That Maritain made such a mistake seems to have been the view of Charles De Koninck.

11. DE KONINCK ON THE PRIORITY OF THE COMMON GOOD

The word "seems" is important. Maritain had delivered his Deneke Lecture at Oxford on 'The Human Person and Society' in 1939. In 1943 De Koninck published *The Primacy of the Common Good against the Personalists*. In it Maritain is never mentioned, but it was widely assumed by readers and reviewers that its sharp polemics were directed against Maritain. Maritain in *The Person and the Common Good* thanks one of those reviewers, the Dominican Father Theodore Eschmann, but nowhere refers to De Koninck, although readers of *The Person and the Common Good* took it that in certain passages Maritain was replying to De Koninck and accusing him of making palpably false accusations against Maritain. All that matters about these unfortunate quarrels is that they distracted attention from what mattered most in what De Koninck had to say, something for which he had only himself to blame. Maritain had argued that the concepts of the person and of the common good were correlative and equally fundamental. Against this De Koninck asserts the primacy of the concept of the common good. Who was right?

It is a fundamental thesis of De Koninck that different kinds of agent—nonhuman animals, human beings, angels—are to be distinguished by the differences in the goods towards the achievement of which they are directed by their specific natures. Human beings do have distinctive worth. In Aquinas's terms, human agents have dignity and to have dignity is to be valued for one's own sake. But they have the dignity that they have by reason of their ultimate end and their freedom to attain that end. Human beings are parts of a number of wholes, most notably of the family, political society, and the universe. We are not to think of them as having each an individual end, an individual good and *also* a set of shared ends, of common goods. They achieve their own good in achieving the common goods that are theirs, for it is in achieving those common goods that they perfect themselves as human beings and so achieve their own individual good.[12] De Koninck presents this as Aquinas's plain view, citing a variety of texts. If he is right, both in his exegesis and in his substantive reasoning, then Maritain errs in supposing that we can give any account, let alone a Thomistic account, of the nature and worth of human individuals prior to and independently of a characterization of their relationships to common goods.

On this, although not on very much else in his polemics, I am in agreement with De Koninck. And, as I have argued earlier, I also take it that we do not have a defensible concept of human rights prior to and independently of our account of common goods. It is because and only because we are directed towards the achievement of common goods as our own goods that we need positive laws which mandate relationships with others partially defined by a mutual regard to their and our rights. So the concept of a right is secondary to and derivable from an adequate account of common goods. And once again I am at variance with Maritain. But we cannot simply move on and leave Maritain behind. For the criticism of his views leaves us with questions rather than answers.

The politics of the common good, as I have reiterated to the point of tedium, can only be a politics of local community. But we, all of us, whatever the political condition of our local communities, inhabit modern states and cannot dispense with a politics that deals with them on their terms. So that, even if we reject Maritain's view of the possibilities of the modern state, we need a politics of the modern state that is consonant with a politics of the common good. And this we do not as yet have. Moreover, the rhetorical politics of universal human rights, the partial definition of conflicts by referring to such rights, is an established fact. So that a skeptical critique of the very idea of a universal human right has to be a prologue to an account of how protagonists of the politics of common goods should position themselves with regard to such conflicts. And this we do not as yet know how to do.

TWENTY-ONE

Practical Rationality and Irrationality and Their Social Settings

This is an exploratory paper in which some points are made at sufficient length, but others much too briefly. I begin by advancing an account of what it is to be a practically rational agent, an account whose central features derive from Aristotle and Aquinas, and I sketch a problem about the ways in which distributions of economic power may undermine rational agency. I then consider the inability of Aristotle's version of Aristotelianism to address this problem and examine an influential contemporary account of practical rationality that also fails to supply what is needed. Finally I identify some large irrationalities in our recent economic and financial

"Practical Rationality and Irrationality and Their Social Settings," paper presented at Centre for Contemporary Aristotelian Studies in Ethics and Politics, London Metropolitan University, 2012.

life and ask what light they throw on what it would be to be practically rational in our economic transactions.

I

Aquinas took it that, if we are to deliberate rationally, even about the achievement of our own individual goods, we need to do so in the company of others, since otherwise our practical reasoning will be one-sided and partial (*Summa Theologiae* Ia-IIae q. 14 a. 3). We might add that we need the criticism of insightful others, if we are not to become the victims of our own wishful, or fearful thinking. But this is not all. The goods that we pursue are many of them common goods, the goods of family, school, and workplace, of clinic, orchestra, and political society, goods that we pursue and enjoy only *qua* family member, *qua* teacher or student, and so on. Hence we need to reason together with other family members, other teachers and students, and the like both as to what in concrete terms our common good consists in here and now and as to the means by which it is to be achieved. Any particular agent therefore is apt to find her or himself engaged in a number of conversations directed towards arriving at practical conclusions. Someone may, for example, at one and the same time need to arrive at agreement on disputed issues with her or his siblings and with other members of her or his trade union branch, while acting easily in concert with members of other groups to which she or he belongs on the basis of past and now settled agreements.

What matters is that these various relationships should be informed by a broadly shared assent to the norms of practical reasoning and consequent agreement in recognizing and responding to violations of those norms. That assent and that agreement will for the most part be tacit and the acknowledgment of the authority of the norms will be a matter of how agents give reasons to others and evaluate those reasons. There will always be room for disagreement about how in this or that particular situation the goods at stake are to be rank ordered, but it is a necessary condition, if this kind of shared rationality is to inform the choices, actions, and transactions of some group, that the members of that group should be in broad agreement as to how goods are to be rank ordered. Without some measure of such agreement they will in particular situations be unable to agree on the premises of the practical syllogisms that issue in their choices and actions, but the extent of agreement will vary from case to case. We can therefore characterize not only individual agents, but also institutions, organizations, and local societies as more or less rational. Insofar as the transactions of an institution, organization, or political society are rational, its members will conform to the precepts of the natural law, since it is conformity to those precepts that requires us to secure the cooperation of others by reason giving rather than by force, fraud, or nonrational persuasion. And, if that conformity is to inform the habits and the transactions of a particular society, then authority and power will have to be understood and distributed in particular ways. Other incompatible ways of understanding and distributing authority and power may make it difficult and perhaps impossible for the exercise of practical rationality to be sustained. What these might be is a question to which I will return.

The goods that rational agents pursue through such relationships and transactions are the particular goods of particular people in particular situations. Practical reasoning, says Aquinas, is concerned with the singular and the contingent (*Summa Theologiae* Ia-IIae 91, 3 a. 3). The generalizations and rules that find application in our reasoning may therefore always have to be revised to take account of the particular features of this or that particular case (Ia-IIae 94 a. 4). So the ends to which we direct our activities are particular ends and about them two questions always need to be answered and will in fact be answered by the way in which we choose and act: 'What place should this end have in my life, in our common lives, here and now?' And 'What resources do I/we have for achieving this end and what means should we employ in achieving it?' Ends are of two kinds. There are those that we can specify adequately prior to taking any action, so that we can also devise whatever means are appropriate in advance. But there are those that we learn to conceive more adequately only in and through the activities that we undertake in order to achieve them, so that our choice of appropriate means may also change. A farmer, having as his end the harvesting of a crop of oats, knows in advance what he must do to achieve it. But the same farmer, having as his end to become a good farmer of this particular land, may over the years have his notion of what it is to be a good farmer transformed, perhaps by his own experience, perhaps by what he learns from others. So it is too with someone whose end is to become a good teacher or a good painter of landscapes or portraits.

It is important then that those social relationships that are informed by the norms of practical rationality are relationships in which the participants are open to learning from each other and that creativity, inventiveness, and improvisation are often needed, if we are to make progress in achieving our individual and common goods. Note too that there are cases where practical enquiry begins not from some conception of an end to be pursued, but from a consideration of the resources available to us and a hunch that we could make better use of them than we have done hitherto. "Given these means," we ask, "to what uses might we put them, to what ends might we direct them?" And so sometimes advances in technology, new forms of art, and even new forms of social life come to be.

A rational institution, organization, or social order is characteristically one that flourishes by transforming itself in various ways. How far it does so and in what ways, how well it is able to sustain itself in hard times, depends in part on the qualities of mind and character of the agents involved in making key decisions. For without the exercise of prudent judgment concerning the ordering of the relevant goods, an exercise that requires the exercise of the virtues of temperateness, courage, and justice, no rational society can sustain itself, let alone transform itself. But it also depends in key part, on the economic resources that it possesses: natural resources, labor, skills, productivity, trade, savings. When such a society is in good order, its economic resources and activities are means to the achievement of the noneconomic goods that agents value, but, as means to the achievement of those goods, they themselves have a more than economic character.

Consider the difference between two cases, in both of which a group of men are digging a ditch. One group are doing so as a punishment drill. The ditch serves no purpose and, when it has been dug, it will be filled in. The other group are members of a farming cooperative constructing a system of irrigation that will allow them to experiment. The physical labor is as taxing and unpleasant in the one case as the other, but for the second group their work has point and purpose and not only as means to their end. It is understood as a necessary component of a shared way of life, the living out of which is itself a good. So more generally economic activities, insofar as they derive their point and purpose from noneconomic goods, have a noneconomic significance. In a rational social order economic resources and activities serve noneconomic ends, but they are indispensable for the attainment of those ends and economic change originating from outside that order may result in radical changes in the ends that its agents pursue.

A first example is that of a tenant farmer confronted by a significant increase in the rent that he has to pay to the owner of the land that he farms. His ancestors have farmed this land for generations and, like his predecessors, he has four aims. The first is to obtain a livelihood for him and his family. The second is to retain the farm by paying the rent. The third is to achieve the first two by being as good a farmer as he has it in him to be, by alternating crops, renewing the soil, irrigating where and when necessary, and integrating his care for his farm animals with his care for his arable land. His knowledge is of and his care is for this particular land and whatever idiosyncrasies are involved in farming it. His fourth aim is to hand on the farm to one or more of his children, having provided the others with the education that they need. A sufficiently large increase in the rent that he owes makes inescapable some large change in one or more of his aims. He can retain his land by making his farm more immediately productive, resorting to an intensive use of chemical fertilizers and weed killers, having an eye only to the short term, making the farm pay by being a less good farmer. And this may be a first move towards acting not as a family farmer, but as an efficient practitioner of agribusiness, as someone engaged in maximizing the profitability of his land. If so, economic reasons will no longer have the subordinate place in his reasoning that they once had. Or he can give up farming.

The point is that his ability to pursue his ends as rational agent and his power so to act depends in part on how economic power is distributed and on how those who possess it use that power. So it is too in a second type of example. A gifted teacher has as her end, the good for the sake of which she teaches, the shaping of children so that they come to recognize and pursue ends that they have made their own. Therefore on the one hand she is concerned to inculcate a range of skills needed by every child, skills at reading prose and poetry, at writing grammatically and at retelling stories, arithmetical, geometrical, and equation solving skills, knowing how to speak and to read a second language, skills in using pencil and paint brush, in singing and playing an instrument. On the other hand she is concerned with the particularities of each of her pupils, with their different potentialities, with different speeds of learning, with what each finds engrossing and what boring. For the development of a child's potentialities is always more than the acquisition of skills. Children have to learn to enjoy what initially is difficult and seems boring.

Education however has to be funded and funding agencies often require some measure of success or failure in making children into what the funding agency believes that they should be. Imagine now a funding agency that aspires to supply the labor market with what the labor market needs and therefore focuses exclusively on English language and mathematical skills, regarding art, music, and poetry as expensive luxuries and a second language as unnecessary. The skills that the funding agency values have the advantage of being testable and funds are allocated on the basis of test scores. So teachers have to teach primarily with an eye to test scores and our imagined teacher has either to revise her aims radically or to take to some other occupation. If she remains as a teacher, she can no longer rank order goods as she formerly did. Her power to act as a rational agent has been undermined. The moral, as with our imagined farmer, is that what goods can be pursued and achieved depends in key part on the distribution of economic power and on how it is exercised by those who possess it. In both cases the agent may be moved by powerfully motivating considerations to act in a way contrary to the requirements of practical rationality, as he or she has hitherto understood them.

At this point someone may well exclaim indignantly "Do you think that we did not know this already? Why labor over the obvious?" To which my reply has to be twofold: first, that my claim is not just that the distribution of economic power affects the goods that each of us are able to pursue, but that some distributions of economic power threaten the very possibility of sustaining those relationships and activities necessary for agents to act as practical reasoners directed towards achieving the human good in the company of others; and, secondly, that by identifying those distributions of economic power that endanger and harm, we take a first step towards identifying the kind of distribution of such power needed to sustain networks of rational agency. To which the retort may well be that I have moved from the boringly platitudinous to the absurdly ambitious.

II

The problem is that of the relationship between economic and other types of consideration in our practical reasoning. Two of the most influential theories of practical rationality are both liable to mislead us. One is Aristotle's. What makes it misleading is twofold. First, Aristotle misunderstood the place of productive work in human life. Productive work is for slaves or for those who will be so burdened by it that they will be unable to develop the virtues of a citizen. What that misunderstanding involves needs to be developed a good deal further, but not here. All that needs to be remarked is that all work that has point and purpose, work for doing which we can give good reasons, like all other such activity, is directed towards the achievement of particular goods of particular people. Secondly, Aristotle's relatively brief remarks on money are inadequate. I take him to be right about two things, although both are plainly controversial.

He is right to deny that for a rational agent the acquisition of money cannot be more than a means to achieving particular goods, nonmonetary goods. And he is right to infer that the life of money making cannot be the good life for a rational agent. Money is to serve nonmonetary ends and there is always a question 'For the sake of what are you making money?' But Aristotle, having recognized money's role in facilitating the division of labor and more generally how it functions as a means of exchange, proceeds to assert that both the acquisition of goods as a result of profitable trading transactions and the practice of lending money at interest are "contrary to nature," lumping together two very different things (*Politics* 1258a38–b8). In medieval Europe the latter assertion, together with the biblical injunction not to charge interest on money lent to one's brother, provided support for the prohibition of usury (Deut. 23:19–20). But what Aristotle had left unexamined was the relationship between a rational agent's aim in acting so as to make money and the goods which provide that agent with her or his reason for so acting. For money makes available to agents a range of genuine goods not otherwise available. Such goods are of at least four kinds.

First, someone who has money is able to choose how to spend it. Markets provide alternative possibilities and so someone may make money, having in mind not this good or that, but the possibility later on of choosing between them. And this freedom to choose can itself be a good. Secondly, by making money now and saving it, I become able to obtain certain goods not now, but at some point in the future. So I am able to provide for future contingencies in ways that without money would be impossible. Thirdly, by saving and continuing to save I may become able in the future to acquire kinds of good that would otherwise be unattainable by me or mine. And, fourthly, money may enable me to acquire means for further acquisition—ploughs, looms, and increasingly sophisticated machines, horses, camels, sailing ships, and increasingly sophisticated modes of travel—that further increase my freedom of choice, my ability to provide for future contingencies, and the kinds of good that I can acquire.

These characteristics of money have at many points in the past made money and its acquisition seem to many to be unqualified goods—and, since neither Aristotle nor his successors had provided any account of them that would have identified their place in the overall scheme of human goods, it is unsurprising that the prohibition of usury was so easily set on one side the moment that it became an obstacle to achieving such goods. So we were left without an ethics of money just at the point when it was most needed. Those of us who now aspire to supply what has hitherto been missing from a Thomistic or any other Aristotelian account of practical rationality arrive on the scene some six hundred years too late. But, when we turn to the most influential contemporary account of practical rationality, we discover that it too fails to provide what we need, although for quite different reasons.

The problem, we should remind ourselves, is of how to relate the economic to the noneconomic in our practical reasoning and of what it is to be practically rational in our economic transactions. Aristotle and Aquinas may teach us what is to be practically rational, but are effectively silent on most matters economic and financial. Contemporary decision theory by contrast provides an account of practical rationality such that all our decisions and our consequent actions and transactions become, as it were, economic decisions, actions, and transactions. And this is unsurprising when we recall the crucial part played by L. J. Savage in formulating the key propositions of rational decision theory and the close relations between Savage and such statistically minded economists as W. Allen Wallis and Milton Friedman.

Rational agents, on the view shared by decision theorists and economists, seek to maximize the satisfaction of their preferences, whatever those preferences happen to be. Gary S. Becker says of his analysis of human behavior that it "assumes that individuals maximize welfare *as they conceive it*, whether they be selfish, altruistic, loyal, spiteful, or masochistic. Their behavior is forward-looking, and it is also consistent over time. In particular they try as best they can to anticipate the uncertain consequences of their actions."[1] It was Becker's great and intended achievement to show how surprisingly much of human behavior could plausibly be explained on this assumption, even if the explanatory power of his analyses is not, I believe, quite what he takes it to be.[2] But his quite as great and unintended achievement was to show how much of what is distinctively human becomes invisible from his standpoint. Consider three features of rational agency that disappear from view.

First, practical rationality, according to Becker and to decision theorists more generally, is a matter of how agents implement their preferences, not of how they arrive at them. It is the individual agent who at each moment of decision is or fails to be rational. The notion that to lead the life of a rational agent is to learn how to form one's habits and preferences through a life increasingly directed towards a final end makes no sense in decision-theoretic terms and with it the notion that the rationality of particular decisions has to do with the part that they play in such a life. Secondly, the notion of a preference has displaced the notion of a good and with it any connection between the rationality of someone's practical judgments and the possibility of their flourishing or failing to flourish as a human being. For here everything turns on what preferences one has and on the grounds for regretting certain kinds of preference. Thirdly, the disappearance of the notion of a good entails the absence of any notion of common goods as providing reasons for concern with the goods of others. What replaces it in Becker's and other such accounts is the notion of altruism. (Becker argues, persuasively enough from within his conceptual scheme, that rational agents, whether initially self-interested or not, will tend towards altruistic behavior, especially towards other family members—see *The Economic Approach to Human Behavior*, Part Seven.) Why does this matter?

Altruistic attitudes are those which express a care for the interests of others rather than our own and they presuppose some large degree of incompatibility between acting out of self-interest and acting benevolently. By contrast, on a Thomistic Aristotelian view, it is for my good that I should act for the common good and I will not achieve my individual good, unless I do so. Moreover I am accountable to those others with whom I share some common good, if my actions do not promote, but hinder and frustrate the achievement of our shared good, while, insofar as my standards are those of an altruist, I ought to do certain things, but I am not accountable for my failure to do them. In this respect as in others what Becker enables us to understand is the extent of the differences between a decision theoretic point of view and any Aristotelian standpoint and so also of the difficulty of thinking about economic and financial matters in anything like Aristotelian terms. To this someone may protest: "But of course! How could it be otherwise? You are setting yourself an impossible task." We have however reached a point at which it is possible to carry the enquiry one stage further.

A good place to begin is with Catherine Cowley's 2006 book, *The Value of Money: Ethics and the World of Finance*, a book in which Cowley identified some of the features of advanced economies that generated the economic and financial crisis by which we are still afflicted. Cowley however, like many subsequent analysts, believes that the central institutions of advanced economies are now indispensable to the achievement of our common good and she argues that, on an adequate view of that common good, it cannot be realized within those kinds of local community in which, as I have contended, a form of Aristotelian politics can still be achieved in the modern world, but only on a larger scale. Cowley acknowledges that on occasion the exercise of the virtues may involve some degree of conflict with the established order, but, in her critique of my work, as in her book more generally, she argues that local goods are achievable only if the financial institutions of the present order can be made to act for the common good and she in effect accuses me of moral irresponsibility with regard to the larger order, speaking of the kind of local community that I have praised as a type of "moral ghetto."[3] So about what is she right and about what is she mistaken?

She is of course right that nowadays only rarely, if at all, can local communities lead a life with anything like economic self-sufficiency. The possibilities of productive work and profitable enterprise almost always depend on patterns of investment determined by individual and corporate decisions often taken far away. The universal need for electric power is by itself enough to ensure a certain kind of dependence of local communities on national and international institutions. So any viable politics of local community will be able to secure the goods of such community only by somehow coming to terms with the demands made upon it by those with the relevant economic and political power and in such a way that the local distribution of economic power is compatible with an Aristotelian politics and ethics. Attempts to achieve this are in the longer run apt to end in failure. The most instructive examples are perhaps those drawn from the history of the *kibbutzim*, first in Palestine under the British mandate and then in Israel. Their socialist and communitarian beginnings come very close to satisfying the requirements for Aristotelian community. Yet over time they have been able to survive only by transforming themselves into capitalist enterprises. Is there then any place left for developing in the contemporary world types of social relationship informed by the norms of practical reasoning and political community, understood as Thomistic Aristotelians understand them? And, if there is, must they be no more than what Cowley calls moral ghettos? I approach answers to these questions by first considering what it is about contemporary beliefs concerning, attitudes towards, and uses of money that is inimical to the development of such social relationships.

III

Those beliefs, attitudes, and uses are intelligible only as the outcome of a long history. Three stages in that history need to be remarked. The first is that initial stage in the development of capitalism during which the appropriation of surplus value by owners of the means of production in the form of money enabled those owners to accumulate, invest, and reinvest capital in unprecedented ways and unprecedented amounts. The second is that long subsequent period in which there is a double movement, one in which money becomes more and more important as a means to the discovery, the making, and the acquisition of goods, some of them goods to be valued for themselves, others — machines — as a means to the manufacture of still other goods, including further machines. So there are more and more impeccably good reasons for valuing money, for wanting to make money, some wanting it in order to acquire the bare necessities of subsistence living, some wanting it in order to build cathedrals or Palladian villas or skyscrapers. And there are of course at the same time more and more bad reasons for valuing money in order to do harm to others or to oneself. But in the same period in which there is this movement in which money functions as a means to more and more possibilities of achievement, good and bad, and more and more choices, good and bad, there is another movement of a sharply contrasting kind.

In that movement money becomes increasingly valued as a means to making money, by trading in currencies, by paying lower rates of interest to depositors and investors in order to lend at higher rates of interest, by selling short, by doing whatever it takes to make more and more and more money. So for a small, but powerful and influential tone-setting and trend-setting section of the capitalist class, the accumulation of money becomes an end in itself. For them investment flows in and out of this firm and that firm, this industry and that industry, this society and that society depending *only* on what maximizes profitability and not at all on what goods are being produced or for whom. Goods come to be valued not for themselves, but as a means to making money, an inversion of what reason requires.

In the history of economic development these two kinds of change occur together as aspects of a single complex and uneven history of growth, growth in areas of local prosperity, growth in national economies, and finally the growth of globalization. And such growth has undeniably positive aspects. It becomes the condition for alleviating and ending poverty. It provides a context in which many kinds of admirable capitalist enterprise—admirable, that is, by Aristotelian standards—can be undertaken, enterprises in which money is valued as a means to achieving goods and not vice versa. Consider two twentieth century cases, those of the early histories of the Cummins Engine Company of Columbus, Indiana, and of Schlumberger then of Paris. The former was founded in 1919, but made its first profits only in 1937. Its aim was to transform the American trucking industry by adapting the kind of engine invented by Rudolph Diesel. Its founders were only prepared to market their product, when it satisfied their own high standards for innovative technology and, after they had marketed it, remained in conversation with their customers, so that they could perfect their technology. More recently they have taken the lead in producing engines that conform to EPA standards, always insisting on thinking in terms of the long run and of goods to be achieved.

The agreement between family members, by which Schlumberger, the most important firm in the oilfield service industry for more than half a century, was founded, also in 1919, laid it down explicitly that "in this undertaking, the interests of scientific research take precedence over financial ones."[4] And a daughter of Conrad Schlumberger, looking back later on, could write that "nothing produced there was mere merchandise . . . This *sonde*, that galvanometer, were not for sale. The tie between the man who makes and the thing made was not cut."[5] Both Cummins and Schlumberger became extremely profitable and without their long run profitability they could not have continued to value what is more and other than profitability. But they provide evidence that within capitalism modes of activity that exemplify rationality, as Thomistic Aristotelians understand it, can continue to flourish, given certain distributions of economic resources and economic power. Exclusive attention to their success, however, would lead us to overlook symptoms of gross irrationality in the larger history in which they find their place.

In that history I distinguished two closely related movements, one directed towards an ever increasing production of goods, the other directed towards an ever increasing acquisition of money. Their outcome is that for many individuals, corporations, and groups nothing is ever enough. Whatever needs are met, more needs are generated. Desires are indefinitely multiplied and so are choices. The successfully acquisitive tend over time to become the limitlessly acquisitive. But to be limitlessly acquisitive is to have just that character trait that Aristotle identifies as typical of the unjust human being, *pleonexia* (*Nicomachean Ethics* 1129b1–2). For Aristotle and Aquinas a failure in respect of the virtues is always also a failure in practical rationality, while for those for whom practical rationality is defined in decision theoretic terms no set of consistent preferences is in itself contrary to reason and among those whose conception of practical rationality is well captured by the decision theoretic account the irrationality of the limitlessly acquisitive must therefore be invisible. Yet it is not invisible to many plain persons who have never heard of Aristotle or Aquinas. How come?

IV

The account of practical rationality drawn from Aristotle and Aquinas that I have presented is, I now want to claim, one presupposed at least on some types of occasion by the choices and judgments of many plain nonphilosophical persons, even in the societies of advanced modernity. It is of course in tension with the modes of practical thought and judgment characteristic of the economic and financial transactions and roles that they inescapably engage in and occupy. But in a variety of practices they continue to recognize, rank order, and pursue goods, distinguishing them from mere objects of desire or preference, so that, implicitly or explicitly, they ask and answer such questions as 'What place should each of these goods have in my life, if I am to flourish as a human being?' Their practical reasoning and their activities more generally are apt therefore to suffer from various kinds and degrees of incoherence and it is one of the functions of the compartmentalizations of the contemporary social order to make this incoherence manageable. But one thing that most plain persons cannot but learn is the importance of observing limits, of having well defined and attainable goals, of recognizing therefore that money is an indispensable means, but only a means to the achievement of those goods in terms of which they define their goals. When confronted by the limitless acquisitiveness of those for whom the pursuit of money is no longer a means, but itself an end, they sometimes begin to pose disturbing questions, expressing their suspicion that what confronts them is irrationality, irrationality understood very much as Aristotle and Aquinas understand it. So it was on occasion in the years before the crisis of 2008 and so it has been ever since. For the rest of this paper therefore I speak both as Thomistic Aristotelian and as plain person in order to ask why in the years that led up to our present crisis so many economically and financially sophisticated people acted in ways that any plain person could have told them were contrary to reason. Note however that this is not a plain person's question.

The thinker from whom we most need to learn, if we are to pose this question rightly, is Georg Simmel. One of the great merits of Cowley's book is her insistence that, if we are to understand the workings of contemporary financial institutions, we must first learn what Simmel has to teach. What Simmel supplies is the outcome of the history constituted by the two movements that I described earlier. Those movements had their beginning in the discovery of how much in the achievement of economic and other goods money as a means made possible. Its outcome, as Simmel understood, is a transformation of money and of money-makers such that more and more of our and their social relationships are transformed into financial relationships, that trustworthiness becomes credit worthiness, that our ends become secondary to our means, that—in a passage that Cowley quotes—"the peripheral in life, the things that lie outside its basic essence, have become masters of its center and even of ourselves."[6] Elsewhere Simmel puts it even more strikingly. Money has become "the secular God of the world." The resort to theological language is not unimportant.

The first of Simmel's essays on money was published in 1889. The culmination of his work was the *Philosophie des Geldes* in 1900. 1889 was also the year of the great dockworkers' strike in East London, notable both for the part that it played in the development of the labor movement and for Cardinal Manning's active identification with the cause of the dockworkers. In 1891 Leo XIII issued the encyclical, *Rerum Novarum*, setting out the Catholic social teaching to which Manning's actions had given expression. That teaching took it for granted that money is never to be valued, except for the nonmonetary goods that can be achieved through its use and thus provides an important counterpoint to Simmel. And from the standpoint of the theology on which that teaching is founded what Simmel describes is a form of idolatry. Idolatry is a sin not only against God, but also against reason, since nothing could be more unreasonable than worshipping something other than God. And it is through its irrationality that the contemporary regard for money discredited itself, as it informed the workings of the economy and above all of the financial sector in the decades before 2008 and in the crisis from 2008 onwards that will be with us for many years to come.

Consider just two aspects of what constituted growth in the financial sectors of advanced economies in these two periods: the willingness by investment bankers to borrow beyond their means in order to make—temporarily—stupendous sums of money and some of the relationships between risk and debt relevant to investment in certain kinds of derivative. Under each of these headings we find irrationalities of two kinds, irrationality in decision making and action and irrationality as an inability to recognize, let alone to understand, the irrationality of decision making and action. The context for decision making and action in the financial sector was provided by the gross inequalities generated in the decades before 2008. Thirty years ago Peter Drucker had argued that the most highly paid executives of a well-functioning corporation could reasonably be paid twenty times the average wage of the workers employed by it. In the United Kingdom by the year 2000 such executives were paid forty-seven times the average wage and by 2009 eighty-one times. In the United States in 2008 the multiple was three hundred and nineteen. This is only one aspect of a more general and worldwide increase in inequality, well documented for the period preceding the crisis of 2008 in an OECD report issued in that year and for the years since then in a second OECD report in 2011. The outcome in some advanced countries is a continuing polarization of opposites, small minorities of ludicrously rich individuals and corporations at one extreme, very large numbers of long term unemployed, too often young men and women without any employment prospects, at the other, with corresponding concentrations of and deprivations of economic and political power. "The *polis* aims to consist of those who are equal and like one another" (*Politics* 1295b25–26). So, whatever such contemporary societies are, they are not *poleis*. But it is in and through the relationships of a polis that human beings become rational. So how in these economic relationships does irrationality become obvious?

I begin with the willingness and the ability of bankers to borrow absurdly beyond their means. Which bankers should we take as an example, considering how many there are to choose from? I choose Iceland's bankers for two reasons. The first is the relative transparency of the Icelandic financial sector, the second the small size of Iceland's population (now about 307,000), its egalitarian and social democratic values, and its exceptionally high standards in health care and educational provision. Its politics exemplify a politics of local community and it had generally structured its external economic relationships with great success.

The major actors were three banks who borrowed money in order to make money and borrowed more money to make more money. The money they borrowed came from interbank loans and from foreign depositors to whom they offered interest rates as high as 15.5% at a time when Eurozone banks were offering 4% and United Kingdom banks 5.5%. By early in 2008 their debt amounted to well over 40 billion euros. (I translate from kronur.) In 2007 Iceland's GDP had been 8.5 billion euros. And the debt was not only the bankers'. The average household debt was 213% of disposable income. That, when those banks needed to refinance their debts, nobody would refinance them, so that the outcome was economic and financial ruin, is scarcely surprising. The irrationality of course was not only that of the bankers. It was also that of the managers of pension funds and the treasurers of municipalities in the United Kingdom and the Netherlands who entrusted them with their clients' money. So how could all of them have behaved so irrationally?

One answer can be ruled out immediately, that they could not have perceived the irrationality of what they were doing, that no one could have perceived it at the time. But this is false. The premiums demanded for insuring against default on their loans by Icelandic banks during the relevant period were unprecedentedly and prohibitively high. The insurance companies, that is to say, had no problem in identifying the irrationality of what was going on. But the data to which they had access was the same data to which everyone had access. So there are two problems, not one. Why did the principal agents in bringing about Iceland's and their own ruin act contrary to reason and why could they not perceive that their actions were contrary to reason?

The same two problems are evident if we consider some of the relationships between risk and debt. Those who bought credit derivatives that made their owners responsible in the case of default on their mortgages by some set of homeowners acted rationally only if they knew what the probability of default was in this or that particular case. Characteristically however the buyers of such derivatives—and often enough the sellers too—had no access to the information that would have enabled them to calculate those probabilities and in many cases would not have known how to calculate them. What they did know was that the more profitable that it was for them to take on the risk of default the more likely it was that the risk was high. It was therefore of the first importance to them to know to whom mortgages were being granted and on what terms, that is, to know the creditworthiness of the relevant sets of homebuyers. But such evidence as we have makes it clear that those who bought the relevant derivatives rarely, if ever, commissioned enquiries about that creditworthiness. Interestingly much of what they needed to know required no high level of mathematical or economic sophistication, so it is the case that much investment in such derivatives was the work of those who not only did not know what they were doing, but to whom it should have been glaringly obvious that they did not know what they were doing. Once again we have to ask both why the agents who in this way brought about their own ruin acted contrary to reason and why they could not perceive that their actions were contrary to reason?

V

I have so far advanced three claims. The first is that the exercise of practical rationality requires the existence of certain kinds of social relationship. The second is that whether or not those kinds of social relationship can be sustained depends in part on how economic power is distributed and exercised and on the part that economic considerations have in the practical reasoning of agents. I then focused attention on how money functions in the societies of advanced modernity in order to argue that under certain conditions new types of practical irrationality have been generated. What might it be about agents in those societies that results in such irrationalities? I remarked earlier that in well ordered societies, where the conditions for practical rationality are generally in place, there must be widespread, if rough and ready practical agreement as to how in particular situations goods are to be rank ordered, an agreement that informs choices and actions. But those whose decisions and actions are for the most part at least informed by their knowledge of how to rank order goods are to that degree virtuous, if we understand the everyday virtues as Aristotle and Aquinas understand them. So a fourth claim emerges, that failures in rationality, in economic and financial matters as elsewhere are failures in the exercise of the virtues.

Note what I am not saying. I am not proposing that we bring some moral standard that invokes the virtues to bear upon our economic and financial affairs, one more exercise in so-called applied ethics. I am arguing that we cannot describe, let alone understand economic and financial activities and the ends to which they are means except in terms that make reference to the table of the virtues inescapable. Economics, if it becomes what I take it to be, will turn out to be a moral science, one that is able to relate economic and financial means to noneconomic ends. This project resembles in some ways the attempts by Sen, Nussbaum, and others, on the one hand, and by Easterlin, Scitovsky, and others, on the other hand to provide measures for economic development other than the familiar measures of growth.[7] However, where the former are concerned with capabilities and the latter with happiness, my attempt is to identify both the types of social order within which practical rationality can be sustained and the relationships in which local communities must stand to the larger social order, if they are not to be the victims of the irrationalities of that order.

What would characterize such local communities would be their norms of public justification. Those engaged in various types of economic activity would be required to show that their activities would not undermine or frustrate the achievement by practically rational agents of the common goods of that community, such common goods as those of the family, the workplace, and the school. So investments and expenditures that would result in the unavailability of prenatal and later child care or in local unemployment or in inadequate provision for school teachers would be unacceptable. To act so as to increase one's own prosperity or so as to promote kinds of growth that would put these at risk would be understood as, would *be*, failures in temperateness, courage, justice, and prudence. How so? To be intemperate is, among other things, to have desires undisciplined by and undirected towards one's own and the common good. To be courageous is, among other things, to be able to distinguish the risk taking necessary to achieve certain goods from the risk taking that frustrates and destroys. To be just is, among other things, to be accountable to all those others whom one puts at risk. And to be prudent, to be practically intelligent, is to act so that goods are rank ordered rightly.

It follows that much trading in derivatives, especially in collateralized debt obligations, has not been adequately characterized until it has been understood as a symptom of a failure in the virtues, something equally obscured by the habits of mind of economists and by the habits of mind of moral philosophers, even Aristotelian moral philosophers. The former take the actions of traders in markets to be intelligible independently of their functioning as expressions of character. The latter believe that what it is to have the virtues can be understood adequately without this being spelled out in economic and financial terms. How then can we begin to think in terms that avoid both errors? Perhaps initially by writing a certain kind of history that is at once a moral, an economic, and indeed a political history. Happily we already have a number of such histories, although they were not of course written with the purpose that I have in mind. So let me recount just one of them.

The original history is to be found in Thomas Højrup's *The Need for Common Goods for Coastal Communities*, a notable contribution to public debate on the European Commission's proposal for a common fisheries policy, central to which is a privatization of fishing rights by means of a system of "Individual Transferable Quotas."[8] What Højrup tells is the story of the destructive effect of such privatization on fishing communities in Denmark and the successful construction of an alternative to it in one particular community, that of Thorupstrand in Northern Jutland. To understand the significance of Højrup's history we need to begin more generally by asking what someone who spends his—and now a little more often her—working life as a member of a fishing crew is doing. There are two very different kinds of fishing and two very different answers. Much deep sea fishing is financed by corporations whose returns depend on the size of their catch and who compete in national and international markets. Their aim is to dominate in the most profitable fishing grounds and to compete successfully in the sale of salted, canned, and frozen fish. To work for such a corporation is to be like any other worker for a typical capitalist enterprise, that is, you are serving *their* ends for the sake of the livelihood of you and yours and there is only or principally a financial connection between your work and the ends that you have as a member of a family and a member of a local community.

Contrast the lives of members of fishing crews in communities where share fishing is practiced, crews who are self-employed, whose fishing grounds are near at hand, and who belong to communities with long experience of this way of life. At Thorupstrand income from fishing was calculated, after variable costs had been paid, so that 40% was allotted for maintenance and repair of boat, nets, and lines, 20% to the skipper (usually also owner of a share of the boat), and 20% each to the other two crew members. When a loss was incurred, it was divided proportionately.

Every member of a crew was therefore a partner in an enterprise, in some communities often a family enterprise, so the individuals in such communities recognized and recognize three closely related common goods, those of family, crew, and local community and find their own individual ends in and through cooperating to achieve those common goods. There are of course complexities here that I will notice only to ignore. School teachers, boat builders, priests and pastors have crucial parts to play in such communities. Some have much richer communal lives than others. What they share is this: that their work is not a means to an external end, but is constitutive of a way of life, the sustaining of which is itself an end.

Around 80% of European fishing crews in various countries are still share fishers. How their communities have fared varies from country to country. Højrup's history begins in 2006 with the approach allocation of fishing quotas to boats, the privatization of quotas, and their acquisition by investors. Those crew members without a share in the ownership of a boat lost out immediately. Those with such a share were confronted with the possibility of making more money than ever before immediately, but of then becoming permanently dependent for employment on those outside the community with even more money. And in some communities in North Jutland there appeared to be no alternative: not so in Thorupstrand. There the possibility of retaining share fishing and with it the forms of community sustained by it was explored and achieved. What had to be done and was done was the formation of a cooperative company that purchased a common pool of quotas.

The purchase was financed by the payment of entrance fees and by substantial loans from two local banks, security for which was provided in large part by the common pool of quotas. Twenty families joined the cooperative in which decisions were made democratically, one member, one vote. So the families engaged in share fishing assumed a new kind of economic responsibility for sustaining the practice of share fishing and with it their way of life. Between 2006 and 2008 they watched others do strikingly well or badly in the market frenzy—all the implications of 'frenzy' are intended—of those years. Between 2006 and 2008 the price of a boat rose 1,000%. But the crisis of 2008 had much the same consequences in Denmark as elsewhere, one of which was the failure of one of the local banks on which the cooperative had relied and a demand for the repayment of their loan. Here the cooperative had to take to politics, which it did and successfully, so that it provides a model for all those engaged in share fishing as they confront the demands, the threats, of the market that would be created by proposed European Union regulations.

Economic theorists, when they recognize that free markets can threaten certain ways of life, conclude that this is because those ways of life are inefficient and therefore obstructive of growth. What is at issue between the share fishing crews of Thorupstrand and elsewhere and such theorists is how efficiency and growth are to be understood. This is not a new quarrel. It was what was at issue between Ricardo and the Luddites. It is a quarrel about ends before it is a quarrel about means. It is a quarrel about how economic resources and economic power have to be distributed, if certain ends are to be achieved. What ends we pursue depends upon what kind of people we are and that is a matter of the virtues and vices.

The fragile success of the *Thorupstrand Kystfiskerlaug* (The Guild of Thorupstrand Coastal Fishermen) so far was made possible only by qualities of mind and character especially in those who provided the community with leadership and the Guild with an articulate voice: prudence increasingly informed by economic and political know how, justice both in the allocation of shares and in the structure of the Guild, courage in taking the right risks in the right way, and temperateness in not being seduced by the promises of the market. Subtract any one of these and you subtract a necessary condition for the community's flourishing. And it matters very much that the Guild is an association of families as well as of individuals. Members of the next generation can join on the same terms as the founders. It also matters that the Guild has had from the beginning to engage with the economics of the market and the politics of the Danish state, that it will survive only if economic and political power in Denmark are distributed and exercised in some ways rather than others. Continuing prudence on the part of its members will require a more extensive capacity for economic and political judgment.

The virtues exercised in the founding and sustaining of the Guild are the same virtues already exercised in pursuing and achieving the goods internal to the practices of traditional share fishing communities. This is not to say—absurdly—that either in the past or the present everyone in those communities was virtuous. It is to say that the shared standards in terms of which excellence was and is judged at the level of practice were and are the standards of the virtues. What this common regard for the virtues sustains is a regard for the norms of practical rationality. To judge as the virtues require is to rank order goods rightly in relationship to the ends that must be ours, if our common and individual goods are to be achieved, and to do so not abstractly or in general, but in decision making and acting in particular situations. To have regard for the virtues is to know how to act as a rational agent acts. So my argument has come full circle. It is not just a truth of theory that practically rational agency can only be embodied in and sustained by certain types of social relationship, but a truth exemplified in the history of certain types of relationship and association. It follows that certain other types of social relationship and association are inimical to and subversive of both practical rationality and the virtues. What my overall argument suggests is that the forms of relationship and association characteristic of the financial sectors of advanced economies are among these.

NOTES

Introduction

1. *After Virtue*, 3rd ed. (University of Notre Dame Press, 2007), 11.

ONE. Plain Persons and Moral Philosophy: Rules, Virtues and Goods

1. T. H. Irwin, "A Conflict in Aquinas," *Review of Metaphysics* 14 (1990), 21–42.

TWO. Does Applied Ethics Rest on a Mistake?

1. Stephen Toulmin, "The Tyranny of Principles," *The Hastings Center Report*, vol. 11, no. 6, December 1981, 31–32.
2. *Summa Theologiae*, I–IIae q. 94 a. 2.
3. Toulmin, cited in n1, above.
4. It was in one recent period the case that the professional code of American psychologists prohibited lying to subjects in the course of their research enquiries, while that of American sociologists permitted such lying in certain circumstances and under certain conditions.

FOUR. The Idea of an Educated Public

1. Richard Peters, 'Motives and Causes', *Proceedings of the Aristotelian Society*, Supp. Vol. 26 (1952), 139–162.

2. J. L. Austin, *Collected Papers* (Oxford University Press, 1961), 219.

3. David Hume, *A Treatise of Human Nature*, L. A. Selby-Bigge, ed. (Oxford University Press, 1975), Bk. II, pt. iii, section 3, 415.

4. Ebenezer Erskine, *The Whole Works of the late Rev. Mr Ebenezer Erskine*, Vol. I. (D. Schaw & Co., 1798), 531.

5. Alexander Carlyle, *Autobiography*, J. H. Burbon, ed. (William Blackwood & Sons, 1860), 561.

6. Samuel Taylor Coleridge, *On the Constitution of Church and State, Collected Works*, Vol. 6. (Harper & Brothers, 1858), 52.

7. John Stuart Mill, 'Coleridge' in *Autobiography and Other Writings* (Houghton Mifflin, 1969), 290.

8. Mill, 'Coleridge', 294.

9. John Stuart Mill, *Utilitarianism* (Dent, 1972), ch. IV.

SEVEN. Conflicts of Desire

1. For an excellent and full account, see Michael D. Resnik, *Choices: An Introduction to Decision Theory* (University of Minnesota Press, 1987).

2. Donald Davidson, "How Is Weakness of the Will Possible?" in *Essays on Actions and Events* (Clarendon Press, 1980), 21–42.

3. *Nicomachean Ethics* 1176a10–24; Aquinas, *Sententia libri Ethicorum* 10.8 (nn. 2059–63), Editio Leonina, 47/2: 576a–b. English translation: *Commentary on Aristotle's Nicomachean Ethics*, trans. C. I. Litzinger, O.P. (Dumb Ox Books, 1993), 616–617.

EIGHT. Interview with Alex Voorhoeve

1. This interview was originally published under the title "The Illusion of Self-Sufficiency" in Alex Voorhoeve, *Conversations on Ethics* (Oxford University Press, 2009). Reproduced with permission of Oxford University Press through PLSclear.

NINE. Danish Ethical Demands and French Common Goods

1. For work contemporaneous with Løgstrup's see, for example, P. M. Van Overbeke, "La loi naturelle et le droit naturel selon Saint Thomas," *Revue Thomiste* 57 (1957): 53–78 and 430–498; Jacques Maritain, *The Person and the Common Good*, trans. J. J. Fitzgerald (University of Notre Dame Press, 1966); for the relevant Aquinas texts see Aquinas, *The Treatise on Law* (*Summa Theologiae* I–II

qq. 90–97), Latin text, translation, and commentary, ed. and trans. R. J. Henle, S. J. (University of Notre Dame Press, 1993).

2. For Lipps see especially *Untersuchungen zur Phänomenologie der Erkenntnis*, in vol. 1 of *Werke* and *Untersuchungen zu einer hermeneutischen Logik*, in vol. 2 of *Werke* (Vittorio Klosterman, 1976), both still untranslated into English. For an excellent discussion see Stefan Kristensen, "Langage et Réalite, Hans Lipps entre Herméneutique de la Perception et Phenomenologie du Langage," in his translation of Lipps's *Untersuchungen zu einer hermeneutischen Logik*, entitled *Recherches pour une Logique Herméneutique* (J. Vrin, 2004).

3. K. E. Løgstrup, *The Ethical Demand* (University of Notre Dame Press, 1977), 45.

4. Løgstrup, *The Ethical Demand*, 27.

5. Løgstrup, *The Ethical Demand*, 115, 137.

6. See in Michael R. Marrus, *The Holocaust in History* (NAL Penguin, 1987), the footnotes to chapter 5, for references to the relevant literature.

7. Løgstrup, *The Ethical Demand*, 100.

8. Løgstrup, *The Ethical Demand*, 85.

9. Aristotle, *Ethica Nicomachea*, ed. I. Bywater (Clarendon, 1894), 1179a33–1179b31; Aquinas, *Sententia libri Ethicorum*, ed. R. A. Gauthier, O. P., 2 vols. (Ad Sanctae Sabrina, 1969); trans. C. L. Litzinger as *Commentary on the Nicomachean Ethics* (Dumb Ox Books, 1993), bk. 10, lect. 14, 2137–2147.

10. Aquinas, *Sententia libri Ethicorum* 1541 and 1592, commenting on Aristotle, *Ethica Nicomachea*, 1155a 20–22 and 1157a 20–25, passages that I discuss in MacIntyre, "Human Nature and Human Dependence: What Might a Thomist Learn from Reading Løgstrup?," in Svend Andersen and Kees van Kooten Niekerk, eds., *Concern for the Other: Perspectives in the Ethics of K. E. Løgstrup* (University of Notre Dame Press, 2007), 147–166.

11. Jørgen I. Jensen, *Den Fjerne Kirke: Mellem kultur og religiøsitet* (Samleren, 1995).

12. Knud J. V. Jespersen, *A History of Denmark* (Palgrave Macmillan, 2004).

13. K. E. Løgstrup, *The Ethical Demand* (University of Notre Dame Press, 1977).

14. Emil Brunner, *Das Gebot und Die Ordnungen* (J. C. B. Mohr, 1932); trans. Olive Wyon as *The Divine Imperative* (Lutterworth Press, 1937).

15. See the critique of Luther in chapter 4 of Løgstrup, *The Ethical Demand*.

16. Bauman, "The Liquid Modern Adventures of the 'Sovereign Expressions of Life'," in Svend Andersen and Kees van Kooten Niekerk, eds., *Concern for the Other: Perspectives on the Ethics of K. E. Løgstrup* (University of Notre Dame Press, 2007), 117.

17. Perpich, *The Ethics of Emmanuel Levinas* (Stanford University Press, 2008), 126.

18. I am grateful to Robert Stern, editor of *The European Journal of Philosophy*, and his editorial colleagues, both for their invitation to deliver this paper as the 2009 Mark Sacks Lecture and for the discussion of it at a workshop. I owe a special debt to Hans Fink.

TEN. On Having Survived the Academic Moral Philosophy of the Twentieth Century

1. David Lewis, *Philosophical Papers*, vol. 1 (Oxford University Press, 1983), x, xi.

2. A. J. Ayer, "Jean-Paul Sartre's Doctrine of Commitment," *Listener*, November 30, 1950, 633–634.

3. J. L. Austin, *Philosophical Papers* (Clarendon Press, 1961).

4. See Peter Geach "'Good' and 'Evil,'" republished in Philippa Foot, ed., *Theories of Ethics* (Oxford University Press, 1967).

5. Peter Geach, "Assertion," *Philosophical Review* 74, no. 4 (1965), 449–465.

6. Simon Blackburn, *Spreading the Word* (Oxford University Press, 1985), ch. 6.

TWELVE. The *Theses on Feuerbach*

1. Lucio Colletti, 'Introduction', in Q. Hoare, ed., *Karl Marx: Early Writings* (Vintage, 1975), 8.

2. George L. Kline, 'The Myth of Marx's Materialism', *Annals of Scholarship* 3, no. 2 (1984); Carol Gould, *Marx's Social Ontology* (MIT Press, 1978), ch. 1, especially 30–39.

3. On the complexity and subtlety of Feuerbach's development see Marx W. Wartofsky, *Feuerbach* (Cambridge University Press, 1977).

4. P. Bourdieu & L. J. D. Wacquant, *An Invitation to Reflexive Sociology* (University of Chicago Press, 1992), 43.

5. E. P. Thompson, *The Making of the English Working Class* (Victor Gollancz, 1963).

6. Thompson, *The Making of the English Working Class*, 295.

7. Thompson, *The Making of the English Working Class*, 302.

8. *Der Neue Merkur*, October 1923–March 1926.

THIRTEEN. Politics, Philosophy and the Common Good

1. See the interview with Giovanna Borradori and the interview for *Cogito* republished in Kelvin Knight, ed., *The MacIntyre Reader* (Polity Press, 1998).
2. *Renewing Philosophy* (Harvard University Press, 1992), 185–186.
3. On compartmentalization see further my 'What Has *Not* Happened in Moral Philosophy,' *Yale Journal of Criticism* 5, no. 2 (1992), 193–199.
4. See my 'Natural Law as Subversive: The Case of Aquinas,' in Alasdair MacIntyre, *Ethics and Politics: Selected Essays, Volume 2* (Cambridge University Press, 2006).
5. See on this the 'Introduction' to the second edition of *Marxism and Christianity* (Duckworth, 1995).
6. *Politics* 1328b33–1329a2.
7. On this see 'The *Theses on Feuerbach*: A Road Not Taken,' above.

FIFTEEN. The Irrelevance of Ethics

1. Eric Schwitzgebel and Joshua Rust, "The Moral Behaviour of Ethicists: Peer Opinion," *Mind* 118 (2009), 1053.
2. D. W. Winnicott, *The Child, the Family and the Outside World* (Pelican Books, 1964) and *Play and Reality* (Tavistock, 1971).
3. Adam Smith, *An Inquiry into the Nature and Causes of the Wealth of Nations* (Harriman House, 2007), 70.
4. Speech at the Federal Reserve Bank, September 9, 1999.
5. Adam Smith, *An Inquiry into the Nature and Causes of the Wealth of Nations* (Harriman House, 2007), 84.
6. Benjamin Nelson, *The Idea of Usury: From Tribal Brotherhood to Universal Otherhood*, 2nd ed. (University of Chicago Press, 1969), 128.
7. Karl Marx, *Capital. Volume I*, trans. Ben Fowkes (Penguin Books, 1990), 92.

SIXTEEN. Four–or More?–Political Aristotles

1. Richard Bodéüs, *Le philosophe et la cité: Recherches sur les rapports entre morale et politique dans la pensée d'Aristote* (Presses universitaires de Liege, Les Belles Lettres, 1982). Translated by Jan Garrett as Richard Bodéüs, *The Political Dimension of Aristotle's Ethics* (SUNY Press, 1993).

2. Francis Sparshott, 'Review of *The Political Dimensions of Aristotle's Ethics,' Dialogue* 36, no. 2 (1997), 410–413.

3. A. W. H. Adkins, 'The Connection between Aristotle's *Ethics* and *Politics*,' *Political Theory* 12, no. 1 (1984), 47.

4. Adkins, 'The Connection between Aristotle's *Ethics* and *Politics*,' 45.

5. R. G. Collingwood, *An Autobiography* (Oxford University Press, 1939), 61.

6. Jean Dunbabin, 'The Reception and Interpretation of Aristotle's *Politics*', in N. Kretzmann, A. Kenny and J. Pinborg eds., *The Cambridge History of Later Medieval Philosophy* (Cambridge University Press, 1982), 730.

7. Charles B. Schmitt, *Aristotle and the Renaissance* (Harvard University Press, 1983).

8. For a fuller account of Case see Charles B. Schmitt, *John Case and Aristotelianism in Renaissance England* (McGill-Queen's University Press, 1983), and my 'John Case: An Example of Aristotelianism's Self-Subversion?' in T. Hibbs and J. O'Callaghan, eds., *Recovering Nature* (University of Notre Dame Press, 1999). For a fuller account of Piccolomini see my 'Rival Aristotles: Aristotle Against some Renaissance Aristotelians' in my *Ethics and Politics: Selected Essays, Volume 2* (Cambridge University Press, 2006). Some of what I say here repeats what I say in these essays.

9. 'Rival Aristotles: Aristotle Against some Modern Aristotelians' in my *Ethics and Politics: Selected Essays, Volume 2* (Cambridge: Cambridge University Press, 2006), 26–27.

10. For a summary see J. W. Binns, 'Elizabeth I and the Universities' in J. Henry & S. Hutton, eds., *New Perspectives in Renaissance Thought: Essays in the History of Science, Education and Philosophy in Memory of Charles B. Schmitt* (London: Duckworth, 1990).

11. Heinz Lubasz, 'The Aristotelian Dimension in Marx,' *Times Higher Education Supplement*, 1 April, 1977, 17.

12. Patricia Springborg, 'Politics, Primordialism, and Orientalism: Marx, Aristotle, and the Myth of the *Gemeinschaft*,' *American Political Science Review* 80, no. 1 (1986), 185–211.

13. T. H. Green, *Lectures on the Principles of Political Obligation* (Cambridge University Press, 1986), 39.

14. A. C. Bradley, 'Aristotle's Conception of the State,' in D. Keyt & F. D. Miller, Jr., eds., *A Companion to Aristotle's Politics* (Blackwell, 1991).

15. Carnes Lord, 'Introduction', in Carnes Lord, ed. & trans., Aristotle, *The Politics* (University of Chicago Press, 1984), 19–20.

16. Richard Kraut, *Aristotle on the Human Good* (Princeton University Press, 1989), 5.

17. Fred D. Miller, Jr., *Nature, Justice, and Rights in Aristotle's Politics* (Oxford University Press, 1995), vii.

SEVENTEEN. Two Kinds of Political Reasoning

1. On the interpretation of Aristotle see G. E. M. Anscombe, *Intention* (Blackwell, 1957), Sections 33–35, and M. T. Thornton, 'Aristotelian Practical Reason', *Mind* 91, no. 361 (1982), 57–96.

EIGHTEEN. Happiness

1. Ed Diener et al., 'The Relationship Between Income and Subjective Well-Being: Relative or Absolute?', *Social Indicators Research* 28, no. 3 (1993), 195–223.

2. See, for example, P. Hills & M. Argyle, 'The Oxford Happiness Questionnaire: A Compact Scale for the Measurement of Psychological Well-Being,' *Personality and Individual Differences* 33, no. 7 (2002), 1073–1082.

3. See Bruno S. Frey & Alois Stutzer, *Happiness and Economics* (Princeton University Press, 2002), and *Happiness, Economics and Politics* (Edward Elgar, 2009).

4. Ruut Veenhoven, interview in *The Irish Times*, June 5, 2009; Richard Layard, *Happiness: Lessons from a New Science* (Penguin Books, 2005), 12.

5. Fred Feldman, *What is This Thing Called Happiness?* (Oxford University Press, 2010), 135.

6. Feldman, *What is This Thing Called Happiness?*, 145.

7. Feldman, *What is This Thing Called Happiness?*, 117–118.

8. Kaare Christensen, Ann Maria Herskind, and James W. Vaupel, 'Why Danes Are Smug: A Comparative Study of Life Satisfaction in the European Union,' *British Medical Journal* 333 (2006), 1289–1291.

9. Shelley E. Taylor & Jonathan Brown, 'Illusion and Well-being: A Social Psychological Perspective on Mental Health,' *Psychological Bulletin* 103, no. 2 (1988), 193–210.

10. *Theory of the Moral Sentiments* (Clarendon Press, 1976), 183.

11. Interview in the *New York Times*, September 4, 2010.

NINETEEN. Political Rhetoric in a Fractured Society

1. Dirk Bezemer, 'No One Saw This Coming: Understanding Financial Crisis Through Accounting Models', MPRA Paper 15767.
2. Dirk Bezemer, *Financial Times*, September 8, 2009.
3. See Aquinas, *Summa Theologiae*, Ia-IIae, q. 1, a. 3c.

TWENTY. Common Goods, Modern States, Rights, and—Maritain

1. A. W. H. Adkins, 'The connection between Aristotle's *Ethics* and *Politics*,' in David Keyt & Fred D. Miller, Jr., eds., *A Companion to Aristotle's Politics* (Oxford: Blackwell, 1991).
2. Jacques Maritain, *The Person and the Common Good* (University of Notre Dame Press, 1966), 37.
3. Maritain, *The Person and the Common Good*, 41.
4. Maritain, *The Person and the Common Good*, 52.
5. Maritain, *The Person and the Common Good*, 49.
6. Jacques Maritain, *Man and the State* (Catholic University of America Press), 23–24.
7. Maritain, *Man and State*, 11–12.
8. Maritain, *Man and State*, 61–63.
9. Maritain, *Man and State*, 104–105.
10. Elinor Ostrom, *Governing the Commons: The Evolution of Institutions for Collective Action* (Cambridge University Press, 1990).
11. Maritain, *Man and the State*, 91–92.
12. *The Primacy of the Common Good against the Personalists* in R. McInerny, ed. and trans., *The Writings of Charles De Koninck*, Vol. Two (University of Notre Dame Press, 2009), 74–76, 83, 88; for an excellent discussion of the larger issues at stake and of their relationship to the thought of Benedict XVI see Jeffery Nicholas, 'Local Communities and Globalization in Caritas in Veritate,' *Solidarity: The Journal of Catholic Social Thought and Secular Ethics* 1, no. 1 (2011).

TWENTY-ONE. Practical Rationality and Irrationality and Their Social Settings

1. Gary Becker, "The Economic Way of Looking at Life," in *Accounting for Tastes* (Harvard University Press, 1996), 139.

2. Gary Becker, *The Economic Approach to Human Behavior* (University of Chicago Press, 1976).

3. Catherine Cowley, *The Value of Money: Ethics and the World of Finance* (T. & T. Clark, 2006), 179–180.

4. Ken Auletta, *The Art of Corporate Success* (G. P. Putnam's Sons, 1984), 24.

5. Auletta, *The Art of Corporate Success*, 160–161.

6. Cowley, *The Value of Money*, 107.

7. See L. Bruni, F. Comim, & M. Pugno, eds., *Capabilities and Happiness* (Oxford University Press, 2008).

8. Thomas Højrup, *The Need for Common Goods for Coastal Communities* (Centre for Coastal Culture and Boatbuilding, 2011).

INDEX

A
Adkins, A. W. H., 298–99, 367
Amis, Kingsley, 222
Anderson, John, 181
Anscombe, Elizabeth, 354, 417
Aquinas, Thomas: 90–95, 169, 268, 380, 412; on common goods and the common good, 315, 325–26, 367–69; on desire and reasons for action, 139–43; interpretation and use of Aristotle, 300–303; on *misericordia*, 154; on moral rules and the precepts of natural law, 37, 155, 259, 270, 384–85; on plain persons, 4–7, 18–23; on practical reason, 318, 388–90, 400–401
Aristotle: 53–59, 146–47, 167, 184–85, 263–64, 269–70, 279, 325–27; on happiness, 341–47; on money and economic reasoning, 394–95, 400–401; on plain persons, 4–5, 8–9, 21–23; political interpretations, 294–311; on political rhetoric, 351; on politics and the common good, 366–69; on the practical syllogism, 318; relationship between theory and practice, 90–92, 100, 111–14, 190–91

Austin, J. L., 65, 184–85
Ayer, A. J., 178–86

B
Bauman, Zygmunt, 174–75
Becker, Gary, 396–97
Belloc, Hilaire, 287
Bentham, Jeremy, 90, 334, 342, 374
Berdyaev, Nikolai, 101
Berelson, Bernard, 210
Berkeley, George, 72
Berlin, Isaiah, 185
Bernstein, Richard, 242
Bezemer, Dirk, 358–59
Binns, J. W., 416
Blackburn, Simon, 187
Bloch, Ernst, 242
Bodéüs, Richard, 296–98
Bradley, A. C., 308
Brown, Thomas, 71, 76
Brunner, Emil, 174

C
Carlyle, Alexander, 72
Case, John, 305–7, 311
Chesterton, G. K., 287, 373
Coleridge, Samuel Taylor, 81–82
Colletti, Lucio, 231
Collingwood, R. G., 87, 300

common good, the: 141, 168–73, 249–66, 270, 296, 301–2, 315–30, 347–48; achievement of, as precondition for achieving our individual goods, 114, 189; educational conditions required for politics of, 360–61; political rhetoric in support of, 350–65

common goods: 121–22, 129, 132, 150–56, 165–69, 190, 232–33, 258–60, 268, 274–75, 280–84, 292, 301–2, 315–30, 350–51; "Common Goods, Modern States, Rights, and–Maritain," 366–87

Condorcet, Marqus de, 199
Cowley, Catherine, 397–98, 401–2
Crosland, Anthony, 198

D

Davidson, Donald, 64, 139–40, 142
Davie, George Elder, 79–80
de Gaulle, Charles, 170–71, 343, 376
De Koninck, Charles, 194, 385–86
desire: 188, 269, 319, 328, 339; conflicts between, 125–26, 138–39; for the good, 136–39; Mill on desire for happiness, 82–83; relationship to moral agency, 104, 110–15; relationship to motives and reasons for action, 127–36, 141–42

Descartes, René, 55–56, 58, 60, 70
Diderot, Denis, 19, 106, 207
Drucker, Peter, 285, 403
Dunbabin, Jean, 304

E

Engels, Friedrich, 181, 207, 209, 230–31, 241–42
Enlightenment: conception of the goals of education, 65–67, 248–49; project of justifying morality, 89–90, 106–7; Scottish, 75–79

Erskine, Ebenezer, 71

F

Feldman, Fred, 334–36
Ferguson, Adam, 71, 77, 230
Feuerbach, Ludwig, 230–43
Fink, Hans, 173
Flaubert, Gustave, 343
Fletcher of Saltoun, Andrew, 76–77, 85
Foucault, Michel, 248
Freud, Sigmund, 221–22

G

Garrigou-Lagrange, Réginald, 158, 170–71, 194
Geach, Peter, 184, 187–88
Gluckman, Max, 192
Gould, Carol, 231
Green, T. H., 65, 308
Guevara, Che, 242

H

Hampshire, Stuart, 48, 185
Hare, R. M., 183
Hegel, G. W. F.: 19, 50, 59, 212–18, 225; on civil society, 230–33; on freedom, 200–203
Heidegger, Martin, 99, 165, 252
Hobbes, Thomas, 114, 216, 300
Højrup, Thomas, 407–8
Horace, 341
Hume, David, 70–72, 76–77, 85, 113, 127, 132
Husserl, Edmund, 50, 158–59
Hutcheson, Francis, 70–71
Huxley, Aldous, 198

I

Ilyenkov, E. V., 88
Irwin, T. H., 7–8

J
Jefferson, Thomas, 121

K
Kant, Immanuel: 6, 31, 42, 58–59, 242; on Enlightenment, 66, 74–76, 248–49; on moral motivation, 15, 145–46; rejection of teleological grounding of morality, 93–94, 113
Kautsky, Karl, 242
Keilson, Hans, 345
Keynes, John Maynard, 228
Kline, George, 231
Knight, Kelvin, 245
Koestler, Arthur, 222
Kraut, Richard, 309–10
Kristensen, Stefan, 413n2

L
Las Casas, Bartolomé de, 92, 304
Lassalle, Ferdinand, 130, 339
Layard, Richard, 333, 342
Lenin, Vladimir, 239, 275
Leo XIII, 287, 371–72, 402
Levinas, Emmanuel, 174–75
Lewis, David, 49, 179–80
Lipps, Hans, 158–60, 165–66, 172, 175
Løgstrup, Knud Eiler, 158–69, 173–75
Lord, Carnes, 309–10
Lucretius, 341
Lukács, Georg, 194, 225, 241–42
Luther, Martin, 173–74

M
Malcolm, Norman, 223
Manning, Henry Edward (cardinal), 372, 402
Maritain, Jacques, 21, 50, 171, 194, 374–87, 412n1 (chap. 9)
Marrus, Michael, 413

Marx, Karl: 88, 92, 223, 264, 292; Aristotle's influence, 92, 308; critique of Hegel, 203; critique of morality, 180–81; on materialism and historical explanation, 208, 211–13; on social structures and moral responsibility, 288–89; *Theses on Feuerbach*, 229–43
Maurras, Charles, 374–76
McNabb, Vincent, 287
Mill, John Stuart, 19–20, 42, 80–83, 90, 94, 225–26, 284, 308, 334, 340, 342
Miller, Fred D., Jr., 310–11
moral dilemmas, 46–48
moral rules, 12–16, 26–42, 93–94, 147, 155, 165–173, 302–3
Mounier, Emmanuel, 375–76

N
Namier, Lewis, 219
narrative unity of life, 9–11, 23–24, 113–14
Newton, Isaac, 72, 207
Nicholas, Jeffery, 418
Nietzsche, Friedrich, 95, 289

O
Oakeshott, Michael, 221
Oresme, Nicole, 304, 311
Orwell, George, 198
Owen, Robert, 239

P
Paine, Thomas, 197–98
Parsons, Talcott, 215–17, 238
Perpich, Diane, 175
Peters, Richard, 64–65
Piccolomini, Francesco, 305–7, 311
Plato, 38, 54, 99, 178, 181, 258, 276, 286, 295, 300
Plekhanov, Georgi, 241
Popper, Karl, 178, 211–15, 220

practices, 8–9, 90–92, 114, 188–89, 242–23, 251–55, 268, 273, 401, 409
Putnam, Hilary, 244, 264

R
Rawls, John, 151
Reid, Thomas, 6, 16–17, 70–72, 76
Resnik, Michael, 412
Ross, W. D., 183–84

S
Sartre, Jean-Paul, 5, 16–17, 64, 179–80, 182, 186, 199, 238
Savage, L. J., 395
Schmitt, Charles, 416n8
Seligman, Martin, 332
Sepúlveda, Juan Ginés de, 92, 304
Sidgwick, Henry, 6, 16–17, 83, 334
Simmel, Georg, 287–88, 401–2
Simon, Yves R., 21, 170–71
Singer, Peter, 153–55
Smith, Adam, 68, 71, 77–78, 85, 90, 280, 283, 343–44
Socrates, 38, 43, 62, 126, 276, 340, 342
Soloviev, Vladimir, 101
state: 270, 300, 370–71; contrast with practice-based communities, 92–93, 260–66, 324; incoherence of modern state's relationship to citizens, 234, 246–48, 256–58; in modern Catholic social teaching, 371–74
Steiner, Franz, 181, 192
Stevenson, C. L., 182–83
Stewart, Dugald, 70–71, 76

T
Thompson, E. P., 240
Thornton, M. T., 417 (chap. 17)
Toulmin, Stephen, 28–29, 37, 39
traditions: encounters between rival traditions of inquiry, 96–98, 264; social and cultural, as starting point for critical inquiry, 258; of textual interpretation as necessary for an educated public, 69
Trotsky, Leon, 228, 242

V
van Fraassen, Bas C., 47
Van Overbeke, P. M., 412n1 (chap. 9)
Veenhoven, Ruut, 333
virtues: 19–24, 54, 90–92, 189–92, 251, 274–75, 296–98, 302–6, 325–29, 367–69, 383, 406–10; and money-making, 276–77, 286–88; relationship to deliberation, 7–8; relationship to rules, 12–14, 37, 93, 260; relationship to social structures, 77, 121–22, 247, 264; role of narrative in understanding, 10; theological, 94–95
Vitoria, Francisco de, 304

W
Wartofsky, Marx, 414n.3 (chap. 12)
Whynott, Douglas, 119–21
Williams, Bernard, 47–48, 53
Winnicott, D. W., 279
Wittgenstein, Ludwig, 50, 56, 221–24, 345
Wright Mills, C., 216–17

KELVIN KNIGHT

is reader in ethics and politics at London Metropolitan University, where he was the director of the Centre for Contemporary Aristotelian Studies in Ethics and Politics from 2009 to 2020. He is the author of *Aristotelian Philosophy: Ethics and Politics from Aristotle to MacIntyre*.

PETER WICKS

is scholar-in-residence at the Elm Institute and lecturer at Yale University.

www.ingramcontent.com/pod-product-compliance
Lightning Source LLC
Chambersburg PA
CBHW071435300426
44114CB00013B/1437